War Without End

War Without End

The Iraq War in Context

Michael Schwartz

In cooperation with TomDispatch

Haymarket Books
Chicago, Illinois

Published in 2008 by Haymarket Books
P.O. Box 180165
Chicago, IL 60618
773-583-7884
info@haymarketbooks.org
www.haymarketbooks.org

Cover image of a Polish soldier stationed at Camp Echo, in Diwaniyah, Iraq. Photo taken
by Tech. Sgt. Dawn M. Price.
Cover design by Eric Ruder

Trade distribution:
In the U.S. through Consortium Book Sales and Distribution, www.cbsd.com
In the UK, Turnaround Publisher Services, www.turnaround-psl.com
In Australia, Palgrave MacMillan, www.palgravemacmillan.com.au
All other countries, Publishers Group Worldwide, www.pgw.com/home/worldwide.aspx

Special discounts are available for bulk purchases by organizations and institutions. Please
contact Haymarket Books for more information at 773-583-7884 or
info@haymarketbooks.org.

Published with the generous support of the Wallace Global Fund.

LIBRARY OF CONGRESS CATALOGING-IN-PUBLICATION DATA
Schwartz, Michael, 1942-
  War without end : the Iraq debacle in context / Michael Schwartz.
    p. cm.
  Includes bibliographical references and index.
  ISBN-13: 978-1-931859 54-7
  ISBN-10: (invalid) 7735837884
  1. Iraq War, 2003---Causes. 2. Iraq War, 2003---Destruction and pillage. 3. United States-
-Politics and government--2001- I. Title.
  DS79.76.S355 2008
  956.7044'3--dc22
                           2008023347

10 9 8 7 6 5 4 3 2 1

Printed in Canada by union labor on recycled paper containing 100 percent post-
consumer waste in accordance with the guidelines of the Green Press Initiative,
www.greenpressinitiative.org

Contents

To my children and grandchildren,
Shanna, Rebecca, Joshua, Julia, Katherine, Mizel, Judah, and Lila.

My generation set out to address and correct the world's problems.
Instead we have bequeathed you dire crises.
I hope this book makes a small contribution to your effort to redeem our failures.

Introduction

It is curious to see America, the United States, looking on herself, first, as a sort of natural peacemaker, then as a moral protagonist in this terrible time. No nation is less fitted for this role. For two or more centuries America has marched proudly in the van of human hatred—making bonfires of human flesh and laughing at them hideously, and making the insulting of millions more than a matter of dislike—rather a great religion, a world war-cry.

—W. E. B. Du Bois, 1919

In the days just after September 11, 2001, as the United States rallied behind President George W. Bush and his newly initiated Global War on Terror, many people visualized the use of America's military might as a fast and efficient way to cut through the Gordian knot of international intrigue that protected al-Qaeda and its terrorist cohort.

The idea in those days was to use America's military preeminence to depose rogue political regimes that provided the safe havens necessary for planning the next inevitable terrorist attacks on U.S. soil. It was said that a few successful thrusts would directly eliminate "states who sponsor terrorism" and quickly liquidate the terrorists they were harboring. The Bush administration identified as many as sixty countries that harbored al-Qaeda cells, and announced that U.S. officials had given each one "a stiff 'with us or against us' message: join 'an international coalition against terrorism' or pay the price. . . . Join the fight against al-Qaeda or 'be prepared to be bombed. Be prepared to go back to the Stone Age.'"[1]

The United States was thus embarking on a series of quick, effective assaults on various offending countries, a kind of international housecleaning that would sweep through country after country. Even after al-Qaeda was liquidated, Secretary of State Colin Powell assured the world, the United States would continue with "a global assault on terrorism" that would last as long as necessary to contain or eradicate any threat to the U.S. "homeland."[2] The saving grace of this potentially endless process was the merciless efficiency of the military instrument, which would guarantee that each battle was quickly won and painless for the United States.

In the imagery of the post-9/11 moment, the conquest of Afghanistan was an immediately successful first thrust; it removed and dismantled the Taliban government, and therefore eliminated al-Qaeda's most important safe haven. Afghanistan's reconstitution as Washington's staunch ally was expected to proceed almost automatically, without conflict or significant investment.

A year later, the attack on Iraq became the next of these military thrusts, this one aimed at eliminating a second hydra head, the long-standing U.S. antagonist Saddam Hussein. In those days, according to the U.S. narrative, the war in Iraq was meant to be a sequel to the war in Afghanistan: efficient, precise, almost sanitary, and—most of all—quick. In a few months, with "major combat operations" successfully completed in Iraq, the job would be done and the next target, probably Iran or Syria, would be selected.

But something went wrong in that second battle. Before the invasion, Bush administration leaders offered a "Global War on Terror" rationale for their choice: left alone, Saddam Hussein would either arm al-Qaeda terrorists with weapons of mass destruction or use such weapons himself to attack the United States or its allies. This was most urgently expressed by National Security Advisor Condoleezza Rice, who commented on CNN's *Late Edition* that "We don't want the smoking gun to be a mushroom cloud."[3] President Bush was more modulated in his 2003 State of the Union address, delivered two months before the invasion: "America's purpose . . . is to achieve . . . the end of terrible threats to the civilized world. All free nations have a stake in preventing sudden and catastrophic attacks."[4]

A year after the start of the Iraq War, any threat that might have existed of a weapons of mass destruction attack had been foreclosed. Instead of ending on schedule, however, the war had been escalated from a regime-changing military thrust into a transformative historical enterprise, the "central battle in the war on terror." Its new goals included implanting democracy int Iraq (and—by quick diffusion—the rest of the Middle East), the definitive defeat of al-Qaeda (fighting them there so "we won't have to fight them here"), and the stabilization of the "arc of instability" that extended from the borders of China to the Horn of Africa.

With this change in status, the war in Iraq had morphed from a one-act performance of shock and awe into a full-length drama that could conceivably continue to the next millennium, with almost daily media images of bombings, beheadings, and torture. To make matters worse, Afghanistan, the previously successful, quick so-called victory, began to drag on, becoming a second endless war.

Justifying an Endless War

By the time of Bush's 2004 State of the Union address, a new rationale had gained pride of place in administration rhetoric. The imagery of the Global War on Terror receded, replaced by America's destiny as bearer of democracy to Iraq and the Middle East: "As democracy takes hold in Iraq, the enemies of freedom will do all in their power to spread violence and fear. They are trying to shake the will of our country and our friends, but the United States of America will never be intimidated by thugs and assassins. The killers will fail, and the Iraqi people will live in freedom."[5] Three years later, the U. S.-sponsored Iraqi government, riddled with visible corruption, despised by its constituency, and indelibly tied to sectarian warfare, had lost the luster of democracy. The rationale for the ongoing military campaign therefore migrated back to terrorism. This time, however, the appeal was devoid of the optimistic imagery of invincibility and quick victory. Instead of imagining the quick elimination of an impending threat, Bush's 2007 State of the Union address invoked the prospect that an ongoing (perhaps endless) military presence in Iraq was necessary to forestall the otherwise inevitable development of new and far more dangerous forms of terrorism:

> The consequences of failure are clear: Radical Islamic extremists would grow in strength and gain new recruits. They would be in a better position to topple moderate governments, create chaos in the region, and use oil revenues to fund their ambitions. Iran would be emboldened in its pursuit of nuclear weapons. Our enemies would have a safe haven from which to plan and launch attacks on the American people.[6]

The migrating goals for the continuing war were a telltale indicator that none of publicly stated justifications were fundamental to Washington's intransigent determination to conquer Iraq. Had weapons of mass destruction been a primary motivation, the affirmation that Iraq had no such weapons should have led to a (perhaps embarrassed) disengagement or at least a modification of on-the-ground military strategy.

Instead, the military campaign continued unmodified, with only the justification altered.

Deputy Secretary of Defense Paul Wolfowitz had explained these migrating public justifications back in 2001, when he told *Vanity Fair*'s Sam Tannenhaus that there were many reasons for the invasion, but—for public consumption—they "settled on the one issue that everyone could agree on, which was weapons of mass destruction."[7] That is, the Bush administration used the argument that they predicted would be most effective in winning over public opinion. It is clear that at each stage they reapplied this same logic—cultivating public opinion with the most appealing argument they could muster at the moment, while remaining silent on other motivations that seemed less appealing.

This book is designed to scrutinize the full range of the Bush administration's ambitions in Iraq. When these hidden aspects of U.S. policy are made visible, they allow us to make sense of what would otherwise appear to be contradictory and paradoxical actions. Instead of seeing these contradictions as expressions of George W. Bush's twisted psyche or mistakes based on limited intelligence, we can discern instead how the choices made at each juncture reflect these enduring ambitions.

In order to understand these policies, we need to look beyond the periodic spectacles that have punctuated the war and scrutinize the day-to-day events that reflect set goals and produce long-term consequences. In order to understand such events, we need to look beyond the pervasive impact of a brutal military occupation to the equally pervasive impact of an equally brutal economic policy.

Bush's 2007 State of the Union address mentioned oil in an oblique but nevertheless instructive way, suggesting that control of oil was a critical determinant in Washington's campaign to convert Iraq militarily from a regional adversary to U.S. outpost.

Bush's assertion that U.S. withdrawal would allow Islamic extremists to "use oil revenues to fund their ambitions" points to a twenty-first-century fact of life—that oil had come to play the role that gold had played in earlier epochs. In the Age of Discovery, many countries and private citizens spent precious resources and fought brutal wars, particularly in North and South America, for access to and control over gold, with the expectation that success would yield not only wealth, but also power on the world stage. Centuries later, oil came to play the same role. By the early twentieth century, the oil-rich Middle East—which for several hundred years had been little more than a way station in international affairs—reemerged as a focal point of big-power politics. As former Federal Reserve Board Chairman Alan Greenspan commented: "The intense attention of the developed world to Middle Eastern political affairs has always been critically tied to oil security."[8]

In this context, the invasion of Iraq was no different from all the previous iterations of Western intervention in the Middle East: the control of Iraqi oil was a prime goal of the invasion, and this control could only be assured if three intermediate outcomes were achieved: a thoroughgoing revision of the way Iraq managed its economy (so that oil could be quickly and efficiently extracted), willing participation by the Iraqi people in this transformation (no matter how much it disrupted or degraded their lives), and an ongoing, dominant military presence (to protect against domestic and foreign resistance to these and other changes that Washington hoped to implement). At the same time, control of Iraq and its oil was itself an intermediate goal in a more comprehensive foreign policy: the establishment of the United States as the preeminent power in the Middle East.

The Paradox of Shock and Awe

The war began with what military strategists called the "shock-and-awe" campaign, which the U.S. media portrayed as a kind of fireworks show, featuring spectacular visuals of explosions in and around Baghdad. Residents of Baghdad experienced it as an enduring nightmare, magnitudes worse than the infamous blitzkrieg of London.[9]

The military rationale for such a strategy lay in its potential to demoralize the soldiers and citizens of the enemy country. In the circumstances just preceding the invasion—with the bulk of the Iraqi population sullenly antigovernment and the military on the verge of collapse—the use of such a strategy would have appeared to be at best unnecessary. At worst, it ran the risk of rallying the Iraqis around their once-hated government and thus stiffening the resistance.

But if we look at the ambitions of U.S. foreign policy, we can better discern the logic of the attack. As Naomi Klein has meticulously documented, a particular logic was enshrined in the economic, political, and military thinking of Washington policy makers. Stated bluntly, this thinking asserts that a sudden devastating shock—whether a large-scale society-wide natural disaster affecting the entire nation or an individual's traumatic injury—make groups and individuals more compliant to disruptions and degradations of their lives.[10] Given the intention to revolutionize Iraq society, demoralizing the population might prove a useful anesthetic.

Viewed through this lens, the shock-and-awe campaign that preceded the invasion makes sense: It can be seen as a softening process that would induce compliance among Iraqi citizens with the radical transformation of their society from a Baathist state-dominated dictatorship to a fully globalized, market-driven ally of the United States. A short review of the events of that campaign will introduce us to the reality behind "shock and awe," and to its connection to the immediate postinvasion attempt at economic revolution.

Shock and Awe

The shock-and-awe strategy was developed in the 1990s by Harlan K. Ullman, a U.S. Navy commander and an influential National War College professor, as a way to "control the adversary's will."[11] Rapid and overwhelming physical and human destruction would, he theorized, "induce sufficient Shock and Awe to render the adversary impotent."[12]

When the concept of shock and awe became a part of public discourse during the run-up to the Iraq invasion, Ullman was asked by CBS correspondent David Martin to portray its projected role in the imminent assault on Iraq. He emphasized that successful occupation of Iraq would depend on annihilating both the physical infrastructure of the country and its military capability. He compared shock and awe to the nuclear attack on Hiroshima:

> We want them to quit. We want them not to fight," Ullman told CBS, explaining that the concept relied on a "simultaneous effect, rather like the nuclear weapons at Hiroshima, not taking days or weeks but in minutes. . . . You're sitting in Baghdad, and all of a sudden, you're the general and 30 of your division headquarters have been wiped out. You also take the city down. By that, I mean you get rid of their power, water. In two, three, four, five days they are physically, emotionally, and psychologically exhausted.[13]

Some of the novel components in this strategy are worth noting. First, we should consider the lack of differentiation between military and civilian space. Targets are no longer to be selected according to their military value, but because they have the potential to induce physical, emotional, and psychological exhaustion. Any target, populated or unpopulated, functional or decorative, public or private, urban or rural, could be appropriate to this purpose.[14]

Such undifferentiated targeting would normally be considered a violation of long-established international law prohibiting civilian targets, but a second innovation by shock-and-awe theorists sidestepped this issue. In modern society, most infrastructure (for example, the power grid, the network of highways, the water purification system, and a multitenant office district) is simultaneously used for civilian and military purposes (known in military jargon as "dual-use" facilities). In principle then this legitimizes them as military targets. Lieutenant Colonel Kenneth Rizer, an airpower strategist, commented on how shock-and-awe advocates exploit this ambiguity to justify attacks on civilian morale:

> The US Air Force perspective is that when attacking power sources, transportation, networks, and telecommunications systems, distinguishing between the military and civilian aspects of these facilities is virtually impossible. . . . Since these targets remain critical military nodes . . . they are viewed as legitimate military targets. . . .
>
> By declaring dual-use targets legitimate military objectives, the Air Force can directly target civilian morale. In sum, so long as the Air Force includes civilian morale as a legitimate military target, it will aggressively maintain a right to attack dual-use targets.[15]

This, in turn, produces a third momentous aspect of shock and awe: that the target population experiences deepening devastation over months and even years after the attack has been completed. As Ruth Blakeley has argued, it is really a "bomb now, die later" policy,[16] since the degraded infrastructure becomes the incubator for a declining quality of life.

Disrupted electrical generation undermines every aspect of social life. Polluted water yields water-borne illness and devastated crops. Direct attacks on crops and the disruption of irrigation yield a declining food supply. A depleted hospital system combined with declining public health creates all manner of medical care crises, including drastic increases in infant mortality. Without vast and comprehensive reconstruction, the impact of shock and awe can continue to deepen over many years.

Finally, the initial devastation combines with this infrastructural decline to undermine the economic viability of the target country. This results in what can best be described as demodernization: urban areas especially lose their capacity to sustain the sorts of facilities that constitute modern society, and they slowly or quickly devolve into the "slum cities" that characterize much of the global South.[17] Stephen Graham has argued that this effect is a key feature of shock-and-awe warfare:

> The forced de-modernization of cities and urban societies through state infrastructural warfare is emerging as a central component of contemporary military strategy. . . . Vast military research and development efforts are fueling a widening range of "hard" and "soft" anti-infrastructural weapons . . . carefully designed to destroy, or disrupt, the multiple networked infrastructures that together allow cities within modern "network societies" to function.[18]

These damaging consequences were wholly inconsistent with the initially stated goals of the war: the surgical removal of Saddam Hussein (who was hated by his own people) and the creation of a responsive government that would attack neither its own citizens nor any outsiders. The outcome of such a surgical removal could best (and perhaps only) be managed if minimum physical damage were caused, allowing the new government to quickly become effective while minimizing psychological damage, so that Iraqi citizens could begin to act on their own behalf after decades of repression.

If however we view the war in light of the political-economic goals of the United States in the Middle East, the physical and psychological devastation of a shock-and-awe campaign begins to make sense. As we will discuss in detail in chapters 1–4, Washington's larger goals centered around transforming Iraq from a state-controlled system to a radically privatized economy that would ratchet up oil production by transferring investment and management of the oil fields to the cash-rich and technologically advanced international oil companies. This sort of transformation was certain to generate ferocious resistance at all levels of Iraqi society. Moreover, it was also certain to generate resistance in neighboring countries, whose governments would see these changes as foreshadowing U.S. demands for similar reforms in their respective countries.

Shock and awe held out the possibility of significantly reducing all this resistance. A brutal military campaign that left the Iraqi people "physically, emotionally, and psychologically exhausted" would pave the way for compliant acceptance of radical economic transformation. In fact, this ambition fit neatly into what social analyst Naomi Klein has identified as the "shock doctrine," an economic reform strategy originally enunciated by Nobel Prize–winning economist Milton Friedman: "Only a crisis—actual or perceived—produces real change."[19]

As she surveyed the history of the late twentieth century, Klein found that Friedman's insight had been applied repeatedly in introducing the sort of economic reform that Washington sought to introduce in Iraq. Over a three-decade period starting in the 1970s—in Chile and then Poland, China, Great Britain, Russia, South Africa, and numerous countries impacted by the tsunami of 2004—economic shock therapy was introduced in the aftermath of political, economic, and natural upheavals. In 2003 Iraq became a new example of this strategy:

> First came the war, designed, according to the authors of the Shock and Awe military doctrine, to "control the adversary's will, perceptions and understanding and literally make an adversary impotent to act or react." Next came the radical economic shock therapy, imposed, while the country was still in flames, by the U.S. chief envoy, L. Paul Bremer.[20]

Thus the initial attack, which might have made the process of military conquest more difficult, was designed to pave the way for a relatively uncontested economic transformation, an example of what Klein calls "disaster capitalism." Even the long-term infrastructural devastation was functional: It cleared away the outmoded existing equipment and facilitated its replacement with the proprietary "state of the art" facilities favored by the foreign companies who would undertake the reconstruction and development of the new Iraq.

The Failure of Shock and Awe

Ironically, the Iraq War did not initially feature a fully developed anti-infrastructural attack of the sort that Ullman felt was necessary to stun and intimidate the enemy.[21] While there was extensive damage to transportation, sewage, and communication, it was not systematic. The United States did not, for example, directly target water purification plants during the initial invasion; the vast majority of them were unharmed and electricity was still on in Baghdad.[22] Ullman himself complained that it "did not bring the great Shock and Awe that we had envisaged."[23]

Perhaps as a result of this moderation in the original plan, there was little overt bitterness when the U.S. military arrived in Baghdad and other cities that had been subjected to the modified shock-and-awe campaign. The initial round of violence involved looting and other actions aimed at targets other than the occupation forces.

On the other hand, resistance began to grow as soon as the social and economic impact of the occupation was felt; that is, as Iraqis grew increasingly suspicious that Washington was intending to occupy and transform the country, rather than liberate and reconstruct it. Looking at the situation from the point of view of shock-and-awe advocates, then, the campaign proved insufficient to pave the way for the economic reforms that L. Paul Bremer sought to enact while the "adversary" was still "impotent to act or react."[24]

As time went on and the economic reforms took their toll, the insurgency increased in breadth and depth, and in its willingness to undertake increasingly violent and destructive methods to expel the occupation forces. This resistance, both in the Sunni areas of active insurgency and in the more quiescent but still rebellious Shia areas, further frustrated efforts to implement economic reform and to ratchet up oil production.

At the end of 2003 the insurgency had become powerful enough to force the Bush administration into a difficult policy choice: to abandon the plan to reform Iraq—and the rest of the Middle East—or to "stay the course." At that moment early in the war against the insurgency, and at each juncture afterward, the Bush administration opted for the full application of military force to rescue the larger plan. Each new strategy sought to achieve what the initial attack had not achieved: to "induce sufficient Shock and Awe to render the adversary impotent," and thus make the population compliant to Washington's policy.[25]

In this way, it was the underlying political-economic ambitions of the Bush administration that determined the strategies adopted by the U.S. military in Iraq. The military campaigns were, in each iteration, needed because they were the only possible way to achieve the political-economic goals. The evolving arguments used to justify the continued military campaigns did not, therefore, reflect evolving goals, but were instead selected as the best choices to win over evolving public opinion.

What Went Wrong?

On the third anniversary of the invasion of Iraq, when U.S. newspapers and TV news reports were filled with retrospectives on the origins of the Iraq War, the question of "what went wrong" in Iraq was almost universally answered as follows:

> The invasion was initially successful, but the plan for the peace was faulty. Bush administration officials misestimated the amount of resistance they would encounter in the wake of Baghdad's fall, and did not deploy sufficient soldiers to definitively suppress the attacks mounted by remnants of the Hussein regime. This blunder allowed what was at best a modest insurgency to grow to formidable proportions, at which point the occupation officials were confronted with the consequences of a second blunder: the dismantling of the Iraqi army, which otherwise could have been deployed to suppress the rebellion.
>
> The bottom line? Army Chief of Staff, General Eric Shinseki, was correct when he recommended before the war that the U.S. should deploy several hundred thousand troops to lock down the country. Had this been done, the rebellion would have been quickly quelled, and the U.S. occupation would have looked more like those of Japan and Germany after World War II.[26]

The problem with this theory—and with the shock-and-awe theory it replaced—was that it underestimated the ultimate resistance to the transformations that Washington tried to implement in Iraq. If either theory were correct, the lack of U.S. troops and the deep chaos created by initial lawlessness and mass looting should have provoked immediate and violent expression of anti-occupation feeling. The fact that there were almost no attacks against the U.S. military at first and that the insurgency only began to build momentum in fall 2003 suggests that other, nonmilitary factors developed during that early period, factors that did not exist when the United States initially took the reigns of government.

To understand the powerful resistance that emerged after that first quiescent period and then continued to amplify for years afterward, we must search for a complex of nonmilitary factors that energized the evolution of social chaos into a guerrilla war aimed at expelling the U.S. military from Iraq. We must in particular ponder the size and resilience of the insurgency, which persisted and grew magnitudes stronger despite the escalating application of overwhelming firepower.

It is here that the accepted wisdom of the U.S. media is grossly inaccurate. The resistance did not arise because of inadequate troops or the absence of a coherent plan; it derived, instead, from the implementation of a familiar formula designed to transform Iraq into a beachhead for U.S. economic and political preeminence in the Middle East. The centerpiece of this transformation was a by then familiar set of policies, known in international development circles as "neoliberal structural adjustment," that had taken decades to complete in other countries. This attempted transformation had a devastating impact on Iraqi society: within a few months Iraqi cities were—as urban historian Mike Davis labeled the process— "rushing backwards to the age of Dickens"—and within three years they had already arrived.[27]

By 2006 Iraqi agriculture was gutted and most Iraqi cities were flooded with new migrants looking for work. The cities, for their part, had lost their historic economic centers of gravity. With their manufacturing sectors idled or decayed, a huge proportion of urban residents were unable to find or keep their jobs. Those who were working had suffered major declines in income that rendered them incapable of affording the imported products and services that now dominated the economy. In short, the cities were populated by an economically marginal population mired in a downward spiral of poverty and desperation. Many became unmoored— jobless and/or homeless—and left for other countries or other Iraqi cities, seeking a new beginning.

It was this process that produced the real war in Iraq—the one that occurred after Bush's declaration that "major combat operations in Iraq have ended."[28]

To understand why things went so wrong—why the quick conquest that was supposed to be battle number two in the endlessly successful Global War on Terror became an endlessly unsuccessful war of its own— we need to heed what President Bush said just after the much-quoted beginning of his victory speech. The very next sentence was "And now our coalition is engaged in securing and reconstructing that country." It was in fact the process of "securing and reconstructing" Iraq that produced the war without end.

Part I

The Almost Invisible Goals
of the War in Iraq

Chapter One

The Oily Origins
of the War in Iraq

*I am saddened that it is politically inconvenient to acknowledge what everyone knows:
the Iraq War is largely about oil.*

—Alan Greenspan, former chairman, Federal Reserve

*An American-led overthrow of Saddam Hussein, and the replacement of the radical
Baathist dictatorship with a new government more closely aligned with the United States,
would put America more wholly in charge of the region than any power since the
Ottomans, or maybe even the Romans.*

—David Frum, presidential speech writer

The United States viewed Middle East oil as a precious prize long before
the Iraq War.[1] Intense attention to the region—from the entire Western
world—started with the discovery of huge, easily accessed petroleum
fields just at the time when oil became the central resource in industrial
life. As a consequence, the Middle East was an important theater of operations during the first World War, with Great Britain emerging as the
biggest shareholder of the Middle East reservoirs of "black gold" and the
arbiter of the peace settlement that created Iraq as a country. From then
on, the region became an uninterrupted focal point of economic, political, and military intrigue (as well as open warfare), with Iraq a key part
of the equation.[2]

The United States, Saudi Arabia, and OPEC

By the Second World War that interest was in full bloom. When British
officials declared Middle East oil "a vital prize for any power interested in

world influence or domination," U.S. officials seconded the thought, calling it "a stupendous source of strategic power and one of the greatest material prizes in world history."[3]

This concern for control of Middle East oil led to a scramble for access during and after the war. The United States staked a claim as the preeminent power of the future when President Franklin Roosevelt successfully negotiated an "oil for protection" agreement with King Abdul Aziz Ibn Saud of Saudi Arabia.[4] That was in 1945. From then on, the United States became actively (if often secretly) engaged in most of the major events in the region, including the overthrow of a democratically elected Iranian government in 1953 to reverse the nationalization of Iran's oil fields, and the fateful establishment of a Baathist Party dictatorship in Iraq in the early 1960s to prevent the ascendance of leftists who, it was feared, would align the country with the Soviet Union, putting its oil in hock to the Soviet bloc.

U.S. influence in the Middle East began to wane in the 1970s, when the Organization of the Petroleum Exporting Countries (OPEC) first proved itself able to coordinate the production and pricing of oil on a worldwide basis.[5] OPEC's power was consolidated as various countries nationalized their oil holdings and wrested decision making away from the Western-owned oil giants that had previously dominated exploration, extraction, pricing, and sales of black gold.

Once all the key oil exporters joined OPEC, it began formally deciding how much oil would be extracted and sold in international markets. After the group established that all members were willing to follow collective decisions—because even one major dissenter might fatally undermine the ability to turn the "spigot" on or off—it could use the threat of production restrictions or the promise of expansion to bargain with its most powerful trading partners. In effect, a new power bloc had emerged on the international scene that could exact tangible concessions even from the United States and the Soviet Union, the two superpowers of the time.

Though the United States was largely self-sufficient in oil when OPEC was first formed, its economy was still tied to trading partners, particularly Japan and Europe, which were dependent on Middle Eastern oil. The oil crises of the 1970s, including the seemingly endless gas lines in the United States, demonstrated OPEC's power.

OPEC's rise to prominence significantly enhanced the importance of the long-term alliance with the Saudi royal family. With the largest petroleum reserves on the planet and the largest production capacity among OPEC members, Saudi Arabia was capable of shaping the cartel's policies to conform to its wishes. In response to this simple but essential fact, successive presidents strengthened the Rooseveltian alliance, deepening economic and military relationships between the two countries. The Saudis, in turn, could be depended upon to use their leverage within OPEC to make the group's actions fit into the broader aims of U.S. policy. In other words, the United States gained favorable OPEC policies by arming and otherwise supporting a Saudi regime that was chronically fragile.

Backed by a tiny elite that used immense oil revenues to serve its own narrow interests, the Saudi royals subjected their impoverished population to one of the most oppressive authoritarian regimes on the planet. Not surprisingly, the United States supplied increasing infusions of military aid as well as political support in situations that were often uncomfortable and sometimes untenable for Washington. For their part, in an era of growing nationalism, the Saudis found overt pro-U. S. policies difficult to sustain, given the pressures of their OPEC partners and their own population.

A key year for U. S. policy in the Middle East was 1979, when Iranians, who in 1953 had lost their government to a coup engineered by the United States and Britain, poured into the streets to overthrow the U.S.-backed Mohammad Reza Shah, an absolute ruler whose brutality toward his own people was legendary. Ayatollah Ruhollah Khomeini succeeded the shah, presiding over the first explicitly Islamist regime in the region.[6] The Iranian revolution added a combustible new element to an already complex and unstable equation. It was, in a sense, the match lit near the pipeline. A regime hostile to the United States and not particularly amenable to Saudi pressure had now become an active member of OPEC, aspiring to use the organization to challenge Washington's economic hegemony.

It was at this moment that the militarization of U.S. policy toward the Middle East became visible to the naked eye.[7] In 1980, in response to the Iranian Revolution and the Soviet invasion of Afghanistan, President Jimmy Carter enunciated what would become known as the Carter Doctrine: that Persian Gulf oil was "vital" to U.S. national interests, and that Washington would use *"any means necessary, including military force"* to retain access to it. To assure this access, Carter announced the creation of a Rapid Deployment Joint Task Force, a new military command structure that would allow the United States to deliver large numbers of personnel from all military services, together with state-of-the-art military equipment, to any location in the Middle East.[8]

Succeeding presidents of various political hues nurtured and expanded the Carter Doctrine. The Reagan administration, in addition to dramatically increasing U.S. military aid to the fragile Saudi regime, repeatedly sought to reassert U.S. influence over Iran. This led to support for Saddam Hussein's regime during its war with Iran as well as to elaborate negotiations and secret agreements with Iran that led to the Iran-Contra scandal.

During the Reagan years the Rapid Deployment Force evolved into the United States Central Command (Centcom), which took charge of all U.S. military activity in the Middle East and surrounding regions, but until George H. W. Bush ascended the presidency, the Carter Doctrine had been invoked only to justify military preparedness.

This changed with Bush's decision to fight the Gulf War in 1991. Though it was not emphasized at the time, the Gulf War was a crystalline application of the Carter Doctrine, implementing for the first time the proposition that "any means necessary, including military force," should be used to guarantee "access" to Middle East oil.[9] That war, in turn, convinced a shaky Saudi royal family—that saw Iraqi troops reach its border—to accept an ongoing U.S. military presence within their country.[10]

Bill Clinton's ascension to the White House after twelve years of Republican rule did not alter the trajectory of American policy in the Middle East or relax the Carter Doctrine. The Clinton administration continued the development of Centcom, enhanced the powerful American presence in Saudi Arabia, and engineered United Nations sanctions on Hussein's regime that severely degraded the quality of life in Iraq. In 1997 and 1998, Clinton added his own enhancement to the growing Carter Doctrine legacy. Whereas the Gulf War had been fought in response to Iraq's military aggression in Kuwait, Clinton ordered "a series of strong, sustained air strikes" provoked only by the refusal of the Iraqi regime to comply with UN inspection protocols. Clinton, in justifying this first aggressive use of military power in the region, invoked the principle of preemptive action that the second Bush would utilize, saying the strikes were "designed to degrade Saddam's ability to develop and deliver weapons of mass destruction."[11]

In 2000, just before the ascension of the George W. Bush to the presidency, James Bodner, Clinton's deputy under secretary for defense for policy, pridefully assessed his administration's extension of the Carter Doctrine, declaring that the "U.S. is better prepared today than ever before to prevent disruptions of energy supplies" in the Middle East. He pointed in particular to "new bilateral agreements that give the U.S. military access to facilities in all countries of the Gulf Cooperation Council." Whereas during the Gulf War the United States had to transport combat troops to theaters of operations from distant bases, these new agreements allowed Centcom a permanent presence of twenty-five thousand military personnel and thirty ships in the Middle East.[12]

The Unipolar Moment

The disintegration of the Soviet Union in the late 1980s, which conferred upon the United States uncontested global military supremacy, set in motion another policy vector that embedded itself in Middle East policy. A debate arose within Washington policy circles about how to utilize and preserve this "unipolar moment."[13] Future members of the administration of George W. Bush were especially fierce advocates of making aggressive use of this military superiority to enhance U.S. power everywhere, but especially in the Middle East.[14] They eventually formed a policy advocacy group, the Project for a New American Century (PNAC), to develop and lobby for their view that the United States should use its advantageous position to extend the unipolar moment indefinitely, establishing what they called "the American peace" based on overwhelming U.S. military supremacy, which they claimed would guarantee world "prosperity" into the indefinite future.[15]

The group, whose membership included Richard Cheney, Donald Rumsfeld, Paul Wolfowitz, and dozens of other key individuals who would hold important positions in the executive branch once George W. Bush took office, wrote an open letter to President Clinton in 1998 urging him to "turn your Administration's attention to implementing a strategy for removing Saddam's regime from power." They cited both the Iraqi dictator's military belligerence and his control over "a significant portion of the world's supply of oil." This proposal, if enacted, would have constituted a dramatic extension of the Carter Doctrine beyond the significant expansion already implemented by the Clinton administration.[16]

Two years later, the group issued a ringing policy statement that would codify their appeal to Clinton for regime change, and would become the guiding text for Clinton's successor. Entitled *Rebuilding America's Defenses*, the document advocated that U.S. military preeminence be utilized to "secure and expand" the United States's influence in the world, including—in the cases of North Korea and Iraq—its use "to remove these regimes from power and conduct post-combat stability operations."[17] The document even commented on the probability of overwhelming resistance by U.S. citizens to such an aggressive use of the military, noting that public approval could probably not be obtained without "some catastrophic and catalyzing event—like a new Pearl Harbor."[18]

The Clinton administration was not unresponsive to appeals from PNAC and others who shared what became known as the neoconservative approach to foreign policy. Though the Clinton administration did not undertake the recommended invasion of Iraq, it endorsed the preservation of the unipolar moment and the ouster of the Hussein regime. It sought to preserve and expand U.S. military preeminence through generous military budgets while applying military power to various issues, including the NATO intervention in Kosovo and the 1998 bombing in Iraq. PNAC activists were not fully satisfied, but they would have to wait until the second Bush administration to undertake a more rigorous application of neoconservative principles.

The Oil Crisis Matures

The 1990s also saw the maturation of the energy crisis, the third vector that would ultimately lead to the invasion of Iraq. The first widely visible sign of this pending crisis was the economic recession that coincided with the Gulf War, beginning in 1990 and ending in 1992.

In response to Iraq's invasion of Kuwait in 1990, the United States organized an international boycott of Iraqi and Kuwaiti oil.[19] Over the next seven months, Iraqi retaliation against the boycott, the ongoing war, and the need to reconstruct oil industry infrastructure damaged during the war meant that world markets were lacking at least four million barrels of oil per day that the two countries had supplied.

During all previous periods of shortage, whatever their origin, Saudi Arabia—with frequent help from other OPEC members—had been able to ratchet up production to cover the demand for oil, thus stabilizing both supply and prices. This did not happen in 1991. The expanding demand for oil on the world market was already straining the capacity of OPEC as a whole and Saudi Arabia was only able to replace two-thirds of the shortage. The result was a huge spike in oil prices and supply shortages, which became major factors leading to a recession. It was this economic downturn that figured prominently in the electoral defeat of George H. W. Bush by Bill Clinton.

Prices and supply stabilized once Kuwaiti oil was brought back on line, and there were even moments when prices fell below OPEC targets. Nevertheless, the world had learned from the Gulf War that the surplus capacity of Saudi Arabia and the other OPEC countries was effectively exhausted. With fears rising that continuing increase in demand would put a real strain on oil resources even without a disruption of production, member states of OPEC began demanding a range of political and economic concessions in exchange for expanded energy production. By this time the United States had joined the ranks of the energy deficient and dependent, as imported oil surged past the 50 percent mark.[20]

By the late 1990s, even while prices were at their lowest of the decade, there was no longer any doubt that increased demand had undermined OPEC's ability to cover even small disruptions, raising the specter that dependent countries would face chronically rising prices as well as increasingly frequent disruptive shortages triggered by small perturbations in the market.[21] Alan Greenspan pointed out: "The buffer between supply and demand has narrowed to the point where [OPEC] is unable to absorb, without price consequences, shutdowns of even a small part of the world's production."[22]

In the meantime, Saudi Arabia was further weakened by the rise of al-Qaeda, which took as its main goal the overthrow of the royal family, and as its key target the thousands of U.S. troops stationed at bases there in the years after the first Gulf War. The bases seemed to confirm "the core grievance" of Osama bin Laden and other Saudi dissidents that the royal family had indeed become a tool of U.S. imperialism. This in turn made the Saudi royals increasingly reluctant hosts for those troops and ever more hesitant supporters of pro-Washington policies within OPEC.[23]

The situation was complicated further by the potential future leverage that both Iraq and Iran might wield—individually or collectively—in OPEC. With the second and third largest oil reserves (Iran also had the second largest reserves of natural gas), their power was enhanced by the tightening oil market. Iraq's, in particular, was significantly amplified in the late 1990s, when UN sanctions were modified to allow Saddam Hussein at least partial control of the amount of oil extracted and exported. As Dilip Hiro commented, this "gave Baghdad a role in oil-price fixing that it had not played before."[24] Moreover, if Iraq could extricate itself from the remaining limitations imposed by post–Gulf War UN sanctions (which prevented it from either developing new oil fields or upgrading its deteriorating energy infrastructure), its influence would certainly increase further.

Though the leaders of Iraq and Iran were enemies, having fought a bitter war in the 1980s, they could agree at least on policies aimed at thwarting U.S. desires or demands—a position that was strengthened in 1998 when the citizens of Venezuela, the most important OPEC member outside the Middle East, elected Hugo Chávez, who shared the views of Iraq and Iran, president.

By January 2001, when George W. Bush took office, the new administration in Washington could look forward to negotiating oil policy not only with a newly resistant Saudi royal family, but also with hostile powers in a strengthened OPEC.

These negative developments were amplified by the underlying structural contradiction between the United States (reduced to the status of oil-dependent consumer state) and OPEC members, who sought to wield their developing petro-power to serve their own interests. The United States and other oil-dependent nations sought maximum development and production of existing oil reserves, along with aggressive efforts to find and develop new fields in the Middle East. OPEC producers, however, did not share these interests; the rising prices during this period gave them more than ample revenue, making them reluctant to increase production. Beyond this, the workings of international markets more or less forced OPEC producers to invest much of their oil earnings in U.S. securities, a strategy that was becoming increasingly problematic as the U.S. economy faltered. Production increases would necessitate further investments in these problematic securities. Moreover, beyond these problems lurked a greater one: that the increases in production demanded by the United States and other customers might not even be possible, if the most pessimistic predictions of actual reserves were correct.[25]

Even if the OPEC countries had the capacity to increase production dramatically, there was little chance of their voluntarily doing so. Such expansion would be very expensive and not particularly appealing, since a slower and steadier exhaustion of the oil reserves would guarantee revenues into the future while assuring that the total return would be much greater as growing scarcity drove up prices.

As the 1990s wore on, it became clear that even Saudi Arabia, the most compliant of OPEC members, would not undertake the production expansion that growing international demand required. Some other form of leverage would therefore be needed or the world would have to begin moving quickly toward conservation and alternative sources of energy. This view was forcefully expressed by the influential Baker Institute in its November 2000 report "Running on Empty?", which warned that OPEC could not be depended on to spontaneously expand production levels:

> Policy makers must focus on the political dimension to the timely development of resources instead of assuming that market forces will always bring these resources to bear in an efficient and timely manner. Political considerations have contributed to a slowing in resource development in recent years and have, in several cases thoughout the history of the oil patch, brought about market failure. There is no question that political factors could still thwart the full development of oil-production capability needed to meet rapidly growing demand in the years to come.[26]

Regime Change as Energy Policy

It is hardly surprising, then, that the newly installed George W. Bush administration—riding the tide of the ever-expanding Carter Doctrine, bent on unipolarity, and dreaming of a global Pax Americana—wasted no time implementing the aggressive policies advocated in the PNAC manifesto. According to then Secretary of the Treasury Paul O'Neill, Iraq was much on the mind of Defense Secretary Donald Rumsfeld at the first meeting of the National Security Council on January 30, 2001, seven and one-half months before the 9/11 attacks. At that meeting, Rumsfeld argued that the Clinton administration's Middle Eastern focus on Israel-Palestine should be unceremoniously dumped. "[W]hat we really want to think about," he reportedly said, "is going after Saddam." Regime change in Iraq, he argued, would enhance the power of the pro-U.S. Kurds, redirect Iraq toward a market economy, and guarantee a favorable oil policy.[27]

The adjudication of Rumsfeld's recommendation was shuffled off to the mysterious National Energy Policy Development Group that Vice President Cheney convened as soon as Bush took office.[28] This task force quickly decided that enhanced influence over the production and sale of Middle East oil should be "a primary focus of U.S. international energy policy," relegating both the development of alternative energy sources and domestic energy conservation measures to secondary or even tertiary status.[29]

The Cheney energy task force decided that the two central goals of the Middle East policy would be to convince or coerce Middle Eastern countries to double their output of oil, an enormously expensive proposition that all Middle East oil countries had been resisting for some years; and to finance and manage this project by opening up "areas of their energy sectors to foreign investment," that is, to replace government control of the oil spigot—the linchpin of OPEC power—with decision making by multinational oil companies headquartered in the West and responsive to U.S. policy demands.[30] If such a program could be extended to even a substantial minority of Middle Eastern oil fields, it would prevent coordinated decision making and constrain, if not eliminate, the power of OPEC, a theoretically enticing way to staunch the loss of U.S. power in the region.

Having determined its goals, the task force began to concretize a strategy for utilizing U.S. military preeminence to accomplish them. Michael Klare summarized the logic of this decision in his authoritative book *Blood and Oil:*

> The Bush-Cheney team could draw only one conclusion: that, on their own, the Persian Gulf countries had neither the will nor the capacity to increase their petroleum output and protect its outward flow. If the administration's energy plan was to succeed, the United States would have to become the dominant power in the region, assuming responsibility for overseeing the politics, the security, and the oil output of the key producing countries.[31]

According to Jane Mayer of the *New Yorker*, the most significant innovation implemented to accomplish this goal was a close collaboration between Cheney's energy crew and the National Security Council. The NSC evidently agreed "to cooperate fully with the Energy Task Force as it considered the 'melding' of two seemingly unrelated areas of policy: 'the review of operational policies towards rogue states,' such as Iraq, and 'actions regarding the capture of new and existing oil and gas fields.'"[32]

Though all these deliberations were secret, enough of what was going on has emerged in these last years to demonstrate that the "melding" process was successful. According to O'Neill, who was a member of both the NSC and the task force, by March 2003 "Actual plans . . . were already being discussed to take over Iraq and occupy it—complete with disposition of oil fields, peacekeeping forces, and war crimes tribunals—carrying forward an unspoken doctrine of preemptive war."[33]

O'Neill also reported that, by the time of the 9/11 attacks on the World Trade Center and the Pentagon, the plan for conquering Iraq had been fully developed. Secretary of Defense Rumsfeld urged that the plan be activated at the first National Security Council meeting after 9/11. After several days of discussion, the attack on Iraq was postponed until after the Taliban was driven from power in Afghanistan. It only took until January 2002 before the "administration['s] focus was returning to Iraq." It wasn't until November 2002, however, that O'Neill heard the president himself endorse the invasion plans.[34]

The Plan for Conquering Iraq

With this background, we can better understand the flurry of controversy over a single sentence in *The Age of Turbulence*, the best-selling, 500-plus-page memoir published in 2007 by longtime Federal Reserve chairman Alan Greenspan. He wrote simply, as if this were utterly self-evident: "I am saddened that it is politically inconvenient to acknowledge what everyone knows: the Iraq war is largely about oil."[35] As the first major government official to make such a statement, he was asked repeatedly to explain his thinking, particularly since his comment was immediately repudiated by various government officials, including White House spokesman Tony Fratto, who labeled it "Georgetown cocktail party analysis."[36]

The book itself contained only this brief explanation of the logic behind the comment: "It should be obvious that as long as the United States is beholden to potentially unfriendly sources of oil and gas, we are vulnerable to economic crises over which we have little control."[37] Later, Greenspan elaborated further to *Washington Post* columnist Bob

Woodward, telling him that because of the hostility of the Iraqi regime to the United States, "taking Saddam out was essential" in order to make "certain that the existing system [of oil markets] continues to work."[38] In a later *Democracy Now!* interview, he amplified this point, explaining that his support for ousting Hussein had "nothing to do with the weapons of mass destruction," but rather with the economic "threat he could create to the rest of the world" through his control over oil.[39]

Greenspan's argument echoes the logic expressed by the Project for a New American Century and other advocates of aggressive military challenges to OPEC's power. He was concerned that Saddam Hussein, who since 1991 had been a major adversary in the Middle East, would control key oil flows. That, in turn, might allow him to exercise economic and political leverage over the United States and its allies. If he were capable of disrupting oil flows sufficiently to threaten U.S. economic health, Hussein might put Washington in the untenable position of having to offer him concessions previously unacceptable to the administration.

Greenspan then elaborated further, arguing that the threat could be eliminated, "by one means or another," either by "getting him out of office or getting him out of the control position he was in." Replacing Hussein with a friendly government, of course, seemed like such a no brainer. Why have a guy like that in a "control position" over oil, after all? Better by far, as the Cheney energy task force put it, "to open up areas of [Iraq's] energy sectors to foreign investment." Like the task force members, Greenspan believed that removing control of oil—not just from Hussein, but from any Iraqi government—would permanently remove the possibility of any Iraqi government wielding economic leverage over the United States.

Revealingly enough, Greenspan saw the invasion of Iraq as a generically conservative action preserving unencumbered access to sufficient Middle Eastern oil. In a world with such energy demands, and whole new energy-devouring economies on the rise in Asia, continued access to sufficient Middle Eastern oil seemed to require stripping economic and political power from key Middle Eastern nations, then extracting oil at a pace far faster than the countries themselves had deemed judicious.

In other words, Greenspan's conservative urge to preserve U.S. access to Middle East oil implied exactly the revolutionary—and disastrous—changes in the political and economic equation that the Bush administration tried to engineer in Iraq in March 2003. It's also worth remembering that Iraq was considered just a pit stop in the Middle East, an easy mark for invasion and occupation. PNAC-nurtured eyes were already turning to Iran. One quip, reportedly circulated among neoconservatives in Washington, expressed this expanded vision: "Everyone wants to go to Baghdad. Real men want to go to Tehran."[40] Moreover, in the twenty-first-century world, expanding demand would, sooner or later, outdistance expanding production even if the Middle East doubled production. U.S. control over Middle East oil would eventually deprive other countries of sufficient oil when chronic shortfalls in production arrived. Greenspan's conservative effort to preserve access to sufficient oil therefore implied a dramatic increase in Washington's leverage over all countries that depended on oil for their economic welfare.

Note that these decisions rested on a vision of an imperial United States that should, could, and would play a uniquely dominant, problem-solving role in world affairs. All other countries would, of course, continue to be "vulnerable to economic crises" over which they would have "little control." Only the United States had the ability to apply (or threaten to apply) overwhelming military power to the "problem" of energy. Only the United States had the ability to subdue any country that attempted to create—or exploit—an energy crisis. Only the United States had the ability to use its military power to take preventive action against a country that had the potential and animus to utilize oil as a political weapon.[41] Vice President Cheney explained this very logic to NBC's *Meet the Press* just before the invasion, telling Tim Russert that only the United States had "the capacity to do anything about" rogue states like Iraq.[42]

None of this was lost on the unipolar officials who made and implemented the decision to invade Iraq—and who were more ready than any previous administration to spell out, shock-and-awe style, a stronger version of the Carter Doctrine. According to Treasury Secretary Paul O'Neill, Rumsfeld offered a vision of the grandiosity of the goals at the Bush administration's first National Security Council meeting: "Imagine what the region would look like without Hussein and with a regime that's aligned with U.S. interests. It would change everything in the region and beyond."[43]

An even more grandiose vision was offered to the *New York Times* by Bush speechwriter David Frum a few weeks later: "An American-led overthrow of Saddam Hussein, and the replacement of the radical Baathist dictatorship with a new government more closely aligned with the United States, would put America more wholly in charge of the region than any power since the Ottomans, or maybe even the Romans."[44]

The soaring worldwide demand for hydrocarbons that threatened to overwhelm supply left the Bush administration with three policy choices: It could lead a national or worldwide effort to combine alternative energy sources with rigorous conservation in order to significantly reduce energy consumption; it could accept the leverage conferred on OPEC by the energy crunch and attempt to negotiate both increased production and an adequate share of what might soon enough become an inadequate supply; or it could use its military power in an effort to coerce Middle East suppliers into raising production, while guaranteeing the United States privileged access at the potential expense of everyone else. Beginning with Jimmy Carter, five U.S. presidents chose the coercive strategy, with George W. Bush finally deciding that violent regime change and extended occupation was needed to make it work.

WMDs, Democracy, and Oil

The primacy of oil does not mean that the various public justifications for the war in Iraq were exercises in empty rhetoric. As Deputy Secretary of Defense Wolfowitz put it, the administration initially emphasized weapons of mass destruction because it was "the one issue that everyone could agree on."[45] How then, did the public justifications fit together with the drive for Middle East oil, and with each other?

The answer lies in following the logic of using U.S. military supremacy to impose economic solutions in the Middle East and elsewhere. As the Project for a New American Century stated in its manifesto, for this strategy to work U.S. troops would have to be regarded by all potential adversaries as "an overwhelmingly powerful force" that could sweep into a country and then perform "constabulatory duties"—that is, quickly overcome any military or violent resistance and then stay to act as a police force until reliable locals could be recruited.[46] It is in this context that weapons of mass destruction became an issue, since any country that possessed WMDs would likely be able to resist such a surgical attack. The PNAC made a particular point of saying that no adversary or potential adversary should be allowed to acquire WMDs, since these would effectively deter an invasion:

> Weak states operating small arsenals of crude ballistic missiles, armed with basic nuclear warheads or other weapons of mass destruction, will be in a strong position to *deter the United States from using conventional force*, no matter the technological or other advantages we may enjoy. Even if such enemies are merely able to threaten American allies rather than the United States homeland itself, America's ability to project power will be deeply compromised.[47] [emphasis added]

Following this logic, it hardly mattered to key strategists in the Bush administration whether Saddam Hussein had arsenals of WMDs, was trying to create such arsenals, or had no plans for developing them. Once they intended to use the military to oust Hussein and install a friendly government, they also made the commitment to prevent him from obtaining any weapon that could deter such an attack. If Iraq already had WMDs, the United States needed to invade before the regime developed an effective delivery system. If there were no WMDs in Iraq, the United States needed to invade before the regime developed them as a defense against the impending attack. Thus, even in their total absence, WMDs constituted a reason for prompt action, once the commitment to regime change had been made.

Connected to these security concerns, but also fundamental to the larger plan, was the establishment of a powerful long-term military presence in the Middle East once the Hussein regime was removed. This ambition was clearly enunciated in PNAC's key document, *Rebuilding America's Defenses*,[48] and it was reiterated by PNAC co-chair Donald Kagan, who answered *Atlanta Journal-Constitution* columnist Jay Bookman's question about bases in Iraq: "I think that's highly possible. . . . We will probably need a major concentration of forces in the Middle East over a long period of time. That will come at a price, but think of the price of not having it. When we have economic problems, it's been caused by disruptions in our oil supply. If we have a force in Iraq, there will be no disruption in oil supplies."[49] The construction of permanent military facilities, though often denied by top U.S. officials, was activated immediately once the Hussein regime was toppled, in the form of what became known as "enduring bases" (see chapter 6). These huge military bases—replete with bus lines, stateside chain restaurants, and varied recreation facilities—were justified, as Zalmay Khalilzad put it just before the invasion, by Washington's responsibility for the "territorial defense and security of Iraq after liberation."[50] Beyond this middle-term goal, however, lay the broader vision, expressed by Brigadier General Mark Kimmitt (the deputy chief of operations in Iraq), who said the bases were a "blueprint for how we could operate in the Middle East."[51] This blueprint involved Iraq becoming the hub of U.S. military and economic presence in the Middle East, a goal that was nicely summarized by author Tom Engelhardt:

> From the first Gulf War on, Saudi Arabia, the largest producer of energy on the planet, was being groomed as the American military bastion in the heart of the Middle East. But the Saudis grew uncomfortable—think here, the claims of Osama bin Laden and Co. that U.S. troops were defiling the Kingdom and its holy places—with the Pentagon's elaborate enduring camps on its territory. Something had to give—and it wasn't going to be the American military presence in the Middle East. The answer undoubtedly seemed clear enough to top Bush administration officials. As an anonymous American diplomat told the *Sunday Herald of Scotland* back in October 2002, "A rehabilitated Iraq is the only sound long-term strategic alternative

to Saudi Arabia. It's not just a case of swopping horses in mid-stream, the impending U.S. regime change in Baghdad is a strategic necessity."

As those officials imagined it—and as Deputy Secretary of Defense Paul Wolfowitz predicted—by the fall of 2003, major American military operations in the region would have been reorganized around Iraq, even as American forces there would be drawn down to perhaps 30,000–40,000 troops stationed eternally at those "enduring camps."[52]

These bases also formed the foundation of Washington's hope that it would not need to physically invade the fifty to sixty countries that might constitute an obstacle to the unipolar power it sought to establish. The war in Iraq and its aftermath were designed to make clear that resistance to American geostrategic claims was fruitless. According to Washington reporter Ron Suskind, a key theme in the National Security Council meetings in which the invasion plans were finalized was that the conquest of Iraq be "a demonstration model to guide the behavior of anyone with the temerity to acquire destructive weapons or, in any way, flout the authority of the United States."[53]

The concerns for installing a democracy in Iraq were only one degree more complex. As Naomi Klein has demonstrated in *The Shock Doctrine*, Washington officials were eager to install a government that was supported by Iraqi public opinion, but only if Iraqi public opinion did not conflict with the occupation's goals.[54] L. Paul Bremer III, the head of the occupation government, expressed it well when he told the *Washington Post* his position on transferring control of Iraq to a democratically elected government: "I'm not opposed to it, but I want to do it in a way that takes care of our concerns." He then explained that early elections might well confer power on those who rejected the U.S. program and/or supported a religiously based government, both unacceptable outcomes: "In a postwar situation like this, if you start holding elections, the people who are rejectionists tend to win. . . . It's often the best-organized who win, and the best-organized right now are the former Baathists and to some extent the Islamists."[55] Vice President Cheney succinctly summarized Washington's attitude toward elections when he told Bremer in May 2003 that they could not be held at that time, since "We are not yet at the point where people we want to emerge can yet emerge."[56]

During the occupation, therefore, Washington's representatives in Iraq regularly ignored Iraqi popular opinion by taking unilateral actions that went against the publicly registered wishes of the Iraqi people and/or their leadership. In the first year, before the formal transfer of sovereignty, this often included canceling or postponing local and national elections when they seemed likely to produce unfavorable outcomes and appointing local officials that U.S. officials felt that they could "work with."[57]

Consistent with Rumsfeld's ambition for a successful invasion, the United States sought to install—at first by appointment and later through elections—"a regime that's aligned with U.S. interests," and then convince, cajole, or coerce the Iraqi people into supporting it. This became the working definition of "democracy," and it made sense out of otherwise nonsensical actions and arguments, such as that of Lieutenant Colonel Nathan Sassaman, who commanded a highly destructive siege on a Sunni village: "With a heavy dose of fear and violence, and a lot of money for projects, I think we can convince these people that we are here to help them." [58]

In the years after the invasion, critics of the war pointed to the myriad ways in which U.S. political and military leadership was unprepared for what it encountered once the Saddam Hussein regime was removed. · This lack of planning, however profound, did not extend to the level of strategic vision. The Bush administration was very clear about its ultimate goals, and was determined to "stay the course" to fulfill them. As the situation evolved, U.S. military and political leadership adjusted strategy with these goals in mind: to "install a regime that's aligned with U.S. interests"; to reconstruct Iraq's economic system to conform to Washington's ambitions for the disposition of Middle East oil; and to use Iraq as the headquarters for hegemonic influence in the Middle East.

No matter how convoluted the situation became as unforeseen circumstances interfered with original strategies, the Bush administration kept its eyes on the prize.

Chapter Two

Toxic Economics

Much of the urban world . . . is rushing backwards to the age of Dickens.

—Mike Davis

Iraq has been fundamentally changed for the better.

—L. Paul Bremer III

As we saw in chapter 1, the United States entered Iraq with the goal of transforming the country from an active adversary to the flagship of U.S. preeminence in the region. To accomplish this, the occupation would need to construct a government that was aligned with Washington's interests; it would need to wrest control of Iraq's oil from government hands, even friendly ones; and it would need to create an environment congenial to multinational oil companies investing the vast billions of dollars that would be needed to double or even quadruple Iraqi oil production. Fulfilling these ambitious goals required a thoroughgoing reform of the Iraqi government and economy, root and branch. The needed reforms would necessarily extend far beyond the oil sector, since the existing political and economic institutions derived their power from the nationalized oil business and were therefore highly likely to resist the U.S.-mandated reforms.

Washington Post reporter Thomas Ricks concluded in his carefully crafted history of the war that the United States sought to "change the politics, economy, and even the culture of Iraq," the first steps in "transforming first Iraq and then the Middle East."[1] In Iraq, the goal was to manage reconstruction through the market, with little or no role for the Iraqi government to supervise or regulate the largely foreign companies that would become the heart of the new Iraqi economy. L. Paul Bremer III—the man placed in charge of this transformation—expressed this double commitment when he promised the U.S. Senate that he would replace the "brutal socialist dictatorship" of Saddam Hussein, with a "democratic government and open economy."[2]

To accomplish the economic part of this project, Bremer and his staff sought to dismantle the state-centered system that had developed for almost fifty years around the extraction of oil, and which accounted for a third of the Iraqi economy. Bush administration officials considered this government dominance to be the major source of the power and corruption that had been the hallmark of the Hussein regime. In its place they sought to erect (after a short but shocking transition) a market economy that would welcome unrestricted trade and investment by multinational corporations.

One novel element in this expansive ambition was the reliance on the military as an instrument of economic change, perhaps best expressed in the decision to place the Department of Defense in charge of post-invasion reconstruction. Stephen Graham, after reviewing the massive U.S. military reform in the fifteen years after the fall of the Soviet Union, concluded that this reconfiguration was designed for exactly the task of making the armed forces into an instrument of economic transformation.[3] *Washington Post* reporter Ricks concluded that it was precisely this military-economic connection that was poorly implemented at the beginning of the Iraq occupation: "The war plan . . . confused removing Iraq's regime with the far more difficult task of changing the entire country."[4] At any rate, the prewar "melding together" of the military and economic realms, so central to the attack on Iraq, was continued in the period after "major combat operations" had been completed.

The Neoliberal Tradition

Though dramatic in its goals and innovative in its means, the program of reform planned by U.S. policy makers was not unfamiliar. The Bush administration chose to embellish a so-called neoliberal strategy that had been applied in many countries. The label *neoliberal*—which at first seems contradictory, considering the very conservative character of the changes undertaken—derived from the effort, spearheaded by a triumvirate of global financial institutions (the World Bank, the International Monetary Fund, and the World Trade Organization), to "liberalize" various economies by replacing state control of economic goods and services with the free market.[5]

◆ ◆ ◆

Starting in the 1970s, transformative neoliberal economic policies had been adopted by many countries, initially in Africa and Latin America and later in Russia and other countries formerly part of the Soviet Union. Most other countries—including the United States, South Korea, and even China—had experienced less encompassing reforms. A small minority—including Iraq, Iran, and other countries governed by regimes hostile to the United States and to its economic allies—had resisted these changes, in good part because their oil revenues made them less dependent on the loans that typically triggered the reforms. Many of the most powerful policy makers had long believed that the continuation of government control over the economy was the principal reason Middle Eastern countries—Iraq and Iran in particular—had failed to increase oil production.[6]

In *The Endgame of Globalization*, historian Neil Smith placed these policies in the broader arc of U.S. foreign policy since the Civil War.[7] The United States formally entered the exclusively European imperialist club during the war with Spain in the late nineteenth century. Though the United States did acquire a handful of formal colonies (Puerto Rico, Guam, the Philippines, and Hawaii) its main goal was to liberalize the economies of politically independent but economically undeveloped countries.

Liberalization, then and now, meant that the economic system would welcome—with as little restriction as could be politically accomplished—imported goods and investment from advanced industrial countries. In practice these changes meant opening the local economies to multinational corporations headquartered outside the country, creating long-term dependencies on foreign trade and investment, and establishing a routinized flow of products and profits from the hinterlands to the core.[8]

Smith notes that a key goal of the more than one hundred military interventions undertaken in the last century by the U.S. military has been the desire to protect or enhance the access of multinational corporations to foreign markets. For example, the CIA overthrow of the elected Iranian government in 1953 reversed the nationalization of Iranian oil fields; the overthrow of the elected Guatemalan government in 1956 prevented the nationalization of foreign-owned banana plantations; and the long war in Vietnam unsuccessfully sought to stop the spread of socialism in Southeast Asia. The U.S. invasion of Iraq, designed to "open up" the Iraqi oil fields to foreign investment, was therefore entirely consistent with the long legacy of military and economic intervention around the world. To use Smith's phrase, the policy that led to the invasion of Iraq was designed "to impose a global capitalism dressed up as liberal democracy" on the Middle East.[9]

U.S. Goals for the New Iraqi Regime

The Coalition Provisional Authority (CPA), the administrative apparatus installed by the United States to run Iraq after the overthrow of the Hussein regime, might have focused narrowly on the oil goals of the Cheney energy task force. Many officials, including its initial head, former General Jay Garner, favored such an approach. Garner sought to preserve the Iraqi Army as well as the entire government structure, and utilized the government-owned enterprises to quickly restart the Iraqi economy.[10]

But the upper reaches of the Bush administration favored introducing the full range of neoliberal reforms into Iraqi society. Their goal was to make Iraq into the exemplar of radical change, the vanguard of an economic transformation that would fulfill Defense Secretary Rumsfeld's ambition to "change everything in the region and beyond."[11] L. Paul Bremer III, who replaced Garner in the second month of the occupation, told the World Economic Forum in June 2003 that replacing the vast government apparatus with the openest of open markets would be the centerpiece of Iraq's reconstruction: "Markets allocate resources much more efficiently than politicians. So our strategic goal in the months ahead is to set in motion policies which will have the effect of reallocating people and resources from state enterprises to more productive private firms."[12]

The specific mechanisms Bremer utilized were comprehensive. Besides dismantling both the army and the state apparatus, he sought to implement virtually every neoliberal reform that had been adopted piecemeal in other countries during the previous thirty years. These included immediately shuttering all state-run (nonoil) enterprises (which were viewed as inefficient, unprofitable, and corrupt); selling those that were potentially viable (at distress prices, if necessary); dismantling tariff and tax barriers that prevented the entry of foreign products and companies (which would be expected to introduce superior products, modern technology, and efficient methods into the economy); voiding state regulations and subsidies that protected domestic businesses (which were accused of selling worse goods at higher prices than foreign competitors); weakening some and outlawing other labor unions (because they produced or protected wages and benefits and therefore created an unprofitable business climate); eliminating laws that restricted the use of foreign workers (who were expected to work harder for lower wages); and removing state sub-

sidies on food and fuel (which gave unemployed workers sufficient resources to demand wages that could undermine profitability).[13]

Ten months later, as he left his position in Iraq, Bremer pridefully
told the *Washington Post* that these reforms were his most important ac-
complishments:

> Bremer maintained that "Iraq has been fundamentally changed for the bet-
> ter" by the occupation. The CPA, he said, has put Iraq on a path toward a
> democratic government and an open economy after more than three decades
> of a brutal socialist dictatorship. Among his biggest accomplishments, he
> said, were the lowering of Iraq's tax rate, the liberalization of foreign-invest-
> ment laws and the reduction of import duties.[14]

Smith's comment about this set of policies points to their deeper significance: "Bremer's emphasis on the liberalization of tax, trade, and investment laws . . . goes to the heart of the construction effort and, even
more, speaks to the larger reasons for the war. . . . Washington wanted
first and foremost to privatize the Iraqi economy."[15]

It is this revolutionary intention that distinguishes Iraq reconstruction
from post–Second World War reconstruction in Germany and Japan to
which it is sometimes compared; in those countries the goal was to recon-
stitute the prewar economy, leaving the maximum number of major institutions intact. And what distinguished Iraq from the earlier military
interventions was the use of the military to *impose* economic change, instead of *preventing* it. In Guatemala, Iran, Vietnam, and countless other previous interventions, the goal was to prevent the nationalization of resources
or the establishment of socialism. In Iraq, the goal was to implement a neoliberal revolution—the denationalization of resources and the disestab-
lishment of what Bremer considered to be socialism.

Accumulation by Dispossession

In a series of books scrutinizing the impact of neoliberal reform in a
range of countries, David Harvey has demonstrated that the apparently
straightforward process of privatization (the heart of the reforms undertaken by Bremer) had myriad other social consequences. Harvey
found that neoliberalism redistributed both power and wealth upward,
concentrating it in the hands of the owners and managers of large businesses; led to a smaller number of ever-larger companies gaining an
ever-expanding proportion of global wealth; and exposed "the least fortunate elements in any society—be it Indonesia, Mexico, or Britain—to
the chill winds of austerity and the dull fate of increasing marginalization." Neoliberalism's "main substantive achievement," Harvey wrote,

has been "to redistribute, rather than to generate, wealth and income."[16] Its record is "nothing short of dismal" when measured against the standard of sustained economic development. At best, neoliberalism generates "spurts of growth followed by economic collapse."[17]

One infernal consistency of neoliberalism's record is that it regularly produces increased inequality. Harvey calls the process that produces this dismal pattern "accumulation by dispossession."[18] "Dispossession" takes place because the owners (state or private) of the now-unprotected local industries are separated from their holdings, either through sale or bankruptcy. "Accumulation" takes place because multinational firms exploit new opportunities for profit, either by selling more of their foreign-made products in local markets or by acquiring devalued local enterprises and operating them at a substantial profit, usually by paying desperate workers lower wages.

To these economic consequences of neoliberalism we must add the decline of meaningful democracy. As sociologist Jackie Smith has shown, privatization, wherever it is practiced, reduces the governing capacity of the state, since it transfers economic decision-making from the government into the hands of private owners working through markets. Moreover, if these new private owners are located outside the country, they are out of reach of even the most activist government. Ultimately, therefore, privatization erodes the reality of (or the potential for) democracy, since elections can reach no further than government capacity. When the government loses the ability to control business decision making and economic trajectories, so do the people. Smith concludes from her survey of the impact of privatization in many countries over several decades that neoliberal reforms "undermine both the legitimacy and political effectiveness of states."[19]

In Iraq neoliberalism was implemented in record time. When the United States entered the country in 2003, Iraq had a quasi-industrial economy, anchored by a weakened but still formidable infrastructure, and was home to several viable manufacturing districts. This foundation should have been capable—with the appropriate exploitation of Iraq's oil resources—of supporting a modern economy. Instead, the lethal combination of violent occupation and neoliberal reform produced very rapid accumulation by dispossession, the erosion of government capacity, and slummification, simultaneously motivating the expansion and resilience of the insurgency.

Chapter Three

The Neoliberal Project in Iraq

What we have done over the last six months in al-Anbar has been a recipe for instability....
Through aggressive de-Baathification, the demobilization of the army, and the closing of
factories, the coalition has left tens of thousands of individuals outside the economic and
political life of the country.

—Keith Mines, U.S. State Department, Fall 2003

The drastic reform that L. Paul Bremer attempted to implement as head of the Coalition Provisional Authority produced a rapid and dramatic decline in the Iraqi economy. The linchpin of his comprehensive effort was the three-pronged dismantling of the entire Baathist state apparatus. This dismantling included two well-publicized and much-criticized actions: the elimination of Hussein's army and the de-Baathification of the government. Disbanding the Iraqi Army left five hundred thousand well-trained (and well-armed) young men unemployed and bitter. De-Baathification separated eighty-five thousand state officials from the government, the core of administrative and technical expertise of the country, including the vast majority of Iraq's precious stock of engineers, technicians, and experienced public works administrators.

Though these demobilizations were publicized as attempts to remove the threat of a Baathist restoration, they also accomplished an important neoliberal purpose. The destruction of the Baathist administrative apparatus and military would guarantee that any new Iraqi government would be incapable of reasserting control over the economy, since the administrative and technical expertise to run or regulate large enterprises would disappear with the departure of the Baathist technostructure, and the ability to undertake large public works projects would disappear with the dissolution of the army. In fact, Bremer's dissolution order countermanded a "detailed plan to use up to one hundred thousand Iraqi troops as the low-technology end of reconstruction projects." In the new Iraq, such projects would get done by private companies, or—as things turned out—not get done at all.[1]

The third, often overlooked, aspect of Bremer's dismantling of the government was the centerpiece of his program of neoliberal economic restructuring—known as "shock therapy" to practitioners of structural adjustment.[2] The plan itself was adapted from programs undertaken by the International Monetary Fund (IMF) and the World Bank in the 1980s and 1990s, including those that deepened the economic crisis of Russia and helped to bankrupt Argentina.[3] Bearing Point, a Virginia-based consulting firm that was paid $250 million to plan the restructuring, called it a "transition from a . . . centrally planned economy to a market economy." Noting that existing Iraqi law was "woefully deficient in terms of establishing a market-friendly legal and regulatory environment," it proposed to transform existing practice:

> It should be clearly understood that the efforts undertaken will be designed to establish the basic legal framework for a functioning market economy; taking appropriate advantage of the unique opportunity for rapid progress in this area presented by the current configuration of political circumstances. . . . Reforms are envisioned in the areas of fiscal reform, financial sector reform, trade, legal and regulatory, and privatization.[4]

The phrase "the current configuration of political circumstances" was a reference to the direct control the United States planned to exercise over Iraq, which would allow for a radical transformation of the economy without resistance from internal Iraqi economic and political forces.

The full scope of Bearing Point's vision was highlighted by the firm's list of areas in which market forces would be introduced: from "major utilities such as gas, oil, water, and power" to virtually all financial operations, including "asset sales, concessions, leases and management contracts, especially those in the oil and supporting industries."[5] These sectors were state-owned or heavily regulated in every advanced industrial country, but in Iraq the plan was to devolve them very rapidly into almost unfettered privatization.

Implementing Neoliberal Policy

By the summer of 2003 the CPA had promulgated all manner of laws implementing Bearing Point's ambitious plan. James McPherson, a key player in enacting the details of the program, told the U.S. Senate that the goal was to create the "foundation for a revolutionized economy" that would "challenge the economic policies and the politics of the whole region. . . . All restrictions [would be] taken off foreign corporations' intent on buying full control of Iraqi enterprises; nor were demands to be made of those companies to reinvest any percentage of profits in Iraq." [6]

It was at this time that the vast majority of state-owned companies were shuttered (with the oil sector the notable exception), based on the principle that "free markets emerge the fastest in countries that quit subsidized industry cold turkey." [7] The few remaining government-owned firms were explicitly prohibited from participating either in repairing facilities damaged during the invasion or in any of the initially ambitious reconstruction projects the United States commissioned. This policy was so strict that enterprises with specific expertise in Iraqi electrical, sanitation, and water purification systems were forbidden from obtaining subcontracts from the multinational corporations placed in charge of rejuvenating the country's infrastructure. The CPA also excluded the government-owned cement and fertilizer plants, phosphate and sulfur mines, and pharmaceutical factories from functioning until and unless they were sold to private owners, thus forcing reconstruction projects to seek these supplies from outside the country.

Thomas Foley, who was placed in charge of "private sector development" for the occupation, developed a plan to sell off 150 of the 192 shuttered enterprises, including "cement companies, fertilizer operations, a phosphate mining operation, sulfur mining and extraction businesses, pharmaceutical companies, and the airline and automobile tire makers." The sell-off plans foundered because foreign companies were unwilling to brave the security risks and because domestic entrepreneurs lacked the capital necessary to buy and energize the businesses. Following neoliberal orthodoxy, Bremer ordered that the factories remain shuttered. [8]

In one crystalline example of neoliberal policy in action, the Bremer regime discontinued aerial spraying of date palms, instructing farmers to hire private services to replace what was formerly a free Baathist government service. The inability of farmers to locate a low-cost private service resulted in infestation that crippled local growers and drastically reduced production of what had been a lucrative crop. After three years many of the trees, which take ten to fifteen years to reach fruit-bearing maturity, had died, leaving the farmers destitute. At that point, over the objections of the U.S. State Department, which insisted that the market be allowed to operate, the U.S. military began spraying the trees, arguing that the devastation of the date business was "fueling the insurgency." In reality, however, it was a full range of neoliberal measures that were immiserating the Iraqi population and therefore fueling the insurgency.[9]

Consider another example, a state-owned tractor factory located south of Baghdad, one of the 192 government-owned enterprises abruptly shuttered by Bremer in summer 2003.[10] The tractor factory, which had been operating at half capacity before the war, dismissed its staff of three thousand, who joined the hundreds of thousands of other demobilized workers, soldiers, and administrators impacted by Bremer's policies. When no private purchaser appeared, the factory lay idle for four years.

The neoliberal scenario expected this shutdown to be part of the transformative process that would "increase unemployment en route to greater employment and greater productivity."[11] Farmers in need of tractors would be initially forced to buy from foreign manufacturers. Only the most prosperous would have enough money or credit to the pay the (unsubsidized) price for imported tractors. Once the purchase was made, however, the superior, imported tractors, together with other improved methods made available by the removal of trade barriers, would increase the yields of their farms.

Those farmers without such resources would be forced into uncompetitive positions that degraded the value of their farms. They would also find themselves in similar binds with regard to seed, fertilizer, and other supplies that had been subsidized before privatization. Under these compromised conditions, the less efficient farms would fall further and further behind, and therefore become less valuable, making their ineffective owners willing to sell at distress prices to more prosperous farmers or outside investors, who had the capital to buy foreign tractors and to apply high productivity methods. These same outside investors—together with the increasingly prosperous surviving domestic farmers—would use their more commanding market position (and the growing rural unemployment) to seek out less expensive domestic or immigrant labor that would further increase the profitability and productivity of the farms. If and when the enhanced profitability of the transformed farms created a strong enough market for tractors, a firm with large capital resources could buy the fully depreciated factory or create a highly productive new one that would outcompete the foreign tractor suppliers.

One problem with this vision of the eventually positive consequences of the neoliberal process is that the profits made by foreign tractor companies and corporate farmers would reside largely in the hands of multinational investors (or local businesses with multinational connections), so the enhanced profits would be mainly reinvested outside the local communities and most likely outside Iraq. Except for those prosperous enough to purchase foreign-made tractors, the original cohort of Iraqi farmers would be displaced from the land (left with only the devalued proceeds from selling their degraded farms), searching for low-paid work in overpopulated farm country or overcrowded cities in a job market containing an influx of other displaced workers. The tractor workers would be unemployed at first because of the initial shutdown and would probably remain so, since if the factory were to reopen, it would do so with much less expensive, perhaps even foreign, labor. Thus, even if the situation developed just as the planners hoped, the benefits would flow primarily to foreign or local corporate investors, with the dispossession side of the equation plaguing small farmers and local workers.

In reality, the balance sheet was even more negative. According to a critical report by one of the officials in charge of economic revival in Iraq, Deputy Undersecretary for Defense Paul Brinkley, the privatization program had wreaked havoc on Iraqi farming and contributed to the slummification of the cities. The shuttering of the tractor factory and parallel demobilization of other farm supports such as date spraying resulted in the bankruptcy of vast numbers of farms, adding to the already tremendous unemployment pool. Even at distress prices, however, there were few internal and no external buyers, so farm production collapsed, falling to half of prewar levels. This farm depression forced people to buy expensive imported food at a time when incomes were dwindling, thus increasing levels of malnutrition to alarming levels.[12]

At the same time, according to Brinkley, "shutting down state-run industries crippled the existing Iraqi private sector." Years of international sanctions, which prevented Iraqi firms from purchasing supplies outside the country, had actually generated some beneficial effects. One of them was the necessity of finding virtually all inputs to the manufacturing sector within Iraq (since importing the inputs was prohibited). As a consequence, the government-owned factories were supplied almost exclusively from privately owned Iraqi firms, whose existence depended on these supply contracts. The shuttering process therefore rippled outward to these suppliers, compromising their viability and leading to the bankruptcy of a large proportion of private sector entrepreneurs.

The final irony recorded in Brinkley's survey of privatization was that the tractor factory—and a great many other factories closed by Bremer's draconian effort at privatization—was not stereotypically inefficient. Instead, it was a modern factory, and its products were fully capable of competing with imports in both performance and price. The shuttering process, therefore, cleared the way for foreign tractors to establish themselves when so-called fair competition would probably have worked in favor of the local factory.

The privatization program had thus fulfilled none of its positive promises. Visions of a more concentrated but more productive agricultural sector, of inefficient government enterprises replaced by efficient private enterprises, and of consumers buying new and better goods all went unfulfilled.

In 2006, Brinkley and a few other officials broke with Bremer's policy and began a campaign within the Bush administration to reopen shuttered factories. The effort, however, made very little headway. One problem was the ongoing resistance within both the State and Defense Departments. Even after Bremer left Iraq, his conviction that the privatization program needed more to time reach fruition had powerful advocates who resisted any compromise of the original vision of full privatization.

Moreover, after two years, the privatization process had become largely irreversible. The destruction of shuttered factories by looters and weather had left many of them beyond repair, and the necessary skilled technicians had been dismissed. Beyond this, the new Iraqi government, constructed according to the neoliberal recipes of the occupation, was not equipped to construct or sustain the sorts of manufacturing enterprises that Brinkley was trying to revive. After eighteen months of effort, Brinkley, operating with a small budget and many restrictions (including a requirement that only factories with a strong potential for successful sale to private entrepreneurs would be reopened) had resuscitated only seventeen factories, employing less than 5 percent of the workers who had been displaced by the shutdowns.[13] The Baghdad tractor factory, like many other resuscitated plants, was operating at only partial capacity. Nearly 150 other facilities were permanently lost.[14]

Sinking into Depression

Although the privatization program was the most significant of Bremer's reforms, other aspects of the attempted economic revolution also contributed to Iraq's economic calamity. Bremer's "Order 39" complemented the shuttering of state-owned enterprises by removing practically all restrictions on foreign investment and marketing within the country. This generated an immediate surge of sales to the Iraqi middle class of previously unobtainable goods like air conditioners, cell phones, and electronic devices. This was interpreted by many as an early sign of coming prosperity—a demonstration of the power of the "open economy" once it was freed from the "undue concentration of economic power" represented by state ownership of major industry.[15]

As it happened, though, this surge did not last even through the winter of 2003. The problem was that the CPA-induced economic "opening" to multinational competition bankrupted a substantial proportion of Iraqi-owned local enterprises and farms. Owner-operated shops lost business to multinationals offering drastically lower-priced goods (either because their cost was actually lower or because they sold at a loss in order to capture the market). A depression swept through the small business sector in Iraq, leaving neighborhoods without their normal complement of shops, and without the income that these shops plowed back into communities.

These devastating effects on Iraqi merchants were not "unintended consequences." As one Bush administration official put it, "One well-stocked 7-Eleven could knock out 30 Iraqi stores; a Wal-Mart could take over the country."[16]

This depression in local business was compounded by the demobilization of the army and the sidelining of state enterprises, producing a constantly escalating unemployment crisis. Though many state enterprises continued to pay demobilized employees half their wages, and the CPA belatedly decided to pay Hussein's former soldiers, this money did not regularly reach the targeted groups, in large part because the state apparatus had been dismantled by de-Baathification. The fragmentary administration set up by the occupation was inefficient at delivering any services, including paychecks, and significant sums were siphoned off by increasingly corrupt denizens of the administrative apparatus. As a result, millions of unemployed workers and soldiers, lacking the money to feed their families, also lacked the money to support local merchants.

All these processes acted together to devastate the leather goods industry that employed about 150,000 workers in about 3,500 private factories before the war. The shuttering of state-owned tanning plants was the first devastating blow, forcing the manufacturers to import their key raw material at dramatically increased prices. The removal of import barriers delivered the second blow, creating an "avalanche of cheap imports from China and Syria." The third blow came from the economic depression, which severely depressed the market for high-end Iraqi shoes, which the imports could not match in quality. By the end of 2003, nearly all of the leather goods plants had shut down.[17]

An additional setback was the almost immediate failure of the high-profile reconstruction program promised by the United States just after the invasion. When Congress allocated almost $20 billion in supplementary funds to the project, expectations were high for expanding electrical production, rapid repair of highways and sewage systems, and a thorough rehabilitation of hospitals and schools. Instead, the high-visibility promises turned quickly into high-visibility failures.[18] Electrical service declined rather than increased in Baghdad, creating countless problems for residents (who could not store perishable food) and businesses (which could not engage in many manufacturing or commercial activities). The failing sewage system created health hazards and a host of new medical problems, and the failure to rehabilitate schools left parents with school-age children to take care of during the day. One Baghdad resident told *Democracy Now!*:

> We have heard a lot of stories about reconstruction during the six months or the first year after the war. And we were living inside Baghdad and watching for them, as an example, for the campaign of maintenance of the schools. We have heard about [the] huge budget for the contractors from Bechtel or other American companies. But the reality on the ground was that . . . they paid it [to] subcontractors [who paid] subcontractors; then—a subcontractor, an Iraqi one, he got it for $2,000 for each school just to put paint and to maintain the broken glass. This is the only thing they have done.[19]

An additional injury to the Iraqi economy was the fact that very few Iraqis were employed in the reconstruction projects. The announced total funding of reconstruction was over $70 billion (though only a small fraction of that was ultimately spent on reconstruction), yet during Bremer's regime, fewer than fifteen thousand Iraqis were employed in the effort, less than 2 percent of those rendered unemployed by the demobilization, de-Baathification, and privatization.[20]

As this crisis deepened, multinational corporations found they had sold just about all the appliances the market could bear, and were no longer making sufficient profit to continue their sales efforts in much of Iraq. Therefore, they withdrew from the now-unprofitable Iraqi market, leaving communities with the empty shops of bankrupt local merchants and bereft of needed products and services. Residents who still had incomes found it difficult to obtain needed products. A reverse multiplier effect began to take hold as Iraqis who remained prosperous were forced to shop, work, or live outside their former communities, further depleting and depressing many neighborhoods.

By fall 2003, what Bremer called the "harsh, immediate consequences" of his program were fully apparent to ordinary Iraqis. With hundreds of thousands of demobilized soldiers and unemployed government workers supplemented by subsequent waves of rural and urban displacement, unemployment soared past 50 percent.[21] Shuttered factories and bankrupt local enterprises stood as constant reminders of the declining fate of local citizens. Highly advertised reconstruction projects visibly faltered and failed after refusing to employ Iraqi workers. The struggle for daily sustenance became grimmer: incomes declined and then disappeared, family savings became depleted and then disappeared, products became more expensive and then disappeared, and local shops became denuded and then disappeared.

The impact of this roiling economic disaster was visible to many of the most embedded U.S. officials. Keith Mines, a State Department diplomat assigned to Anbar Province, reported to his superiors in November 2003 that the Bremer program had created a tinderbox: "What we have done over the last six months in al-Anbar has been a recipe for instability. . . . Through aggressive de-Baathification, the demobilization of the army, and the closing of factories, the coalition has left tens of thousands of individuals outside the economic and political life of the country." [22]

The result was a crescendo of protest. Individual demands for government aid became complaints to occupation officials about the occupation's imposition of neoliberalism, and then developed into local protests, followed by national protests. [23] During summer 2003, there were almost daily demonstrations demanding restoration of jobs lost due to demobilization, de-Baathification, and privatization. At the same time, newspapers and other media arose to protest what Bremer called the "harsh, immediate consequence of economic modernization." [24] Everywhere in Iraq, people organized politically to create or take over local government, and to demand that a nationally elected government be installed to address the growing problems. When Bremer refused to schedule elections, national protests were mounted, including a march of one hundred thousand in Baghdad.

Ironically, this consequence had been anticipated by L. Paul Bremer himself when he warned in 2002—before the invasion—that the sort of program he later instituted in Iraq would typically "create real tensions in emerging markets" because the "painful consequences . . . are felt long before its benefits are clear." His recommendations before, during, and after his experience in Iraq were unaltered: stay the course, since the programs were "good for the economy and society in the long run." [25]

A Response of Savage Repression

The economic debacle affected various parts of Iraq with differing degrees of severity, and this differential was then reflected in the levels of protest. Baghdad, the capital, contained a large proportion of the government apparatus and the commerce of the country; so it was hit with cata-strophic force by the surge in unemployment.[26] Predominantly Sunni cities outside Baghdad, where the largest proportion of state facilities were located and many government employees lived, were similarly dev-astated.[27] Many predominantly Shia cities in the South were strongly af-fected, but not as profoundly as the predominantly Sunni cities.

Iraqi Kurdistan—to the north of Baghdad—was largely shielded from the immediate impact of Bremer's policies. The region had always been discriminated against by the Hussein regime, so few government jobs and factories were located there. During the twelve years following the Gulf War, the region had largely been left to rule itself and establish eco-nomic ties to neighboring countries. This segregation from the Iraqi economy insulated the Kurds from the "shock treatment" instituted by the U.S. occupation, though Kurdistan was impacted by the longer-term economic decline.

This differential impact, exacerbated by subsequent decisions and events, marked the beginning of the sectarian divisions that would later become such a visible part of Iraqi life. Though Sunni and Shia had lived together peacefully for more than one thousand years, the eco-nomic discrimination practiced by the Hussein regime became bla-tantly visible under the occupation, as Sunnis were hardest hit not only by the economic depression, but also by de-Baathification and the de-mobilization of the army. In response, Sunnis organized the earliest and most visible protests against the occupation, which encouraged occu-pation officials to use military force most ferociously against Sunnis, creating a cycle of violence between occupation forces and the Sunnis that would eventually contribute to further sectarian divisions.

Anger mounted as economic depression took hold, with the largest and most insistent protests coming from predominantly Sunni cities and Sunni-dominated areas of Baghdad. The rebellion was made more pro-nounced by the residual loyalty of many Sunni communities to the Hussein regime and by the U.S. military's initial focus on those commu-nities, from which it expected the most resistance.

At first, most protests were peaceful, focusing either on local eco-nomic issues or on general conditions that were worsening in the initial weeks and months of occupation. Typically, Iraqis demanded services and jobs from the CPA. The run-up to the ferocious first battle of Fallujah in April 2004 actually began with a protest demonstration a full year earlier, only weeks after the fall of the Hussein regime. When two hundred protesters demanded that the U.S. military vacate a local school so that it could be reopened, U.S. troops responded with overwhelming force to what they believed was rifle fire from the crowd, killing thirteen and wounding seventy-five Iraqis.[28] For the soldiers and officers involved, the incident illustrated the policy of choking off violent protest before it gathered steam, even if the shooter was surrounded by civilians; for the citizens, it illustrated the intention of the United States to use maximum force to take control of Iraqi institutions, including even elementary schools.

This incident was a microcosm of the combination of material oppression and ferocious repression that provoked what would become an ongoing rebellion. This cause and effect was expressed by two residents of Fallujah to Reuters reporter Edmund Blair shortly after the schoolyard violence.

> "They are stealing our oil and they are slaughtering our people," said Shuker Abdullah Hamid, a cousin of one of the victims, 47-year-old Tuamer Abdel Hamid.
> "Now, all preachers of Falluja mosques and all youths . . . are organizing martyr operations against the American occupiers," said a man cloaked in white, using the term often used to describe suicide attacks in the Israeli-Palestinian conflict.[29]

In 2003, even before growing discontent had matured into a well-organized armed rebellion, the U.S. National Intelligence Estimate (NIE), the summary of consensus thinking among the numerous intelligence agencies, officially designated the conflict as an insurgency that "was driven by local factors, and that drew its strength from deep grievances and a widespread hostility to the presence of foreign troops."[30] The Bush administration "essentially ignored the NIE," and instead interpreted both peaceful demonstrations and the growing violence as ongoing Baathist attempts to organize their return to power, much as they would later classify anyone who resisted the occupation as a member of al-Qaeda. The U.S. military applied the occupation's iron heel, on the theory that forceful suppression would soon defeat or demoralize the few "dead-enders" intent on restoring the old regime.

Peaceful protest was met with arrests, beatings, and overwhelming and often lethal military force. Home invasions of people suspected of anti-occupation activities—or named as suspects by informers who used U.S. forces to advance their own campaigns of reprisal—became commonplace, resulting in thousands of arrests and numerous firefights. Detention and torture at Abu Ghraib and other U.S.-controlled prisons were part of a larger strategy designed to get information about the growing resistance, and therefore facilitate harsh, often deadly, strikes. In general, the Iraqi population came to understand that resistance to the U.S. occupation—no matter how it was conducted—would be met by savage repression.

This policy might have worked if, as Bush administration officials claimed, the resistance had indeed been nothing but remnants of the Hussein regime, thirsting for a return to power. It might even have worked if the growing resistance had rested only on the anger people felt about the occupation of their homeland by a brutal alien army. Under those conditions, protestors might have decided to bide their time in the face of overwhelming demonstrations of force, waiting either for a voluntary withdrawal or a decrease in the level of repression once the occupiers felt secure in their rule. In any case, they might have felt that the injuries suffered if they resisted would be more grievous than the injuries suffered if they submitted to domination.

In the context of deepening economic disaster, however, Iraqis had little choice but to protest, since passivity would yield a worse situation tomorrow than today, and still worse in the coming months. Submission would mean destitution. Iraqi citizens felt compelled to try to forestall their ongoing economic decline, and many of them turned to protest, with a growing number embracing violent protest.

Ignoring Eternal Verities

Many have argued that a better-managed occupation could have quelled these problems. However, this argument is without merit. Could the United States have suppressed this economically driven rebellion if, for example, it had flooded the country with several hundred thousand troops, as Army Chief of Staff General Eric Shinseki had recommended? Shinseki's recommendation rested on World War II experiences, when occupation forces were charged with suppressing the remnants of previous regimes in Japan and Germany, not a major revolt against economic destitution. More U.S. troops might have delayed the economic revolt, but as long as Washington's administrators were intent on privatizing the country, the discontent—and various forms of protest—would have continued to mount. The cycle of protest, repression, and escalation would have eventually run its course.

What about the preservation of Hussein's army and use of it to suppress the growing revolt? This might have had some impact, but the contention of Bremer and others that the Baathist Army would be unreliable was more than justified. CPA officials rightly feared major resistance from all institutions that were supported by the old system, including the military, which benefited from government-controlled enterprises as much as any other part of the establishment. The military might have refused to suppress economic protesters, might have bolstered efforts by workers to reopen shuttered factories, and might have even provided the labor to help rehabilitate damaged government facilities. Moreover, the Baathist military had never, under Hussein, been asked to suppress Sunni protests. There was no guarantee that it would do so under Washington's leadership, and every reason to fear that it might become an anchor of anti-occupation resistance. Given these doubts, the U.S. military and political leadership had logical reasons not to risk the preservation of Saddam Hussein's army.

Forced to impose order directly, the Bush administration saw its policy of repression backfire, stoking an ever angrier, more popular, more widespread, and better equipped resistance. By early 2004, what the occupation commanders called "the insurgency" had reached critical mass, concentrated in predominantly Sunni areas, but also viable in Baghdad and in the Shia-dominated cities in the south of the country. A resistance that had mounted fewer than twenty attacks each day in the summer of 2003 was averaging one hundred per day a year later.[31]

An alien army entered Iraq, destroyed that country's sovereignty, and stoked nationalist resentments.[32] The unrelenting brutality inflicted upon resisting communities further angered and incited the Iraqi population. But neither of these provocations, alone or together, could have triggered the fierce resistance that arose so decisively in all areas of the country except Kurdistan. The willingness to fight and die requires something more than insult and injury: it is almost always animated by the conviction that otherwise things will only get worse. It was the downward trajectory of the Iraqi economy, rising levels of unemployment as government and private businesses were shuttered, decreasing wages as neoliberal reform took hold, the ongoing failure of the agricultural economy, and the steadily fading hope of better days for the next generation that guaranteed and sustained the Iraqi insurgency.

Chapter Four

The Struggle
for Iraqi Oil

Iraqi public opinion strongly opposes the handing of authority and control over the oil to foreign companies that aim to make big profits at the expense of the people. They aim to rob Iraq's national wealth by virtue of unfair, long-term oil contracts that undermine the sovereignty of the State and the dignity of the Iraqi people.

— **Excerpt from joint statement of Iraqi labor unions**

During the early days of the war, some observers suggested that "The Bush administration should declare victory and bring the troops home." The idea, though never seriously considered in Washington, had its seductive appeal. Since the official reasons for the war were to eliminate the Hussein government as a threat to its neighbors and haven for international terrorists, regime change made the declaration of success credible. When news emerged that there were no weapons of mass destruction and no terrorist haven, the idea took on more weight, since the raison d'etre for the war no longer applied. Why, then, did the Bush administration seek to subdue Iraqi society instead of looking for a face-saving way to depart? The problem, which grew more pronounced as time went on, was that such a withdrawal would not accomplish the geopolitical goals of the war: the conversion of Iraq into an outpost for U.S. Middle East policy. These goals required that Iraq transfer its oil production from the government to international oil companies, that Iraq be ruled by a stable, powerful, and friendly regime, and that Iraq be a home base for U.S. military presence in the Middle East.

It was in the context of these larger goals that the "declare victory and withdraw" scenario was a nonstarter. Later, as efforts at pacification generated increasing resistance, withdrawal would have represented an even larger setback. Iraq became a fundamental test of America's ability to impose its will, not only on Iraq, but also on Iran and other recalcitrant members of OPEC. In that emerging context, withdrawal from Iraq meant abandoning the goal of achieving the dominant role in the Middle East necessary to execute the Cheney energy plan.

The Bush administration's determination to see its plans reach fruition was expressed both in its escalating military efforts to subdue the insurgency, which we will address in chapters 5 through 8, and in its escalating political-economic efforts to transform the oil industry, which is the subject of this chapter.

Neoliberalism in the Oil Industry

When the United States arrived in Baghdad and disbanded the police force, the military was careful to abide by Defense Secretary Donald Rumsfeld's insistence that Iraqis be allowed to fully enjoy their newfound freedom: "Freedom's untidy and free people are free to make mistakes and commit crimes and do bad things." Under orders from their commanding officers, U.S. soldiers stood aside as looters used large trucks to remove the cradle-of-civilization-era treasures from the National Museum, stole enough equipment and drugs from hospitals to compromise their ability to operate, stripped many government offices of anything that could be sold on the black market, then moved on to looting individual homes.[1]

The principle exception to this "stuff happens" approach was the oil industry. Rumsfeld was not willing to let Iraqis "do bad things" with Iraqi oil. Even before the invasion, during the shock-and-awe air assault that was designed to paralyze Iraqi resistance, U.S. airships patrolled the pipelines and other vulnerable installations to prevent sabotage. Once the ground assault began, combat brigades peeled off from the invading force to guard oil facilities in southern Iraq. And when Baghdad fell, occupation soldiers immediately deployed to the oil ministry and its associated holdings, preventing anyone from tampering with records, equipment, or the oil itself. Others moved quickly to guard facilities north and west of the city. A few other locations were protected (notably the interior ministry, which contained political records and buildings that were designated as possible U.S. facilities) but, aside from these exceptions, the invading troops were specifically instructed that their jobs did not include protection of property.[2]

Though the plan for privatizing Iraqi business had been developed to complement and facilitate the exploitation of Iraqi oil, the oil industry was not treated like the rest of the Iraqi economy. Above all, any disruption of oil production was unacceptable. The Bush administration was very hopeful that Iraq would, as Deputy Defense Secretary Wolfowitz put it, "finance its own reconstruction, and relatively soon."[3] Therefore, Washington had good reason to avoid the sort of drastic changes that would decrease current production in favor of strong future increases. Beyond this, U.S. policy makers publicly acknowledged their concerns about the fragility of the international oil markets, which could be expected to experience price spikes and possibly permanent increases in oil in reaction to any interruption of production.

All these factors led to special treatment of the oil industry. In contrast to the immediate shuttering of other state enterprises, occupation authorities left the existing Iraqi oil industry intact initially, and temporarily postponed efforts to remodel it.

Perhaps even more important than the urgency attached to maintaining and increasing oil production was the fear that immediate and overt privatization—the plan implemented for other industries—would trigger major and perhaps uncontrollable protests. Iraqis, like the citizens of other oil-bearing Middle East countries, had a ferocious attachment to their oil. Just after U.S. troops entered Baghdad, opinion polls indicated that almost 50 percent of Iraqis believed that the U.S. purpose was "to get oil," and the numbers increased regularly thereafter.[4] Clearly, any overt effort to privatize the oil fields would run the risk of generating exactly the sort of protest that would at least disrupt production, and possibly postpone and even prevent the transformation of the Iraqi oil industry that Bush administration policy required.

One inflammatory exception to this conservative oil strategy revealed the degree to which specific actions in Iraq were tied to a larger project of maximizing Middle East oil production under Washington's leadership. During the initial offensive, U.S. forces bombed the small Iraq-Syria pipeline, which had been a key outlet for Iraqi oil.[5] This assault reflected the Bush administration's hostility toward the Syrian regime. With no change in Syria's status as an adversary, the next three years passed without any effort made to restore the historic pipeline. Like the policy of which it was a part, the U.S. management of Iraqi oil was a less-than-smashing (or perhaps an all-too-smashing) success. The destruction and disruption of the U.S. invasion, the dismantling of the police and of other state agencies and enterprises, and the rise of the insurgency produced regular interruptions of production. The chronic uncertainty of Iraqi oil combined with broader supply problems (which had motivated the invasion in the first place) to trigger constantly increasing prices. Instead of the hoped-for decline from $30 to $20 dollars per barrel, the price of oil on international markets approached $100 per barrel by late 2007.

As the occupation proceeded, the strategy for reconstituting Iraqi oil production reflected these negative developments without deviating from the long-term goal of drastically increased production under the aegis of international oil companies.

The Prize

According to U.S. Energy Information Administration estimates in 2006 Iraq had 115 billion barrels of proven oil reserves—that is, oil known to exist that can be extracted using current methods—the third-largest holdings in the world (after Saudi Arabia and Iran). About two-thirds of these known reserves are located in predominantly Shia southern Iraq, and the final third in the north, largely in the three Kurdish provinces. Even if these estimates were severely inflated, as some informed experts believe, Iraqi oil fields would certainly be capable of producing far more than the 2.5 million barrels that the Hussein regime had been extracting each day.

However, only about 10 percent of the country had actually been explored by 2003, and there was every reason to believe that modern methods—which had not been applied since the beginning of the Iraq-Iran War in 1980—might well uncover magnitudes more oil. Estimates of the possible new finds offered by officials of various interested governments ranged from 45 billion to 214 billion additional barrels, depending on the source, but some nongovernmental experts saw Iraqi reserves exceeding 400 billion barrels. If the latter figure were correct, then Iraq would likely become the world's largest source of oil. Even if the more conservative figures were accurate, Iraq would be the country most able to expand production to meet the increasing demands in the world market.[6]

These estimates were disputed by some experts, who believed all the figures for oil reserves in the Middle East had been severely inflated because of the advantages that accrued to countries that declared large amounts of as-yet-untapped resources. These pessimistic experts tended to estimate proven reserves at as little as one third of the claimed volumes, and similarly to discount the amount yet to be discovered.[7] However, if this discounting were accurate, it would make Iraqi oil all the more precious since any shortage in supply would be that much more severe.

For the most part, Iraq's petroleum is considered to be of very high quality. Moreover, both existing and potential fields are extremely cheap to access. James Paul of the international policy monitoring group, the Global Policy Forum, points out that "according to *Oil and Gas Journal*, Western oil companies estimate that they can produce a barrel of Iraqi oil for less than $1.50 and possibly as little as $1. . . . This is similar to production costs in Saudi Arabia and lower than virtually any other country."[8]

Before the war, the price of crude oil was about $30 per barrel, but it steadily soared after the U.S. invasion, approaching $100 in fall 2007. If official estimates of Iraqi reserves are accurate, then even with no new discoveries the profits would be stupendous—at $30 per barrel, the total value was $3 trillion; with new discoveries reaching the most optimistic estimates, and with oil priced at 2007 levels, the value would be $30 trillion.[9]

Once the invasion toppled the Hussein regime, the principal questions became: Who would control the extraction of Iraqi oil? Who would decide who the privileged customers would be? Who would pocket the profits? And could Iraq substantially increase its rate of production? From the U.S. government's point of view, there was no debate. The United States had every incentive to wrest the control of oil from the Iraqi government and deliver it to the oil companies. And the oil companies had every incentive to desire control. In a market that was growing more uncertain and competitive, any firm able to claim a significant portion of the Iraqi oil spoils could vastly increase its market share and profits.

Under Saddam Hussein, Iraqi oil never fulfilled the potential of its proven oil fields. A modest goal for the country's oil industry would have been continuing the 3.5 million barrels per day achieved in 1979, but the disruptions caused by the Iraq-Iran War in the 1980s and by UN sanctions imposed after the Gulf War in 1991 severely limited production. From the late 1990s until the invasion in 2003, Iraq averaged around 2.5 million barrels per day.[10]

Knowledge of this level of underproduction was certainly one factor in Deputy Secretary of Defense Paul Wolfowitz's prewar prediction that the invasion and occupation of Iraq would pay for itself. Wolfowitz hoped for a quick postwar increase in production to 3.5 million barrels per day (at the $30 per barrel price of oil at that time, close to $40 billion per year in revenue).[11] A predicted expansion in production levels (once the oil giants were brought into the mix) to perhaps 6.5 million barrels, through the development of new oil fields or more efficient exploitation of existing fields, would have the potential to more than cover expected short-term military costs while giving the Bush administration a strong foundation for its goal of doubling Middle East oil production—putting into action the melding of energy policy and military policy that Cheney's energy group and allied administration officials envisioned.

The Plan of Attack

In 2002, just a year after Cheney's energy task force completed its work, and before the United States had officially announced its decision to invade Iraq, the State Department "established a working group on oil and energy," as part of its Future of Iraq Project. It brought together influential Iraqi exiles, U.S. government officials, and international consultants associated with the major oil companies. (Several Iraqi members of the group not coincidentally became part of the U.S.-backed Iraqi government.) The result of the project's work was a "draft framework for Iraq's oil policy" that would form the foundation for the energy strategy that the Bush administration would continually press for during the first several years of occupation.[12]

The State Department placed Bearing Point, a well-connected international consulting firm, in charge of developing a concrete program that would sustain and even increase Iraqi production immediately after the invasion, and that would also encourage the big oil companies to invest huge amounts of development capital to ensure a doubling or even tripling of Iraqi production in the near future. The solution they arrived at was to utilize production-sharing agreements (PSAs), a form of temporary privatization that transferred all decision making about development and rate of production to private leaseholders, while leaving the technical ownership in the hands of the host government.

Production-sharing agreements were originally devised for circumstances in which there is a strong possibility that oil exploration will be extremely costly or even fail, and/or where extraction is likely to prove prohibitively expensive.[13] The contracting company promises to supply the investment capital for the enterprise and absorb all losses if no oil is found. To offset the huge risks in such a venture, the contracting company is usually given a long-term lease (usually between fifteen and thirty years) on the oil field, with virtually full ownership rights. The firm makes the decisions about how to approach exploration and drilling, and then—if oil is found—takes control of the extraction and selling process, deciding on the all-important rate of extraction, pricing of the extracted oil, and the customers who will receive the delivered oil.

The licensing country is guaranteed a proportion of the profits, if and when oil is extracted and sold. Commonly, the proportion is quite low at first, usually considerably below half, until the investing company recoups the costs of exploration and drilling. After these costs are amortized, the proportion taken by the country increases, though it never approaches the level of return of nationalized oil industries. In the current production environment most oil fields remain productive for about thirty years;

thus the typical PSA is likely to last through most of the productive life of the oil fields, so that this form of temporary privatization actually works like the old oil concessions that signed away ownership, which had become anathema among all OPEC members in the 1970s and 1980s.

For U.S. planners, the PSAs were a perfect vehicle by which to answer all their long-term needs. The occupation could leave existing oil fields—at least for the short term—in the hands of the government-owned companies, and thus maintain production and avoid popular protest. Since the existing fields represented only a small fraction of the proven reserves, PSAs could be executed with large and wealthy oil companies who had access to vast amounts of investment capital (as retained earnings or easily borrowed capital) to develop these already-proven fields, bringing production on line quickly, and boosting Iraqi production very significantly in a few years.

The oil industry could be expected to embrace PSAs, once the occupation successfully shepherded their acceptance by the Iraqi government and people. The inducements for the companies were manifold: the contracts would be enormously lucrative, since they would allow the companies to obtain a large share of the revenues that had previously been monopolized by the Iraqi government; there was little risk because the Iraqi oil fields were large and already proven, and the oil was high grade and easy to extract; the companies would have virtually unfettered decision-making control, thus guaranteeing maximum profits; the length of the contracts guaranteed long profits; the contracts would be protected by international law, so that successor governments could not erode or void their favorable features; and accounting procedures allowed them to add oil resources held under PSAs to their store of proven reserves, so they would be factored into the companies' stock prices as though they were fully owned. With this sort of reward, the large oil companies could be expected to invest lavishly in rapid and state-of-the-art development of Iraq's unexploited oil fields.

Imposing the Plan

Unfortunately, the new Iraqi government, which U.S. occupation officials would select a year after the invasion, was certain to oppose the plan to use PSAs to develop the oil industry. In the first place, no ruling group is anxious to reduce its own power. Thirty years of OPEC control of the oil spigot in the Middle East had accustomed both the Iraqi elite and its citizens to the exercise of this power. The new government of Iraq would expect to inherit this control, and would not be eager to transfer it to private oil companies that were explicitly mandated to use it to deplete the nation's chief source of wealth.

Second, the spectacular profits that the oil companies could expect to gain from their control of oil extraction would be at the expense of the Iraqi government. As its neighbors continued to accrue the profits from the extraction and sale of crude oil, the Iraqi government would be sharing these profits—often giving up the lion's share—with the oil companies.

Finally, the new government would almost certainly oppose the Bush administration's plan of dramatically increasing production. In the 1990s all the OPEC producers, even America's then-most loyal ally, Saudi Arabia, had become increasingly sensitive to their own finite supplies, and growing demand would increase prices on a steady basis. In the short run, therefore, they had little interest in substantially increasing production, since it would lower prices and decrease their return. In the longer run, they also had little interest in increasing production, since such increases might interrupt the upward trend in prices.

Given this interest in delaying the extraction of finite reserves, Middle East governments were unwilling to invest the vast amounts of capital needed for maximum extraction. They preferred to develop new fields at a moderate pace, perhaps as slowly as simply replacing old fields as they were exhausted. Even the most compliant Iraqi regime would likely resist the execution of PSAs that allowed outside oil companies to claim a large share of the profits while depleting their reserves and drastically reducing oil revenues in the future.

Because of this, governments have been willing to execute PSAs only when oil exploration and extraction is extremely risky. If the host country had neither the expertise nor the financial resources to undertake such a risky venture, PSAs were used to induce outside companies to take on the task.

None of these conditions applied in Iraq, though. Huge reservoirs of easily accessible oil had already been identified, and any new fields were likely to be easily discovered and developed. That is why none of Iraq's neighbors had ever utilized PSAs. Saudi Arabia, Kuwait, Iran, and the United Arab Emirates all paid the multinationals a fixed rate to explore and develop their fields, and all the profits became state revenues.

The advocates of PSAs in Iraq justified their use by arguing that $20 billion would be needed to develop the Iraqi fields fully, and that favorable PSAs were the only way to attract such heavy doses of finance capital under the dangerous circumstances prevailing after the fall of Saddam Hussein.[14] Moreover, Iraq could neither generate the money from existing revenues nor borrow against later cash flow because Saddam Hussein had accumulated $120 billion in debt and reparations obligations from his invasion of Kuwait. The only way to generate capital would be to give the multinational oil companies PSAs that would make the risks worthwhile.

This assertion seemed, however, to be little more than a smokescreen.[15] No major oil companies were willing to invest in Iraq immediately, no matter how sweet the deal, since they had many reasons to doubt that their rights to the oil would remain secure once the situation in Iraq stabilized. However, once the situation in Iraq stabilized sufficiently to allow for orderly development of the oil—that is, once things were calm enough to start work on the PSAs—there would be no need for PSAs, since the government would have no trouble attracting finance capital to develop reserves that could well be worth in excess of $10 trillion.

This very visible conflict of interest made Washington's planners unsure that even the most compliant client government would be willing to double production and follow U.S. leadership in selling it. PSAs, if they could be implemented, would resolve this problem and would also answer the second—and far more significant—half of Greenspan's argument about the importance of replacing Saddam Hussein: that it was essential to get him "out of the control position" he held over the production of oil.[16] PSAs would not only deliver the oil fields into the hands of capital-rich oil companies eager to extract large amounts of oil as quickly as possible, they would take decision making out of the hands of any government.

The Initial Campaign to Capture Iraqi Oil

In light of this history, the particular way in which the United States sprang into action as soon as its forces arrived in Baghdad was hardly surprising.[17] Not long after President Bush declared "major combat operations in Iraq have ended," L. Paul Bremer promulgated a series of laws designed, among other things, to jump-start the development of Iraqi oil. While he left the operating oil wells under the control of Northern Oil Company and the Southern Oil Company, the two Iraqi government companies that had run them for the past thirty years, he announced the transfer of remaining existing oil refineries, pipelines, and shipping to Halliburton subsidiary KBR. And he began the process of negotiating production-sharing agreements that would place foreign oil companies in control of Iraq's valuable undeveloped reserves.[18]

All these efforts were, however, quickly frustrated, both by the growing insurgency and by civil resistance. Iraq's oil workers quickly unionized—even though Bremer extended Hussein's prohibition on unions in state-owned companies, one aspect of the Iraqi dictatorship he was happy to keep intact. The workers quickly brought the southern oil fields and pipeline back on line even before KBR had arrived on the scene. They then successfully resisted the transfer of pipeline and port management duties to foreign companies. In one noteworthy moment, the oil workers actually refused to take orders from KBR officials and stopped any exports from the oil hub of Basra. After a two-day strike, the KBR officials withdrew, thus preserving its members' jobs (which were threatened by KBR's policy of employing Western administrators and South Asian workers) and keeping the state-owned Southern Oil Company in control of operations in the region. KBR's management contract was subsequently voided, and Bremer abandoned his effort to transfer the management of facilities to outside companies.[19]

At the same time, the growing insurgency, acting on the already prevalent belief that a major goal of the occupation was to steal Iraqi oil, systematically began to attack the oil pipelines that traveled through the largely Sunni areas of the country. Within a few months, all oil exports in the northern part of Iraq were interrupted—and the northern export pipelines remained unusable from then on. The pipelines in the south were protected by the workers, who had useful ties to the mainly Shia resistance in the southern part of the country and who advocated the continuation of oil exports as long as the state-owned company was left in charge.

Another key player in Iraqi oil politics during these early years were the major U.S. corporations involved in the so-called reconstruction of Iraq, notably Halliburton and Bechtel. These crony corporations with close ties to the Bush administration accepted huge fees to rehabilitate dilapidated or damaged oil facilities.[20] Almost without fail, they chose not to repair existing plants locally or to employ the skilled Iraqi technicians who had ingeniously maintained those facilities during more than a dozen years of UN sanctions that had deprived the country of needed parts.[21] Instead, working under cost-plus agreements that guaranteed a fixed profit rate no matter how much an operation ultimately cost, the contractors preferred to install expensive, new, proprietary equipment. Then, in the absence of any outside oversight, they ran up huge expenses and frequently failed to complete their contracts, leaving the oil facilities they were servicing in states of disrepair or partial repair—and equipped with technology that local technicians could not service. Damaged oil facilities, particularly in the north where no union could protect them, were left unrepaired.

Meanwhile, the major oil companies refused Bremer's invitation to invest their own money in Iraqi projects, pointing out that the insurgency and spreading chaos made such investments unwise. In addition, they were well aware that Bremer's regime in Baghdad lacked clear authority to sign contracts with them, since international law requires occupying powers to leave intact the basic laws of the country they occupy. Bremer's willingness to ignore preexisting Baathist law that kept all oil production in the hands of the state was not shared by the oil companies, since even the most airtight PSA might be overturned as illegal in the very international courts that were expected to protect them. This, in turn, meant that their investments might be in jeopardy once a legitimate Iraqi government took power.[22]

At least in part because of this refusal by oil companies to sign development contracts, the United States appointed an Interim Governing Council, which was asked to approve Bremer's directives, including his oil program, and thus provide an Iraqi validation of U.S. policy. This did not sufficiently reassure the oil companies and eventually, in June 2004, Bremer "transferred sovereignty" to a U.S.-appointed Iraqi Interim Government headed by former CIA asset and Iraqi exile, Iyad Allawi. The new premier embraced Bremer's policy, explicitly inviting the oil companies to sign PSAs, but to no avail. International oil companies were no more confident in Allawi's future than they had been in Bremer's, and weren't willing to risk their capital in such dangerous and legally ambiguous circumstances.

As a result, the first two years of Bush administration efforts to open up the Iraqi oil industry failed dismally. The insurgency had kept the northern oil pipeline closed, with more than 226 pipeline attacks.[23] The union kept the southern pipeline opened and pumping, but prevented any intrusion of outside contractors into the existing production system. Halliburton and other contractors failed to bring shuttered facilities on line. And throughout this unsettled period, international oil companies refused to sign any contracts for new development.

As a result production never even approached the 2.5 million barrels Hussein's regime had managed to extract on its worst days. In fact, there was not a single month when production exceeded 2 million barrels. In the third and fourth years of the occupation, production improved somewhat, but only a single month reached the 3.5 million barrels that Wolfowitz had expected to average right away.[24]

Dealing with the Iraqi Government

It is difficult to judge how much Bremer's inability to impose plans for Iraq's oil industry contributed to the Bush administration's decision to abandon its plans for Bremer to be—as historian Juan Cole put it—"a

MacArthur in Baghdad for years." As it happened, nothing substantive was attempted on the oil front until January 2005, when the first elections for a temporary Iraqi government were completed. Almost immediately, U.S. officials began a new campaign to "capture . . . new and existing oil and gas fields" in Iraq.[25] Wary of being seen as imposing oil privatization on the Iraqi people, the Bush administration concocted a strategy that would enlist the international community in pressuring the new Iraqi government and various regional and provincial authorities to adopt its program.

This strategy involved making the International Monetary Fund (IMF) a key player in Iraqi oil policy.[26] Through loans in the 1980s and reparations imposed for his invasion of Kuwait in 1990, Hussein had accumulated $120 billion in external debt, the largest per capita debt in the world and a potentially insurmountable obstacle to economic recovery, even in oil-rich Iraq. One option available to the new government was to declare this debt "odious," a technical term in international law referring to debt accumulated by authoritarian rulers for their own personal or political aggrandizement.

Hussein's expansionist war against Iran, his use of public funds to build ostentatious monuments and palaces, his transfer of billions to his personal accounts, and his failure to maintain the infrastructure of the country were all excellent evidence that the debt was indeed odious. The United States claimed as much for almost $40 billion of it, held by nineteen industrialized countries known as the Paris Club of lenders. Instead of seeking to cancel this debt (and the remaining $80 billion) entirely, however, the Bush administration sent James Baker, secretary of state under George H. W. Bush, to the Paris Club to negotiate conditional forgiveness. The resulting agreement immediately forgave $12 billion but left $28 billion of Paris Club debt on the books. A second $12 billion would be forgiven if the Iraqi government signed on to "a standard International Monetary Fund program," while an additional $8 billion would be abrogated three years later, if the IMF confirmed Iraqi compliance. Even if "successful," almost $8 billion would still be outstanding to the Paris Club—together with $80 billion not covered by the agreement.

The standard International Monetary Fund program not surprisingly included a requirement that the Iraqi government pass legislation enacting the familiar U.S. policies regarding Iraqi oil, including the use of PSAs, as well as a host of other provisions that would force the continuation of Bremer's privatization program. Among the most punitive of the IMF provisions was one that Bremer had announced but failed to implement: an end to the economic breadbasket that guaranteed all Iraqi families low prices for fuel and certain food staples. In a country with anywhere between 30 percent and 70 percent unemployment depending on the source, average wage levels under $100 per month, and escalating inflation, these Hussein-era subsidies meant the difference between basic subsistence and disaster for a large proportion of Iraqis. Noted independent journalists Basav Sen and Hope Chu: "A move that appears on the surface to be beneficial for Iraq—debt cancellation—is being used as a tool of control by the World Bank, the IMF and the wealthy creditor countries. What is more, it is a tool of control that will last long after the withdrawal of U.S. combat forces."[27] Zaid Al-Ali, an international lawyer working on development issues in Iraq, described the agreement as a "perfect illustration of how the industrialized world has used debt as a tool to force developing nations to surrender sovereignty over their economies."[28]

The Iraqi National Assembly, elected in January 2005 just as the IMF contract was activated, promptly denounced the agreement as "a new crime committed by the creditors who financed Saddam's oppression." This forceful expression reflected the opinions of the Assembly's constituents: opinion polls showed that 76 percent of Iraqis believed that a major reason for the Bush administration's invasion was "to control Iraqi oil."[29] The insurgents denounced both the IMF and the United States.

The protest from parliament, negative public opinion, and the implacable opposition of the insurgents did not prevent Iraq's government from endorsing the deal. The institutional leverage it faced was simply too great. Aside from the U.S. monopoly on institutional violence (the meager and ineffectual Iraqi police and military forces were controlled by the occupation), the United States also had operational control over Iraqi finances. If the Iraqi government resisted, the United States could simply appropriate the bulk of oil revenues for debt service, thus bankrupting the government. When the agreement was announced, interim oil minister Thamir Ghadbhan, a British-trained technocrat, publicly protested the provisions eliminating fuel and food subsidies. He was subsequently pushed out.[30]

The United States then began pressuring the Iraqi government to draft an oil law that would conform to IMF guidelines. Given high levels of resistance to the very idea, this work was conducted in secret. Independent journalist Joshua Holland described the process:

> Just months after the Iraqis elected their first constitutional government, USAID [the U.S. government's official foreign aid organization] sent a Bearing Point [the consulting group that had designed the U.S. plan for Iraqi oil policy] adviser to provide the Iraqi Oil Ministry "legal and regulatory advice in drafting the framework of petroleum and other energy-related legislation, including foreign investment." . . . The Iraqi parliament had not yet seen a draft of the oil law as of July [2006], but by that time . . . it had already been reviewed and commented on by U.S. Energy

Secretary Sam Bodman, who also "arranged for Dr. Al-Shahristani to meet with nine major oil companies—including Shell, BP, ExxonMobil, ChevronTexaco and ConocoPhillips—for them to comment on the draft."[31]

The pressure from Washington was not limited to the Bush administration and its representatives. When Congress appointed the bipartisan Iraq Study Group (ISG) to evaluate the Iraq War, it fully supported the effort to force Iraqi compliance with the IMF demands. The ISG's final report devoted three pages to proposals for U.S. policy regarding Iraqi oil that sought to enact two key principles: to "encourage investment in Iraq's oil sector by . . . international energy companies" and to "assist Iraqi leaders to reorganize the national oil industry as a commercial enterprise."[32] This support for privatization should not be surprising, since the ISG was co-chaired by former Secretary of State Baker, who had brokered the original "odious debt" relief that triggered the IMF guidelines.

In the summer of 2006, a draft of the proposed hydrocarbon law that fully conformed to the demands of the United States and the IMF was presented to the Iraqi cabinet. There it encountered the expected resistance, but institutional leverage exercised by the occupation prevailed. A fragile alliance among Shia, Kurdish, and Sunni ministers was forged, and the bill was presented to Parliament in early 2007.

The Proposed Petrochemical Bill

Starting in the fall of 2006, key provisions of the pending law were leaked to the Iraqi public. Astute observers could see that it was, once again, the original Bearing Point plan, developed before the invasion and then unsuccessfully promulgated as policy by the CPA under Bremer, and the interim government led by Iyad Allawi. Virtually every element in Iraqi society except the top officials of the Iraqi government immediately opposed the law. The majority of parliament, a wide range of government officials, the leadership of major Sunni political parties, the oil worker's union (which had support of the entire union movement), and the leadership of both Sunni and Shia insurgent groups all registered their opposition and vowed to use all means at their disposal to resist its enactment and implementation.[33]

All this opposition led to many changes in the law even before it was delivered to the Iraqi parliament and to the public on February 18, 2007. The amended version mandated oil company control of production under conditions identical to PSAs, but removed the explosive designation from the actual wording of the law.[34] It also removed the explicit statement that the oil companies would receive 70 percent of profits from newly developed fields until development expenses were amortized, earning 20 percent thereafter. This would have guaranteed them many times the typical profit margin during the initial years, and then at least twice the typical profit margin for the remainder of the contract. In the later version, no such division was specified, but neither was it excluded; the division was left to be negotiated contract by contract.

Many other elements of the original law that were considered deal-breakers by most Iraqis remained in the amended law.[35]

• Insofar as PSAs or their legal equivalent were enacted, the investing oil companies and not the Iraqi government would determine the level of production and the ultimate destination of the oil.

• The law would allow the oil companies to repatriate all profits from oil sales, all but guaranteeing that the proceeds would not be reinvested in the Iraqi economy.

• The Iraqi government would not have control over oil company operations inside Iraq. Any disputes would be referred instead to pro-industry international arbitration panels. This meant that wage levels, working conditions, and environmental protection would be outside the purview of the Iraqi government.

• The oil contracts would be secret documents, thus depriving the Iraqi public and even the parliament of information about the terms negotiated.

• Contracting companies would not be obligated to hire Iraqi workers, and could therefore continue the policy of Halliburton and other foreign firms operating in Iraq of employing Western technicians and South Asian manual laborers.

This proposed law was a clear indication of the unwavering commitment of the Bush administration to its original Middle East plan. All the bill's provisions aimed at advancing Washington's goal of removing Iraqi oil from government control while dramatically increasing production. Despite more than three years of failure to lay a foundation for the transfer of Iraqi oil production from the government to foreign companies, and despite the failure of the occupation to significantly increase levels of Iraqi oil production, the administration elected to stay the course in terms of oil policy just as it continued to stay the course militarily.

In fact, the parallel between oil and military strategy was not accidental. The original invasion was expected to produce a doubling of Iraqi oil production by allowing the oil companies to apply their expertise and resources to the undeveloped Iraqi reserves, then to provide the United States with a military platform from which to influence other Middle Eastern oil states—most importantly Iran—to follow suit. After three years of frustration, abandoning the transformation of the Iraqi oil sector would mean abandoning the larger ambitions for the Middle East. Without a strong Iraqi government and a strong U.S. military presence to pressure Iran and to provide incentive and protection for the Saudis, the Kuwaitis, and the other states, the United States would face a huge setback in implementing the energy policy that had guided U.S. policy since president Carter— resolving energy shortages by guaranteeing access to sufficient oil to provide for growing demand both domestically and among key U.S. trading partners. Since foreign policy had largely been built around this goal, the foundations of Washington's foreign policy were at stake.

The Resistance

Resistance to the U.S.-sponsored law—and more broadly to any privatization scheme—spread throughout Iraqi society. Even in the early days of the occupation, Iraqis sabotaged oil lines in Anbar province and other strongholds of the insurgency. As time went on, the resistance became increasingly unified and threatened to overwhelm the dwindling power of the occupation.[36]

When the formal law was finally formulated by the Iraqi government in 2006, the Iraqi parliament was its most visible opponent. Parliament had unsuccessfully challenged the original IMF agreement, and then—even before they were officially given a copy of the proposed law—passed a sense-of-the-body motion opposing any form of privatization, including PSAs. Once the bill arrived, parliament delayed its debate month after month and finally adjourned in the summer of 2007 without ever officially considering it as proposed legislation. In doing so, parliament defied a March 2007 deadline for passage that Washington politicians of both the Democratic and Republican parties had pronounced an important "benchmark." Even Iyad Allawi, who as prime minister had attempted to impose the law, joined the parliamentary opposition.[37]

In addition, the officials responsible for administering the oil industry constituted a strong opposition within the government bureaucracy. Rafiq Latta, a London-based oil analyst, told *Nation* reporter Christian Parenti, "The whole culture of the ministry opposes [the law]. . . . Those guys ran the industry very well all through the years of sanctions. It was an impressive job, and they take pride in 'their' oil."[38]

Perhaps most formidable of all was the Federation of Oil Unions, with twenty-six thousand members and its allies among the other Iraq labor unions. The oil workers had overturned contracts in 2003 and 2004 that would have placed substantial oil facilities under multinational corporate control, and they initiated a vigorous campaign against the U.S.-sponsored oil program in June 2005, soon after the IMF plan became public, calling a conference to oppose privatization that was attended by workers, academics, and international civil society. In January 2006 the federation convened a convention composed of all major Iraqi union groups in Amman, Jordan; the convention issued a manifesto opposing the entire U.S. neoliberal program for Iraq, including any compromise on national control of oil production.[39]

At a second Amman labor meeting in December 2006, the Federation of Oil Unions announced its opposition to the pending law: "Iraqi public opinion strongly opposes the handing of authority and control over the oil to foreign companies that aim to make big profits at the expense of the people. They aim to rob Iraq's national wealth by virtue of unfair, long-term oil contracts that undermine the sovereignty of the State and the dignity of the Iraqi people."[40] When the bill was made public, oil union president Hassan Jumaa denounced it at another protest meeting, stating: "History will not forgive those who play recklessly with our wealth. . . . We consider the new law unbalanced and incoherent with the hopes of those who work in the oil industry. It has been drafted in a great rush in harsh circumstances."[41]

Jumaa then called on the government to consult Iraqi oil experts who had not participated in drafting the law, and "ask their opinion before sinking Iraq into an ocean of dark injustice."[42] These words were followed by two short labor strikes in Basra province during March 2007, which included a demand for a voice in the final disposition of the oil law.

Finally, the armed resistance registered its opposition, most spectacularly by attempting to assassinate Vice President Adel Abdul Mahdi, a major advocate of the pending law, on the day the bill was made public.[43]

By September 2007 delays and conflicts in parliament had effectively delayed passage of the law.[44] The announcement by the regional government of the Kurdish provinces that it had signed an agreement with Texas-based Hunt Oil for developing an oil field in Kurdistan signaled the collapse of any federal agreement. The Iraqi Oil Ministry declared the Kurdish deal void, invoking the petrochemical law that parliament had not yet considered. The ensuing controversy led to the collapse of the already fragile alliance among Shia, Kurdish, and Sunni ministers and the bill was never passed.

Beneath this factional controversy lay the resistance to the U.S. plan. The Kurds declared that they needed to begin developing the very rich oil lands within their regional boundaries, and that the time had come for them to stop waiting for the United States to either implement or abandon its plan. The Kurds' decision to stop waiting was symptomatic of the on-the-ground reality in Iraq. The U.S. plan was not going to be implemented through legislative action any time soon. And, more generally, the chances that any Iraqi government with even the smallest nationalist or democratic pretensions would enact such an agreement were nil. The resistance—from government officials, unions, the insurgency, and ordinary citizens—would delay or defeat any such program, for at least as long as Iraq remained contested terrain.

Therefore, the success of the Bush administration program necessitated the dismantling of institutional resistance and defeat of the insurgency, in order to impose U.S. will on an Iraqi society rendered compliant through force.

◆ ◆ ◆

As the war progressed, therefore, withdrawal from Iraq also meant abandoning America's energy policy, its foreign policy in the Middle East, and the attempt to prolong the unipolar moment that had occurred when the Soviet Union collapsed.

At each juncture in the war, therefore, the Bush administration faced a huge choice: either abandon the main thrust of the U.S. energy and foreign policy since the Carter administration, or else stay the course in Iraq, using any means necessary to install a friendly regime that would allow international oil companies to develop and pump Iraqi oil.

Part II

Fighting to Capture and Control Iraq

Chapter Five

Collective Punishment

"You know why those people get killed? It's because they're letting insurgents hide in their house."

—U.S. Marine

The die was cast in Iraq as soon as the program of radical reconstruction initiated by L. Paul Bremer began to take hold. The combination of a demobilized Iraqi Army, a dissolved police force, and a dismantled government created a perfect storm of social chaos in communities around the country.

Massive unemployment, ranging up to 70 percent in many localities where government facilities had dominated the economy, created crises for those directly impacted, for the surrounding community, and for the entire country as it attempted to absorb the first of several waves of displaced families.[1] The discontinuation of government services added to the first-order agony of job loss by crippling social services, particularly targeting the poor and unemployed. The shuttering of government enterprises accelerated the degradation and decay of public infrastructure—most immediately electricity, water, and sewage grievously damaged by the war. The occupation's commitment to an immediate shift to private enterprise starved publicly financed local institutions, including hospitals, road maintenance, and agricultural support, and sent them into precipitous decline. The absence of police unleashed a nationwide crime wave that started with the looting of depopulated public buildings and spread to businesses, homes, and individuals, as kidnapping of prosperous citizens and their families became a major source of income for organized crime.[2]

In each city, existing or newly formed organizations, mostly connected to local mosques, sought to stem the tide of chaos with stopgap measures. They distributed meager food baskets, provided inadequate employment services, and moved displaced families to temporary housing. They organized distribution of whatever resources were made available by the crippled government. Most significantly, in virtually every city, religious or secular groups formed local militias to enforce a modicum of order in place of the dissolved police force.

Throughout the country people protested to whatever representatives of the occupation (and later the Iraqi government) they could find. As a consequence, U.S. military units—the only organization represented in most places—were faced with constant complaints, sometimes registered individually, sometimes by religious, tribal, or political representatives, and sometimes through collective protest, often angry and occasionally violent.

Bremer and the occupation military leadership were well aware that discontent would not soon dissipate, since the U.S. program of social and political transformation involved a period of economic shock treatment before the hoped-for benefits would reach the discontented neighborhoods. The possibility of abandoning economic revolution in favor of short-term amelioration of local crises was never considered, and it therefore became the military's responsibility to suppress all protest until the process of transformation was complete. In June 2003 the choice had already been made, as Bremer indicated to BBC correspondent Peter Sissons: "We're going to fight them and impose our will on them and we will capture or if necessary kill them until we have imposed law and order on this country. . . . We dominate the scene and we will continue to impose law and order and impose our will on this country."[3]

The dissolution of the Iraqi military and police, one of the most widely criticized of Bremer's initial actions, might appear to have made it difficult to impose law and order, since the occupation was deprived of what might have been its best tool for local operations. But the long-term strategy had called for a permanent U.S. military presence, since Iraq was slated to become the military, political, and economic hub of Washington's hegemony in the Middle East. As soon as the occupation was officially established, work began on the construction of four "enduring" bases, replete with the full amenities of U.S. military life (fast food, movie theaters, officers' clubs, discount electronics stores, and gyms with swimming pools). Though the original occupation plan projected a total capacity of about fifty thousand troops, who would be used as a rapid deployment force on a regional basis, the bases were easily adapted to a larger campaign to pacify Iraq itself.[4] By April 2004, then, the number of large U.S. bases expanded to fourteen, with the capacity to maintain one hundred thousand troops. Occupation spokesman Brigadier General Mark Kimmitt described these bases as part of "a blueprint for how we could operate in the Middle East."[5]

At Bremer's urging, the military, working from their already functioning large bases and more than one hundred smaller facilities around the country, applied tried-and-true methods: the use of overwhelming force to suppress any sign of violent resistance.[6] In the wake of aggressive or violent protest, they sent patrols into offending communities to question, arrest, or kill suspected insurgents or their supporters. Nir Rosen, a U.S. reporter who also speaks Arabic, was embedded in summer 2003 with the Third Army Cavalry Unit in Husaybah, a small town near the Syrian border where the United States suspected foreign fighters were crossing the border and then joining with local insurgents. He described a nighttime patrol undertaken by his host unit aimed at apprehending sixty-two individuals that U.S. intelligence had identified as key players in the local insurgency, the "guys who actually do the shooting."

> After half an hour of bumpy navigating in the dark the convoy approached the first house and the vehicles switched their lights on, illuminating the target area as a tank broke the stone wall. "Fuck yeah!" cheered one sergeant, "Hi honey I'm home!" The teams charged over the rubble from the wall, breaking through the door with a sledgehammer and dragging several men out. The barefoot prisoners, dazed from their slumber, were forcefully marched over rocks and hard ground. One short middle-aged man, clearly injured and limping with painful difficulty, was violently pushed forward in the grip of a Brobdingnagian soldier who said, "You'll fucking learn how to walk." Each male was asked his name. None matched the names on the list.[7]

With the help of the terrified innocents, the correct residence for their first target was found and invaded. When the suspect's son asked to be taken instead of his aged father, the soldiers arrested both and marched them off. The rest of the night reenacted these initial incidents. Most of the targeted homes—whether or not they contained listed suspects—were ransacked, with doors smashed, closets broken, and dressers emptied onto the floor. Families were terrorized by the violent entries, the angry English-language orders, and by the physical assaults administered to the residents. Men were arrested indiscriminately, whether or not they were on the list.

> Prisoners with duct tape on their eyes and their hands cuffed behind them with plastic "zip ties" sat in the back of the truck for hours, without water. They moved their heads toward sounds, disoriented and frightened, trying

to understand what was happening around them. Any time a prisoner moved or twitched, a soldier bellowed at him angrily and cursed. Thrown among the tightly crowded men in one truck was a boy no more than 15 years old, his eyes wide in terror as the duct tape was placed on them. . . .

The soldier guarding them spoke of the importance of intimidating Iraqis and instilling fear in them. "If they got something to tell us I'd rather they be scared," he explained. An Iraqi policeman drove by in a white SUV clearly marked "Police." He too was stopped at gunpoint and ordered not to move or talk until the last raid was complete. From the list of 34 names, the troop I was with brought in about 16 positively identified men, along with 54 men who were neighbors, relatives or just happened to be around. . . .

In Baghdad, coalition officials announced that 112 suspects had been arrested in a major raid near the Syrian border, including a high-ranking official in the former Republican Guard.[8]

The denouement of this, and so many other U.S. raids and patrols, was the incarceration of the suspects and the other captured residents suspected of having information about—or sympathy for—the suspects. Rosen offered this ironic portrait of the outcome of the raid:

That night the prisoners were visible on a large dirt field in a square of con-certina wire. Beneath immense spotlights and near loud generators, they slept on the ground, guarded by soldiers. One sergeant was surprised by the high number of prisoners taken by the troop I was with. "Did they just ar-rest every man they found?" he asked, wondering if "we just made another 300 people hate us."[9]

Based on the accounts of twenty-four U.S. soldiers, *Nation* reporters Chris Hedges and Laila Al-Arian offered a more general description of these raids:

The American forces, stymied by poor intelligence, invade neighborhoods where insurgents operate, bursting into homes in the hope of surprising fighters or finding weapons. But such catches, they said, are rare. Far more common were stories in which soldiers assaulted a home, destroyed prop-erty in their futile search, and left terrorized civilians struggling to repair the damage and begin the long torment of trying to find family members who were hauled away as suspects.[10]

Hedges and Al-Arian conclude that these house-by-house acts of ter-ror became a "relentless reality" in the predominantly Sunni areas of Iraq. Among the soldiers they interviewed, many reported invading sev-eral hundred homes, with one claiming to have participated in "thou-sands" of house raids. Many home invasions were punctuated with gratuitously brutal acts, including killing family dogs, emptying refriger-ators onto the floor, and destroying sofas and other furniture. In the overwhelming majority of cases, the soldiers concluded that the resi-dents were not involved in the insurgency.

The outcome of this campaign was to crystallize the already growing resistance to the occupation into an organized insurgency, supported by the same civic organizations that had arisen in response to the post-invasion chaos. Militias originally formed to restore law and order became an organized force against the U.S. military, mounting ambushes and attacks designed to frustrate the U.S. raids, intercept supply convoys, and assault the bases where U.S. troops were stationed. Within a few months, formidable guerrilla armies were operating in many localities around the country, adopting names such as the Mahdi Army, Islamic Army in Iraq, al-Mujahideen Army, Ansar al-Sunna, al-Fatiheen Army, Islamic Front for the Iraqi Resistance, Iraqi Hamas, and the 1920 Revolution Brigades.[11]

Predictably, the U.S. military responded by using its superior might to suppress the now-organized guerrillas. Tactics involved applying a microversion of shock and awe—including air assaults in crowded communities. These crushing attacks, which often destroyed one or more homes, were intended not only to suppress those who violently opposed the occupation, but also to deter others in the targeted community from the supporting or "harboring" insurgents. What appeared to the naked eye as indiscriminate violence was instead a part of U.S. strategy to collectively punish communities that housed insurgents.[12]

All this remained under the radar of the U.S. press because these confrontations took place in obscure neighborhoods with small units of occupation troops confronting a handful of Iraqi insurgents, far from the Green Zone where U.S. journalists congregated. But this daily drumbeat of small, deadly confrontations—punctuated by occasional high-profile, citywide search-and-destroy operations—was at the heart of the process that would generate sixty thousand U.S.-caused deaths in the first fourteen months, and that would contribute a disproportionate share of more than one million deaths in fifty months.[13]

To see how all this came about, we need to look at examples of the tiny battles that made up the day-to-day reality of the war in Iraq.

The Incident at Haditha

On November 19, 2005, in town/city of Haditha, a small city of one hundred thousand located about one hundred miles west of Baghdad, an improvised explosive device (IED) exploded under an U.S. military supply convoy, killing one and wounding two members of Kilo Company, Third Battalion, First Marine Regiment. Later that day, a Kilo Company patrol was ordered to investigate the explosion, in search of the perpetrators of the attack. This led to a small firefight that might have gone unreported were it not for an Iraqi human-rights worker who videoed the aftermath, and a *Washington Post* team, led by Ellen Knickmeyer, that investigated charges by local residents that the marines had deliberately executed—with point-blank head shots—nineteen unarmed women, children, and older men in a single room, apparently in retribution for the earlier IED attack.[14] These horrific charges, supported by lurid pictures of nineteen unmistakably civilian bodies lying together in a single room, made the incident newsworthy and propelled an extensive investigation and subsequent prosecutions.

It is actually the defense's version of the story—and the testimony of the various officers that supported the accused marines—that makes the Haditha incident useful in understanding the translation of U.S. patrols into collective punishment involving hundreds of thousands of Iraqi deaths. Consider the key testimony of First Lieutenant William T. Kallop, the officer who sent out the patrol with orders to "clear" the building that was the apparent source of the IED attack.[15] He told the military hearing that he personally inspected the building after his marines returned to the base, and was shocked to discover that only civilians had been killed. Here is the *New York Times* account of his testimony:

> He inspected one of the homes with a Marine corporal, Hector Salinas, and found women, children and older men who had been killed when marines threw a grenade into the room.
> "What the hell happened, why aren't there any insurgents here?" Lieutenant Kallop testified that he asked aloud. "I looked at Corporal Salinas, and he looked just as shocked as I did."[16]

We should take note that Lieutenant Kallop testified that the civilians died from a grenade, not execution-style shots in the head; the two accounts of the incident differ in this important respect.

It is more important, however, to note that Lieutenant Kallop was not shocked or surprised that the incident caused the death of many civilians. His alarm at the carnage was a result of the absence of insurgents among the dead. What made the situation problematic was that *all the fatalities were civilians*, and it led to the possibility that the Kilo Company unit had not been in hot pursuit of an enemy combatant.

Later, however, after questioning Staff Sergeant Frank D. Wuterich (who had led the patrol and commanded the military action), Lieutenant Kallop decided that the incident involved no misbehavior on the part of his troops: "Sergeant Wuterich had told him that they had killed people [in the house] after approaching a door to it and hearing the distinct metallic sound of an AK-47 being prepared to fire. 'I thought that was within the rules of engagement because the squad leader thought that he was about to kick in the door and walk into a machine gun,' Lieutenant Kallop said." [17]

According to Kallop, then, the soldiers were following the rules of engagement because if the squad leader sincerely (but incorrectly) "thought" that he was going to be attacked (based on recognizing a noise through a closed door), he was authorized to use the full lethal force of the patrol (in this case a hand grenade), enough to kill all the people huddled within the apartment.

First Lieutenant Max D. Frank, sent to investigate the incident after it broke in the newspapers, emphasized this to the marine prosecutor, Lieutenant Colonel Sean Sullivan: "It was unfortunate what happened . . . but I didn't have any reason to believe that what they had done was on purpose." [18]

Note that intentionality is the key to the rules of engagement. If the soldiers had known that only civilians were behind the door, then their actions would have been unjustified. If, however, they believed that their attack might capture or kill an armed insurgent—something that can be claimed by U.S. troops in nearly any imaginable situation, given the conditions of the occupation—the rules of engagement justified and mandated their action, including the deaths of nineteen civilians.

Note here that other alternatives were *not* considered. The soldiers could have decided that there was a good chance of hurting civilians in this situation and therefore retreated without pursuing the suspected insurgents. This would have allowed the guerrillas (if they were actually present) to get away, but it would have protected the residents of the house. This option was not chosen, even though many of us might feel that letting one or two or three insurgents escape (in a town filled with insurgents) might be acceptable, instead of risking (and ultimately ending) the lives of however many civilians were huddled behind the closed door.

Later in the hearing, Major General Richard Huck, the commanding officer in charge of the marines in Haditha, underscored these rules of engagement in more general terms: "[The deaths] had occurred during a combat operation and it was not uncommon for civilians to die in such circumstances. 'In my mind's eye, I saw insurgent fire, I saw Kilo Company fire,' Huck testified. . . . 'I could see how 15 neutrals in those circumstances could be killed.'" [19]

For General Huck, and for other commanders in Iraq, once "insurgent fire"—or even the threat of insurgent fire—entered the picture (as it did with the real or imagined metal click behind the door), the actions reported by the marines in that Haditha home were not just legitimate but exemplary. As long as they weren't lying about what happened, they were responding appropriately in a battlefield situation, and the death of "15 neutrals" was not only fully justified, but "not uncommon." This is perhaps the most telling part of the story: commanding officers were used to hearing about, and approving without further investigation, the deaths of a dozen or so civilians.

This same logic applies to the almost routine killing of Iraqis at U.S. military checkpoints. With all cars subject to inspection before passing through roadblocks guarded by U.S. or Iraqi troops, the checkpoints themselves were targets for either sniper fire or car bombs detonating from approaching cars. For that reason, any suspect behavior at or near the checkpoints—most often cars that failed to slow down or stop according to directions—could trigger lethal responses from soldiers who did not want to make the mistake of permitting an attack by an assassin or suicide bomber.

The rules of engagement called for the firing of warning shots, but if the vehicle did not stop, to then "shoot to kill." In one all-too-typical instance, a bus bringing workers to the Rasheed bank approached a "cars-only" checkpoint and did not stop when warning shots were fired. The subsequent attack killed four passengers and wounded several others.[20]

In many instances the location of the checkpoint and/or distracting events nearby meant that oncoming vehicles were fired upon before they realized that they were approaching U.S. soldiers. This sort of confusion was the cause of the widely publicized checkpoint attack near the Baghdad airport on the automobile carrying Italian reporter Giuliana Sgrena, who had just been freed after a month as a hostage.[21] A more mundane incident of the same sort was reported by *Rolling Stone* correspondent Evan Wright during the first year of the war at a roadblock near the city of Nasiriyah:

> Because these sites tend to be poorly marked, many Iraqi drivers fail to stop at them. When U.S. soldiers fire warning shots, the Iraqis often speed up. As a result, many are killed. After one car has been shot at, a Marine named Graves goes to help a little girl cowering in the back seat, her eyes wide open. As he goes to pick her up, "thinking about what medical supplies he might need to treat her...the top of her head slides off and her brains fall out," . . . . As Graves steps back in horror, his boot slips in the girl's brains. "This is the event that is going to get to me when I go home," he says.[22]

Checkpoints, then, operated in parallel to patrols: if there was the perception of potential danger (for example, when the bus did not stop when warned) the appropriate response was the use of lethal force. Hundreds of thousands of vehicles passing through checkpoints created thousands of incidents each day. Even though only a tiny minority of these confrontations resulted in fatalities, they nevertheless contributed to the drumbeat of death across the country.

The same logic applied to the protection of countless U.S. convoys moving people and supplies across the Iraqi countryside and through Iraqi cities. Soldiers and private contractors charged with protecting these convoys from attack or hijacking were mandated to use lethal force in any threatening situation. In the case of convoys, this meant that they were mandated to fire at pedestrians who might block or slow passage, cars that followed too close behind, and vehicles on side streets that could possibly ram the convoy. Most of the time, such situations involved Iraqi civilians with no malicious intent, but the security personnel had to decide such matters in a split second, when a better-safe-than-sorry attitude dictated opening fire.

The international scandal that erupted when employees of Blackwater, a private security firm hired by the United States to perform military duties in Iraq, fired into a crowded plaza in September 2007, was far from typical.[23] A more common example was described by a grief-stricken soldier who described a gruesome incident in a blog on Operation Truth, a Web site devoted to firsthand descriptions by U.S. military personnel of daily events in Iraq:

> Last night we had a young girl run out in front of my Humvee. We slammed into her and her body fell and slid on the ground. We were going about 55 mph. I immediately turned around and watched as 8 of the convoy trucks right behind us trampled her body to pieces. Her head was gone and I was frantically trying to get the trucks to move over, but they just kept coming. I jumped out of my turret and dragged what was left of her to the side of the road. I couldn't stand to see her trampled like a dog anymore.
>
> Sorry for the graphic story, just a bit stressed lately. I'll be fine. It's the nature of running the gauntlet.[24]

The tragic irony of this incident is that the soldier was subject to discipline for stopping and tending to her body. Since there had been documented cases in which convoys had stopped to avoid hitting pedestrians (including children playing in the street) and had then been attacked, soldiers were under strict orders not to stop for anyone. By stopping, the Humvee driver had broken the rules and could have been court-martialed for exposing the convoy to attack.[25]

With convoys crisscrossing Iraq carrying food, supplies, weapons, ammunition, and personnel, there were constant chances for pedestrians to stray into the street, for cars to follow too close, or for vehicles on side streets to roll toward the convoys. These tiny mistakes could, and did, turn into lethal encounters with U.S. soldiers or private contractors, another drumbeat of death in occupied Iraq.

Mayhem in Baiji

The firefights erupting from military patrols in insurgent neighborhoods, from checkpoints under threat of sniper and car-bomb attack, and from convoys wary of ambush all point to one key aspect of U.S. military policy in Iraq: the safety of U.S. troops was paramount, justifying the application of lethal firepower at the slightest hint of danger. It was this logic that led Major General Huck to accept the deaths of "15 neutrals" in Haditha, since in his "mind's eye," his own soldiers were in danger.[26]

But another aspect of this policy was just as important as the protection of U.S. soldiers: killing or capturing suspected insurgents was also paramount, and the chance to do so justified killing numerous civilians, even when U.S. lives were not at risk. This policy was built into the fabric of Washington's policy in Iraq.

Another incident (not worthy of front-page coverage in either the *New York Times* or the *Washington Post*) provides crystalline evidence that risking (and taking) the lives of civilians in order to kill or capture suspected insurgents was a fundamental feature of Bush administration policy.[27]

The incident took place in Baiji, a small city 130 miles north of Baghdad that suffered severe economic decline after its industrial district was shuttered by L. Paul Bremer's policy of closing all government-owned manufacturing establishments.[28] Protests against the closures were met with overwhelming force, which, in response, fueled a strong insurgency that soon controlled many neighborhoods of the city.

Here is the initial *New York Times* account of what happened on January 3, 2006, in one of those neighborhoods, based on interviews with various unidentified "American officials":

> A pilotless reconnaissance aircraft detected three men planting a roadside bomb at about 9 p.m. The men "dug a hole following the common pattern of roadside bomb emplacement," the military said in a statement. "The individuals were assessed as posing a threat to Iraqi civilians and coalition forces, and the location of the three men was relayed to close air support pilots."
>
> The men were tracked from the road site to a building nearby, which was then bombed with "precision guided munitions," the military said. The statement did not say whether a roadside bomb was later found at the site. An additional military statement said Navy F-14's had "strafed the target with 100 cannon rounds" and dropped one bomb.[29]

Crucial to this report is the phrase "precision guided munitions," an affirmation that U.S. forces used technology less likely than older munitions to hit the wrong target. It is this precision that allowed us to glimpse the targeting of civilians that is integral to U.S. military strategy in Iraq.

The target was a "building nearby," identified by the officers who viewed the drone's video record as the insurgents' hiding place. According to local residents who witnessed the attack and spoke to *Washington Post* reporters, the air assault demolished the building and damaged six surrounding buildings. In a perfect world the surrounding buildings would have been unharmed; but the reported amount of human damage in them (two people injured) suggests that, in this case at least, the claims of "precision" were at least fairly accurate; that is, the bomb demolished its designated target and little else.

The problem arises with what happened inside the targeted building, a house inhabited by a large Iraqi family. Piecing together the testimony of local residents, the *Times* reporters concluded that fourteen members of the family were in the house at the time of the attack and nine were killed.[30] The *Post* reporters Ellen Knickmeyer and Salih Saif Aldin reported twelve killed, and offered a chilling description of the scene: "The dead included women and children whose bodies were recovered in the nightclothes and blankets in which they had apparently been sleeping. A *Washington Post* special correspondent watched as the corpses of three women and three boys who appeared to be younger than 10 were removed Tuesday from the house."[31]

It is significant that there were no ground troops involved. Their absence indicated that—unlike the Haditha incident—sparing the building would have posed no immediate threat to U.S. soldiers, and therefore the unspoken option of allowing the suspected insurgents to escape could have been pursued without endangering U.S. lives. Moreover, the decision to attack was made by officers far from the scene, and not by potentially emotional soldiers who might have been influenced by their dangerous situation or by the death of their comrade earlier in the day. Unlike the incident in Haditha, the attack in Baiji was pure "policy."

Because in this case there was on-the-spot reporting by U.S. newspapers, the U.S. military command was required to explain this "collateral damage," despite the use of "precision bombing." Without conceding that the deaths actually occurred, Lieutenant Colonel Barry Johnson, director of the Coalition Press Information Center in Baghdad, explained: "We continue to see terrorists and insurgents using civilians in an attempt to shield themselves."[32]

This comment tells us why the precision bombs were deliberately aimed at a building containing at least some fourteen civilians: it was U.S. policy to attack a building where insurgents might be hiding among civilians. (This same policy was invoked in the investigation of the Haditha case: the investigating officer, Lieutenant Colonel Paul J. Ware, recommended against prosecuting Sergeant Wuterich because the "killings should be viewed in the context of combat against an enemy that ruthlessly employs civilians as cover."[33])

Notice that—in the context of the Baiji incident—this justification based on human shields underscores a little appreciated fact: that the "precision guided munitions" were not used to avoid civilian casualties, but rather to strike the exact location of the insurgents and their alleged civilian "shields."

Notice also that in Baiji, as in Haditha, there were options not chosen. First and foremost, the U.S. commanders could have aborted the air strike. Second, they did not issue a warning that would have allowed for the evacuation of civilians before the building was demolished. Such a warning— or any delay at all in the attack—would have given the insurgents a chance to escape, either disguised as civilians or through prearranged escape routes from the building. In fact, the unspoken implication of Lieutenant Colonel Johnson's statement was that any such forbearance would only encourage the insurgents to "shield themselves" with civilians in the future. By attacking this time, perhaps the insurgents would learn that such "human shield" tactics would not work, or civilians would refuse to allow themselves to be used in this way.

At the top echelons of the occupation military, then, the incidents at Baiji and Haditha were both part of U.S. strategy. This strategy did not call for the overt barbarism of choosing civilian targets, but it did call for the covert barbarism of targeting insurgents even when this also meant killing civilians.

With this logic operating at the command level, we should not be surprised that combat soldiers were familiar with the experience of killing civilians. As early as December 2003 a group of Walter Reed Hospital physicians conducted a study of three army and marine combat brigades as they returned from deployment in Iraq. At that early point in the war, when the number of engagements averaged less than thirty per day, fully 21 percent reported being "responsible for the death of a noncombatant."[34] Though no subsequent statistics on this issue were collected, as the number of daily engagements increased to fifty and then one hundred and finally higher during the surge in 2007—and as soldiers were returned for second, third, fourth, and even fifth deployments—these percentages certainly rose to include the vast majority of combat personnel.[35]

Rules of engagement that sanctioned killing civilians who were proximate to suspected insurgents made death and injury to family, friends, and neighbors a familiar experience for millions of Iraqis. By late 2007, almost one quarter (22 percent) of all families reported at least one member dead "as a result of the conflict in Iraq since 2003," with a similar number (26 percent) reporting an injury.[36] While these figures included deaths from car bombs, death squads, and other sectarian violence, the preponderant source of death was U.S. ordnance.[37]

This horrific daily reality was reflected in Iraqi attitudes toward the occupation. In an August 2007 poll commissioned by the U.S. network ABC and the British network BBC, Iraqis were asked how they felt "about the way in which the United States and other coalition forces have carried out their responsibilities in Iraq." Fully 80 percent gave negative evaluations, with the number rising to 98 percent among Sunnis, who lived in the neighborhoods most likely to experience occupation patrols and checkpoints. Perhaps more important were the attitudes toward President Bush's surge, which had begun six months earlier, and was advertised as an effort to bring security to the predominantly Sunni neighborhoods in Baghdad where the insurgency was strongest. Fully 70 percent of Iraqis said that the surge had made security worse, not better, with the number rising to 89 percent among Sunnis.[38]

Civilians: Collateral Damage to Collective Punishment

But these horrific figures leave one question unanswered: why did U.S. military leaders adopt a policy of sacrificing civilians when it generated widespread antagonism among Iraqis? While Bush administration officials and top U.S. military officers often referred to the residents of communities like Haditha and Baiji as innocent victims of insurgent intimidation and terrorism, the reality was that most of them were not unwilling shields for the guerrillas. They were actively harboring and supporting the insurgents, who were most often relatives, friends, or neighbors. Moreover, this protection of the guerrillas was seen by U.S. military and political leadership as a critical obstacle—perhaps *the* critical obstacle—to successful counterinsurgency.

We can get a perspective on this situation (and the U.S. military reaction to it) from the following blog entry by U.S. soldier Alex Horton, describing what happened in the town of Baqubah during the surge in spring 2007, when his unit's first operation in a hostile neighborhood was interrupted by a very powerful and deadly improvised explosive device.

> Two hours into the first mission, my friend was killed in a massive IED blast that busted the hell out of the squad leader's face, resulting in traumatic

brain injury and facial reconstruction surgery. The vehicle commander tore his ACL from the concussion. Shrapnel being thrown around the inside of the truck caught one dude in the knee as a dude in the back hatch got rattled around, bruising his back as the other in the hatch was thrown completely out of the vehicle. He's been quiet since then, and was sent home soon after.

Returning fire from us and the Bradleys killed an untold number of kids unlucky enough to be in the school next to our position.

A wrecker sent out to pick up the destroyed Stryker was the next victim of an IED explosion, killing two men inside. Two more wreckers were sent out, one for the Stryker, one for the now totaled wrecker.

As we pulled out that evening, local Iraqis, men, women and children, danced in celebration by the massive crater where the Stryker had been.[39]

Though the gruesome deaths and injuries to U.S. soldiers were in the foreground of this account, Horton himself was painfully aware of the disaster wreaked upon the neighborhood, captured in his ironic reference to having "killed an untold number of kids." He was also painfully aware that the local residents did not view the U.S. troops as liberators but as invaders (as evidenced by their "celebration by the massive crater where the Stryker had been").

Later in the same post, Horton demonstrated that he was aware that the celebration by the local citizens meant that occupation soldiers were unwelcome in the neighborhood, and therefore—in his judgment—had no legitimate reason to be there. In fact, despite the horrific sacrifices made by his unit that day, he laid the blame for that incident on the U.S. military: "In the future, I want my children to grow up with the belief that what I did here was wrong; in a society that doesn't deem that idea unpatriotic."

But the generals who set the rules of engagement extracted a very different lesson from such celebrations and myriad other indications that local Iraqis supported the violent efforts of the insurgents to expel the United States from their communities and from Iraq in general, a fact that was repeatedly driven home by opinion polls that showed that the vast majority of Sunnis and (as early as summer 2005) a majority of all Iraqis supported violent attacks on the U.S. military.[40] In the view of commanding officers, this opposition to "pacification" was the critical element in the failure to root out insurgents, and this active partisanship was therefore a major reason for ordering attacks that endangered and injured civilians.

During the hearing on the Haditha massacre, Lieutenant Max D. Frank, the first officer to investigate the incident, placed the blame squarely on the civilians, characterizing the deaths as an "unfortunate and unintended result of local residents' allowing insurgent fighters to use family homes to shoot at passing American patrols." A marine calling a radio talk show stated the argument more precisely: "You know why those people get killed? It's because they're letting insurgents hide in their house."[41] Extending this logic, First Lieutenant Adam P. Mathes, the executive officer of the company involved in Haditha, argued against issuing an apology to local residents of Haditha for something that was clearly their own fault. Mathes advocated instead that they should issue a warning that the incident was "an unfortunate thing that happens when you let terrorists use your house to attack our troops."[42]

This view—that these attacks on civilians were necessary to teach civilian families in insurgent strongholds a lesson—was first articulated as part of the "get tough" policy announced by Lieutenant General Ricardo Sanchez, the top U.S. commander in Iraq, when the depth and resilience of the opposition first became apparent in late 2003. *New York Times* reporter Dexter Filkins, citing unnamed "American officers," reported that the new policy was designed to use military power to "punish not only the guerrillas, but also make clear to ordinary Iraqis the cost of not cooperating" with U.S. counterinsurgency operations.[43] It was expressed in a more direct way by an anonymous Pentagon official who told *Newsweek* reporters Michael Hirsh and John Barry, "The Sunni population is paying no price for the support it is giving to the terrorists. . . . From their point of view, it is cost free. We have to change that equation."[44]

Perhaps the best measure of the commitment of the U.S. military to this strategy was the institutionalization of the Baiji drone operation, under the name Task Force ODIN ("observation, detection, identification, and neutralization"). This military campaign was devoted to "hunting IED emplacers with unmanned aerial vehicles, attack helicopters, and spotters in C-12 airplanes." A "senior Army official" told *Washington Post* columnist Rick Atkinson that Task Force ODIN was killing an average of seventy-one "suspected" insurgents per week in 2007. He offered no estimates of the number of civilians (who let "insurgents hide in their house") who were also killed.[45]

Another way to measure the centrality of collective punishment to the U.S. strategy in Iraq is to catalog the multitude of innovative methods that were developed to insure that the Sunni civilian population was "paying a price for the support it is giving the terrorists." These included bulldozing houses and crops (including palm trees that take fifteen years to reach fruit-bearing maturity) as retaliation for refusing to inform on local insurgents, cutting off food and water supplies to force residents to inform on insurgents or evacuate, and arresting most or all the men accused of hiding resistance fighters in a given neighborhood.[46]

Collective Punishment and Terrorism

In any war, both sides have partisans who provide support without participating in the violence itself. The rules of war dictate that the warring parties restrict themselves to targeting only enemy combatants. Troops are prohibited from targeting civilians (people not part of an opposition fighting force), no matter how supportive they are to the other side.

The Geneva Conventions (which have the force of law in the United States despite Attorney General Alberto Gonzales' characterization of them as "obsolete")[47] specifically exclude the type of attacks undertaken by the United States in Haifa and Baiji. After first stating that "parties to the conflict shall at all times distinguish between the civilian population and combatants . . . [and] direct their operations only against military objectives," the Geneva Conventions then assert that the "presence within the civilian population of individuals who do not come within the definition of civilians does not deprive the population of its civilian character." Stated simply, it is illegal to kill a group of civilians because a combatant is hiding among them, whether or not the fatalities are intentional.[48]

When noncombatants are subjected to such violence, this is "collective punishment," a term that is associated with the Nazi practice of executing local residents for not revealing the identities of resistance fighters in Eastern Europe and the Soviet Union. It is also a form of terrorism. The *Merriam-Webster Dictionary* defines terror as "violent or destructive acts (as bombing) committed by groups in order to intimidate a population."[49] While there is much scholarly and policy discourse about the exact way to interpret these words, there is no disagreement that the use of violence to intimidate a civilian population is terrorism.[50] While the incidents at Haditha and Baiji were certainly efforts to capture or kill insurgents, it is also true that they were, as *Times* reporter Filkins put it, attempts to "make clear to ordinary Iraqis the cost of not cooperating." That is, they were intended to "intimidate" the local civilian population into withdrawing their support of the insurgency. Therefore they were acts of terrorism.

By 2007, when one in five families had lost at least one member to postinvasion violence, the terrorist essence of this policy was visible to most Iraqis. Abu Taiseer, a resident of Baquba, spoke for the majority of Iraqis, who by then were registering support for attacks on U.S. troops, when he told independent reporter Ahmed Ali:

> At the very beginning of the occupation, the people of Iraq did not realize the U.S. strategy in the area. Their strategy is based on destruction and massacres. They do anything to have their agenda fulfilled. Now, Iraqis know that behind the U.S. smile is hatred and violence. They call others

violent and terrorists while what they are doing in Iraq and in other countries is the origin and essence of terror.[51]

The policy of collective punishment, enacted in myriad incidents involving checkpoints, convoys, and home invasions, amplified the insurgency by creating more insurgents than it intimidated. This dynamic was visible to some of the American soldiers fighting the war, as Nir Rosen reported in summer 2003, when he was embedded with the Third Army Cavalry Unit in Husaybah near the Syrian border. At the end of a long day of house searches and arrests sprinkled with violence, he was sitting with the soldiers observing the punishment being meted out to recently captured suspects:

> A dozen prisoners could be seen marching in a circle outside the detention center, surrounded by barbed wire. They were shouting "U.S.A., U.S.A.!" over and over. "They were talkin' when we told 'em not to, so we made 'em talk somethin' we liked to hear," said one of the soldiers guarding them, grinning. Another gestured up with his hands, letting [the prisoners] know they had to raise their voices.
>
> A sergeant quipped that after such treatment the ones who were not guilty "will be guilty next time."[52]

The sergeant was prescient. Under the pressure of General Ricardo Sanchez's program for implementing L. Paul Bremer's decision to "impose law and order and impose our will on this country," Iraqis reacted with greater and greater violence of their own.[53] Monthly attacks by insurgents increased from fewer than two hundred fifty in June 2003 to almost a thousand by December and surpassed fifteen hundred by the end of spring of 2004. Virtually all these attacks were aimed at Americans, their partners in the "Coalition of the Willing," and Iraqis recruited to the reconstituted army and police. The few suicide bombs were directed at military or law enforcement personnel, and death squads would not come into prominence for another year.[54]

Chapter Six

Insurgent Strongholds

The situation is not going to improve until we clean out Fallujah. In the next ninety days, it's vital to show that we mean business.

—L. Paul Bremer

By early 2004, the Bush administration faced the choice it would confront repeatedly over the next four years. The insurgency, fed by the ongoing social and economic crisis and inflamed by the U.S. military's attempts at suppression, had become a major impediment to the already fragile revolution that Bremer was attempting to engineer. Iraq could not become the economic, political, and military hub of a dominant U.S. presence in the Middle East unless the insurgency was fully pacified.

The political and economic decisions made during 2004—to transfer sovereignty to the Iraqis, to schedule elections, and to enlist the aid of the International Monetary Fund—were all part the effort to save the occupation from early failure. So was an aggressive new military posture, which applied shock-and-awe principles to attacks on insurgent neighborhoods. And so was the campaign to pacify Fallujah, known to Iraqis as the City of Mosques, and famous for its distinctive kabobs served in outdoor cafes.

Fallujah Becomes a Center of the Resistance

Fallujah, like most Sunni cities, welcomed the fall of Saddam Hussein, and it capitulated to the invading army without a ground assault. Nevertheless, most residents were suspicious of U.S. goodwill due to a legacy of infrastructure attacks during the 1991 Gulf War, when the U.S.

air assault on a local bridge produced over one hundred deaths in nearby neighborhoods.[1]

This ambivalence crystallized into anger when units of the 82nd Airborne division commandeered the al-Qaed School as its base of operation in the city. After three days of frantic appeals from local religious and tribal leaders failed to effect an evacuation in time for the coming school week, the anger found expression during an April 28 march that started at the downtown U.S. military headquarters and ended with three hundred demonstrators shouting "No to Saddam, No to the U.S.!" in front of the school. In an altogether typical incident, several members of the U.S. unit believed that they heard sniper fire or saw muzzle flashes in the crowd. Following the rules of engagement established by U.S. military command, the soldiers shot into the crowd, killing, according to Iraqi cyewitnesses and medical personnel, seventeen unarmed demonstrators and wounding seventy-five others. A second protest with over one thousand demonstrators gathered at occupation military headquarters two days later to protest the shooting incident. U.S. troops again opened fire on the protesters, leading to two additional deaths and a dozen injuries.

These deaths reverberated through the tightly woven tribal and religious networks around Fallujah. Fueled by extensive coverage in both the Arabic and English language media, the incidents became a signal moment in the early occupation, shining the spotlight on Fallujah for the first time and triggering the seemingly inexorable process by which antagonism to the occupation evolved into guerrilla war.[2]

Two other less visible forces conjoined with these violent moments to assure Fallujah's destiny as a center of the insurgency. One was the creation of a local government within Fallujah in the wake of the overthrow of the Hussein regime. With all formal government abolished by the U.S. occupation, local tribal leaders and clerics moved quickly on their own to form a civic management council led by a mayor and city manager. Other governance structures for local institutions soon followed, including an ad hoc militia, led by tribal elders and religious leaders and endorsed by the government, that kept the peace and limited the looting that ravaged other Iraqi cities. These militias were being formed at the same time that the al-Qaed School crisis was developing. As local anger mounted in response to the two incidents, the militia became the organizational home for the insurgency. Later, when the U.S. military sought to recruit an Iraqi military to fight against the insurgency, the most likely candidates were already enlisted in the local militias and allied with the resistance.[3]

These local developments might have subsided after brief flurries of violent retaliation were it not for the deepening economic and infrastructural disaster. When independent reporter Christian Parenti visited Fallujah in January 2004, local citizens "were angry about chronic water and electricity shortages. Power plants, telephone exchanges and sewage systems all remain looted and bombed out."[4]

A *USA Today* poll completed at the beginning of April 2004 offered numerical evidence of this daily decline. In March 2004 more than half of all Iraqi city residents had endured electrical outages beyond scheduled shutdowns, fully a third had been forced to purify contaminated drinking water, a quarter had been deprived of needed medicine, and a fifth had gone hungry. Put bluntly, daily life of Iraqis constituted an indictment of the occupation, creating a reservoir of combustible antagonism to U.S. presence that could explode when ignited by incidents like that at the al-Qaed School.

One typical problem that affected Fallujah, as well as many other cities, was the deterioration of the hospitals, which had been unable to maintain supplies or repair equipment during the prewar sanctions, resulting in a precipitous decline in public health from 1991 to 2003. Then, after the invasion toppled Saddam Hussein, criminals set loose by Bremer's dismantling of the police and army systematically looted expensive equipment and remaining pharmacies.

Instead of utilizing the existing system to supply and repair the hospitals, Bremer's administration dismantled the state-run bureaucracy and negotiated contracts with U.S. companies to handle rehabilitation of the healthcare system. By early 2004, little work had been done in any hospital and the Iraqi minister of health, although he was appointed by occupation officials, could not tell hospital directors whom to contact for supplies or repairs. Then, in March 2004, U.S. Health and Human Services Secretary Tommy Thompson added insult to injury when he declared that Iraqi hospitals would be just fine if the staff "just washed their hands and cleaned the crap off the walls." This comment was broadcast to all Iraqis by the two most watched cable channels in the Middle East, Al Aribiya and Al Jazeera.[5]

These problems generated increasing protest at all levels, and the larger goals of the occupation precluded any ameliorative action to defuse the anger. The program of economic shock treatment dictated that Iraqis wait for the workings of neoliberalism to produce improved employment, hospitals, and electrical power. With no national Iraqi government, and with the local governments in Fallujah and elsewhere developing into centers of resistance, the occupation military was the only available vehicle for suppressing the increasingly unruly protests.

Taken as a whole, the texture of daily life—combined with the dismissive and violent reaction of the occupation to any complaints—gave the impression that the Iraqi economy would continue to decline as long as the United States remained in Iraq. Encouraged by religious leaders and organized by quasi-official local governments, insurgency became the accepted solution to the ongoing crisis.

Abu Muhamad, a prominent Fallujah resident and former Baathist official, explained the rise of the insurgency to independent reporter Nir Rosen:

> We expected things to improve, but everything became worse—electricity, water, sewage, drainage—so mosque speakers openly spoke of jihad and encouraged people to join [the insurgency] after a month of occupation. . . . Nobody in Fallujah opposed the resistance and many different resistance groups came in. Weapons were very available. All soldiers and security personnel took their weapons home [when they were mustered out of the dismantled army] and the Baath party had also distributed weapons.[6]

Even U.S. intelligence agencies were aware that the failure of the occupation to attend to constantly escalating economic and social problems was the engine of rebellion. One intelligence report, leaked to *New Yorker* reporter Seymour Hersh, concluded: "The disaster that is the reconstruction of Iraq has been the key cause of the insurgency."[7]

The Insurgents Take Over in Fallujah

The majority of Iraqis did not become insurgents. In early 2004, an occupation-sponsored survey found that, while 80 percent of Iraqis wanted the United States to leave within six months, only 13 percent "fully supported" armed force as the way of accomplishing the U.S. departure. This combination of attitudes, however, constituted fulfillment of the primary prerequisite for successful guerrilla war: it that meant that virtually no one was willing to report insurgent activity. In addition to supporting the goals of the guerrillas, most of the population in cities like Fallujah knew them as relatives, friends, or neighbors who, as the local militia, protected the community from criminals and adjudicated various local disputes. As Abu Muhamad told Nir Rosen, "Nobody in Fallujah opposed the resistance . . ."[8]

The relationship of the Fallujah insurgents, who called themselves mujaheddin, to the local population was described during later fighting by independent reporter Rahul Mahajan, one of two reporters who witnessed the April siege from inside the city:

> Among the more laughable assertions of the Bush administration is that the mujaheddin are a small group of isolated "extremists" repudiated by the majority of Fallujah's population. Nothing could be further from the

truth. Of course, the mujaheddin don't include women or very young children (we saw an 11-year-old boy with a Kalashnikov), old men, and are not necessarily even a majority of fighting-age men. But they are of the community and fully supported by it. Many of the wounded were brought in [to the hospital] by the muj and they stood around openly conversing with doctors and others. They conferred together about logistical questions; not once did I see the muj threatening people with their ubiquitous Kalashnikovs. . . .

I spoke to a young man, Ali, who was among the wounded we transported to Baghdad. He said he was not a muj but, when asked his opinion of them, he smiled and stuck his thumb up.[9]

After the two fatal incidents in April 2003, U.S. troops withdrew to a base outside Fallujah and rarely ventured into the city.[10] Violent confrontations became relatively rare events, though the insurgents achieved a measure of nationwide fame during the winter of 2003 when they shot down a U.S. Chinook helicopter, killing sixteen soldiers.[11] Inside Fallujah, the insurgency was visibly dominant, politically as well as militarily. Various factions contended for power and favor, but all were antagonistic to any U.S. presence. The main thoroughfare, was a major route linking the Baghdad and the Syrian border, was too dangerous for Westerners to travel without armed convoys. Fallujah became a national symbol of successful resistance to the occupation.

The Marines Attack Fallujah

In January 2004 Major General Charles Swannock, commander of the 82nd Airborne, announced that his work in Fallujah "was on a glide path to success."[12] This evaluation was not altogether disingenuous: U.S. military units in the Fallujah area fought far fewer engagements than in localities where the occupation was actively attempting to subdue the insurgency. If the occupation was willing to recognize the legitimacy of the existing government in Fallujah, then all that remained was to negotiate some kind of truce that would allow non-Iraqis associated with the occupation unfettered access to the highway running through the city. Swannock felt that such an accommodation was negotiable, declaring that "we have turned the corner, and now we can accelerate down the straightaway."[13]

Swannock's logic did not, however, take into account the larger goals of the occupation. His view made sense if the ultimate U.S. goal was to establish order or self-rule in various cities, transfer sovereignty to whatever national government was elected, and remove U.S. troops. L. Paul Bremer, however, was committed to the much more ambitious project of laying the "foundation for a revolutionized economy" that would "challenge the economic policies and the politics of the whole region."[14] He could not tolerate a high-visibility city ruled by a "semi-autonomous" Fallujah government, dominated by tribal and religious leaders identified with the insurgency and "patrolled by local militias" whose members were also guerrilla fighters. This would be a long-term impediment to his goals, since the city as a whole would continue to resist the privatization campaign; continue to demand that government services be renewed, sustained, and increased; and oppose the long-term presence of the U.S. military, which was essential for enforcing America's Middle East interests. Because Fallujah had become a beacon of the insurgency, occupation authorities were "determined to make an example of the city."[15]

It is important to reiterate that the U.S. campaign to pacify Fallujah was not an attempt to reduce violence within the city. While there had been some violence among factions since the U.S. withdrawal in summer 2003, this period of insurgent control was far calmer than the previous period when the United States contested for dominance.[16] The effort to recapture the city was animated by the desire to wrest control from the insurgency, not reduce violence or lawlessness. L. Paul Bremer was thus thinking of the already faltering long-term goals of the occupation when he declared, "The situation is not going to improve until we clean out Fallujah. In the next ninety days, it's vital to show that we mean business."[17] The policy of collective punishment was now going to be applied to whole cities, instead of to individual families and neighborhoods.

◆ ◆ ◆

The guerrillas also made a fateful decision—they decided that they had the ability and the popular mandate to resist any incursion into the city. A senior tribal leader made this clear by sending a message to the marines through the *Washington Post*: "If they want to prevent bloodshed, they should stay outside the city and allow Iraqis to handle security."[18]

The battle began in late March, when the First Marine Expeditionary Force replaced General Swannock's 82nd Airborne and immediately initiated patrols designed to capture suspected guerrillas inside the city. One of the first patrols met with intense resistance. U.S. Marines killed fifteen Iraqis in the ensuing confrontation, including at least a few civilians. It was clear to everyone that this was only the beginning.

The next few days saw repeated violent confrontations as the marines persisted and the guerrillas resisted. It was during this tense period that the internationally publicized attack on four Blackwater mercenaries, followed by the mutilation of their bodies, occurred. The attack may or may not have been planned, but it certainly was well organized, and it relied on the insurgent organization that had been developing over the past year.

The Blackwater operatives were providing armed security for a convoy that was headed through Fallujah on the highway that ran through the middle of town. The insurgents apparently had spies inside Blackwater, since they knew the route and likely time of arrival of the convoy. At the appropriate moment, the insurgents cleared the street, a common guerrilla tactic designed to limit civilian casualties. (One shopkeeper on his way to work was stopped by a black-robed stranger, who told him to turn around, saying "something is going to happen.") He did so, and returned only after the mercenaries had been murdered. The celebrations and mutilations that followed put an exclamation point on what was already a noteworthy event: a public statement by the insurgents in Fallujah that they would defend their turf against any outside incursion.[19]

The huge battle that followed is generally portrayed as the U.S. military's reaction to the attack on the Blackwater "civilian contractors," and the subsequent mutilation and gruesome display of their burnt body parts. The nature, timing, and ferocity of the U.S. offensive may well have been a response to the Blackwater incident, but the battle itself had started earlier, and its escalation had become inevitable, once Bremer decided to "clean out Fallujah."[20]

The Marine Battle Plan

The battle plan—application of overwhelming military force to defeat the strengthened insurgency—had already been implemented several times in smaller towns in Iraq.[21]

Washington Post reporter Karl Vick summarized U.S. strategy in terms that evoke the logic of collective punishment: "military doctrine that unites terrifying firepower with almost zero tolerance for casualties in its own ranks."[22] The plan called for surrounding the offending village, town, or city to cut off all escape routes for the insurgents. Women, children, and older men were allowed to evacuate, but fighting-age men were all to be treated as suspected insurgents and therefore refused exit. Troops then searched the area, street by street, house by house, breaking down doors and invading homes, looking for incriminating evidence, until all guerrillas or suspected guerrillas were caught. Any resistance was met with overwhelming force, including destruction of any buildings that housed insurgents. As one army commander told Vick, "If we take fire from it, we destroy the whole building," using "tanks, howitzers, Apache attack helicopters and carrier-based bombers."[23]

The presence of civilians was not a deterrent to overwhelming force. In fact, brutality toward civilians might convince them to identify the insurgents rather than continue to suffer themselves. In one village where this strategy was applied, the local commander told *New York Times* reporter Dexter Filkins that he would not allow villagers to travel to their jobs outside the town unless they identified some insurgents first. Brigadier General Mark Kimmitt justified these tactics, as well as the attacks on civilian-occupied buildings, by invoking the "human shield" argument, blaming what he called the "collective punishment" on "those terrorists, those cowards who hunker down inside mosques and hospitals and schools, and use the women and children as shields to hide against the marines." [24]

The underlying premise of this strategy was bluntly expressed by Captain Todd Brown, a company commander who had applied the plan in the village of Abu Hishma: "You have to understand the Arab mind . . . the only thing they understand is force—force, pride, and saving face." [25] This comment expresses the degree to which racism toward Iraqis is embedded in campaigns of collective punishment, which make terrorism the centerpiece of U.S. counterinsurgency strategy. The military's new plan—first utilized in Abu Hishma and other small towns, then extended to the city of Fallujah, and applied thereafter during battles in many other cities—targeted the community or city as a whole, treating everyone as the enemy until and unless they abandoned the city or helped to defeat the guerrillas.

The First Siege of Fallujah

On April 4, 2004, the United States initiated Operation Vigilant Resolve, the first siege of an Iraqi city since President Bush had declared the end of "major combat operations" a year before. [26] Two brigades of U.S. Marines began the operation by sealing off the city of Fallujah. In the process, they closed the bridge over the Tigris River, cutting off access to the only full-service hospital. They then took control of the hospital—in contradiction to Geneva Convention provisions protecting medical personnel and facilities—and prohibited medical personnel from treating any wounded insurgents. Difficulty in distinguishing injured civilians from potential insurgents made it impossible to treat any victims of the fighting in the hospital, and eventually doctors set up poorly equipped temporary clinics on the other side of the river.

The invasion of Fallujah started with air attacks on electrical power plants and other public services, a standard shock-and-awe technique designed to deprive the resistance of needed resources and undermine the morale of the insurgents and their supporters. Ground forces then assaulted the three neighborhoods that marines believed were most supportive of the guerrillas.

New York Times reporters Jeffrey Gettleman, John Burns, and Ian Fisher, embedded with the marines, compiled this description of the rules of engagement applied to the ongoing siege:[27]

1. Snipers on the top of buildings were instructed to shoot anyone approaching any U.S. positions.

2. A dusk-to-dawn curfew, designed to prevent guerrilla movements in the dark, was imposed. The troops were under orders to "shoot any male of military age on the streets after dark, armed or not."[28]

3. Coalition soldiers were expected "to shoot anyone with a gun," male or female, young or old, whether or not the gun holder was shooting at them.[29]

4. If there was hostile fire, troops returned fire, then called in helicopter and C-130 gunships to annihilate enemy positions. If this failed, they ordered air strikes, nearly seven hundred over the course of the battle. Everyone inside the city was considered an enemy combatant.

5. No one was allowed to enter or leave town without undergoing careful inspection at a check point. No men were allowed to leave town at all, because they could be insurgents.

6. No civilians were allowed on the main highways outside of town. The U.S. military posted a warning on all affected roads that read "If civilians drive on the closed sections of the highways, they may be engaged with deadly force."[30]

The occupation brought the full strength of its technological superiority to bear: armored vehicles that could blast holes in any cover used by the guerrillas, automatic salvos from helicopters and C-130 gunships that could shoot through the walls of most buildings, and—when the return fire was not silenced by these weapons—air strikes featuring bombs (some as large as two thousand pounds) that annihilated large structures in a few seconds.

Yet the progress was very slow. After almost a year of practice and planning, the mujaheddin knew how to exploit the tools available to urban guerrillas against an invading army. They had already dug their hiding places before the attack, they were well-camouflaged inside pre-selected buildings, and they knew the passages from one structure to another. They could stash their armaments in one place, move to another without any visible weapons, then pick up arms cached in the new location.

Advancing U.S. troops found that no success was permanent. The guerrillas flowed back into any captured area as soon as U.S. troops left. To maintain control of even small neighborhoods, vast numbers of troops were needed, most of them to guard against the return of guerrillas to already cleared areas. Ironically, even total destruction was no indication of success. As Lieutenant Colonel B. P. McCoy told the *New York Times*, "we don't want to rubblize the city. That will give the enemy more places to hide."[31]

Many people chose to leave Fallujah, but those who made it to the town boundaries discovered that no males teenage or older were allowed to leave. This meant that many whole families took the drastic step of staying in the city rather than split up, while others took the equally drastic step of leaving men and boys behind, exposed to the fighting. Those that escaped the city could not travel on main roads to Baghdad, so many refugees spent long hot days in transit in the desert between the two cities.

Estimates of at least seven hundred killed, many thousands wounded, and tens of thousands rendered homeless seem moderate. Independent journalists Dahr Jamail and Rahul Mahajan, who risked death and injury to see the damage first-hand, corroborated the stories of refugees: Two football fields filled with new graves (because the cemeteries were inaccessible outside the ring of marines); women and children shot dead by sharp-shooting marine snipers (because they were out after curfew or were thought to be men or armed); ambulance drivers shot in the chest through their ambulance windows (because they were men out at night, or might be transporting guns or insurgents instead of wounded); city blocks annihilated by bombs (because they housed insurgents who could not be silenced by marines); and gravely wounded patients removed from hospitals for interrogation (because they might be insurgents with timely information about others).[32]

Why the U.S. Withdrew after the First Battle of Fallujah

While U.S. leaders pondered whether to renew the marines' advance into the city, official and unofficial observers inside and outside the U.S. government argued that the U.S. military should use its overwhelming firepower to sweep away the resistance, even if that meant destroying much of the city. Included among the many advocates of this option was FOXNews military analyst Lieutenant General Tom McInerney (retired), who advocated attacking the entire remaining civilian population, emulating Rome's most famous act of state terrorism, the destruction of the competitive city of Carthage: "We must be ruthless, especially in the area of collateral damage....We shouldn't be concerned about collateral damage. All the good civilians are gone. If we must make Falluja Carthage, then let's make Falluja Carthage."[33]

The editors of the *Wall Street Journal*, the preeminent business periodical in the United States, were more analytical in their argument: "Sooner or later," its editors wrote, "the insurgents have to be defeated, and at the point of a gun, not by diplomacy." Anything less would be interpreted as a "sign of weakness" that would encourage the insurgents to "ramp up their attacks [in Fallujah] and elsewhere."[34]

Nevertheless, the U.S. military chose to withdraw, and these dire predictions were fulfilled. Most people in Iraq viewed the withdrawal as a classic guerrilla victory: the mujaheddin had gained uncontested control of the city while inflicting significant casualties on the much larger and better equipped U.S. Army. The guerrilla casualties, though substantial, were more than offset by new recruitment. Just as the *Wall Street Journal* predicted, and even before the battle ended, other cities began to emulate Fallujah, counterattacking whenever U.S. troops entered the community and establishing tribal- and clerical-based alternative governments. Over the next few months, the predominantly Sunni cities of Samarra, Ramadi, Baquba, and Mosul and many smaller towns had success in emulating Fallujah. So did at least eight Shia cities, including Basra, the second-largest city in Iraq, and the holy cities of Karbala and Najaf. Perhaps most important of all, Sadr City—the immense Shia ghetto in Baghdad—became a semi-independent city-state under the leadership of revolutionary cleric Muqtada al-Sadr.[35] *Washington Post* reporter Thomas Ricks summarized the broad impact of the battle: "Fallujah, which the Marines had hoped to make a showcase for how to fight smarter and better in Iraq, instead had become an international rally point for anti-American fighters." On-the-ground Marine Regiment Commander Colonel John Toolen was more poetic: "Fallujah" he said, "was like a siren, calling to the insurgents."[36]

Given that these dire consequences were foreseen by respected strategists inside and outside the government, why did the U.S. choose to withdraw? The *Wall Street Journal* gestured at the reasons when it reported this hesitation: "There's no doubt Marines could retake the city by force, but the fear is that al-Jazeera and other anti-American media would portray the campaign in the worst possible light and perhaps prompt uprisings elsewhere in Iraq."[37]

Though it conferred far too much power on the pro-insurgency media, the *Wall Street Journal* analysis was certainly right that the ferocious and destructive house-to-house fighting needed to retake Fallujah would detonate "uprisings elsewhere in Iraq." In fact, these insurrections

had already begun before the *Journal* predicted them. Once the guerrillas survived the initial thrust, the rebellion began to spread. It started
with denunciations of the U.S. offensive (which extended even to officials of the U.S.-appointed Iraqi Governing Council) and widened into
declarations of support for the insurgents—from inside and outside
Iraq, by Sunni and Shia alike. It soon amplified into food and blood collection drives designed to aid besieged Fallujah residents and guerrillas,
delivered by convoys that evaded the U.S. checkpoints. And, within two
weeks, the rebellion had spawned uprisings around the country, most
alarmingly for occupation authorities in the formerly quiescent Shia
areas.[38]

In numerous cities, the rebellions swept away the Iraqi police or recruited them to the insurgency. Spanish, Polish, and British garrisons in
the Shia south withdrew to their bases outside the cities. In the holy city
of Najaf, a second major battle was being fought—also initiated by the
United States—between U.S. forces and the Mahdi Army, a Shia militia
organized by the Sadrist movement.[39]

Finally, insurgent groups systematically attacked the weakest link in
the U.S. presence: the overland highways that brought military weapons
and supplies into the country from Kuwait and then carried them out to
the fighting units. U.S. forces "lost control of long sections of the 375
mile highway leading west from Baghdad to Jordan," the same highway
that traversed Fallujah. Disruptions then spread to the highway from
Kuwait, through which all incoming supplies were funneled. Eventually,
Iraqis targeted the third main artery, which ran north through Kurdistan
to the Turkish border. U.S. military spokesman Brigadier General Mark
Kimmitt called these attacks "a concerted effort on the part of the enemy
to try to interfere with our lines of communication, our main supply
routes."[40] The effort was successful, at least until airlifts and armed convoys were implemented. In mid-April commanders were "rationing use
of critical stockpiles," even at the highly secure "enduring" bases around
the country.[41]

Once the guerrillas had halted the initial attack in Fallujah, the damage was done. The occupation leadership could either concede defeat in
Fallujah, then try to figure out how to win the next battle (the option it
chose), or it could have fought on in Fallujah, generating concentric circles of new outrage and new rebellions that would become unmanageable immediately (given the limited number of coalition troops
available). In this context, it is not surprising that military strategists
chose waiting. By doing so, they were able to select the time and location

of the next big confrontation (which would come only five months later) and, in the interim, develop new strategies that might be more effective.

In Fallujah, the previously overwhelming U.S. military was suddenly undermanned and outflanked. The United States could have conquered Fallujah, but it might have lost as many as fifteen other cities. The U.S. command chose strategic retreat instead of strategic defeat. This judicious decision did not, however, halt efforts by other cities to emulate the Fallujah strategy. City after city became what the U.S. forces called "no-go" zones.

Chapter Seven

Torture, Death Squads, and the Second Battle of Fallujah

A desolate world of skeletal buildings, tank-blasted homes, weeping power lines, and severed palm trees.

—**New York Times reporter Erik Eckholm describing post-conquest Fallujah**

The CPA described the withdrawal of the marines from Fallujah as a negotiated cease-fire, with responsibility for security in the city officially transferred from the U.S. military to the newly formed Fallujah Brigade. U.S. media portrayed this development as a truce with no clear winner, even though the composition of the Fallujah Brigade suggested otherwise—it had been recruited exclusively from Fallujah-vicinity residents and was led by former Baathist military general Jassim Huhamad Saleh.

The people of Fallujah considered it a monumental victory by the Fallujan David against the U.S. Goliath. Dahr Jamail, the only English-language journalist remaining in the city after the the last marine units departed, described the residents' reaction:

> Clustered together in the back of a Stryker vehicle, peering out from under their black helmets, the embedded reporters saw the scene only from the perspective of the U.S. soldiers they relied on for their safety. Thus, they could not see what I was about to witness after they departed with the soldiers.
>
> As the patrol receded, spontaneous celebrations erupted, and crowds of residents flew into the street. Iraqi flags appeared everywhere. People began chanting and waved the flags wildly. Members of both the Iraqi police and the ICDC [Iraq Civil Defense Corps—the American-sponsored Iraqi military] joined in the celebration, waving their guns in the air and giving the victory sign. A parade was quickly formed. Trucks with boys and men riding in the

backs lined up, their horns blaring. Policemen who were there to guard the
marines promptly turned into parade escorts, as well as participants.

The ruckus began to inch down the street. An old Fallujan man riding
in the back of a truck waving a tattered Iraqi flag yelled, "Today is the first
day of the war against the Americans! This is a victory for us over the
Americans!" Mujahedeen brandishing RPGs [rocket-propelled grenade
launchers], Kalashnikovs, and hand grenades were paraded on trucks as
thousands of residents began to move up and down the main street in the
victory parade. Loud music blared from the minarets of mosques. . . .

The celebrations continued throughout the day. After several hours the
parade dispersed but small groups of honking cars full of triumphant flag-
waving Iraqis continued to buzz around the streets. Children ran around
carrying flowers toward mosques. People planned more celebrations for
the evening."[1]

There were certainly a few Fallujans who did not welcome the insurgent victory, but they were too small a minority either to dampen the enthusiasm of the others or to have an impact on subsequent events.

The ensuing five months—until the second U.S. assault—were certainly marked by complex and sometimes violent political maneuvering
among a host of political tendencies within the city, but a fundamental
anti-occupation consensus united the contending parties. Ali A. Allawi,
the Iraqi defense minister, described the local government as a "form of
Islamic rule," forged from a "fusion between the insurgents, the Fallujah
Brigade, the police and the imams." Nir Rosen, the only journalist to report from city during this period between the two battles, described it as
"a city run by the Iraqi resistance."[2]

The first battle of Fallujah was the culmination of a growing crisis in
the U.S. strategy for pacifying Iraq. As early as fall 2003, the U.S. military command and civilian leadership had begun to appreciate that
they were not fighting remnants of the old Baathist regime; on the contrary, the Baathists were by and large hated by ordinary Iraqis for the
years of misery they had helped to impose. Instead, the insurgency was
a popular rebellion, supported by the residents of the communities in
which it was active, and rapidly extending its popularity to the Iraqi
people as a whole.

This popular support caused two major problems for the occupation.
The first was a question of intelligence, a problem that had been apparent
even before the first battle of Fallujah. Because the guerrillas were embedded in supportive communities, it was virtually impossible for the occupation to obtain useful intelligence about the activists, leaders, and strategy of
the insurgency. The military had to devise a way to extract such information if it was going to effectively target the individuals who set IEDs, shot
at U.S. patrols, or provided the logistical support for these operations.

The second major problem was crystallized by the first battle of Fallujah. The marines could have completed their conquest of the city and were angry that they were not allowed to do so.[3] The siege was called off because its completion might have triggered multiple uprisings across Iraq, particularly in Shia areas of the south. In order to successfully subdue Fallujah, therefore, steps had to be taken to prevent uprisings elsewhere, no matter how ugly the situation in Fallujah became.

In answering these challenges, the U.S. political and military leadership fulfilled its destiny as an occupying power by incorporating two types of state terrorism—torture and death squads—as central features of its pacification strategy.

The Inexorable Logic of Torture

In late spring 2004, just at the time when the Americans were invading Fallujah, photographs of torture at Abu Ghraib prison surfaced in a report on the CBS news show *60 Minutes II*.[4] The ensuing controversy, which lasted more than a year and was never resolved, raised a number of serious issues about the treatment of detainees at Abu Ghraib and elsewhere in Iraq. The initial revelation left the indelible impression on Iraqis, the world public, and large segments of the U.S. electorate that the United States had made torture a central part of its intelligence-gathering operation in Iraq. For many who followed the controversy more closely, it revealed the ways in which state terrorism had become a centerpiece of U.S. policy in Iraq and elsewhere.[5]

The reasons for this gruesome development are not hard to discern: occupying powers fighting a popular insurgency will almost inevitably resort to torture. The causal factors are lamentably straightforward.[6] During a successful guerrilla war, insurgents fight a battle then melt into the population. The occupying power therefore cannot identify them via positions behind barricades, by their uniforms, or because they are carrying guns. Only their friends and neighbors know who the insurgents are. Very often even other units of the guerrilla army do not know the identities of their comrades who live in nearby neighborhoods.

If a substantial portion of the local population dislikes the guerrillas, then they will quietly inform on them to the occupying power, allowing for their arrest or facilitating attacks on safe houses. These attacks are usually precisely targeted and therefore do not harm other residents of the community. But when residents support and protect the guerillas, as they did in Fallujah and most other Iraqi cities, the occupying power must either resign itself to failure in its search for guerrillas or use imprecise methods that alienate noncombatants, such as the brutal house invasions that the Americans used from the beginning of the occupation.

In this circumstance, the occupation often finds, as it did in Fallujah and elsewhere, that counterinsurgency creates more guerrillas than it captures. The occupation is left with the choice of ceding local control to—or finding accommodation with—the insurgents, attacking whole neighborhoods or even cities, or finding a way to force people to inform on the insurgents. In Iraq, U.S. commanders were not willing to withdraw; nor were they willing to reach an accommodation with the insurgents, as Major General Charles Swannock had suggested in Fallujah.[7] They opted instead to implement the two other options, treating all residents of neighborhoods and cities as the enemy and forcing people to inform on the insurgents.

However morally opposed the invading army is to the use of torture in theory, those in charge of determining rules of engagement and interrogation policy will likely be persuaded to mandate torture because it follows so logically from the exigencies of the war.[8] If a captive can be forced to talk, then more of the enemy is captured or killed while fewer of "our" side are killed or wounded. Even though the process of coercion involves incredible brutality, the controlling argument is that it is better for the enemy to suffer than for "our" side to suffer. So if torture works—or even if it might work—it will be worth it because it can "save lives," that is, it "might save the lives of our side." The collateral dehumanization of the "enemy"—usually in the form of racism—becomes the justification for this "necessary" tactic (for example, "the only thing they understand is force"[9]).

Following this logic one step further, detaining and torturing innocent individuals who are not part of the resistance is actually a useful strategy. Such brutality, particularly if it is well publicized, holds out the possibility of convincing residents of insurgent communities to stop "harboring" guerrillas. Latin American historian Greg Grandin, who documented the development by U.S. intelligence operatives of what he called the "holy trinity" of state terrorism—torture, disappearances, and death squads—concluded that one of the primary goals of such tactics is to "keep potential rebel sympathizers in a state of fear and anxiety." In Latin America, Grandin found, specific techniques were chosen because they were expected to generate "a chilling ripple effect" on sympathizers of the insurgency.[10]

In the case of Abu Ghraib and other U.S. detention facilities, the torture was conceived, developed, and authorized in Washington, and implemented by trained personnel from various U.S. intelligence agencies.

The actual process began with the realization in summer 2003 that Iraqi civilians were unwilling to report the identities of the guerrillas among them. A key intelligence report stated the problem bluntly: "Human intelligence is poor or lacking" because the community and the police "are rife with sympathy for the insurgents."[11] Undersecretary of Defense for Intelligence Stephen Cambone was placed in charge of remedying the situation, and he decided to adapt an already existing CIA program, which applied "enhanced," "harsh," or "aggressive" interrogation to a small number of "high value" detainees considered leaders of al-Qaeda and other international jihadist organizations. This program was operating in a number of clandestine sites around the world and at the Guantánamo Bay detention center, where prisoner treatment had already become a subject of substantial controversy. The program was exposed to unwanted publicity in late 2007 when news emerged that the CIA had destroyed the video records of two detainees, including suspected al-Qaeda leader Abu Zubaydah, apparently to protect its operatives from prosecution for using torture.[12]

Cambone's innovation was to apply the program's methods on a mass scale, in an attempt to identify and destroy "the broad middle of the Baathist underground."[13] He brought in General Geoffrey Miller, the commander at Guantánamo, to " 'Gitmoize' the prison system in Iraq—to make it more focused on interrogation," using methods that included "sleep deprivation, exposure to extremes of cold and heat, and placing prisoners in 'stress positions' for agonizing lengths of time." Soon afterward, Abu Ghraib operatives were authorized to expand their repertoire to the full range of techniques used by the CIA on the high-value prisoners.[14]

One final bottleneck needed to be addressed: There were not nearly enough intelligence officers to handle the huge number of prisoners in Abu Ghraib. Cambone's solution to this bottleneck was to involve the regular MPs at the prison in the interrogations, teaching them the various techniques that had been developed, and adding new elements to suit the Iraqi context. According to one of Seymour Hersh's informants, even the highly publicized pictures of naked detainees in bizarre sexual postures may have been part of a plan to use the threat of public exposure to recruit spies against the insurgency:

> The government consultant said that there may have been a serious goal, in the beginning, behind the sexual humiliation and the posed photographs. It was thought that some prisoners would do anything—including spying on their associates—to avoid dissemination of the shameful photos to family and friends. The government consultant said, "I was told that the purpose of the photographs was to create an army of informants, people you could insert back in the population." The idea was that they

would be motivated by fear of exposure, and gather information about pending insurgency action, the consultant said.

Hersh then commented, "If so, it wasn't effective; the insurgency continued to grow."[15]

This new plan was implemented beginning in summer 2003 and it immediately changed the flow of intelligence. One former intelligence officer involved in the operation told the before-and-after story to *New Yorker* reporter Seymour Hersh:

> They weren't getting anything substantive from the detainees in Iraq. . . . No names. Nothing that they could hang their hat on.
> Cambone says, "I've got to crack this thing and I'm tired of working through the normal chain of command. I've got this apparatus set up—the black special-access program—and I'm going in hot."
> So he pulls the switch, and the electricity begins flowing last summer. And it's working. We're getting a picture of the insurgency in Iraq.[16]

The system soon generated resistance from the CIA leadership, who opposed the conversion of their targeted torture program into an instrument of mass interrogation. According to Hersh, the CIA withdrew from the program just after it was rolled out, in fall 2003: "By fall, according to the former intelligence official, the senior leadership of the C.I.A. had had enough. "They said, 'No way. We signed up for the core program in Afghanistan—pre-approved for operations against high-value terrorist targets—and now you want to use it for cabdrivers, brothers-in-law, and people pulled off the streets.'"[17] The program continued without the CIA and became an integral part of the occupation effort.

Death Squads

Military patrols and home raids could not be expected to capture or kill even a small proportion of the suspected resistance fighters the U.S. military was identifying through enhanced interrogation. Active insurgents melted away as soon as U.S. units appeared in the neighborhood, leaving behind civilians who were then gathered up in the dragnet. Moreover, as the insurgency grew, it more frequently ambushed U.S. patrols. These firefights might result in killing or capturing the insurgents who set bombs and sniped the patrols, but they interrupted or aborted the house raids, making it far more difficult to capture or kill targeted suspects.

The answer provided by Stephen Cambone's strategic brain trust was described by a U.S. adviser in Iraq in these graphic terms: "The only way we can win is to go unconventional. We're going to have to play their game. Guerrilla versus guerrilla. Terrorism versus terrorism."[18]

The plan was simple. Armed with names and other identifying information of suspected activists and leaders of the insurgency, clandestine units would hunt down and apprehend or kill their targets, using the cover of disguise and darkness to penetrate hostile communities. The first of these units were U.S. Special Forces assigned to hunting Saddam Hussein and other high-profile Baathist leaders. In 2004, however, the mission was expanded. First, the failure of home invasions led the commanders to target rank-and-file insurgents with these death squads, vastly increasing the scope of the operation. Second, faced with insurmountable obstacles to using U.S. soldiers in clandestine operations in tight-knit Iraqi neighborhoods, they began recruiting Iraqi units to take on the task of "apprehending Saddam loyalists and other insurgents around the capital."[19] These Iraqi units, whose members were drawn largely from the Badr Brigade, the militia associated with the Supreme Council for the Islamic Revolution in Iraq—Washington's closest ally within the Iraqi government—were slated to consist of about eight hundred elite troops trained, supervised, and supported by the U.S. Special Forces. Like other clandestine programs, the death squads soon disappeared from the mainstream media.[20]

One year later, the existence of these units was once again made visible by a brief flurry of new coverage, most notably a *Newsweek* article that described the Iraqi units as "Special-Forces-led assassination or kidnapping teams." According to *Newsweek* they were housed in the newly formed Iraqi Ministry of the Interior and tasked with killing men in Sunni neighborhoods suspected of planning or supporting the suicide bombers. By then the program was informally known as the "Salvador Option," reflecting its similarity to the death squads that operated under CIA guidance during the insurgency in El Salvador in the 1980s.[21]

Seymour Hersh labeled this program a "bottom-up" strategy, since it sought to defeat the insurgency by starting at the bottom: arresting sympathizers and local activists, then using "enhanced interrogation" to identify higher-level leaders, who would then be captured and interrogated—or killed—by the Special Forces units or their Iraqi subordinates. Starting with the bottom layers of the organization and working their way upward, the teams hoped to reach the top and therefore eliminate the whole structure in a city, region, or eventually the whole country.

While this strategy inevitably involved capturing, torturing, and killing many uninvolved or peripherally involved individuals, such collateral damage was, as we have seen, viewed as useful in creating "a chilling ripple effect" on sympathizers of the insurgency.[22] The participants in the program appear to have understood this aspect of the operation very well. One of Seymour Hersh's informants told him, "We've got to scare the Iraqis into submission."[23]

As with so many other strategies developed and implemented by U.S. military theorists, the use of torture and death squads did not have the expected effect. As these methods were more generally applied, the support for the insurgency grew, and the number of battles between U.S. troops and guerrillas increased dramatically.

Plan of Attack

These new programs of enhanced interrogation and special operations could not, even with the best results, eliminate the need for full-scale assaults on insurgent strongholds like Fallujah. No amount of intelligence or targeted assassination would overthrow the entrenched regimes within these cities. The first battle of Fallujah, however, had demonstrated that frontal assaults on insurgent strongholds were fraught with the unacceptable risk of spreading the battle to new and distant cities, as well as creating a more general, national mobilization against the occupation. Before challenging the Fallujah resistance a second time, the U.S. military sought to demonstrate that it could mount a major attack on Fallujah—or some other target city—without triggering uprisings in too many others, particularly in the Shia regions that contained the majority of the cities in the country. During the summer of 2004, several developments, some designed for this purpose, helped the U.S. military accomplish this goal.

The most visible was the nominal transfer of sovereignty on June 28, 2004, from the CPA led by L. Paul Bremer to the Iraqi Interim Government led by Iyad Allawi. Though Allawi was appointed by the Americans, the Bush administration hoped that an "Iraqi face" on the government would frame military engagements as U.S. support for an indigenous government's effort to restore order, instead of the near-universal image (everywhere except in the United States) of an invader seeking to crush resistance to a foreign occupation. From the beginning of his regime, Allawi played this role well, calling the insurgency an effort by defeated Baathists to regain power and repeatedly vowing to crush it. In the second battle of Falluja, Allawi took on the task of ordering the attack, so that the battle was technically the execution of his policy.[24]

About the same time as Allawi was assuming the leadership of the newly created interim government, sectarian tensions between Shia and Sunni began to find violent expression. From the beginning of resistance in Sunni cities, there had been a small jihadist element, including a few foreign nationals, who argued that the U.S. presence was facilitated, if not welcomed, by the Shia majority. Ironically, this assertion echoed the very public expectations of many Washington officials, including Vice President Dick Cheney, who commented just before the invasion—presumably with the Shia majority in mind—that "my belief is we will, in fact, be greeted as liberators." [25] While the reception was much more measured than anticipated by Cheney and others, many Sunnis were worried that the jihadists and Cheney were right: that Shia would support the U.S. presence, and therefore provide a critical resource for continuing both the occupation and the pacification. [26]

Before the first Fallujah battle, there had been a few violent sectarian clashes, but these were overshadowed by the solidarity the battles produced. In all parts of the country residents brought food, medicine, and other products to local mosques, Shia as well as Sunni, for transport to Fallujah, while the Mahdi Army, the most visible Shia militia, sent a token unit to fight alongside the Fallujah resistance. [27]

Muqtada al-Sadr, the leader of the most important Shia resistance movement and commander of the Mahdi Army, issued a ringing statement celebrating the unity: "You are witnessing the union of Sunnis and Shiites toward an independent Iraq, free of terror and occupation. This is a lofty goal. . . . Our sentiments are the same, our goal is one, and our enemy is one. We say yes, yes to unity, yes to the closing of ranks, combating terror, and ousting the infidel West from our sacred lands." [28]

Residents of Fallujah and other Sunni cities expressed the same sentiment with banners and graffiti containing slogans that explicitly called for unity—such as "Sunni + Shia = Jihad against Occupation"—or that grouped together Sunni and Shia centers of insurgency, such as "The Martyrs of Fallujah, Najaf, Kufah, and Basra Are the Pole of the Flag that Says God Is Great." [29]

The U.S. military command fully grasped the significance of this developing cross-sectarian unity for the future of the occupation. General Ricardo Sanchez, commander of U.S. forces in Iraq, stated the problem bluntly: "The danger is we believe there is a linkage that may be occurring at the very lowest levels between the Sunni and the Shia. . . . We have to work very hard to ensure that it remains at the tactical level." [30]

This unity proved short-lived. [31] The outpouring of support for Fallujah died down with the fighting after the first battle, leaving the Fallujans to pick up the pieces of their lives without help from around the country. The image of united struggle evoked by the statements and slogans never matured into formal alliances.

These developments contributed to efforts by the jihadists to recruit supporters for their campaigns against Shia communities. Their appeal was straightforward, perhaps best expressed by al-Qaeda's Ayman al-Zawahiri, Osama bin Laden's second in command. Asked about the causes of sectarian violence in Iraq, Zawahiri labeled the Shia as the "aggressor" because they had cooperated with and fought alongside, the "Crusader occupier." His account of the early history of the war included this indictment of the major Shia political forces as simultaneously agents of the United States and Iran: "The Shiite militias trained, funded, and armed by Iran for years advanced violently and quickly into Iraq following the collapse of the Saddam regime. They were merged into the Iraqi Army and other Iraqi security services. They were and remain the Crusader occupier's paws used to strike at Muslims in Iraq."[32]

The translation of this indictment into justification for attacks on Shia civilians focused on the newly installed Allawi government, which was sponsored by the Americans but populated by Shia leadership associated with militias, many of which had been trained in Iran before the fall of Hussein. In the view of the jihadists, this alliance between the new Iraqi government and the U.S.-led occupation could not survive without the support of the Shia community. If the Shia community could be made to withdraw that support, then the government would be forced to oppose both U.S. economic policy and its military offensives, and to work for an end to the occupation. Shia citizens, then, should be "made to pay" for their support of devastating attacks on Fallujah and other Sunni cities. Once they realized that their own comfort, safety, and lives were at stake, they would be intimidated away from the Allawi government.[33] Zawahiri expressed this logic succinctly, offering a formula for ending sectarian strife in Iraq: "Those who cooperate with 'the Crusader occupier' should stop doing so 'and should be engaged in jihad against the Crusaders.'"[34]

The logic was not any different from that applied by the occupation in attacking insurgent communities. Whereas military strategists expected that offensives in predominantly Sunni neighborhoods would convince them to withdraw support from the guerrillas, jihadists expected that violence against Shia would convince Shia communities to withdraw support from the Allawi government and the U.S. occupation. Both fit comfortably into the definition of terrorism: that is, attacks on civilians to coerce a change in their political behavior.[35]

◆ ◆ ◆

The emergence of jihadist attacks on Shia civilians—usually spectacular suicide bombings in crowded public places—dovetailed with the renewed effort of the U.S. military to recruit Iraqi soldiers to participate in the pacification campaigns. Though the first Fallujah battle had taken place almost a year after the dissolution of the Baathist army, the United States found it could not rely at all on the Iraqi military. Recruitment had been difficult, but when the April 2004 attacks began, there had nevertheless been almost a thousand Iraqi troops present, slated for support roles while the marines did the heavy fighting. Even this modest role, however, never materialized.[36] The Iraqi troops, recruited mainly from cities near Fallujah, disappeared before the battle began, mutinied when ordered to march forward, or deserted during the battle. The recruits told the U.S. commanders, "We did not sign up to fight Iraqis."[37]

This pattern was repeated in other localities, most emphatically by the behavior of the Fallujah Brigade, the newly formed military force that was supposed to maintain order in Fallujah after the marines retreated to the outskirts of town. That force, also recruited from around the region, was quickly integrated into the local militias, becoming in effect a functioning part of the insurgency and openly hostile to the occupation.[38]

With the installation of the Allawi government, the recruitment of Iraqi military units trained to fight on the side of the United States became even more important, since framing the pacification efforts as an Iraqi government project required an authentic Iraqi military force. Occupation officials devoted more resources to the project, transferring large sums from reconstruction budgets implied, and sought ways to guarantee against the sort of mutiny that had occurred in Fallujah. One precedent that must have influenced their thinking was the experience during the battle of Najaf against the Shia Mahdi Army. Although locally recruited Shia army and police units had melted away, the Kurdish *peshmerga*, sent down from the northern provinces, had fought effectively.[39]

A logical implication of this experience was that Shia troops might fight effectively in predominantly Sunni areas. The escalating jihadist violence in Shia communities provided a recruiting tool, since angry Shia could be offered the opportunity to avenge their own injuries and suppress further attacks by serving in the Sunni communities that were the source of suicide car bombs.

By the second battle of Fallujah, then, the U.S. military did not use any locally recruited soldiers. The two thousand Iraqi soldiers were made up of Kurdish peshmerga and new units consisting of Shia recruits from the southern areas of Iraq. In this way, all the soldiers they utilized were separated by physical and sectarian distance from those they were fighting.

The second battle of Najaf, fought in August 2004, provided some evidence that various developments over the summer had substantially weakened Sunni-Shia unity. While the U.S. military did not have Sunni units with which to fight the Shia Mahdi Army, it once again successfully used Kurdish peshmerga in the assault. More significantly, during a sustained siege aimed at expelling the Mahdi Army from the tomb of Imam Ali (a major destination for Shia pilgrims), there was no outpouring of support from Sunni areas and no significant spread of the uprising to other cities, particularly Sunni cities. The stage was thus set for the second battle of Fallujah.

The second battle of Fallujah

In November 2004, after three weeks of aerial attacks on neighborhoods that U.S. intelligence designated insurgent strongholds, ten thousand U.S. soldiers, accompanied by two thousand Iraqi national guards, marched into Fallujah.[40] By early December, the city was a wasteland. Erik Eckholm of the New York Times described it as "a desolate world of skeletal buildings, tank-blasted homes, weeping power lines and severed palm trees."[41] At least a quarter of its homes were destroyed, and most of the others were substantially damaged. Blown-out windows, wrecked furniture, three-foot blast holes in walls, and disintegrated doors demonstrated that U.S. troops had relentlessly applied what they jokingly called the "FISH" strategy (Fighting in Someone's House), which involved "throwing a hand grenade into each room before checking it for unfriendlies." Since, in the words of a U.S. commander, "each and every house" was searched, few homes were livable afterward.[42]

Embellishing the strategy of the first battle, U.S. forces surrounded the city and barred entry to everyone. Even humanitarian and medical personnel were not allowed to enter for the next two months. The commanders of the siege then invited all women, children, and older men to leave through a few of heavily guarded checkpoints. All fighting-age men were prohibited from exiting, since they might be disguised guerrillas. Civilians who stayed in the city during the fighting, estimated to be about fifty thousand of the two hundred fifty thousand residents, found themselves in a kill-anything-that-moves free-fire zone.[43] Captain Paul Fowler, a company commander during the fighting, commented, "I really hate that it had to be destroyed. But that was the only way to root these guys out . . . The only way to root them out is to destroy everything in your path."[44]

When the first medical teams were finally allowed into one section of the city in January 2005, they collected more than seven hundred unburied and rotting bodies (reputedly including those of five hundred fifty women and children). They did not include the dead already buried or hidden under debris.[45] Al Jazeera reported, "the smell of corpses inside charred buildings pervades the atmosphere."[46]

More than two hundred thousand residents were estimated to have fled the battle, many without even a change of clothes, just as the Iraqi winter set in. The lucky ones crowded into the homes of friends and relatives in other cities, sometimes as many as thirty people to a small apartment. The unlucky ones created ad hoc refugee camps and shantytowns almost anywhere they could squat, most without any facilities. One family moved into the bumper-car arena of an abandoned amusement park.[47] Independent journalist Dahr Jamail reported that the daily life of these refugees consisted of "searching for food, medical attention, warmth, and clean water." One refugee told Jamail, "We are living like dogs."[48]

◆ ◆ ◆

In an instant of history, Fallujah was transported, as Mike Davis had put it, "backwards to the age of Dickens."[49] A town whose economy rested on its reputation as the "City of Mosques," where great shish-kebab could be purchased at hospitable restaurants and eaten next to a beautiful river, was reduced to rubble. A city previously able to house, feed, and employ its residents was transformed into a political-economic basket case, with multitudes of homeless, no facilities, and no medical care.

The second battle of Fallujah was as vicious as the first if not more so, but it did not generate the national outrage and rebellion of the first battle. While predominantly Sunni cities took advantage of the huge concentration of U.S. forces in Fallujah to stage uprisings throughout Anbar province, the multiplex political developments of the summer had taken their toll on Iraqi solidarity, and quieted the outrage in the vast Shia areas of the south. Muqtada al-Sadr, whose Mahdi Army had just fought a huge battle against the Americans in Najaf without any support from Sunni insurgents, returned the favor with a emphatic lack of rhetorical, logistical, or physical support. Other Shia groups also remained silent or—worse yet—vocally supported the Allawi government's portrayal of battle as a necessary step to eliminate anti-Shia terrorists from a city that had harbored and nurtured them.[50]

Nor did the second battle of Fallujah produce the mass Iraqi military defections that had marked the first battle. The Kurdish peshmerga, who had fought reliably against the Shia Mahdi Army in Najaf, credited themselves again in Sunni Fallujah. The nascent Shia units, recruited in the south where jihadist bombings had produced, at least among a substantial minority of young men, the desire for revenge against Sunnis, were less effective but they neither mutinied nor deserted in large numbers. In the aftermath of the battle, they were willing recruits to the occupation police force that was quickly assembled to manage the city, adopting in full measure the U.S. system of harsh enforcement in an ultimately failing effort to prevent a renewal of the insurgency.

As a result of the battle, the residences, livelihoods, and lives of several hundred thousand Fallujans had been destroyed and at least five hundred children were permanently handicapped.[51] The people of Fallujah were permanently embittered toward the United States and its presence in Iraq, and the insurgency, despite devastating losses, soon replenished its ranks and renewed its attacks. Nevertheless, the conquest of Fallujah was viewed by U.S. military and political leadership as a resounding success, since it accomplished its main goal—the spectacular annihilation of the most visible center of resistance—without triggering the generalized rebellion that had caused the military to abort the earlier effort. As Lieutenant Colonel Paul Newell, a battalion commander during the battle put it, they had delivered a message to the residents of Fallujah and all other cities of Iraq that "This is what happens if you shelter terrorists."[52]

Deconstructed Fallujah

With the occupation in full control of Fallujah, the city became the perfect laboratory for the economic program that the United States was attempting to implement in Iraq. The imagery of the neoliberal planners, epitomized by the comment that "Iraq is like a firm that is putting a business together for the first time,"[53] assumed that neoliberal reform would work best in areas where occupation officials started with a clean slate, where it could move ahead without the encumbrances of the "brutal socialist dictatorship" of Saddam Hussein.[54]

This belief was explicitly expressed by Americans involved in Fallujah and its aftermath. Derrick Anthony, a twenty-one-year-old navy corpsman, surveyed the desolate Fallujah landscape and commented, "It's kind of bad we destroyed everything, but at least we gave them a chance for a new start."[55] The point was elaborated on by Colonel John R. Ballard, one of the reconstruction planners, who told the New York Times, "The best place to bring a model town into place is Fallujah." He promised that Fallujah would become a showcase for the rest of the country to admire and emulate—"a feat of social and physical engineering . . . intended to transform a bastion of militant anti-Americanism into a benevolent and functional metropolis."[56]

This vision, however, was never enacted. In the first couple of months after the conquest, the only new construction in the city consisted of a series of checkpoints (where soldiers recorded the fingerprints and retina scans of returning residents) and the newly bulldozed main streets (the use of which was restricted to U.S. military vehicles). This work prefigured the establishment of the tightest security system of any city in Iraq, before or after the fall of Saddam Hussein, a police-state approach that reflected what Charles Hess, the director of the Iraq Project and Contracting Office and the man in charge of the city's reconstruction, called a "near term . . . focus on operational security measures." [57]

But the deepest tragedy lay not in the "near term," but in the long term, as the promised reconstruction failed to get started and was later canceled. The monetary commitment cited by U.S. officials escalated from a pre-attack $50 million to an early January 2005 estimate of $230 million. But this figure, which Hess claimed to be adequate for the job, was actually a fraction of what would be needed to recreate a modestly working city and a minuscule proportion of the total required to create "a benevolent and functional metropolis." [58]

The inadequacy of the allocation can be judged by considering that the official estimate for repair of Fallujah's sewers and water treatment plants was about $250 million. This repair alone would have exhausted the entire $230 million allocation originally promised by the occupation. [59] The electrical system, which needed to be "ripped out and rebuilt from scratch," [60] would have cost at least as much as the sewers. The cost of replacing or repairing some thirty thousand homes would be several hundred million dollars, while repair of commercial establishments would have added perhaps another $100 million. Rejuvenating the medical system, rebuilding the schools, and clearing and rebuilding the streets would likely have claimed at least $300 million. In addition, many of Fallujah's famous mosques—particularly the minarets, which were actual or suspected locations of snipers—were damaged during the fighting. Taken as a whole, the reality on the ground in Fallujah made the $230 million in promised funds an insulting underestimate of the damage done.

But it would not be long before injury was added to the insult: within six months, it emerged that the United States would not deliver even the modest sums it promised. The new laissez-faire attitude was made official when Deputy Secretary of State Robert B. Zoellick visited the city, and was asked by various local leaders to "get involved" and to "start reconstruction on a big scale." Zoellick replied that "we can help," but "to bring a city back to life, it has to be done by the people of the city." [61]

The subtext of this comment was that Fallujah, like the rest of Iraq, was expected to finance its own reconstruction through private investment. Reconstruction funds would arrive only when and if profitable opportunities made it attractive to domestic or international investors. The magic of the neoliberal market would decide whether and when Fallujah

would be economically revived. The United States accepted as its obliga-
tion the task of removing the threat of insurgency (though it never succeeded in accomplishing even'that), thus creating a favorable investment
climate, and the implication was that the citizens of Fallujah could do
their part by refusing to support the sort of protest that had brought
about the destruction of the city. After that, if the City of Mosques was attractive economically, then private capital would flood into the city and
create "a benevolent and functioning metropolis."

This approach stood in sharp contrast to the reconstruction projects
in post–World War II Germany and Japan, where the Marshall Plan had
placed huge sums of money into the government's hands for reconstituting cities, many of which were even more devastated than Fallujah. In
Iraq, however, the neoliberal doctrine under which reconstruction was
managed demanded that the market, rather than government intervention, animate the reconstruction process. The Iraqi government was
therefore constructed without either the monetary or organizational resources to take the activist role that the occupation governments in Japan
and Germany had performed. Inevitably, then, the approach to Fallujah's
reconstruction was to be replicated in all the battlefield cities: neither the
occupation nor the Iraqi government would make any serious commitment to rebuilding the physical infrastructure of these cities or reconstituting their economies.

The Return to the "Age of Dickens"

By summer 2005 the only ongoing projects in Fallujah were the draconian
measures adopted to prevent the reignition of resistance among the sullen,
demoralized, and economically disconnected citizens of the city.[62] There
were two checkpoints through which all traffic into and out of the city was
funneled (replete with multihour waits, retinal scans, and obtrusive in-
spections fraught with the threat of violence and arrest). Five thousand
U.S. soldiers (augmented by police recruited from among the most angry
and vindictive Shias) patrolled all parts of the city day and night, armed
with rules of engagement that called for maximum firepower in response
to minimal provocation. Major Francis Piccoli, a spokesman for the First
Marine Expeditionary Force that established the system of control, explained to Associated Press reporter Katarina Kratovac: "Some may see
this as a 'Big Brother is watching over you' experiment, but in reality it's
simply a security measure to keep the insurgents from coming back."[63]

Even the resilient Fallujans were staggered by the weight of the occupation.[64] Eighteen months after the U.S. conquest, the city remained a

virtual prison camp, with access so limited that normal economic life was impossible. After promising meager amounts of $100 million in reconstruction funds and $180 million in housing compensation, the Iraqi government diverted between 25 percent and 30 percent of the funds to security expenses, while "even more has reportedly been siphoned off by corruption and overcharging by contractors."[65] A spokesman for the city government estimated that some sixty-five thousand former residents could not return to their homes, while those who did had few basic services and less than four hours of electricity per day. A UN report on conditions concluded:

> Very little can be seen visibly on the streets of Fallujah in terms of reconstruction. There are destroyed buildings on almost every street. Local authorities say about 60 percent of all houses in the city were totally destroyed or seriously damaged and less than 20 percent of them have been repaired so far. . . . Power, water treatment and sewage systems are still not functioning properly and many districts of the city are without potable water.[66]

Seventeen-year-old Ali Ahmed expressed the opinion of many when he told Inter Press Service: "The Americans and Iraqis in power accused us of terror, killed thousands of us and now they are just talking about reconstruction. Well, they are all thieves who only care for what they can pinch off the Iraqi fortunes. Just tell them to leave us alone as we do not want their fraudulent reconstruction."[67]

In early 2006 a U.S. soldier on duty in Fallujah testified to the absence of public services while commenting on the demoralization of the city's residents:

> Trash is everywhere. Heaps upon mounds upon piles of trash of every kind litter every single street in every single direction. I saw many houses where I believe the residents were throwing trash bags from their house directly into the street. It's insane. There is also rubble and debris everywhere. I am not sure how much of this is the result of Al Fajr ("The Dawn," the 2nd battle for Fallujah), but I can confidently say there is no effort on the part of the citizens to clear the bricks and mortar blocks from their own front yards.[68]

In fall 2007 fully three years after the battle, an *Economist* reporter, embedded with the five-thousand-strong garrison in and around the city, joined a U.S. patrol and provided a succinct portrait of the condition of the city that, three years earlier, U.S. military and political leaders had promised would become "a model town":

> In the precinct of Nazal—one of Falluja's nine, each with a joint American-cum-Iraqi police station—locals watch warily as a dozen helmeted young American marines, their guns pointed at the ground, tramp slowly past, avoiding puddles of sewage and piles of rubbish (much favoured by insurgents as a place for planting roadside bombs), and smiling at the knots of

ragged children who shout "Chocola, meester" and are sometimes given pencils instead.

After every ten steps or so, the marines swivel round and walk backwards, giving themselves a maximum field of vision. A couple of local Iraqi volunteers, clad in blue jeans and without helmets, accompany the patrol. Locals politely exchange "*salaams*"; veiled women with babies in arms retreat hastily behind high metal doors. But the marines say the mood has been transformed. No marine has been killed in Falluja since the summer's surge. The patrol stops from time to time as its leader, a fresh-faced corporal from Chicago, engages passersby, via Dave, the newly coiffed interpreter from Baghdad, in amiably stilted badinage. A boy is asked about football. A shopkeeper talks about his oranges, and how business is only slowly improving. The Shia-led government in Baghdad, it is plainly believed, is loath to give much help to the Fallujans, with their reputation for Sunni extremism.

After the Americans' ten-day attack on Falluja in November 2004, much of the city was a mess of rubble; despite a spate of building that started in the summer, also thanks to the surge, the marks of destruction are still visible everywhere. At least 1,500 Islamist militants, most of them members of [al-Qaeda in Iraq], many of them foreign, were said to have been killed in the siege, but until this spring the city remained a smouldering hub of insurgency.[69]

BBC reporters Mike Lanchin and Mona Mahmoud added texture to the *Economist* description, drawing direct connections between the ongoing occupation, the ongoing threat of violence, and the ongoing economic devastation. One telling point was a comment from a local insurgent leader, who told the BBC that the lull in fighting would be temporary if there were not tangible improvements in local conditions: "If the occupier doesn't respond to our demands, then the fight continues."[70]

Perhaps more significant was the possibility that the underlying economic degradation had reached the point of no return. Though the decline in overt violence had been largely a consequence of replacing U.S. patrols with locally recruited police, it was also a consequence of banning the use of cars within the city. This ban, like so much else connected to the U.S. pacification scheme, had further eroded commerce. Most significantly, it had contributed to the economic stagnation of the Sinaa district, once "a thriving area of small industry and work shops." A local tribal leader saw no hope for reviving a district that might be essential for any economic revival in Fallujah: "Sinaa is dead," he said.[71]

Perhaps the most direct expression of Fallujah's status three years after the Americans vowed to create a model city was carried in this report from Muslim Hands International, a relief organization, which designated the city as one of the most desperately depressed in the country: "In response to the most pressing needs of ordinary Iraqis, much of our work is focused on delivery of emergency aid to vulnerable groups in

Baghdad, Mosul, Fallujah, Karbala and Najaf."[72] Or perhaps its status was best described by *Independent* reporter Patrick Cockburn, who commented in early 2008 that Fallujah "had been sealed off from the outside world since it was stormed by the US marines in November 2004."[73]

In a few days, the U.S. military machine had transformed Fallujah into a slum city—comparable to the slum cities of the Global South, which resulted from decades of economic desperation. The new Fallujah, replete with fragile dwellings lacking basic utilities erected in the rubble of formerly substantial homes, featuring elementary education conducted in tents where schoolyards used to be, and debilitated by communicable disease caused by filth and pollution flowing out of the wrecked sewers, was indeed "a feat of social and physical engineering."

Chapter Eight

The Human Toll

I am not here to win hearts and minds; I am here to kill the enemy.

— **Unnamed U.S. army officer**

From the first days of the invasion onward, the human toll of the war in Iraq was virtually unreported in the United States. Establishment media outlets gave the impression that the Bush administration was fighting a "virgin war" in which precision bombing and restrained rules of engagement had reduced civilian casualties to a tiny number of accidental deaths.

The real situation was dramatically different. From the beginning, when the strategy of using overwhelming force to discourage protests was first instituted, through countless home raids aimed at detaining and killing insurgents, through the collective punishment of neighborhoods, through the use of torture and death squads, and finally to the annihilation of Fallujah and parts of other cities, the lethality of the U.S. occupation was commensurate with that of its most brutal historical forebears.

In late 2004 a group of Johns Hopkins researchers reported that during the war's relatively unferocious first fourteen months about one hundred thousand Iraqi civilians—about seven thousand per month—had died violently, with about sixty thousand of the deaths directly attributable to military violence by the United States and its allies.[1] The study, published in the highly respected British medical journal the *Lancet*, applied the same rigorous, scientifically validated methods that the Johns

Hopkins researchers had used in estimating that 1.7 million people had died in the Congo in 2000.[2] Though the Congo study had won the praise of the Bush administration, and had become the foundation for UN Security Council and State Department actions, the Iraq figures were quickly declared invalid by the U.S. and UK governments and by other supporters of the war.[3]

This dismissal was hardly surprising, since the study severely undermined the Bush administration's portrait of itself. After a brief flurry of protest, even the antiwar movement (with a number of notable exceptions) abandoned the issue.[4]

Almost exactly two years later, in October 2006, the same research team published an updated study, this time reporting that six hundred thousand Iraqis had died violently due to the war in Iraq.[5] The average of about fifteen thousand deaths per month over the course of the war was twice that of the earlier report, reflecting the upward trajectory of violence. Even more dramatic was their breakout for the first six months of 2006, which showed a precipitous increase to thirty thousand Iraqi deaths per month. This dramatic turn for the worse apparently reflected events on the ground: the bombing of the Askariya "Golden Dome" early that year had triggered death squad murders of Sunnis and suicide attacks against Shia that dwarfed earlier periods, while the U.S. military was systematically bombing, shelling, and invading "insurgent strongholds" from Baghdad to the Syrian border. The mayhem continued without abatement for the next year, as the second Golden Dome bombing and the U.S. surge added to the deadly mix. By late 2007, the number of Iraqi deaths due to the war, based on extrapolations from the *Lancet* reports and a new survey, had exceeded one million.[6]

Reputable researchers accepted the *Lancet* study's results as valid with virtually no dissent. Juan Cole, the most visible U.S. Middle East scholar, summarized it with a particularly vivid comment: "The US misadventure in Iraq is responsible [in a little over three years] for setting off the killing of twice as many civilians as Saddam managed to polish off in 25 years."[7]

Despite the scholarly consensus, the U.S. and British governments' denials were once again quite effective from a public-education standpoint, and the few news items that mentioned the *Lancet* study bracketed it with official rebuttals. One BBC report, for example, mentioned the figure in an article headlined "Huge Rise in Iraqi Death Tolls," but quoted at length from President Bush's public rebuttal, in which he said that the methodology was "pretty well discredited," adding that "six hundred thousand or whatever they guessed at is just . . . it's not credible."[8] (In a never-released-to-the-public document, the British government later admitted that the study had utilized "a tried and tested way to measuring mortality in conflict zones"; but never publicly admitted its validity.[9])

As a consequence of this sort of coverage, the majority of the U.S. audience thought the war was virtually casualty free for the Iraqis. In a national poll taken by the Associated Press in February 2007, the North American public knew that three thousand U.S. military personnel had died, but they believed that fewer than ten thousand Iraqis had died, less than two percent of the actual total.[10]

Counting How Many Iraqis the United States Killed

Even among those few who had heard and accepted the six hundred thousand figure, only a tiny minority were aware that the majority of Iraqis killed had been killed by the U.S. military. This point is worth repeating—it may be the least publicized fact about the invasion of Iraq: the U.S. military was responsible for more Iraqi deaths than all car bombings, death squads, and other causes combined.

Here is how we know: the *Lancet* interviewers asked their Iraqi respondents how their loved ones died and who was responsible. More than half the casualties (56 percent) were due to gunshots, with about an eighth due each to car bombs (13 percent), air strikes (13 percent), and other ordnance (14 percent). Only 4 percent were due to unknown causes or accidents.

Many times, the families could not tell for sure who was responsible for their loved ones' deaths. Only half were certain, and the interviewers did not record their opinion about who was responsible if "households had any uncertainty" as to who fired the death shot. But even these partial results are staggering: among the cases when the victims families knew for sure who the perpetrator was, U.S. forces (or their "coalition of the willing" allies) were responsible for 56 percent of the killings.

Even though the families could not be sure, we can, using simple statistics, conclude that the United States was responsible for more than half the unattributed deaths.[11] We know this because the vast majority of all unattributed deaths, about two hundred thousand of them, were due to gunshots. Since we also know—from the families who did know the perpetrator of gunshot deaths—that U.S. military action caused over 80 percent of all gunshot deaths, we can calculate that the United States was responsible for about one hundred sixty thousand more deaths. Adding these to the one hundred eighty thousand deaths that the victims' families knew were caused by the United States, *at least* three hundred forty thousand deaths, *at least* 57 percent of the total Iraqi fatalities, were caused by the United States and its allies.

This conclusion seems to contradict some obvious facts about the war. For one thing, how could the United States be responsible for so many gunshot deaths when we hardly ever heard about such deaths, except for occasional incidents at checkpoints and the few atrocities that were prosecuted? The answer lies in the way the Bush administration chose to conduct the war. Their principal military tactic called for house-to-house searches by small units in insurgent strongholds. To stop the occupation military from completing these missions, the guerrillas typically planted roadside bombs and took cover on top of or inside buildings, waiting to detonate IEDs or fire at patrols to halt their progress.

Once the war began heating up, these patrols engaged in firefights at a rate of about one hundred per day. These battles usually occurred after an IED exploded or a sniper fired on a patrol. It was these battles that generated the overwhelming majority of gunshot deaths. Although frequently both the guerrillas and the U.S. military were firing, the insurgents by and large fired into battle-emptied streets where patrols were located, whereas U.S. soldiers expended 1.8 billion bullets each year firing into the structures, often occupied by civilians, where guerrillas were hiding.[12] Even if, as occupation military commanders often claimed, the civilians in these buildings were being used as willing or unwilling "human shields," it was U.S. soldiers, artillery, or airpower that fired the death shot.

What about the IEDs? The headlines of U.S. papers suggested that roadside bombs—the biggest killer of occupation soldiers—must have accounted for a very large proportion of Iraqi deaths. Indeed, U.S. military statistics indicated that, by mid-2006, some eighty thousand IEDs—two thousand every month—been set by the insurgency.[13] These bombs, however, were almost all aimed at U.S. patrols.[14] Iraqi citizens learned very quickly that they should scatter when U.S. armored patrols entered their neighborhood, not only to avoid the IEDs, but also to avoid provoking fire from anxious U.S. personnel. This double-edged caution meant that streets were virtually deserted when bombs exploded or snipers opened fire. The *Washington Post*, citing U.S. military sources who were likely to *overestimate* the destructiveness of the IEDs, reported "an estimated 11,000 Iraqi civilian casualties" due to roadside bombs as of mid-2007.[15] Given that about half these casualties died, IEDs had accounted for only six thousand Iraqi deaths, just about one percent of the total.

What about the death squads? Death squad victims, who were left in conspicuous places with overt signs of torture and telltale execution-style kill-shots in the head, were prominent in the media for a year and a half after the Golden Dome bombing in early 2006, and were counted with considerable accuracy by the hospital officials that received the bodies.[16] These murders rose dramatically that year, peaking at just under eighteen hundred in October and then subsiding, never exceeding five hundred per month in the first half of 2007.[17] They therefore did not, even in peak months, account for more than 15 percent of the approximately fifteen thousand shooting deaths per month during this period, and the usual proportion was considerably less than 5 percent. In all, death squad executions could not have exceeded twenty thousand— about 3 percent of all Iraqi deaths.

Finally, our impression that car bombs account for a preponderance of the fatalities derives strictly from their high visibility in both the print and electronic media. They were certainly the most publicized source of Iraqi deaths and the source of the most spectacular carnage, sometimes causing more than one hundred deaths in a single incident. Through the summer of 2006, however, there had been less than one car bomb per day across the country, with the highest months registering fewer than five per day. The truly lethal bombs, registering three or more deaths, reached a monthly peak of forty-six bombs in September 2005, to which U.S. officials attributed 481 deaths. (A higher peak of sixty-nine lethal bombs and 862 deaths would be recorded in December 2006).[18] Even if the fatalities were many times greater than the official U.S. figures (e.g., two thousand per month) they would still pale in comparison to the ten thousand people per month killed relentlessly by the United States and other members of the "coalition of the willing."[19]

The *Lancet* study, in fact, provides a precise measure of how many people died from car bombs, because this was the easiest source of death for victims' families to identify. Vehicle bombs were responsible for 13 percent of the deaths, about eighty thousand people, by mid-2006, and they certainly killed tens of thousands more as their use peaked the following year. This was a horrendous number, but it was less than a quarter of the total inflicted by the United States, which had reached three hundred forty thousand by that point in the war.

These figures sound impossible to most people who relied for their information about the war on the mainstream U.S. media. Certainly ten thousand Iraqis killed by the United States every month—about three hundred each day—should have been headline news, over and over again, in the United States and elsewhere. Yet, the establishment media simply did not tell us that the United States was killing so many people. Instead, the mainstream media wrote and broadcast stories about car bombers and death squads (despite their *relatively* meager comparative totals), with little coverage of U.S. armed forces killing Iraqis.

One Thousand Patrols Each Day

To complete our understanding of this death toll and why it was not re-ported, we need to examine another amazing statistic, this one released by the U.S. military and reported by the highly respected Brookings Institution: before the surge began in February 2006, the U.S. military was sending out about one thousand patrols each day into hostile neigh-borhoods. Once President Bush's surge strategy was implemented start-ing in early 2007 the number more than doubled, and it was further augmented by an equal number of patrols by Iraqi troops working under U.S. supervision.[20]

These thousands of patrols regularly turned into thousands of Iraqi deaths. As independent journalist Nir Rosen described vividly in his in-dispensable book, *In the Belly of the Green Bird,* these patrols involved brutality that was only occasionally reported by the embedded reporters of the corporate press. The approach was characterized by a brigade commander who told Rosen, "I am not here to win hearts and minds; I am here to kill the enemy." One U.S. commander ordered his troops "to bulldoze any house that had pro-Saddam graffiti on it. He gave half a dozen families only a few minutes to remove whatever they cared about most before their homes were flattened."[21]

This brutality is all very logical once we understand the goals of these patrols and the rules of engagement that guided their actions. From the very beginning of the occupation, and with accelerating frequency as the economic depression generated increased discontent, U.S. troops found that nearly the entire Iraqi population supported the insurgency. (By early 2005, 52 percent of all Iraqis supported armed attacks on U.S. sol-diers.[22]) Troops often had a list of suspects' addresses. Their job was to search the house for incriminating evidence—particularly arms and am-munition, but also literature, video equipment, and other items that the insurgency used for its political and military activities. They were also tasked with interrogating the suspect and, if he seemed guilty, arresting him, and if he resisted or evaded capture, killing him. When they lacked lists of suspects, they conducted house-to-house searches, looking for suspicious individuals.

In this context, any fighting-age man was not just a suspect but a po-tentially lethal adversary. U.S. troops were told not to take any chances: knocking before entering, for example, could invite gunshots through the doors. The instructions in such situations were to use the element of surprise—to break down doors, shoot at anything suspicious, and throw grenades into rooms or homes where there was any sign of resistance. If

the unit encountered tangible resistance, they were expected to call in fire
from artillery or armored vehicles and airpower, rather than risk U.S.
lives by invading a possibly fortified building.

Here is how two Iraqi civilians described these patrols to *Asia Times*
reporter Pepe Escobar: "The Americans usually 'come at night, sometimes by day, always protected by helicopters.' They 'sometimes bomb
houses, sometimes arrest people, sometimes throw missiles.'"[23]

If the patrols encountered no violent resistance during an eight-hour
patrol, they could track down thirty or so suspects or inspect several
dozen residences. Consequently, the one thousand or so patrols could invade thirty thousand homes in a single day. If, however, an IED exploded
under a Humvee, or a sniper shot at them from a nearby rooftop, then
their routine was disrupted and the job at hand was transformed into
finding, capturing, or killing the perpetrator of the attack, a task that
typically took several hours. Iraqi insurgents often set off such IEDs or
shot at the patrols to divert the soldiers from forcibly entering homes.
For insurgents, this represented protection of the neighborhood from a
destructive invasion, even if it provoked a firefight that could risk the
lives of their neighbors.

The battles triggered by IEDs and sniper attacks almost always spread
to the structures surrounding the incident, since that is where the insurgents took cover to avoid the U.S. counterattack. If a perpetrator was
likely to be holed up in a building, the rules of engagement made it clear
that capturing or killing the insurgents was paramount, and therefore
sufficient justification for risking civilian casualties.

Chapter Nine

Creating Slum Cities

They bombed the power stations, water treatment facilities, and water pipes. This house is destroyed, that house is destroyed. You will see poverty everywhere. The things that the simplest human in the world must have, you won't have it there.

—**Sheikh Majeed al-Ga'oud, regarding Ramadi**

So many problems are happening in the city. . . . Where do I start—water, electricity, security, unemployment or health? . . . This is not a life. This is hell.

—**Mohammed Sarhan, regarding Dora district, Baghdad**

The history of war in the twentieth century, as philosopher Eduardo Mendieta observes, "has been the history of the destruction of cities."[1] After an auspicious beginning with the Falange air attack on Guernica during the Spanish civil war, attacks on cities became a centerpiece of the Second World War, which featured the "flattening" of the Warsaw Ghetto, the "rape" of Nanking, the blitzkrieg of London, the firebombing of Hamburg, Tokyo, and Frankfurt, and the nuclear devastation of Hiroshima and Nagasaki. Many later wars have also featured the destruction of cities, from Vietnam to Chechnya.

But even this systematic annihilation, however horrible, has in some situations been reparable. After the Second World War, even the most devastated cities, among them Hamburg, Frankfurt, Hiroshima, and Nagasaki, began to revive as soon as the inhabitants returned and initiated reconstruction, sometimes even before the end of hostilities. Even in Vietnam, the resilience of local residents ultimately reversed the downward economic and social trajectory once the war was ended.

In Iraq, however, this resilience was dampened and perhaps defeated by a new, ambitious, twenty-first-century strategy that sought to induce permanent changes rather than restore livability to the country. In Germany and Japan, the government—supported by the occupation— underwrote and organized the reconstruction of the devastated cities, investing or mobilizing vast monetary and human resources without requiring that they make themselves attractively profitable to risk-averse foreign investors. In Fallujah, however, this sort of commitment was not only unavailable, it was anathema to occupation policy. The U.S. policy that guided the occupation of Iraq sought to transform the Middle East political economy, and this required that Fallujah be made fully accessible to outside investors.

To guarantee this openness, the city was not allowed to reconstruct on its old economic foundations, based, as they had been, on state subsidies, government enterprises, and the economic leverage exercised by empowered technicians and skilled workers committed to the system they had built and maintained. Therefore, even spontaneous reconstruction by local citizens had to be carefully controlled and monitored. In Fallujah, this policy yielded uncounted thousands of refugees, who were deprived of resources with which to rebuild their city and eventually settled elsewhere.

As is always the case in such refugee crises, it was the most prosperous, the most skilled, and the most respected who could find tolerable conditions elsewhere and were thus most likely to leave, taking with them valuable financial, human, and social capital. These losses contributed to the ever-growing combination of anger and despair among those still residing in the city, waiting for some sign of economic and social revival. This anger and despair, in turn, animated a renewed insurgency. The ongoing insurgency then became the rationale for the occupation to keep Fallujah "sealed off from the outside world" and prevented from becoming a functioning city.[2]

A pervasive U.S. military presence became the most visible obstruction to a revived economy. Even three years after Fallujah was reconquered, all commerce waited hours to enter or leave the city, or even to move from one concrete-enclosed neighborhood to another.[3] Reconstruction efforts— almost all initiated and financed by Fallujah's resilient residents—were thwarted by occupation checkpoints, the absence of even minimal public services, and the loss of skills that the city's exiles had taken with them.[4]

As the occupation continued, therefore, the city's potential was systematically compromised. Physically, the decay of infrastructure was a cancerous process, with sewage, water treatment, electrical power, roads, schools, and hospitals slipping further away from viability as months and years passed without reconstruction. The manufacturing and commerce that had sustained Fallujah economically and the mosques and other institutions that provided the foundation for its community life also began to atrophy. Once the human and economic resources for reconstruction fell below critical mass, Fallujah fit the neoliberal mold: a slum city, sitting at the periphery of global society, waiting for economic revival from private investors who had no incentive to risk capital in shantytowns populated by penniless consumers and unemployable workers.

The Destructive Routine of Urban Warfare

U.S. military strategy in 2004 was formulated around the proposition that the destruction of Fallujah would be a deterrent against insurgency elsewhere. A high-ranking Pentagon official told *New York Times* reporters Thom Shanker and Eric Schmitt the larger logic of the battle: "If there are civilians dying in connection with these attacks, and with the destruction, the locals at some point have to make a decision. Do they want to harbor the insurgents and suffer the consequences that come with that, or do they want to get rid of the insurgents and have the benefits of not having them there?"[5] The U.S. military thus expected that the devastation of Fallujah would convince its residents and Iraqis in other cities not to "harbor" the resistance, and therefore obviate the need for further destructive attacks. Here, then, was the ultimate application of the theory of collective punishment (banned under international law), in which a whole city was subjected to house-to-house military invasion as punishment for harboring what the occupation claimed was a small number of allegedly unpopular terrorists. It was, in the vocabulary of twenty-first-century warfare, the application of shock and awe to a single city.

The ferocity of the U.S. attack in Fallujah did not, as the Pentagon official hoped, have this chilling effect. Even with an ongoing presence of five thousand U.S. combat personnel in and around the city, Fallujah continued to harbor considerable insurgent activity for at least three years after the battle.[6] More important, the battle did not mute the resistance in other Sunni cities. While Shia cities did not respond with any signs of support and collateral uprisings, Sunni insurgents took advantage of the U.S. focus on Fallujah during and after the battle to gain control of a number of cities, including Mosul, the third-largest city in Iraq. The number of insurgent attacks against U.S. troops thus remained at the same average level in the six months following the battle, and increased measurably thereafter. By the end of 2005, the number of insurgent attacks on occupation military personnel had reached almost one hundred per day, compared to about fifty in the months before the conquest.[7]

Beginning as soon as the sweep through Fallujah was completed and the city sealed off, the United States withdrew half its ten-thousand-strong military force and used it to mount major operations aimed at maintaining, recapturing, or establishing control of key insurgent strongholds throughout the Sunni areas of Iraq. The biggest confrontations took place in Ramadi, Mosul, Tal Afar, and Haditha.[8]

In these and other cities and towns, the fighting and its aftermath set in motion the same slum-city dynamics as in Fallujah.

The Deconstruction of Ramadi

Ramadi, where *Washington Post* reporter Ellen Knickmeyer reported that "heavy fighting" had left the city "a bombed-out, weed-overgrown, deserted wasteland,"[9] illustrates the central role that attacks on infrastructure—so critical to Pentagon theories of modern war—played in the military strategy of the U.S. occupation and in the subsequent economic marginalization of the cities involved.

U.S. troops did not enter Ramadi during the first days of the occupation, reportedly because a deal was made to allow local tribal leaders to form an indigenous government.[10] In summer 2003, therefore, there was little looting as local tribes policed the city and few armed conflicts as the U.S. military kept its distance. Eventually, as economic depression took hold, various forms of protest began, directed mainly against the occupation. A relatively mild thirty-person "peaceful demonstration against the occupation" marked the moment when occupation officials decided that Baathists were regaining power within the city. Patrols were ordered to enter the city and quell the protests, using the typical portfolio of U.S. military methods: lists of suspected insurgents, surprise nighttime raids on suspects' homes, and the use of overwhelming force at any sign or suspicion of resistance. According to Inter Press Service reporter Brian Conley, "Iraqis were killed, and, following tribal policies of revenge, a cycle of violence began."[11] The insurgency gained strength and support and soon became the dominant force within the city.

Three years later, occupation officials conceded to reporters that the city was "under insurgent control" and claimed that Abu Musab al-Zarqawi (the Lebanese jihadist portrayed by occupation officials as the leader of the resistance) had made his headquarters there.[12] The use of patrols, however intensive, had failed to dislodge him or the insurgency, so air attacks on insurgent "safe houses" were initiated. Sheikh Majeed al-

Ga'oud, a frequent visitor to the besieged city, told Conley that Ramadi was "a city where the fighters are very much in control. . . . They are controlling the ground and they are very self-confident. They don't cover their faces with masks, and the Americans are running away from them. The Americans cannot win an infantry war with them, so they began using massive airpower to bomb them."[13]

When the aerial assault did not convince Mosul civilians to expel the insurgents, the U.S. military amplified its offensive, utilizing the four-pronged strategy they had applied in Fallujah. First, they cut the city off from the outside world, closing all entrances except two checkpoints and searching all people and vehicles for signs of insurgent sympathies. This had the devastating side effect of choking off the social and economic life of the city. A refugee described the grim passage to Conley: "To enter Ramadi . . . you have to pass the bridge on the Euphrates and the electrical station for Ramadi. This is occupied by the U.S. troops. The checkpoint is there, the glass factory nearby is occupied by American snipers. Here they inspect cars and you will need more than four hours just to pass the bridge."[14]

Aside from the four-hour wait that made some commerce difficult (such as the transport of perishable goods) and other commerce impractical (such as commuting to jobs), note that the soldiers occupied a glass factory, thus immobilizing a key manufacturing plant. The ripple effect of the lost wages of workers there—and others who previously worked outside the city—would contribute to the collapse of the already crippled Ramadi economy.

Second, the U.S. offensive targeted the Ramadi infrastructure, following military theorist Kenneth Rizer's observation that by "declaring dual-use targets legitimate military objectives, the Air Force can directly target civilian morale."[15] In Ramadi, this meant that by mid-2006 "there were no civil services functioning." Al-Ga'oud told Conley, "They bombed the power stations, water treatment facilities, and water pipes. This house is destroyed, that house is destroyed. You will see poverty everywhere. The things that the simplest human in the world must have, you won't have it there."[16]

A Ramadi resident added: "The phone station was attacked by U.S. troops, and now even the building is completely destroyed. And the train station also, 100 percent destroyed; day after day, F16s bomb it."[17] Hospitals, though not attacked directly, were not allowed to bring in needed medical supplies and equipment, and thus were of declining usefulness as the medical emergency amplified. Deteriorating public services, even in neighborhoods where there was little or no fighting, created a stream of refugees, setting in motion the sort of dislocations that rob cities of their economic, political, and cultural vitality.[18]

Third, the U.S. military commanders demanded that Ramadi residents turn over guerrilla fighters or face further assault. Mauricio Mascia, an Italian relief worker, told the Inter Press Service about the choice offered local residents on a neighborhood-by-neighborhood basis:

> Similar to the tactics used during the U.S. assault on Fallujah in November 2004, the U.S. military continues to use loudspeakers to ask people to either hand over "insurgents" who are present in their neighbourhoods, or to evacuate their homes and flee the city. ICS reports that some of the messages have specifically made reference to what happened in Fallujah.[19]

Fourth, after many of the residents left rather than hand over the guerrillas, the United States invaded the city neighborhood by neighborhood using all the weapons at their disposal, including snipers, airpower, tanks, and artillery. One resident, Qasem Dulaimi, told Conley how his house was commandeered by U.S. snipers while his family was held hostage inside, apparently to deter insurgents' counterattacks: "They crushed the main doors and entered the house. I got out of my room and said some words in English, 'We are a peaceful family, OK it's OK.' But the family members were locked up in a small room downstairs. From time to time we heard shooting from our roof. They used our house as a killing tool; they used the roof as a killing tool." Eventually the family was released and the U.S. troops moved on.[20]

Another resident described how U.S. snipers in tall buildings along the main downtown street had converted the thoroughfare into a free-fire zone: "[Main Street] is blocked, not by concrete, but by snipers. Anyone who goes ahead in the street will be killed. There's no sign that it's not allowed, but it's known to the local people. Many people came to visit us from Baghdad. They didn't know this and they went ahead a few meters and were killed."[21] As the siege of Ramadi wore on, it was clear that the effort to find, capture, or kill insurgents would not succeed. After the experience in Fallujah, the guerrillas chose to melt away rather than fight and, despite the best U.S. efforts to trap them in the city, all but a handful slipped through the cordon to join other displaced inhabitants outside the military encirclement.

The U.S. hope for success, therefore, rested on using collective punishment to demoralize the local population and convince Ramadi civilians to expel or demobilize the resistance. In this effort, crises caused by the destroyed infrastructure, the paralyzed economy, and the spread of hunger, disease, and homelessness were viewed by occupation military planners as useful leverage against civilian support for the insurgency. Nevertheless, the residents simply did not give in to the pressure, and the invasion was aborted without working its way through the entire city.

Despite the incomplete conquest, the combination of infrastructure damage, evacuation, and economic disruption had converted Ramadi, like Fallujah, into the economically dysfunctional and marginalized city that *Washington Post* reporter Knickmeyer would later describe as "a bombed-out, weed-overgrown, deserted wasteland."[22]

The Deconstruction of Baiji

The city of Baiji presents yet another facet of this deconstruction process: the physical damage of the war was the least important part of that city's decline.[23]

As the site of the largest oil refining plant in Iraq, Baiji had strategic importance beyond what its moderate population of seventy thousand would suggest. During the Hussein regime its 98 percent Sunni population was supported by well-paying jobs in the government-owned industrial district around the oil refining facilities. Baiji fell onto hard times, however, when coalition administrator L. Paul Bremer's privatization program demobilized most government-owned enterprises. Though the oil industry itself was spared, other industries were shuttered, and unemployment swept through the city, generating deep bitterness among local residents and inspiring a variety of protests against the U.S. presence.[24]

In late 2003, in its typical response to the growing discontent, the U.S. initiated the standard-operating-procedure patrols that General Sanchez had mandated for predominantly Sunni areas with signs of a developing resistance. *Washington Post* reporter Ann Tyson characterized them as "heavy-handed sweeps through Baiji by U.S. forces . . . [that] left many people angry, frightened and humiliated." Adil Faez Jeel, the director of the oil refinery in the town, told her that these sweeps, along with the economic depression, solidified local support for armed resistance: "Most of the people fighting the Americans tell me they do nothing for us but destroy the houses and capture people. . . . There are no jobs, no water, no electricity."[25]

By late 2004 Baiji guerrillas were strong enough to assert control of the town while the U.S. was busy fighting in Fallujah, thus joining many other Sunni-majority towns that became centers of resistance during that period. In addition to skirmishes with U.S. troops and Iraqi police, the guerrillas shut down pipelines from the oil refinery and hijacked trucks transporting oil both to Baghdad and to export. The biggest battle occurred in the center of town when guerrillas launched a mortar attack against a joint U.S. and Iraqi National Guard patrol, triggering two days of battles. A doctor at the local hospital told Agence France-Presse that at least ten civilians were killed and twenty-six wounded.[26]

For the next year, Baiji was out of the news, largely because the U.S. military was busy with massive military sweeps in the west of Anbar province. This quiescence ended in late 2005 when occupation troops returned to Baiji, characterized by Tyson as "a Sunni city long neglected by American forces and still firmly in the grip of insurgents."[27]

According to U.S. military sources, the new attempt at pacification was provoked partly by suspicions that local guerrillas were using Baiji as a staging area for attacks in Mosul and Baghdad. The more immediate motivation was, however, the decision to wrest control of the city's oil business from the insurgency. The guerrillas had begun systematically depriving the occupation and the Iraqi government of any and all oil deriving from the Baiji complex. At the same time, insurgents and their allies among local tribal leaders were siphoning off a share of the oil refinery output and selling it on the black market. The proceeds were then used for local projects controlled by the tribal leaders and to supply the ongoing insurgency. A resistance supporter in Baiji told Inter Press Service reporters Brian Conley and Isam Rashid that that their actions were an attempt to stop U.S. theft of Iraqi oil: "This petrol will go to Turkey and is stolen by the occupation forces; or, when Turkey buys this petrol, the money is taken by the occupation forces."[28]

The resistance thus justified both the attacks on pipelines and convoys and the appropriation of the oil for their own purposes, which, in their view, served the interest of the local community and the Iraqi people. According to reporter Oliver Poole of the British *Telegraph*, nationally the resistance was acquiring tens of millions of dollars per year from their siphoning operations, with comparable amounts being appropriated by other groups, ranging from criminal gangs to mosques, which delivered various local services that the government was no longer providing.[29]

To prevent the resistance from appropriating the oil, occupation forces occupied and closed the Baiji refinery in late 2005 and sent in the U.S. Army's 101st Airborne Division to secure town. The campaign extended into summer 2006 without resolution, replete with ferocious ground battles and U.S. bombing attacks on houses and communities in which resistance fighters were thought to be hiding. Sergeant First Class Danny Kidd, a veteran of both the Afghan and Iraqi occupations, attributed the hard going to the fact that Baiji residents supported the guerrilla fighters: "They have the place locked down. We have almost no support from the local people. We talk to 1,000 people and one will come forward."[30]

The ferocity of the resistance led to an official escalation of the assault. According to the *Army Times,* the new strategy was modeled after "walls built around Falluja and Samarra in recent months [that] have quelled restive insurgent cells." The assault began with the construction of an earthen barrier around Siniyah, the most rebellious neighborhood in the city, with check points set up to inspect "all vehicles leaving or entering . . . for known insurgents, bomb-making materials and illegal weapons."[31]

These draconian measures ended all normal life in Siniyah. Anyone with business outside the community could not reliably pass through the checkpoint: college students discontinued their education, employees lost their jobs, and local commercial establishments could not function. Sumiya, a 33-year-old Siniyah housewife, who spoke on the phone to Inter Press Service reporters Brian Conley and Isam Rashid, described the situation inside the community of three thousand:

> Siniyah has become a real battlefield now, and the occupation forces have destroyed many of our homes. . . . There is no security inside Siniyah and it is worse than any place in Iraq now. The occupation forces and Iraqi National Guard are raiding Siniyah houses every day and arresting many people. There is a curfew from 5 p.m. to 5 a.m.; in Baghdad it is only midnight to 5 a.m.[32]

One resident told Conley and Rashid that "we live in a very big jail for three thousand." A local cleric told the *Army Times* that Siniyah had become "a concentration camp."[33]

As in most other Sunni cities, the fighting in Baiji had occurred episodically, cresting during U.S. efforts at pacification, and subsiding during the much longer periods of local rule (in league with resistance fighters) while the United States was busy elsewhere. But the physical, economic, and infrastructural decline of the city was continual. With no resources available to reconstruct the city, each episode left the electrical, water, and hospital systems further degraded. Economic depression not only eliminated the possibility of physical reconstruction, but also hindered even a minimally adequate existence.

Beyond the ongoing physical damage, there are three elements to the Baiji story that bear further scrutiny because they exemplify the ways in which the occupation created a "slum city" dynamic. These elements were the demobilization of state-owned industrial plants at the beginning of the occupation (part of the original neoliberal reforms instituted by the occupation), the ultimately successful campaign by the U.S. military to end the siphoning of oil (the refinery was reopened in mid-2006 under strict occupation control), and military encirclement of the

Siniyah neighborhood. Taken together, these actions definitively undermined the viability of the city.

The initial demobilization of state-owned factories did more than
create crippling unemployment; it threatened to destroy an entire industrial district that could have supplied Iraq with a variety of manufactured
goods, and could have formed the foundation for expanded production
and modernization. Such industrial districts are precious and fragile. As
numerous scholars have documented, they are the heartbeat of industrial
development.[34] Once the shuttering lasted more than a few months, key
personnel began to leave in search of new jobs, while the idle factories
corroded or were looted for parts (by criminals and/or former employees). The support network for the industrial district—suppliers, educational institutions, and financial sources—atrophied. Once these
processes reached a certain point, they proved irreversible, even with
huge infusions of capital.

The siphoning off of oil represented an Iraqi solution to the economic
shocks that had begun under the Hussein regime.[35] (Like many primary
industries around the world, the oil industry is susceptible to local theft,
with economically stressed communities using these illegally acquired as-
sets to tide them over financially.[36]) During the last economically desperate years of the Hussein regime, local tribal leaders had systematically
siphoned off oil, escaping government retribution by threatening to attack
the pipelines if the government moved to stop them.

A British *Telegraph* report in February 2006 indicated that this informal system had been operating in Baiji since U.S. occupation began, and
might have been cushioning or forestalling the inexorable process of economic decline. One of Baiji's tribal leaders, Meshaan al-Jaburi, the leader
of the Jaburi tribe and a member of parliament, had been entrusted with
forming and commanding seventeen battalions of security officers to
guard the pipeline near Baiji. The government charged that he had not
formed the security force and had instead kept the payments and helped
to organize attacks on government shipments of the oil, while "funneling
a portion of the money to rebel groups." In other words, the Jaburi tribe
was using local oil to enrich themselves, fuel the local economy, and support the resistance to the occupation.[37] The successful effort to choke off
this flow of revenues (Jaburi himself fled the country) deprived the city
of an economic lifeline that might have helped it to sustain its people and
keep its facilities in workable order until they could be more fully revived.

Finally, the encirclement of Siniyah represented yet another crippling
blow to the social system of the city. Although it offered the occupation
the possibility of containing or even defeating the resistance by limiting

its supplies and its mobility, the barrier deprived the larger community of the economic resources that Siniyah residents provided. No city can function when a substantial fraction of its productive citizens are demobilized, so Baiji—already prostrate from earlier economic shocks—was dealt another blow. The isolation, unemployment, and the daily struggle for survival meant that key family members within Siniyah could not lend each other support, that local mosques were strained beyond the limit of their social and personal resources, and that the routines of daily life in the city as a whole were ruptured.

These three developments created a dynamic of economic and social strangulation, which—continued long enough—could convert Baiji into the same hopeless wasteland as Fallujah and Ramadi, even when and if the fighting subsided. By mid-2006, after three years of occupation and war, this slum-city dynamic, in different incarnations, had become daily reality in many Iraqi cities.

Mohammed Sarhan, age fifty, a grocer in the southern Baghdad neighborhood of Dora, spoke for the residents of many Iraqi cities when he told the *Washington Post*: "So many problems are happening in the city. . . . Where do I start—water, electricity, security, unemployment or health? . . . This is not a life. This is hell."[38]

Part III

Deconstruction, Not Reconstruction

Chapter Ten

The Saga of the Al-Fatah Pipeline

The Al Fatah pipeline repair "looked like some gargantuan heart-bypass operation gone nightmarishly bad."

—James Glanz, *New York Times*

Fallujah, Ramadi, and Baiji shared a similar fate. The occupation, through the midwife of war, reduced them to Dickensian cities, populated by economically destitute populations residing in shanties without potable water, electricity or social services. Many areas of Iraq, however, escaped the direct devastation of major military actions. For the first three years, fighting was concentrated in the predominantly Sunni cities located to the west and north of Baghdad, and in the predominantly Sunni areas of the capital.[1] While the vast majority of Shia were anxious for the United States to leave—despite noteworthy military moments in Shia areas of Sadr City, Najaf, and Maysan province—most predominantly Shia cities were not subjected to the sort of focused destruction that the war brought to the Sunni cities.[2] In Kurdistan, which broadened the autonomy it had gained under Saddam Hussein, there was even less fighting, though Kirkuk, a key city claimed by the Kurds, was the scene of serious battles led by Sunni and Turkmen insurgents against the Kurdish-dominated local government.[3] As time went on, violence spread to new areas, with Basra becoming a focus of a four-way struggle among the British and three competing Shia political formations, and Baghdad erupting in early 2006 as the center of violence in the country as a whole.

But even before this malignant metastasis infected new areas with violence, the degradation of daily life had spread to every corner of Iraq. Military quiescence did not insulate predominantly Shia and Kurdish areas from the stranglehold of slumification; it only meant that the degradation was slower.

The main locus of decline—and the greatest source of irreversible damage—was the Iraqi infrastructure. The initial U.S. bombing and artillery barrage had added to the degradation accomplished previously by air attacks during and after the 1991 Gulf War, the UN sanctions that prohibited import of materials needed for upkeep and repair, and the malignant neglect of the Hussein regime. The coup de grace, however, was administered by the George W. Bush administration reconstruction effort, which—despite its advertised goal of modernizing and reviving the Iraqi economy—actually transformed progressive degradation into irreversible decline. In many cases, the damage done in the name of reconstruction was more destructive than even the most intensive assaults performed by the U.S. military.

Perhaps the first definitive proof that reconstruction was strangling rather than reviving the Iraqi infrastructure was the December 2004 report card issued by the Center for Strategic and International Studies' Post-Conflict Reconstruction Project.[4] At that time, the major reconstruction projects mandated by L. Paul Bremer's CPA should have been nearing completion, with the water system, education systems, and electrical grid projected to be functioning at levels well beyond those of the Hussein regime. Instead, very little tangible progress had been recorded. The report began: "The substantial U.S. funding for the reconstruction effort in Iraq is expected to have a significant impact on the ground. Our analysis, however, shows that the impact will be diffused in a number of ways." It then pointed out that only 27 percent of funding committed up to that point had been invested in reconstruction, while 30 percent had been spent on security, 12 percent on insurance and international salaries not associated with reconstruction, 10 percent on overhead and 6 percent on profits. The remaining 15 percent had been frittered away on what the CSIS called "fraud, corruption, and mismanagement." Even so, other informed observers considered these figures a dramatic overestimate of the amount devoted to actual reconstruction.[5]

A closer look at the dynamics of reconstruction gives us a better sense of this failure, and it also allows us to see how the U.S. economic presence—like its military operations—created the downward dynamic toward slumification. This devolution proceeded much faster than neoliberal processes elsewhere in the world, though it did not match the rapid degradation of Baiji and Ramadi and the supersonic destruction of Fallujah.

Repairing the Oil Pipeline at Al-Fatah

In the spring of 2006, reporter James Glanz of the *New York Times* offered a neat window into the dynamics of this downward spiral with his report of the occupation effort to repair an inoperative oil pipeline in Al-Fatah, a village about 130 miles north of Baghdad and on the main pipeline from Baiji.[6] The pipeline had been broken at the beginning of the war by a U.S. air attack on the bridge that had carried it across the Tigris River.

The CPA was eager to access the $5 million per day in oil revenues that a reconnected pipeline promised, and it therefore became one of the first reconstruction projects. Original estimates indicated that restoring the bridge would cost $70 million, and then it would cost some $5 million to reactivate the pipeline. The contract with KBR, the Halliburton subsidiary in charge of the project, was signed in April 2003 and stipulated a completion date in early 2004.

Problems began to arise almost immediately, initially because CPA officials decided that bridge repair was not urgent and that only pipeline repair should proceed on an accelerated schedule. KBR was therefore authorized to develop an alternate method of laying the pipeline across the Tigris. This turned into a daunting project, and eventually the entire $75 million budget originally designated for both bridge and pipeline repair was reallocated just to the pipeline project. The deadline was extended to May 2004.

When Robert Sanders of the Army Corps of Engineers arrived to inspect the work during July 2004, two months after the contracted completion date, the project was in disarray. What Sanders found, according to Glanz, "looked like some gargantuan heart-bypass operation gone nightmarishly bad." Sanders decided that the entire enterprise was unredeemable and had to be reconceived. His recommendation was not implemented, however, because by that time "the project had burned up all of the $75.7 million allocated to it, [and] the work came to a halt. . . . A supervisor later told Sanders that the project's crews knew that [the plan for laying the pipe] was not possible, but that they had been instructed by the company in charge of the project to continue anyway."[7]

Sanders issued a scathing report detailing what he called "culpable negligence" on the part of KBR. His report had little impact: although the Army Corps of Engineers withheld KBR's small bonus fees, nothing was done to recover the wasted millions or to force the completion of the project.

Five important points emerge from this story: First, the bridge and pipeline were destroyed by the U.S. military. The attack was ordered during the initial fighting on April 3, 2003, by U.S. general T. Michael Moseley "to stop the enemy from crossing the bridge on which the original pipelines had run through openings beneath the road."[8] This is typical of the infrastructural damage caused by the United States in Iraq. During the initial battles of the invasion, and during subsequent sweeps against the Iraqi resistance after the occupation was underway, the United States destroyed or damaged roads, bridges, electrical transmission, oil facilities, sewage lines, water treatment plants, commercial and industrial structures, and even mosques and hospitals.[9] While the resistance also targeted such structures, particularly oil pipelines and electrical transmission lines,[10] its destructive powers were modest relative to what U.S. airpower could accomplish with bombs of five hundred to two thousand pounds.[11]

Second, instead of simply repairing the damage, the United States undertook a major overhaul of the pipeline system. Occupation authorities vetoed the original plan to repair both the bridge and pipeline and substituted one to sink a new pipeline into the bed of the Tigris, in the process escalating the cost of pipeline repair from $5 million to $75 million. KBR was therefore replacing relatively old-fashioned engineering with state-of-the-art methods that only the most advanced multinational corporations could undertake. Moreover, if the buried pipeline had been successfully installed, maintenance and repair would also have required specialized and even proprietary methods that only KBR or perhaps another major multinational firm could offer. Successful completion of the project would have integrated the Al-Fatah crossing into the international oil industry.

This strategic decision reflected the larger project of economic reform in Iraq, which involved demobilizing Iraqi state enterprises (including those with experience in just this sort of repair work) and bringing the Iraqi economy— and most importantly its oil industry—into the global system for good.[12] Modern equipment and infrastructure, introduced largely by U.S.-owned multinational corporations, would then have to be maintained by those same corporations. This project was typical of the reconstruction projects authorized by the CPA.[13]

Brigadier General Robert Crear, the U.S. Army Corps of Engineers officer in charge of reconstructing the oil industry, summed up this "replace everything" approach to *Houston Chronicle* reporter David Ivanovich: "It's nation building. It's starting from scratch."[14]

Third, the contractor knew beforehand that the project might fail. The Al-Fatah crossing project was one of many undertaken by KBR, the omnipresent Halliburton subsidiary, without competitive bidding. In implementing its ambitious plan, KBR officials ignored at least three of their own technical reports that "warned that the effort would fail if carried out as designed." A later investigation by the United States special inspector general for Iraq reconstruction concluded: "The geological complexities that caused the project to fail were not only foreseeable but predicted." [15]

So why did KBR proceed after three dire warnings? Glanz does not address this question, but the answer can be found in the combined impact of two elements of U.S. reconstruction policy: lack of competitive bidding and self-regulation by contractors. In the absence of competitive bidding, there is an incentive to propose and execute the most ambitious and expensive versions of any project, and to squirrel away unused funds during its execution. In this case, the cancellation of the bridge reconstruction project by the occupation authorities created exactly such an incentive, resulting in the unspent bridge-repair budget being reallocated to the pipeline repair budget. [16]

The tendencies toward overambition and corruption that are inherent in noncompetitive projects can normally be restrained by tight oversight procedures. The standard procedure for the vast army of Defense Department contractors who supply the U.S. military in normal times requires constant oversight by the Defense Contract Management Agency. DCMA personnel are technical experts in the areas of the various contracts they monitor, and they scrutinize the original contract, and then monitor projects as they proceed, so that below code materials, poor construction methodology, and faulty intermediate parts are corrected in a timely fashion. The agency is equipped with a variety of sanctions that compel compliance when they decide a problem has arisen.

In Iraq, no such oversight system was implemented. The contractors were expected to monitor themselves under the threat of "market discipline"—that is, the threat that a poor job would result in no further contracts. A final inspection, like that administered by Robert Sanders, was the only oversight, and it occurred after nearly all payments had been made, with no provision for enforcement. As a result, there was no effective way to sanction companies for failure to execute a contract as promised. [17]

By the third anniversary of the invasion, the consequences of this fatally flawed contracting system were visible all over Iraq. Inappropriate, inadequate, incomplete, or never-started projects were legion; yet in almost every case, contractors received full payment on expensive contracts, regardless of outcome. Media reports on such cases cited the ferocity of the insurgency as the primary cause of escalated cost, compromised quality, and/or complete failure—even in areas where there was no insurgent violence. Glanz put this explanation in proper perspective: "Although the failures of [reconstruction] are routinely attributed to insurgent attacks, an examination of this project shows that troubled decision-making and execution have played equally important roles."[18]

The General Accountability Office of the United States, in its report to the Senate Foreign Relations Committee in February 2006, extended Glanz's conclusion to the entire reconstruction effort (though in much more diplomatic language):

> While poor security conditions have slowed reconstruction and increased costs, a variety of management challenges also have adversely affected the implementation of the U.S. reconstruction program. In September 2005, we reported that management challenges such as low initial cost estimates and delays in funding and awarding task orders have led to the reduced scope of the water and sanitation program and delays in starting projects. In addition, U.S. agency and contractor officials have cited difficulties in initially defining project scope, schedule, and cost, as well as concerns with project execution, as further impeding progress and increasing program costs. These difficulties include lack of agreement among U.S. agencies, contractors, and Iraqi authorities; high staff turnover; an inflationary environment that makes it difficult to submit accurate pricing; unanticipated project site conditions; and uncertain ownership of project sites.[19]

The general rule became that every project was subject to some kind of delay, and that actual completion was unpredictable and often never achieved, at least by the first contractor. Without adequate oversight, there was little chance that inadequate work would be corrected before it resulted in fatal damage to the project as a whole.

For the contractors, the most profitable projects were those that promised ambitious results for very high prices, and which buried bonus profits in inflated prices for materials, imported labor, and other unmonitored costs. Often a failed project was the most profitable, since failure might allow the firm either to siphon off funds into profits and/or receive an additional highly profitable contract to redo or complete the job.[20]

Fourth, it took over three years for a six-month project to be completed. When inspector Sanders arrived in July 2004, the project was already overdue by two months, after having been granted a four-month extension. At that point, Sanders determined the project was doomed, that "it was just the wrong place for horizontal drilling [the technique used]." But since "all the money had been spent," there were no funds left for KBR to implement a new strategy.[21] No effort was made to find KBR financially negligent or to recover any of the funds already paid.

Almost two years later, in April 2006 when Glanz undertook his investigative report, a new project had been commissioned. This project, like its predecessor, avoided the straightforward plan of repairing the bridge and the pipeline together, perhaps using Iraqi technicians or even state-owned enterprises. Instead it once again sought to sink the pipeline under the river, utilizing the expertise of two other foreign firms at an additional cost of $40 million.[22]

According to Colonel Richard B. Jenkins, the army officer in charge of the new effort, the repair was "essentially a finished project" in April 2006 when Glanz arrived at the scene. An official at the Iraqi Northern Oil Company, however, disagreed. No oil, he pointed out, had yet been transported through the pipeline. Moreover, if and when the project was actually completed, it would remain vulnerable to attack along its entire length by the resistance. U.S. officials even acknowledged that increased production "will only happen if Iraqis can protect the entire pipeline."[23]

The repair was eventually completed and the pipeline brought on line. True to the Iraqi reality, however, the pipeline remained vulnerable to accident and sabotage. In late 2007 the northern pipeline was still only sporadically open.[24]

The timeline for Al-Fatah—more than three years to complete a project that well-qualified, state-owned Iraqi companies could have completed in several months—was all too representative of the handling of Iraqi reconstruction by the U.S. occupation. Though the original intention was a quick return of the pipeline to usefulness, timeliness was a secondary or perhaps even tertiary priority. The quickest fix would have utilized state-owned Iraqi enterprises to jerry-rig the bridge and pipeline to get it running again, but this would have violated the larger program of removing the Iraqi government from the center of the economy. The original plan, for KBR to repair the bridge and pipeline together, would have been quicker than the actual program undertaken, but this would have perpetuated the out-of-date pipeline technology that Iraq had been using. The U.S. economic program for Iraq called for a vast expansion of production, and therefore it made sense to replace outmoded technology immediately rather than redo the work when increased production required a larger pipeline.

The rapid return to production, then, was less critical than providing for economic transformation, and the United States was willing to sacrifice short-term oil production (as well as Iraqi employment and even economic viability) in order to implement the neoliberal reform that was central to the U.S. program for post-Hussein Iraq.

Fifth, the Iraqis were left with a project they could not repair or maintain. Because Iraqi engineers were excluded from the project from the beginning, because U.S. contractors chose new technology that dropped the pipeline onto the bottom of the Tigris River (instead of attaching it to a rebuilt bridge), and because there was no training for local technicians to master the new technology (and no educational institutions teaching it), the Iraqis were dependent upon foreign expertise into the foreseeable future to repair and maintain the crossing.

This sort of manufactured dependency became part of occupation policy. For projects that remained unfinished, even a remobilized Iraqi contractor did not have the expertise to complete the job. For completed projects, like the pipeline, Iraqi engineers had no expertise to address maintenance or repair problems. Without any indigenous expertise, Iraq was forced to hire foreign contractors for maintenance at often prohibitive costs, or else see their new technology fall into disrepair—an all too common outcome.

In the meantime Iraqi technicians, left idle or semi-idle by occupation-sponsored projects that made their skills obsolete, left the area, the industry, or the country in search of work, thus depleting the talent pool available for reconstruction.

This dynamic was a key impetus for the downward spiral of the Iraqi infrastructure.[25] In all areas of Iraqi life, even those most insulated from the war and from the U.S. presence, the changes wrought by the occupation were designed to create dependence on outsiders for basic infrastructural building blocks, while reducing the reservoir of usable expertise within the country. As the reconstruction failures multiplied, Iraqi society was intentionally made less and less able to address the problems that plagued it.

Chapter Eleven

The Degradation of the Iraqi Infrastructure

I don't think anybody has a problem in principle with the idea that if you can put people back to work that is a good thing . . . but the question is at what cost are you going to be doing that? And if the cost is taking a lot of electricity from the grid, maybe you want to look at what the alternative uses of that might be.

— U.S. State Department official, speaking about the availability of electricity to reopen Iraqi clothing factories

The Bush administration initially allocated $18 billion to reconstruction. This was augmented by an unknown amount of oil revenues left over from the Hussein era and perhaps $5 billion in donations and loans from other countries.[1] This total was substantially below the initial UN estimate that $56 billion would be needed to restore the country to infrastructural health, an estimate that increased dramatically as fighting continued and the decrepit state of the infrastructure became fully apparent.[2] Although it was never explicitly stated, the U.S. government intended to make up the difference with oil revenues, since its original plan called for an immediate and dramatic increase in oil production. This intention was implicit in Deputy Secretary of Defense Paul Wolfowitz's testimony to the House Appropriations Committee just a week after the war began: "The oil revenues of that country [Iraq] could bring between $50 [billion] and $100 billion over the course of the next two or three years. Now, there are a lot of claims on that money, but . . . we are dealing with a country that can really finance its own reconstruction and relatively soon."[3]

Like so many of the original U.S. plans, the increased oil production did not materialize, and, as the military situation deteriorated, substantial chunks of reconstruction funds were utilized to cover the increased costs of security and insurance. As a result, only about a quarter of the allocated budget was actually spent on in-country reconstruction. While escalating oil prices eventually allowed the Iraqi government to develop a reconstruction budget, at no point in the first five years were enough funds available to restore Iraq to economic and social viability.

Five years into the war effort, the telltale signs of locked-in infrastructural decay were legion.

The Short Circuit in Electrical Power

Electrical power is the centerpiece of economic infrastructure. Virtually all manufacturing and commerce depend on electricity. Electricity supplies refrigeration that allows city dwellers to preserve food, powers the lights that make life after sundown possible, and fuels communication and transport.

The U.S. offensive during the Gulf War in 1991 had targeted electrical facilities throughout Iraq. Most electrical service was quickly restored, due to the intensive work of Iraqi technicians, engineers, and administrators employed by various government-owned enterprises. The underlying damage, however, was never fully repaired: the predatory nature of the Hussein regime, combined with UN sanctions that prohibited the import of "dual use" materials (any items that could, in principle be used for both civilian and military purposes), prevented electrical engineers from purchasing parts and materials needed to repair, sustain, and upgrade the power grid. No major modernization projects could be undertaken, and the undersupplied technical staff devoted themselves to keeping the increasingly decrepit system functioning. By the time of the U.S. invasion in 2003, the electrical system, beginning with generators and ending with household connections, was extremely fragile and could not meet all the needs of the Iraqi economy.

The aerial barrage that preceded the 2003 invasion was less intense than the more comprehensive air attack in the 1991 Gulf War, but it was more than sufficient to demobilize the Iraqi electrical network. Moreover, there was no quick fix available. The shuttering of state-run enterprises that would have been in charge of repairs, combined with the chaos of looting and the fragile condition of the system, meant that months passed before any real repair work was undertaken. When work began, U.S. occupation authorities insisted that repairs be designed and executed by foreign firms.

The electrical situation just after the invasion was succinctly summarized by *Washington Post* reporter Anthony Shadid, who was in Baghdad before, during, and after the invasion.

> For weeks, the capital's two antiquated power plants were barely running, and the long blackouts in searing heat that began toward the war's end remained the norm. Everything followed from electricity, the cornerstone of modern life. With electricity went water, sanitation, air-conditioning, and the security brought by light at night. With electricity went faith in what the Americans, so powerful in war, were prepared to do after.[4]

By December 2007, when the electrical work commissioned by the United States was declared completed, there had been no tangible improvement in the performance of the electrical system.[5] Electrical generation had averaged 4,100 megawatts in 2007, about the same as prewar level, and well below the 6,000 megawatt target the United States had promised to reach three years earlier. Since demand had increased substantially, averaging about 8,500 megawatts, the shortfall during the year averaged over 50 percent. When unusually cold weather hit the country in January 2008, the U.S. State Department reported that the deficit had risen 65 percent—that is, Iraq was producing about a third of the electricity needed to meet demand.[6]

Because priority was given to "essential services," government buildings and other key facilities were fully supplied with electrical power, while ordinary citizens and small businesses had no electricity available for more than half the day. This was a significant decline from prewar years, and it was a constant and painful reminder of the U.S. promise to provide twenty-four hours of electricity each day to all Iraqis. A cottage industry of petroleum-fueled generators developed in many cities, providing electricity on an hour-by-hour basis to better-off families, but these did not come close to filling the unmet demand. Their usefulness was further undermined when the IMF-mandated reforms reduced the subsidies on fuel prices, resulting in a dramatic increase in the cost of running the generators, pricing all but the most prosperous residents out of the market.[7]

Perhaps the most telling expression of the desperate shortage of electrical power was its impact on commerce and manufacturing. Inter Press Service reporter Ahmed Ali found that many businesses shut down during the chronic electrical outages. Jabar Ameen, a Baquba blacksmith, told him, "If there is no electricity, there is no work. . . . We go back home without doing anything."[8] The impact on industry was underscored during summer 2007, as State Department official Paul Brinkley continued his effort to reopen shuttered state-owned factories. Among his projects was a campaign to revive the Iraqi clothing industry, once a core sector of the economy. In addition to the opposition he faced from privatization loyalists who opposed any state ownership of manufacturing facilities, he also encountered U.S. officials who doubted that there would be sufficient electricity to power the factories, which were "very large consumers of electricity." As one official explained to *New York Times* reporter Stephen Farrell, "I don't think anybody has a problem in principle with the idea that if you can put people back to work that is a good thing . . . but if the cost is taking a lot of electricity from the grid, maybe you want to look at what the alternative uses of that might be."[9]

Because Iraq's electrical system was based on a national grid in which all manufactured power was, in principle, transmittable to any location around the country, the government was charged with equitably distributing this scarce resource.[10] As the post-invasion shortages continued and worsened, various provincial governments, faced with rising discomfort and anger among their citizens, began disconnecting their local electrical plants from the national grid. By doing this, they hoarded all their production for themselves, and starved areas with fewer power plants of their share of the electricity.

By mid-2007, at least five provinces in the Shia south and the three Kurdish provinces in the north had disconnected power plants from the grid. The resulting shortages, compounded by the sabotage and failure of transmission lines into the capital, left Baghdad, which had few plants of its own, with significantly fewer hours of power than any other province.

The national government complained bitterly about this form of local mutiny but lacked the leverage to reverse these actions. Provincial officials had physical control of the switching system and could resist any effort to capture them, since their hoarding decisions were motivated or supported by armed local militias and insurgents who had proven time and again that they were capable of resisting the Iraqi military. Aziz al-Shimari, an electricity ministry spokesman, told *Guardian* reporter Steven Hurst, "Many southern provinces—such as Basra, Diwaniya, Nassiriya, and Babil—have disconnected their power plants from the national grid. Northern provinces, including Kurdistan, are doing the same. . . . We have absolutely no control over some areas in the south."[11] Shimari then added a dire warning: "The national grid will collapse if the provinces do not abide by rules regarding their share of electricity. Everybody will lose and there will be no electricity winner."

Shimari was responding to a tangible problem: Iraq had suffered four brief national blackouts in a two-day period the week before. The threat of a more serious collapse was confirmed on August 14, 2007, when 60 percent of national generation was lost for eight hours. After interviewing Electricity Minister Karim Wahid, *New York Times* reporters James Glanz and Stephen Farrell concluded that these events "deeply undermine an Iraqi government whose popular support is already weak."[12]

With the United States withdrawn from the electrical reconstruction project, the Iraqi government sought to restore its legitimacy by finding alternate methods of repairing and expanding the system. In December 2007, fueled by the huge increase in oil prices that had provided $3 billion per year for an electrical reconstruction fund, the government announced contracts, despite U.S. protests, totaling $1 billion with Chinese and Iranian companies to build new generating capacity in Baghdad, Wassit, Karbala, and Najaf provinces. While these projects and others that might follow had the potential to resolve the crisis in six or so years, the use of foreign contractors also left open the possibility of increasing the debilitating dependency of the Iraqi economy on technology that it could not effectively manage or maintain.[13]

This dire possibility was starkly illustrated by an Iraqi government contract with Japanese companies to refurbish and upgrade an electrical power plant in al-Muthanna. Though the eighteen-month project was scheduled for completion in November of 2007, the core machinery was only 60 percent complete by spring of 2008. With Japanese withdrawal looming on the unfinished plant, local officials told Japanese reporters that the Iraqis lacked "the technical training necessary to complete and operate" the power plant.[14]

One Step Forward, Two Steps Back

Just after President Bush declared "major combat operations" ended in May 2003, the United Nations developed a preliminary set of estimates for the repair Iraq's infrastructure.[15] This initial inventory indicated that $12 billion would be needed to restore Iraq's electrical grid to its unsatisfactory prewar status. The United States allocated only about two-thirds of the needed funds, then substantially reduced the allocation to cover the escalating costs of security and insurance.[16]

The estimated costs escalated dramatically during 2004, as the magnitude of the task became more apparent, and as electrical installations became frequent targets for both the resistance and the U.S. military, each seeking to deprive the other of needed power. The bulk of the destruction in these battles over access to electricity was caused by the occupation. Whereas the insurgents sabotaged transmission lines and occasionally were able to assault switching stations, the United States used airpower to attack major facilities in cities where the resistance was dominant, destroying power plants in Falluja, Tal Afar, Ramadi, and elsewhere.[17]

Though there was a steady stream of new electrical capacity coming on line, the new capacity just managed to keep up with the ongoing destruction and therefore fell further behind the dramatically increased demand, which had been generated by a combination of new electrical appliances belonging to the Iraqi middle class and the huge presence of the military occupation.[18]

The degradation of existing grid capacity occurred not only in battle zones, but also in areas largely unaffected by the fighting. A typical instance occurred in Basra, one of the most peaceful cities in Iraq until violence began escalating in early 2006. In late 2003 the aging turbines at the Najibiya plant—until then unaffected by the war—began to fail.[19] According to Yaruub Jassim, the manager of the plant, the problem was his staff's inability to obtain replacement parts, which had delayed the October 2003 scheduled maintenance and resulted in breakdowns two months later. Bechtel, the U.S. contractor in charge of supplying and reconstructing the plant, was unresponsive to Jassim's requests: "We asked Bechtel many times to please help us," but the only response had been an apparently erroneous delivery of air conditioners.[20]

In this case, the key to Bechtel's unresponsiveness was the fact that the turbines in the Najibiya plant had been built in Russia. Bechtel's ultimate goal was to modernize the plant, replacing the Russian turbines with its own proprietary technology. In the meantime, investing money in maintaining machinery in the Najibiya plant might undermine Bechtel's proposal for the project, which was still awaiting approval.[21]

Unfortunately, similar incidents were multiplied many times around the country. After the occupation began, plant managers found it difficult to obtain even the most rudimentary maintenance supplies and impossible to obtain replacement parts for turbines and other important equipment, particularly if the parts came from countries that had not participated in the invasion.[22] As a consequence, each passing month saw more equipment fail followed by the approval of ambitious contracts to modernize the plants.

Electrical reconstruction projects were rife with the same sorts of corruption and inefficiency that characterized the Al-Fatah oil pipeline project.[23] In early 2006 the Iraqi electricity minister, Mohsen Shlash, declared that "some of the work carried out was worth just one-tenth of the money being spent." Shlash estimated that, despite the near-exhaustion of the original $8 billion allocation, an additional $20 billion would be needed to repair the system, nearly twice the original UN estimate.[24] At almost exactly that moment, the Bush administration announced that there would be no further U.S. investment in electrical reconstruction.[25]

The failure of U.S. companies either to repair or to successfully replace existing electrical facilities was so endemic that it created the impression that the occupation could not compel adequate work from any contractor. This, however, was only partly true. There were symptomatic exceptions to this dreary track record that made it clear that these failures were focused in specific realms, while other projects were completed on time and without the sort of inefficiency that plagued most reconstruction. As independent reporter Pratap Chatterjee commented:

> Certain infrastructure repair projects did get more than empty promises—the dredging of the Umm Qasr seaport and the Baghdad airport got top priority. These projects were quickly executed because the military needed to bring in equipment for the occupation. And within weeks in the spring 2003, mobile phone towers had sprung up to provide MCI service to American officials and their appointed Iraqi advisors.[26]

Using Oil in Gas Turbines

The process by which Iraqi infrastructure was degraded was most visible in the installation of electrical turbines fueled by natural gas.[27] Once again, the problem originated in the U.S. master plan for the Iraqi economy.

Iraq had little capacity to transport and utilize natural gas. Most of the gas found in Iraq's oil fields was simply burned off. The absence of gas pipelines meant that whatever small proportion was captured had to be utilized close to its source. U.S. planners had intended to remedy this situation. Capturing and shipping gas was expected to become a part of the increased production of hydrocarbons, thus helping to resolve world energy shortages while providing a revenue stream for reconstructing Iraq.

When Bechtel began work on its contract to rehabilitate the electrical generation industry in Iraq, it chose to install twenty-six turbines driven by natural gas rather than oil, even though natural gas was available only at a few of the new facilities. Bechtel's plan relied on the intention of the occupation to stimulate the capture of natural gas while installing a pipeline system that would deliver gas both to Iraqi cities and the world market. Considering Bechtel's involvement in the turbine installation and its expertise in other aspects of the extraction and delivery process, the company was well positioned to claim a large share of expected work in this area as well. It made sense for Bechtel to fit its turbine work into this ambitious plan, particularly since gas-driven turbines were highly efficient.

This expectation—by the U.S. occupation and Bechtel—failed to materialize. Along with other ambitious plans for Iraqi energy production, the planned gas production remained a vague hope for the next four years. As the twenty-six turbines came on line, therefore, they faced an immediate crisis: only seven—those located near existing gas fields—could be supplied with natural gas.

Bechtel's contract did not require it to provide fuel for the turbines, and so it was not considered responsible for remedying the problem, and there was no additional U.S. funding available to re-employ Bechtel to handle the new problem. The Iraqi government, which might have been expected to take on this responsibility, had no domestic ability to resolve the crisis since the engineers still employed by the decaying state enterprises had no expertise in these areas. The U.S. Army Corps of Engineers therefore stepped in with a jerry-rigged solution: it reconfigured the turbines to accept a specific form of readily available oil, "a tarry byproduct of Iraq's primitive refineries." Unfortunately the use of this alternate fuel decreased generation capacity by 50 percent and created challenging maintenance problems.[28] Iraqi technicians were incompetent to manage these alien systems, and the U.S. experts who might have addressed this new challenge had moved on to Bechtel's next project. The original contract had not provided for any training of Iraqi technicians to manage the plant under optimum conditions, let alone these much more complicated circumstances.

A few months after the gas turbines began operating, *Los Angeles Times* reporter T. Christian Miller reported that fuel oil had "wreaked havoc on the natural gas generators. One turbine installed by the U.S. at a cost of $40 million at the Baiji power complex in north-central Iraq already needs replacement." One by one, the generators were either reduced to generating a fraction of their authorized capacity or were taken off line altogether.

This incident illustrates the destructive impact of introducing new technologies that are not complementary to existing expertise or infrastructure. Beyond the immediate debacle, the gas turbine generators required Iraqis to develop expertise in operating such turbines and then to reconfigure their energy sector to deliver natural gas. Given the practical impossibility, despite the ambitious plans of Cheney's energy task force, of such wholesale changes, the short-term disaster—operating inefficiencies, increased maintenance, and equipment failure—was an inevitable (and foreseeable) consequence. The long-term disaster—the possible loss of the entire new system—was perhaps not as inevitable, but was certainly foreseeable.

Losers and Worse Losers

When occupation authorities approved Bechtel's plans for gas-driven turbines, both parties expected the project to produce a vast increase in the generating capacity in the country, and therefore lay a foundation for expanded industrial production and improved living conditions. The failure of this project to produce these expected results was certainly a setback for the Bush administration's project in Iraq and for the financial ambitions of Bechtel, which surely hoped for a series of follow-up projects and long-term maintenance and supply revenues that would add substantially to its profits. In that sense, then, the gas turbine fiasco was a disaster shared by the Iraqi people, the Iraqi government, Bechtel, and the U.S. occupation. Everybody lost.

But the losses were greater on the Iraqi side. The calamitous consequences for the Iraqis were made visible to all during the unusually cold winter of 2007–2008, when an intermingled oil and energy crisis left millions of Iraqis without either heat or electricity.[29] The already woefully inadequate electrical grid failed completely, due mainly to a shortage of oil needed to fuel the generators. Two of the three Iraqi oil refineries—sources of both heating oil and the bulk of fuel oil for electrical plants—were idled, mainly by shortages of electrical power needed to power the machinery. It was, as one U.S. official told Reuters reporter Ross Colvin, "a vicious circle," and the Oil and Electrical Ministries each blamed the other for the crisis.[30] But more than anything the intertwined crisis reflected both the fragility of the systems and their severe undercapacity. This was underscored further when the Electricity Ministry announced during the crisis the initiation of a ten-year plan to add 1.5 megawatts to the electrical system; this project, even if it was successfully completed, would leave the country 2.5 megawatts short of fulfilling 2008 demand without even beginning to meet the inevitable increases during the next decade.[31]

The impact of the outages on ordinary Iraqis was dire. All provinces north of Baghdad, more than one third of the population of the country, had no electrical power during January, and many others had less than two hours per day. Kerosene was scarce and prices ranged upward from one dollar per liter; the average monthly wage (for Iraqis with jobs) could therefore pay for no more than a week's worth of kerosene to fuel heating and cooking. Baghdad resident Jaafar Dhia Ali described the impact on his family, swollen to twenty people after two displaced brothers moved their families into his house: "We have not had electricity for a week now and it took me about four hours to buy fuel for my car." Kerosene supplies quickly ran low, and high prices made new purchases impossible.[32]

On the U.S. side, however, the outcome was mixed. Bechtel failed to achieve its long-term connection to the Iraqi electrical grid and it was not contracted to build the natural gas supply system; on the other hand it had made a more-than-adequate profit on a very large project worth well over one billion dollars. Because Bechtel was not deemed responsible for the subsequent calamities, it could therefore expect to do further business with the U.S. government in Iraq or elsewhere.

The Bush administration did suffer a severe setback for its ambitions to develop Iraq into a prosperous Middle East client state that would be the envy of and therefore the exemplar for other countries in the region, and the manifold problems of the improvised fuel system meant that the project would never be deemed a resounding success. Despite these negative outcomes, the electrical reconstruction still contributed to the economic integration of Iraq into the world capitalist economy, and therefore supported the long-term goals of the invasion.

The old power grid that represented the insular, prewar Iraqi economy was destroyed. Although the new system was dysfunctional, it was compatible with and dependent upon the global economy. Any further work or development of the system—even by Chinese and Iranian firms who had no loyalty to U.S. technology—would likely be forced to fit into the framework established by Bechtel. The threat of permanent damage to the turbines from continued misuse might have impelled the Iraqi government to begin negotiations in early 2008 for Shell Oil to capture and market Iraqi natural gas for internal and external consumption.[33]

It was this logic that explained the tolerance of occupation authorities for the multiple disasters and the massive corruption that befell the reconstruction project. Each infrastructural area experienced decline that was hardly what the U.S. government and its private contractors had hoped for, and some became public disasters. Each of these clouds, however, had silver linings of nurturing the bottom line of the contracting company while contributing to the larger Bush administration project of dismantling Iraq's state-centered economy.

For the Iraqis, there were no such silver linings. In early 2008, the International Committee of the Red Cross offered this bleak assessment of the electrical system:

> The electricity supply network has been deteriorating further over the past year, except in the northern governorates and the Babil and Thi Qar governorates. As a result, many water-treatment plants are completely shut down or operating at reduced capacity. Parts of Baghdad, where temperatures reach 50 degrees centigrade in the summer, often have only one hour of electricity per day. The situation is similar in Anbar province. This crisis is caused by poor maintenance, insufficient supplies of refined fuel, the use

of heavy fuel oil instead of natural gas in gas-turbine plants, acts of sabotage, and, last but not least, a failure to carry out necessary repairs and to
boost generating capacity. As a result, water-treatment plants, primary
health-care centers and hospitals have to rely on generators for much of the
time, but even this back-up mechanism regularly fails because of overuse
and an increasingly acute shortage of refined fuel.[34]

Umm Ali, a Baghdad housewife, found an ironic and vivid way to describe the situation "Electricity in Prime Minister Nouri Al-Maliki's
times comes one hour every three days. In the era of Saddam Hussein
power was off for two hours during the day and two hours at night and
there was one rest day when electricity was not turned off at all. I hate
and fear Saddam and his era yet I regret that his days are past now."[35]

Chapter Twelve

The Downward Spiral

Sometimes we have to reuse IVs, even the needles. We have no choice.
—Dr. Qasim al-Nuwesri

The Ebb Tide for Clean Water

The Iraqi sanitation system, which had eroded dramatically during the sanctions period from 1991 to 2003, was further damaged by the U.S. invasion.[1] Though the United States did not target the water supply during the initial fighting, the kinetic force of heavy bombs used on roads and buildings demolished underground waste disposal conduits, releasing sewage into the streets, the ground water, and the country's two main rivers.[2] The thoroughfares of many cities were inundated with health-threatening garbage.[3]

The electrical outages that became endemic in postwar Iraq exacerbated the sewage problem further, since water treatment plants could not operate with sufficient consistency to purify the contaminated water for household use. A growing proportion of Iraqi families had no access to potable water.

Initially the occupation appeared to recognize the urgency of the problem, and the $680 million, limited-bid, cost-plus water reconstruction contract granted to Bechtel in spring 2003 contained a clause calling for the water supply to be repaired within a year: "Within the first 6 months the contractor will repair or rehabilitate crucial water treatment, pumping and distribution systems in 15 urban areas. Within 12 months potable water supplies will be restored to all urban centers."[4]

Even after it failed to fulfill any significant part of this first contract, Bechtel was selected as the prime contractor for the bulk of the $4.6 billion in water and sewage projects funded by the U.S. occupation.[5] As with the electrical grid, much of the allocation was frittered away through inefficiency and corruption, and the sewage system was worse off when Bechtel finished.

By late 2005, the number of people served by sewers had dropped to just over 4.5 million, compared to prewar levels of 6.2 million. Unprocessed filth often flowed down city streets, befouling the air and threatening the adjacent neighborhoods with disease. Once it exited the streets, garbage contaminated the rivers and the underground water supply, rendering ineffective the shrinking number of functional water-purification systems and creating a threat to public health all along the Tigris and Euphrates, even in downstream areas where there had been little actual fighting.[6] This traveling contamination vastly expanded the need for water treatment plants all along the length of these rivers, since before the war many downstream cities and towns had relied upon untreated river water for drinking and cooking.

This need was not met. The CPA had promised to triple water treatment volume from three to ten million cubic meters per day; instead capacity declined by almost two-thirds, to 1.1 million cubic meters.[7] In an August 2005 poll, when Iraqis were asked how often they had "safe, clean water" 71 percent of the respondents said "never."[8] Outbreaks of filth-borne diseases became commonplace.[9]

To make matters worse, by September 2005 nearly half (44 percent) of the original $4.6 billion allocation for the water system was reallocated to what the occupation officials considered more pressing projects.[10] Stuart Bowen, the special inspector general for Iraq reconstruction, reported this shift to Congress in early 2005: "Initial plans to rehabilitate large portions of the country's water and wastewater system through the IRRF have been curtailed. . . . Water resources and sanitation sector funds have been reallocated to security, governance, debt relief and efforts to boost Iraqi employment opportunities."[11]

In June 2005, fully a year after Bechtel had been contracted to bring potable water to all the cities of the country, the *Los Angeles Times* quoted a Bechtel executive as saying that not a single one of the forty projects it had so far completed was operating properly.[12] A few months later, the U.S. military commander in Iraq, Lieutenant General Peter Chiarelli, acknowledged that "only about a quarter of the nation" had "drinkable water." State

Department officials announced that huge new infusions of money would be needed to reverse the downward trend.[13] Bechtel estimated that the true cost of water reconstruction would be $16 billion, more than three times the original estimate, and more than five times the actual expenditure. Nevertheless, in early 2006 U.S. occupation authorities announced that no more than 40 percent of the water-purification program would be completed and that no further projects would be initiated.[14]

How the Water System Failed in Hilla

The sewage and water systems went into sharp decline as the U.S. occupation took hold, even in cities where there was little or no ongoing insurgency (and therefore no need for the elaborate "security" expenses occupation authorities reported were draining the budgets). Hilla, a mainly Shia city south of Baghdad, had been the site of a substantial battle during the initial invasion but was relatively quiet afterward. The aging water plant had survived the fighting unscathed, but maintenance to replace old pipes and pumps was needed before the end of 2003 to forestall outages and serious breakdowns.[15] Even under the extreme austerity of the Hussein regime, these sorts of replacement parts had been available and the system had been trudging along, providing adequate water supplies without interruption before and during the war.

But the occupation changed all that. The shuttering of government-owned enterprises and the dismantling of the Baathist state apparatus made the mundane process of supplying replacement parts administratively daunting. At the same time Bechtel, the key contractor in the water sector, had little interest in spending its resources to maintain or repair facilities that it hoped to replace with new ones.

As a consequence, none of the needed supplies were shipped to the Hilla plant, and local technicians were unable to sustain the fragile water treatment machinery. These problems were measurably exacerbated by the failing electrical infrastructure, and parts of the Hilla system were shut down while the technical staff waited for parts to arrive. The shuttered facilities were an easy target for looters, who inflicted permanent damage to the idled machinery. By spring 2004, only a year after the invasion, the Hilla plant may have passed the point of no return. The plant's chief engineer, Salmam Hassan Kadel, told Pratap Chatterjee that the city of Hilla had only 50 percent of the water it needed, and that the villages outside town were facing a major health crisis: "The surrounding villages had no water, nor had they been supplied with the pipes they needed to get work done. Kadel reported that his plant has had no contact with Bechtel, or any of its subcontractors, despite complaints of massive outbreaks of cholera, diarrhea, nausea, and kidney stones in his area."[16] Independent reporter Dahr Jamail offered this grim portrait of the situation in one of the villages outside the city:

> There was no running water to speak of and barely two to four hours of electricity per day, during which they tried to run their feeble pumps to draw contaminated water from a polluted stream for the families to use. An old man named Hussin Hamsa Nagem bemoaned: "We are all sick with stomach problems and kidney stones. Our crops are dying."[17]

As with electrical power, Bechtel focused its attention on installing brand-new systems. Because these were incompatible with the existing system, the new construction often became unworkable. The most destructive of these incompatibilities was the negative impact on Iraqi expertise, since local technicians and engineers were unfamiliar with the new equipment. Despite vigorous Iraqi complaints, Bechtel and its subcontractors refused to adapt the new system to take advantage of Iraqi human capital and also failed to train Iraqis to use the new equipment. When the units malfunctioned, however, they blamed Iraqi inexperience, telling *Los Angeles Times* reporter T. Christian Miller that unsatisfactory performance of the new facilities resulted from the failure of Iraqi technicians "to maintain and operate them properly."[18] The U.S. Government Accountability Office (GAO) highlighted this problem in its February 2006 evaluation of the work on the water and sanitation system:

> As of June 2005, approximately $52 million of the $200 million in completed large-scale water and sanitation projects either were not operating or were operating at lower capacity due to looting of key equipment and shortages of reliable power, trained Iraqi staff, and required chemicals and supplies. For example, one repaired wastewater plant was partially shut down due to the looting of key electrical equipment and repaired water plants in one southern governorate lacked adequate electricity and necessary water treatment chemicals. In addition two projects lacked a reliable power supply, one lacked sufficient staff to operate properly, and one lacked both adequate staff and power supplies.
>
> In the water and sanitation sector, U.S. agencies have identified limitations in Iraq's capacity to maintain and operate reconstructed facilities, including problems with staffing, unreliable power to run treatment plants, insufficient spare parts, and poor operations and maintenance procedures. [See note 15.] The U.S. embassy in Baghdad stated that it was moving from the previous model of building and turning over projects to Iraqi management toward a "build-train-turnover" system to protect the U.S. investment. However, these efforts are just beginning, and it is unclear whether the Iraqis will be able to maintain and operate completed projects and the more than $1 billion in additional large-scale water and sanitation projects expected to be completed through 2008.[19]

In addition to the destructive impact of the insertion of state-of-the-art technology into the existing Iraqi infrastructure, we see in this evaluation another element in the downward spiral of Iraqi infrastructure: the ceaseless looting by criminal gangs who sold stolen machinery and parts on the black market. The GAO report quoted above mentioned a specific wastewater plant in which criminal gang activity had caused the same sort of destruction in this "peaceful" area that the war had generated in other areas.

Organized looting can operate only in the vacuum created by a broader dynamic of decline. The looting of the Hilla water treatment system, for example, took place in idled and abandoned facilities, and this idleness was a consequence of the mismatch between the existing Iraqi infrastructure and U.S.-sponsored new construction.[20]

The failure of the Iraqi water system was a setback for Bechtel and the other contractors that the United States recruited to do reconstruction work. Their biggest loss was the second-generation business they were positioned to obtain if the company's very ambitious overall vision was fulfilled. Bechtel might have obtained long-term contracts to supply the imported chemicals that its newly installed sewage treatment system required, and they would have been in an excellent position to bid for contracts to build the new electrical facilities needed to serve the sewage systems. Inadequate initial funding, the abandonment of reconstruction by the U.S. occupation, and the awesome costs of fulfilling the grandiose requirements of the Bush administration's vision, however, made these secondary projects impractical. As a consequence, crippled or unworkable sewage treatment facilities contributed to the dynamic of decline through inadequate supplies, unqualified technical support, or looting.

This disappointing result was not, however, a disaster for the U.S. contractors, who collected the full amount (including "cost-plus" profits) for their initial work. Speaking to the *Washington Post* about the reconstruction as a whole, one of Bremer's senior advisors summarized the overarching impact of these projects: "This was supposed to be our big effort to help them—18 billion of our tax dollars to fix their country. . . . But the sad reality is that this program won't have a lot of impact in it for the Iraqis. The primary beneficiaries will be American companies."[21]

Life Without Potable Water

By late 2007 the water system in Iraq was thoroughly degraded. Although U.S. officials reported the completion of 1,500 water treatment and sewage projects, the percentage of Iraqis with potable water had declined from 50 percent to 30 percent during the occupation. Fully 80 percent lacked adequate sanitation. A water treatment project in the previously unserviced Sadr City slum, originally scheduled for 2004 completion, was still unfinished and abandoned at the end 2007, leaving feces-filled sewage in various locations.[22] The water in the Tigris and Euphrates was by and large too contaminated to drink and, in many places, too contaminated to use in agriculture. U.S. officials, who had originally contracted with Bechtel to deliver potable water to all Iraqis by mid-2004, were offering a far more modest goal of 55 percent before the final allocation of funding was exhausted.[23] However, with only one hundred fifty projects still in process, this goal was clearly out of reach, and prospects of reversing the downward trend seemed dim.[24]

The problem was exemplified by the water project in Nassariya, a southern Iraq city that had been the site of a battle during the invasion but had been quiescent afterward. The city waited more than four years (until September 12, 2007) for its water purification system to come on line, only to discover that it was operating at 6 percent of capacity. According to the U.S. Department of Defense, the low output was a result of "lack of permanent [electric] power and insufficient numbers of trained [Iraqi] operators." With no immediate possibility of increased electrical power, prospects for improved performance in the near future were dim. Moreover, despite the mismatch between Iraqi training and the skills needed to run the new equipment, the United States withdrew its technicians just two months later, raising the possibility that the facilities would fall into decline without ever reaching their rated output. When questioned about this pattern of withdrawing U.S. technicians from such projects, Bill Taylor, the U.S. Embassy official in charge of reconstruction, told *Los Angeles Times* reporter T. Christian Miller,[25] "This is their country. This is their water-treatment plant. They need to take responsibility. We're not going to be responsible for it. If they run it into the ground, we'll be disappointed. But this is their country."[26]

The village of Sadiyah in southern Iraq, far from the center of the insurgency, typified the dire circumstances faced by many Iraqis on a daily basis. By November 2007 tap water had been undrinkable for years because raw sewage from upstream cities had contaminated the Euphrates River. According to McClatchy News reporter Bobby Caina Calvan, the water "looks clean enough, but it coats the palate with a thin, slick brine that sometimes smells sour." With no water treatment plant, villagers depended on bottled water, shipped in on an irregular basis. Unfortunately even this water was suspect. As local resident Kayria Fayhan told Calvan, "They say the [bottled] water is clean, but sometimes the water is green. Sometimes, there's rust floating in it." Nevertheless, the villagers used it for cooking and drinking and "for washing up if itching from the groundwater becomes unbearable."[27]

Sadiyah residents, like Iraqis all over the country, feared that their community would be struck by cholera. The disease, which is carried by impure water, spread southward from the northern Kurdish provinces in summer 2007, with over three thousand cases confirmed and as many as thirty thousand suspected in nine of Iraq's eighteen provinces.[28]

The presence of cholera was symptomatic of the compromised condition of the Iraqi water system, but specific features of the epidemic underscored the depth of the crisis after four years of U.S. occupation.

First, the outbreak began in the Kurdish provinces, the region that was not only most insulated from the violence of the invasion and the insurgency, but also partially shielded from the economic depression brought on by the occupation. Because of this insulation, the Kurdistan water system was therefore less degraded than elsewhere, and its citizens were healthier and more resistant to infection. Moreover, because Kurdistan lay upstream from the most devastated areas of the country, it was not subject to contamination transmitted by the rivers. The fact that the outbreak began in this less susceptible area demonstrates that the entire system, not just a few vulnerable parts, was profoundly degraded.[29]

Second, the epidemic was not halted by human intervention. The Iraqi water system was so compromised that neither the U.S. occupation nor the Iraqi government could provide—even on an emergency basis—enough potable water or sufficient medical intervention in affected areas to control it. Instead, the outbreak was finally halted by cold weather, which killed the cholera germ.

Third, the outbreak was almost certain to return when warmer weather combined with contaminated water to regenerate the cholera bacteria. Abdul Yones, the Iraqi minister of health, warned of "more outbreaks" in coming years: "The problem is still there; that is why I'm saying we might have the same next summer and the summer after."[30]

Finally, the water purification facilities may have become part of the problem rather than part of the solution. According to Dr. Said Hakki, head of the Red Crescent Society in Iraq, one symptom of the failing system was "poor control of chlorination levels." This problem was partly a consequence of machine failure and partly a consequence of U.S. limitation on the import of chlorine into Iraq because it could be used to fabricate explosive bombs.[31] The low chlorine levels resulted in cholera bacteria colonizing in the treatment plants themselves. In that case, when warm weather returned, the disease could spread like "fire in a haystack" and even "hopscotch" from Kurdish regions in the far north to Basra in the far south, ensuring a much wider and deeper distribution of the disease.[32]

The Poor Prognosis for Health Care

The Iraqi health care system, the best in the Middle East during the 1970s, was already suffering before the war began.[33] Few hospitals were damaged in the initial U.S. offensive, but with the rise of the insurgency many facilities in embattled cities were damaged by U.S. artillery, air attacks, or infantry invasions. Some invasions were aimed at preventing guerrilla fighters from using the facilities either for sniping or obtaining medical care, and others in retaliation for the hospitals were releasing civilian casualty and death statistics that increased anti-U.S. sentiment locally and nationally.[34]

In late 2005, for example, when Ramadi was the site of major fighting, a local hospital administrator told independent reporter Dahr Jamail that the two main hospitals were "raided regularly by the U.S. military": "The maternity hospital and the general hospital in our city are the two biggest hospitals. . . . These have both been raided twice a week by the American forces with the excuse that they are searching for militants. They break every door which is closed, play with our records and sometimes even detain some of our staff."[35] Even the threat of insurgents using a hospital was sufficient reason to interfere with its functioning. In one instance, the U.S. military shuttered a hospital because its location on a hill overlooking a military base made it potentially useful for insurgent snipers.[36] Regardless of the motives, these attacks—only sometimes denied by U.S. officials—were direct violations of international law, which prohibited any military interference with medical facilities.

Starting in the 1960s Iraqi health care was an expensive, state-funded, hospital-based system paid for with large amounts of oil revenues. The Iran-Iraq war in the 1980s placed a huge strain on the system, which was intensified by Saddam Hussein's diversion of resources to fund his military campaigns. The decline accelerated during the 1990s when UN sanctions curtailed oil revenues and prohibited the purchase of new or replacement equipment and supplies.[37] All these problems were in turn exacerbated by the occupation, as the CPA mandated a drastic reduction in the size and scope of the government. These restrictions were perpetuated by the IMF debt relief agreement, which gave outsiders veto power over the use of oil revenues.[38] These measures, according to the medical NGO MedAct, were particularly harmful to the Iraqi hospital system, since the "drive for privatization" was guided by the U.S. Department of Defense belief that "there was no health infrastructure worth preserving."[39]

The U.S. plan for rebuilding Iraqi medicine centered on the transfer of primary care out of state-run hospitals. The most important program in the health sector therefore became a $243 million no-bid contract awarded to the multinational Parsons Corporation to construct one hundred fifty medical clinics around the country.[40] As with other projects, these clinics were designed to be the hub of a new system in which general practitioners, equipped with the latest technology and expertise, handled most routine health issues and referred more difficult cases to specialized care. The almost instantaneous effect was the dramatic decline in the already compromised care available in the hospitals. The reconstruction budget had allocated about $550 million to sustaining the hospital system—less than 10 percent of the $7 to $8 billion that the Iraqi health ministry estimated would be needed over the next four years.[41] To make matters worse, by the end of 2005 less than a third of this allocation had been spent.[42] An unknown portion of the remainder was lost to the corruption endemic in both the occupation's and the Iraq government's administrative apparatus.[43]

In the meantime Iraqi hospitals, starved for resources, continued their downward trajectory. Baghdad's Medical City, one of the principal medical centers in the country, appeared to be a typical case. Dr. Hammad Hussein told independent reporter Dahr Jamail in late 2004:

> I have not seen anything which indicates any rebuilding aside from our new pink and blue colors here where our building and the escape ladders were painted. . . . What this largest medical complex in Iraq lacks is medicines. I'll prescribe medication and the pharmacy simply does not have it to give to the patient. [The hospital is] short of wheelchairs, half the lifts are broken, and the family members of patients are being forced to work as nurses because of a shortage of medical personnel.[44]

At Chuwader General Hospital, the key facility for the huge Shia slum in eastern Baghdad, hospital director Dr. Qasim al-Nuwesri gave a similarly negative account of conditions:

> "We are short of every medicine," he said, something that had not previously been as severe, even under the economic sanctions. "It is forbidden, but sometimes we have to reuse IVs, even the needles. We have no choice." . . . . Another major problem that all the doctors mentioned was lack of potable water. "Of course we have typhoid, cholera, kidney stones . . . but

we now even have the very rare Hepatitis Type-E . . . and that has become common in our area." Hepatitis Type-E is transmitted primarily via ingestion of feces-contaminated drinking water. I had been in people's homes where they had run the tap to show me the brown water that gurgled out. Water the color of a wet dirty sock that smelled of gasoline.

Inside the hospital, we saw open sewage in the bathroom.[45]

A year later, Jamail reported even worse conditions in Baghdad and elsewhere:

Dr. Abdul Qader, who works at Ramadi General Hospital, told IPS that the critical care unit there lacked monitors, the CT scan was broken, and many other instruments were not working. Such problems are now common around the province. . . .

"In addition to lacking electricity, we often lack fuel deliveries for our generators," said Dr. Qader. "Our machines often break down, which puts our patients in very critical situations."

Similar problems have been evident in Baghdad since last year. "We had a power outage while someone was undergoing surgery in the operating room," Ahlan Bar, manager of nurses at the Yarmouk Teaching Hospital in Baghdad told IPS. "He died on the table because we had no power for our instruments."

The health official said ongoing attacks by militants could provoke U.S. forces to detain more doctors. "We have only 40 percent of staff we need to operate effectively," he said. "Even now, we don't have a specialist in anaesthesia, so this is being handled by the nursing staff. Most medical staff now are too afraid to work in our province."

The doctors expressed frustration at the U.S.-imposed curfew which begins at 7 pm daily. Health services at Ramadi General Hospital end at 5 pm so that medical staff can be home before the curfew begins.[46]

By early 2008 the hospital system was moribund, "all but incapable of caring for" war injuries or serious illnesses.[47] Yarmouk Hospital, one of Baghdad's biggest, was so degraded that a Red Crescent report declared that it should be "leveled." The Red Crescent director told the *Washington Post*, "It's not fit for animal treatment." He then added, "There is no medical system in Iraq to speak of. It doesn't exist."[48]

Malign Neglect of Hospitals

Neither the U.S. occupation authorities nor their major contractors had much incentive to nurture the hospital system, which lay at the heart of the state-run medical establishment that the United States had decided to jettison.[49] Money spent on upkeep, on medicine, and on other needed equipment would not contribute to their long-term program, which sought to construct a new system around the primary care facilities that Parsons was building. Quarterly reports of the U.S. occupation to Congress did not mention the hospital system as a locus of U.S. reconstruction efforts.[50] Iraqi medical personnel working within the doomed system found that officials were unresponsive to their requests, no matter how insistent, for needed materials.

In early 2006 Ammar al-Saffar, the Iraqi Health Ministry's second in command, implicitly acknowledged that the United States was not going help repair the Iraqi hospital system. In announcing to the World Bank that Iraq had insufficient funds, he expressed the hope that aid might be forthcoming from other countries: "'Over the next four years, we need $7 to $8 billion just for reconstruction. This does not include the operational budget.' He warned, however, that Iraqi coffers alone were incapable of funding such an investment. 'We are looking here and there for donations from the international community.'"[51]

In the meantime, primary care centers flashed into the headlines in early 2006, when a U.S. government investigation found that only six of one hundred fifty planned clinics had been completed by the due date, while fourteen others *might* be completed in the foreseeable future. The investigation found that "remedial actions were unable to salvage the overall program" and that the remaining one hundred thirty facilities, completion of which would become the responsibility of a new contractor, might never become functional. Parsons suffered few sanctions for its failure: the contract was "terminated by consensus, not for cause" in January 2006 after the full contract price had already been collected.[52]

As it turned out, Parsons was not even required to complete the fourteen centers for which it retained responsibility. The negotiated settlement called only for Parsons to "*try* to finish 14 more clinics by early April [2006] and then leave the project."[53] In January 2008, with U.S. reconstruction funds virtually exhausted, thirty-nine of the centers had been opened with several under threat of closure for lack of personnel.[54]

By mid-2007 Oxfam reported that health services in every part of Iraq were "generally in a catastrophic situation." MedAct arrived at the same conclusion in early 2008, reporting that the war and its aftermath had had a "disastrous impact" on Iraqi health care.[55] The occupation had drastically reduced the list of drugs available from the national dispensary (twenty-six of thirty-two drugs used to treat chronic diseases were no longer available), and hospitals had no funds with which to purchase imported substitutes from the U.S.-designated providers. The stripped-down government administrative apparatus meant that the surviving distribution system for supplies and medicines was "crippled," resulting in shortages even for materials that had not been taken off the list. In 2007 this administrative incapacity had become so severe that the Ministry of Health did

not spend its entire allocation, despite desperate shortages almost everywhere. Fully 90 percent of Iraqi hospitals lacked "key resources." Doctors
relied on the relatives of patients to "search local pharmacies for blood
bags" and other needed drugs and equipment. Many complex surgeries
were being performed with "only the most basic equipment."[56]

The degradation of the Iraqi health system was underscored by the
one success reported in UNICEF's late 2007 survey of children in Iraq.
National immunization campaigns against polio and measles had essentially eradicated both diseases in the previous year, but these campaigns
had been conducted outside the faltering health care system through
house-to-house canvassing.[57]

This pattern of continued decline in existing facilities while construction of a new system faltered and then failed was exacerbated by an exodus of health professionals. Doctors, nurses, and technicians in Iraqi
medical facilities had ample reason to leave their positions. The failing
system often made their working conditions intolerable, while the endemic violence in Iraqi society hit medical professionals with particular
force. By late 2006 at least two hundred doctors had been killed, and at
least two hundred fifty had been kidnapped for ransom by outlaw gangs,
who targeted any prosperous families. By that summer some eighteen
thousand of the thirty-four thousand Iraqi doctors had left Iraq, part of
a mass exodus that was symptomatic of (and which contributed to) the
escalating humanitarian crisis in the country.[58] In late 2007 the Iraqi
Ministry of Health reported that it had only 35 percent of the physicians
needed to staff the hospital system. At Diyala General Hospital, the largest
in the province, a staff member told the Inter Press Service that there were
times when "we hardly see one physician in the whole hospital."[59] In
many small towns and rural areas, medical professionals were "almost
completely absent." If the primary care centers in those areas were to be
completed, they might well be idled by the absence of trained personnel.[60]

Deconstruction, not Reconstruction

By late 2007 the deterioration had become self-sustaining, as conditions
continued to worsen, even where neither violence nor active efforts at
radical transformation were underway.

Perhaps the most telling indicator of this almost inexorable decline
could be found in the news about the embassy that the United States was
constructing in Baghdad. Referred to as "George W's palace" by Baghdad
residents, the huge self-contained complex was described by the *Times of
London* as "the biggest embassy on earth," featuring "impressive resi-

dences for the Ambassador and his deputy, six apartments for senior officials, and two huge office blocks for 8,000 staff to work in. There will be what is rumoured to be the biggest swimming pool in Iraq, a state-of-the-art gymnasium, a cinema, restaurants offering delicacies from favourite US food chains, tennis courts and a swish American Club for evening functions."[61]

The embassy construction was not immune to the various problems endemic in the U.S. effort, including cost overruns that added almost $150 million to the original $592 million budget. Self-regulation by contractors led to reports of irremediable structural problems, most notably in the fire control system, that one official told the *Washington Post* were "serious enough to get someone killed."[62]

Whatever its vulnerabilities, however, the embassy would not be subject to the vagaries of the Iraqi infrastructure, since it would have "its own power and water plants," and thus would be insulated from the outages and pollution suffered by Baghdad's Iraqi residents. That is, U.S. authorities, in preparing for their new embassy, were not depending on the rejuvenation of any element in the Iraqi infrastructure in the foreseeable future.

In January 2006 the United States announced that there would be no new U.S. allocations for Iraqi reconstruction. A U.S. official told the *Times of London*: "US reconstruction is basically aiming for completion (this) year. No one ever intended for outside assistance to continue indefinitely, but rather to create conditions where the Iraqi economy can use reconstruction of essential services to get going on its own."[63]

At about the same time, the U.S. Department of Energy estimated the cost of Iraqi reconstruction at "$100 billion or higher," fully $40 billion above the original UN estimate.[64] On the question of whether the Iraqi government could handle these costs alone, the *Financial Times* reported that "most of the government's purchases are for short term needs" and therefore "little cash has been available for Iraqi-funded reconstruction."[65]

The *Los Angeles Times* reported on Washington's attitude toward this apparent dilemma:

> The $18.6 billion approved by Congress in 2003 will be spent by the end of this year, officials here say. Foreign governments have given only a fraction of the billions they pledged two years ago.
>
> With the country still a shambles, U.S. officials are promoting a tough-love vision of reconstruction that puts the burden on the Iraqi people.
>
> "The world is a competitive place," Tom Delare, economics counselor at the U.S. Embassy, said this month during a news briefing. "You have to convince the investor that it is worth his while to put his money in your community."[66]

This comment placed in bold relief the overarching logic of the U.S. presence in Iraq, encompassing both the destruction wrought by the war and the deconstruction wrought by U.S. economic policy there. Iraq's economy had arrived at a point where it would "have to convince the investor that it is worth his while to put his money" into Iraqi communities. The neoliberal project had reached its defining moment: Iraq's economic infrastructure would remain dysfunctional until the global financial community found profitable investment opportunities there. This perspective was summarized concisely in the Defense Department's report to Congress in December 2007: "The Government of Iraq will have to accelerate its economic reform programs in order to build a strong private sector capable of attracting more foreign investment and supporting long-term self-sustaining growth and stability."[67]

The process of accumulation by dispossession had been fully realized.

In only four years, the U.S.-sponsored nexus of decline had placed Iraq—in terms of natural resources one of the richest countries in the world—in such dire economic straits that the Iraqi government placed itself under the receivership of the IMF, the same institution that had supervised the neoliberal erosion of Latin America and Africa, and (together with the World Bank and the World Trade Organization) the key force in the creation of slum cities in those continents. In this vein, Matthew Rothschild, writing in the *Progressive*, reported this symptomatic bit of news:

> The International Monetary Fund, in exchange for giving a loan of $685 million to the Iraqi government, insisted that the Iraqis lift subsidies on the price of oil and open the economy to more private investment.
>
> As the IMF said in a press release of December 23, the Iraqi government must be committed to "controlling the wage and pensions bill, reducing subsidies on petroleum products, and expanding the participation of the private sector in the domestic market for petroleum products."[68]

These measures, which if enacted would further reduce wages and income for the already impoverished Iraqi consumers, were the neoliberal recipe for attracting—through private investment—the $100 billion needed to reconstruct the economy.

This enterprise was destined to be fruitless. With this agreement, Iraq joined the company of dependent economies unable to engineer their own prosperity and therefore subject to international financial discipline. This then was the moment when the dynamics of the Iraqi war melded into the dynamics of neoliberal reform.

As the occupation dragged on it was apparent that the U.S. reconstruction program had not met even the modest goal of laying a foundation for Iraq to "get going on its own."[69] In an official accounting during summer 2007, U.S. officials conceded that only $5.8 billion of the original $18 billion allocation had actually been spent on Iraqi reconstruction and that there was no accurate accounting for the remainder, though much had been transferred to security expenses, including a $5 billion allocation for training Iraqi police and military personnel. Moreover, among the 2,797 completed projects, the Iraqi government had accepted administrative responsibility for fewer than a quarter of them (435), either because it deemed them inadequately constructed to perform the designated function or because Iraqis were not qualified to manage them.[70] In either case, the reconstruction effort had by and large contributed to the growing incapacity of Iraqi society to take care of itself.

In the meantime, conditions faced by Iraqis continued to degenerate.[71] By March 2007, as the occupation began its fifth year, a survey of Baghdad residents found that over half had unsatisfactory service in all four of these day-to-day essentials: electricity, trash removal, potable water, and fuel. Ten months later, in the grip of the coldest winter in years, official U.S. State Department documents reported that electricity availability "was the lowest since at least December 2003."[72]

The UN estimated unemployment at 60 percent nationwide, with many others underemployed. More than 90 percent of Baghdad residents reported that their employment situation was unsatisfactory. Inflation rates, which exceeded 30 percent in 2005 and 50 percent in 2006, dropped to a still unmanageable 20 percent in 2007, while the salaries of those still employed lost ground. Over half the population (54 percent) was living on less than $1 a day, a level that placed Iraq below many of the poorest countries in the world. According to Oxfam, nearly half of Iraqis (43 percent) were living in "absolute poverty." According to the UN, nearly a third (eight million people) were in need of "immediate assistance." Fully 11 percent of newborns were clinically underweight. More than a quarter of children (28 percent) were not getting enough food to sustain normal growth.[73]

In the midst of this crisis the Iraqi government announced, following the guidelines in the U.S.-sponsored contract with the IMF, that it would cut by half the size of the food ration to which all Iraqis had been entitled since the Gulf War began in 1991. Since the start of the occupation, coverage by the food-ration program had declined from 96 percent of all Iraqi families to only 60 percent, as displaced people lost rights to rations and earlier IMF-mandated cutbacks had been enforced. Among the remaining sixteen million recipients, approximately ten million depended on the ration as their main source of sustenance.[74]

The 2007 reductions were necessary, according to the Iraqi government official in charge of the program, because "the prices of important foodstuff doubled in the past year," increasing the cost of the program from $3.2 billion to $7.2 billion, well beyond the capacity of the impoverished Iraqi state.[75] This became, then, another ironic result of the U.S. program of opening the Iraqi economy to global competition. First, the inability of local farmers to compete with imported products, combined with the depredations of the war and elimination of government subsidies, caused a decline in Iraqi agriculture, making millions of former self-supporting farmers dependent on the food subsidy system. Later, with the increase in international food prices, the subsidies themselves were cut, and the now-dependent former farmers found themselves below the nutritional threshold.

One Iraqi sarcastically summarized the situation to Inter Press Service reporter Ahmed Ali: "No security, no food, no electricity, no trade, no services. So life is good."[76]

◆ ◆ ◆

Misery does not necessarily produce protest, but when inaction corresponds to increasing misery, people feel compelled to halt or reverse the situation. When inaction invites a life-threatening situation or—more urgently—a danger to the lives of children in a community, the energy for collective action is substantially amplified.[77] While the reaction among Iraqis to their eroding welfare took many forms, including migration away from degraded areas and the formation of local self-help projects, it was often channeled into protests.

These protests—whether expressed in elections, in peaceful demonstrations, or in violent confrontations—inevitably led to further frustration, since sooner or later the protesters experienced the iron fist of repression, usually from occupation forces since the Iraqi military and police were often reluctant to fight their own people and almost always ineffective when they did so. These confrontations contributed to misery and anger, and therefore contributed to support for violent expulsion of the United States from Iraq.

Chapter Thirteen

The Tidal Wave of Misery

Not so much a migration as a forced exodus. Scientists, engineers, doctors, architects, writers, poets, you name it — everybody is getting out of town.

—Iraqi blogger AnaRki13

By 2008 a giant wave of misery was engulfing Iraq, but it was only indirectly related to the horrific events that were regularly featured in U.S. media coverage. Though it was connected to the car bombings and death squads that made the evening news, this tsunami of misery was social and economic in nature. It dislodged people from their jobs, it swept them out of their homes, it tore them from their material possessions, and carried them off from families and communities. It left them stranded in hostile towns or foreign countries with no anchor to help them resist the next wave of displacement.

The victims of this human tsunami were called *refugees* if they washed ashore outside the country, or *IDPs* (internally displaced persons) if their landing place was within Iraq's borders. Either way, they were typically left with no permanent housing, no reliable livelihood, no community support, and no government aid. All the normal social props that support human lives were gone.

Overlapping Waves of the Dispossessed

In its first four years the Iraq war created three overlapping waves of refugees and IDPs.

It all began with the CPA, which the Bush administration set up inside Baghdad's Green Zone and in May 2003 placed under the control of L. Paul Bremer III. When the CPA began disassembling Iraq's state apparatus, thousands of Baathist Party bureaucrats were purged from the government, tens of thousands of workers were laid off from shuttered state-owned industries, and hundreds of thousands of Iraqi military personnel were dismissed from Hussein's dismantled military. Their numbers soon multiplied as the ripple effect of their lost purchasing power rolled through the economy. Many of the newly unemployed found other (less remunerative) jobs, some hunkered down to wait out bad times, and still others left their homes and sought work elsewhere, with the most marketable going to nearby countries where their skills were still in demand. They were the first wave of Iraqi refugees.

As the postinvasion chaos continued, kidnapping became the country's growth industry, targeting any prosperous family with the means to pay ransom. This accelerated the rate of departure, particularly among those whose careers had already been disrupted. A flood of professional, technical, and managerial workers fled Iraq in search of personal and job security.

The spirit of this initial exodus was eloquently expressed by an Iraqi blogger with the online name AnaRki13:

> It's just not worth it staying here. Sunni, Shiite, or Christian—everybody, we're all leaving, or have already left.
>
> One of my friends keeps berating me about how I should love this country, the land of my ancestors, where I was born and raised; how I should be grateful and return to the place that gave me everything. I always tell him the same thing: "Iraq, as you and me once knew it, is lost. What's left of it, I don't want . . ."
>
> The most famous doctors and university professors have already left the country because many of them, including ones I knew personally, were assassinated or killed, and the rest got the message—and got themselves jobs in the west, where they were received warmly and given high positions. Other millions of Iraqis, just ordinary Iraqis, left and are leaving—without plans and with much hope.[1]

In 2004 the occupation triggered a second wave of refugees when it began to attack and invade insurgent strongholds, such as the predominantly Sunni city of Fallujah, using the full kinetic force of its military. Large numbers of local residents were forced to flee battleground neighborhoods or cities. The process was summarized in a thorough review of the history of the war compiled by the Global Policy Forum and thirty-five other international nongovernmental organizations:

Among those who flee, the most fortunate are able to seek refuge with out-of-town relatives, but many flee into the countryside where they face extremely difficult conditions, including shortages of food and water. Eventually the Red Crescent, the UN, or relief organizations set up camps. In Falluja, a city of about 300,000, over 216,000 displaced persons had to seek shelter in overcrowded camps during the winter months, inadequately supplied with food, water, and medical care. An estimated 100,000 fled al-Qaim, a city of 150,000, according to the Iraqi Red Crescent Society (IRCS). In Ramadi, about 70 percent of the city's 400,000 people left in advance of the U.S. onslaught.

These moments mark the beginning of Iraq's massive displacement crisis.[2]

Although most of these refugees returned after the fighting, a significant minority did not, either because their homes or livelihoods had been destroyed, or because they were afraid of the continuing violence. Like the economically displaced of the previous wave, these refugees sought out new areas that were less dangerous or more prosperous, including neighboring countries. And, as with that first wave, it was the professional, technical, and managerial workers who were most likely to have the resources to leave Iraq.

In early 2005 the third wave began, increasing steadily through 2006 into a veritable tsunami of ethnic cleansing and civil war that pushed vast numbers of Iraqis from their homes. The precipitating incidents, according to Ali Allawi—the Iraqi finance minister at the time—were initially triggered by the second-wave refugees pushed out of the Sunni city of Fallujah in winter 2004:

> Refugees leaving Fallujah had converged on the western Sunni suburbs of Baghdad, Amriya, and Ghazaliya, which had come under the control of the insurgency. Insurgents, often backed by relatives of the Fallujah refugees, turned on the Shi'a residents of these neighbourhoods. Hundreds of Shi'a families were driven from their homes, which were then seized by the refugees. Sunni Arab resentment against the Shi'a's "collaboration" with the occupation's forces had been building up, exacerbated by the apparent indifference of the Shi'a to the assault on Fallujah.
>
> In turn, the Shi'a were becoming incensed by the daily attacks on policemen and soldiers, who were mostly poor Shi'a men. The targeting of Sunnis in majority Shi'a neighbourhoods began in early 2005. In the Shaab district of Baghdad, for instance, the assassination of a popular Sadrist cleric, Sheikh Haitham al-Ansari, led to the formation of one of the first Shi'a death squads. . . . The cycle of killings, assassinations, bombings and expulsions fed into each other, quickly turning to a full-scale ethnic cleansing of city neighbourhoods and towns.[3]

The process accelerated in early 2006 after the bombing in Samarra of the Golden Dome, a revered Shiite shrine. It crested in 2007 when the U.S. military "surge" in Baghdad loosened the hold of Sunni insurgents on many mixed as well as mostly Sunni neighborhoods in the capital. At the end of the surge all but twenty-five or so of the approximately two hundred mixed neighborhoods in Baghdad had become ethnically homogenous.[4] A similar process took place in the capital's southern suburbs.[5]

As minority groups in mixed neighborhoods and cities were driven out, they joined the army of displaced persons, often settling into vacated homes in newly purified neighborhoods dominated by their own sect. But many, like those in the previous waves of refugees, found they had to move far away from the violence, including, once again, a large number who simply left Iraq. As with previous waves, the more prosperous were the most likely to depart, taking with them professional, technical, and managerial skills.

Among those who departed in this third wave was Riverbend, the anonymous "Girl Blogger from Baghdad," who had achieved international fame for her beautifully crafted descriptions of life in Iraq under the U.S. occupation.[6] Her account of her journey into exile chronicled the emotional tragedy experienced by millions of Iraqis:

> The last few hours in the house were a blur. It was time to go and I went from room to room saying goodbye to everything. I said goodbye to my desk—the one I'd used all through high school and college. I said goodbye to the curtains and the bed and the couch. I said goodbye to the armchair E. and I broke when we were younger. I said goodbye to the big table over which we'd gathered for meals and to do homework. I said goodbye to the ghosts of the framed pictures that once hung on the walls, because the pictures have long since been taken down and stored away—but I knew just what hung where. I said goodbye to the silly board games we inevitably fought over—the Arabic Monopoly with the missing cards and money that no one had the heart to throw away. . . .
>
> The trip was long and uneventful, other than two checkpoints being run by masked men. They asked to see identification, took a cursory glance at the passports and asked where we were going. The same was done for the car behind us. Those checkpoints are terrifying but I've learned that the best technique is to avoid eye contact, answer questions politely and pray under your breath. My mother and I had been careful not to wear any apparent jewelry, just in case, and we were both in long skirts and head scarves. . . .
>
> How is it that a border no one can see or touch stands between car bombs, militias, death squads and . . . peace, safety? It's difficult to believe—even now. I sit here and write this and wonder why I can't hear the explosions. . . .[7]

The Human Toll

The number of Iraqis who flooded neighboring lands or became internal refugees remains notoriously difficult to determine. Even the most circumspect of observers, however, have reported huge rates of displacement since the Bush administration's March 2003 invasion. These numbers quickly outstripped the flood of expatriates who had fled the country during Saddam Hussein's brutal era.

By early 2006 the United Nations High Commissioner for Refugees was estimating that 1.7 million Iraqis had left the country and that perhaps an equal number of internal refugees had been created in the same three-year period.[8] The rate rose dramatically yet again as sectarian violence and ethnic expulsions took hold. The International Organization for Migration estimated the displacement rate during 2006 and 2007 at about sixty thousand per month. In mid-2007 Iraq was declared by Refugees International to be the "fastest-growing refugee crisis in the world," while the UN called the crisis "the worst human displacement in Iraq's modern history."[9] Veteran Middle East reporter Patrick Cockburn concluded that the "Iraqi refugee crisis is now surpassing in numbers anything ever seen in the Middle East, including the expulsion or flight of Palestinians in 1948."[10]

Syria, the only country that initially placed no restrictions on Iraqi immigration, had (according to UN statistics) taken in about 1.25 million displaced Iraqis by early 2007. In addition, the UN estimated that more than five hundred thousand Iraqi refugees were in Jordan, seventy thousand in Egypt, sixty thousand in Iran, thirty thousand in Lebanon, two hundred thousand spread across the Gulf States, and one hundred thousand in Europe, with fifty thousand in other countries around the globe.[11] The United States, which had accepted about thirty thousand Iraqi refugees during Saddam Hussein's years, admitted only 463 between the start of the war and mid-2007.[12] Its chief invasion partner, Great Britain, admitted no more than 150 per year.[13]

President Bush's "surge" strategy—which added thirty thousand U.S. combat troops to the already intense fighting in Baghdad in the first six months of 2007, further amplified the human flood, especially of the internally displaced. According to James Glanz and Stephen Farrell of the *New York Times*, "American-led operations have brought new fighting, driving fearful Iraqis from their homes at much higher rates than before the tens of thousands of additional troops arrived." The combined effect of the surge and accelerated ethnic expulsions generated an estimated displacement rate of one hundred thousand per month in Baghdad alone during the first half of 2007, a figure that surprised even Said

Hakki, the director of the Iraqi Red Crescent, who had been monitoring the refugee crisis since the beginning of the war.[14]

During 2007, according to UN estimates, Syria admitted an additional one hundred fifty thousand refugees. With Iraqis by then constituting almost 10 percent of the country's population, the Syrian government, feeling the strain on resources, began putting limits on the influx and attempted to launch a mass repatriation policy.[15] These repatriation efforts—in Syria and elsewhere—were, however, largely fruitless. Even when violence in Baghdad declined in late 2007, refugees attempting to return found that their abandoned homes had been irreversibly damaged in U.S. offensives, had been appropriated by strangers (often of a different sect), or were located in newly "cleansed" neighborhoods that were now inhospitable to them.[16] These barriers, however, did not stop Syria and Jordan from closing borders and attempting to expel large numbers of already settled Iraqi refugees.

In the same years the weight of displaced persons inside Iraq grew ever more quickly. Estimated by the UN at 2.25 million in September 2007, this tidal flow of internally displaced, often homeless families began to weigh on the resources of the provinces receiving them.[17] Najaf, the first large city south of Baghdad, where the most sacred Shiite shrines in Iraq are located, found that its population of seven hundred thousand had increased by an estimated four hundred thousand displaced Shia. By mid-2007 three other southern Shia provinces struggled to integrate IDPs who by that point constituted half the population.[18]

The burden was crushing. By 2007 Karbala, one of the provinces most affected, was attempting to enforce a draconian measure passed the previous year: new residents would be expelled unless officially sponsored by two members of the provincial council.[19] Other governates also tried in various ways, largely without success, to stanch the flow of refugees.[20]

Whether inside or outside the country, even families who had been prosperous before the war faced grim conditions. In Syria, where a careful survey of conditions was undertaken in October 2007, only 24 percent of all Iraqi families were supported by salaries or wages. Most families were left to live as best they could on dwindling savings or remittances from relatives, and a third of those with funds on hand expected to run out within three months.[21]

The experience of Mohammed Saleem, who had run a successful supermarket in Baghdad during the austere years before the U.S. invasion, was typical. "The big suffering," he told Inter Press Service reporter Maki al-Nazzai, "started with the 2003 occupation that brought closed roads and reduced income for people." With his business faltering, sectarian violence provided the impetus for departure. Local militias told him to "leave within 24 hours," and he quickly gathered his family and left for Syria. Safe but unable to find work or start a business, Saleem's brother in Baghdad was "selling our property piece by piece so that we can survive."[22]

Under this kind of pressure, increasing numbers of people were reduced to sex work or other exploitative or illegal sources of income.[23] According to independent journalist Deborah Campbell, Damascus nightclubs were "filled with tens of thousands of Iraqi girls and widows who supported their family by selling themselves."[24]

Food was a major issue for many refugee families. According to the UN, nearly half needed "urgent food assistance." A substantial proportion of adults reported skipping at least one meal a day in order to feed their children. Many others endured foodless days "in order to keep up with rent and utilities." One refugee mother told McClatchy reporter Hannah Allam, "We buy just enough meat to flavor the food—we buy it with pennies."[25] Another, the wife of a formerly prosperous construction engineer, told independent reporter Carolyn Bancroft, "In Iraq, we are not safe but we can eat. Our family helps us. In Egypt, we are safe but we can't eat."[26]

According to a rigorous McClatchy survey, most Iraqi refugees in Syria were housed in crowded conditions with more than one person per room (sometimes many more). Twenty-five percent of families lived in one-room apartments; about one in six refugees had been diagnosed with a (usually untreated) chronic disease; and one-fifth of the children had had diarrhea in the two weeks before their parents were interviewed.[27] Although Syrian officials had aided refugee parents in getting more than two-thirds of school-age children enrolled in schools, 46 percent had dropped out—mainly due to lack of appropriate immigration documents, insufficient funds to pay for school expenses, or a variety of emotional issues. The dropout rate was escalating. According to independent reporter Deborah Campbell, education became the exception rather than the rule:

> One of the things that really struck me about the refugee crisis is the way— Iraq had once been, before the war, the most educated country in the Middle East, and all of these [refugee] children that I met . . . were in school before the war. And now, 70 to 90 percent of those in Syria are not in school, although the Syrian government is allowing them. Syrian schools now have sixty, seventy children per classroom. If you don't have documents, and if you're fleeing with twenty-four-hours' notice, you're not going and getting your children's report cards before you leave. Or they've missed three, four years already, and they don't go to school. And many of

them are starting to work now to support their families, whether shining shoes or selling things on the street.[28]

As the numbers of refugees increased these problems amplified. Overcrowding in the receiving cities meant increased rents; in Syria rents had doubled and tripled during the huge influx between 2005 and 2007. Food prices there also tripled as more families competed for limited supplies. Competition for jobs, even sex work, led to lower wages. Fewer and fewer children attended school.[29]

Like the expatriate refugees, internally displaced Iraqis faced severe and constantly eroding conditions. The almost powerless Iraqi central government, largely trapped inside Baghdad's Green Zone—and under continuing pressure from the IMF to reduce the cost of its welfare system— instituted a policy that required people who moved from one place to another to register in person in Baghdad in order to maintain eligibility for the national food subsidy program. Such registration was impossible for most families driven from their homes in the country's vicious civil war. With no way to register, families displaced outside of Baghdad entered their new residences without even the shrinking safety net offered by guaranteed subsidies of basic food supplies.[30]

To make matters worse, almost three-quarters of the displaced were women or children, and very few intact families had working fathers. Unemployment rates in most cities were already at or above 50 percent, so prostitution and child labor increasingly became viable options, when available. UNICEF reported that a large proportion of children in such families were hungry, clinically underweight, and stunted in their growth. "In some areas, up to 90 per cent of the [displaced] children are not in school," the UN agency reported.[31]

Ruba, a thirty-eight-year-old internally displaced widow, told an unfortunately representative story to the Red Cross:

> My children and I left my home in Anbar governorate almost two years ago. My husband had been killed right in front of us. I had to protect my children, so we fled the same night with nothing but some money. For me, today, there is no past and no future, only a horrible present. I only wish I had some photos of my husband and my family. I can see it all in my mind but I don't know how long I will remember. There was a time when we always sat down together for lunch and laughed. Today we are living with my cousin's family. There are 12 of us in one room. I don't want my old life again because I know it is impossible without my husband. All I want is for my children to go to school and lead a normal life.[32]

Ali, a thirteen-year-old, told the Red Cross an even more heart-wrenching tale:

Two years ago, my three-year-old sister and I left our home in Basra and went to stay at our aunt's house. My parents said that everything was okay and that they would join us in a week. We took some clothes and my sister took her doll. We waited for weeks but my parents never came. My aunt told me that I am the man of the family now and that I should take care of my sister. She doesn't know our parents are dead and always asks when we will go back home. But when I am older I will take her home and I will take care of her.[33]

The Collapse of Education

One area that could be seen as a remedy for much that ailed Iraqi society was education, where a new generation of professional and technical personnel could be trained to replace or even upgrade Iraq's lost human capital. Such a vision certainly informed the initial promises of the U.S. leadership, but hopes faded as the reality of occupation policy took hold.

Before 1980 the Iraqi education system was the best in the Middle East, with the university system regarded "as the centre of academia in the Arab world."[34] The educational failures of the Hussein regime were manifold, both in the content of the curriculum and in the isolation of educational professionals from scholarly and scientific advances in the rest of the world.[35] The CPA promised an educational and intellectual renaissance and at first these promises were reflected in increased school enrollments, the rebirth of dissenting intellectual communities, and the explosion of newspapers and other periodicals advocating a full range of political and social viewpoints.[36] It soon became apparent however that Iraq's education system was moving backward, not forward.[37]

One small but highly symptomatic sign was the friction over U.S. military occupation of elementary schools. For an invading army, schools are tempting locations: they have many rooms for headquarters and barracks, open spaces for parking vehicles and mustering soldiers, and are separated from surrounding communities by walls, fences, and natural barriers that can be used as defensive perimeters. In Iraq hundreds of schools became temporary homes for military units.[38] The fierce resistance in the city of Fallujah began when U.S. soldiers fired on a protest against such an occupation. The incident in Haditha discussed in chapter 4 involved a U.S. military unit that had commandeered a local school.[39]

Besides generating ferocious anger among residents of these communities, school occupations caused considerable damage that required repair before the schools could become functional again. For $50 million, occupation authorities hired the ubiquitous Bechtel Group in summer 2003 to "provide a 'quick fix,' repairing war damage and reversing the accumulated degradation endured by the schools before the school year started."[40] By early fall Bechtel had published a list of nearly sixteen hundred "rehabili-tated" schools and—per U.S. policy that reconstruction contractors would be disciplined solely by market forces—the CPA accepted Bechtel's report without any formal inspection. Visits by *Newsweek* reporters to five Baghdad schools listed as "rebuilt" by Bechtel, however, found that "none had enough textbooks, desks or blackboards. Most had refuse everywhere, nonfunctioning toilets and desks made for two kids that were accommo-dating four."[41] When independent reporters Pratap Chatterjee and Herbert Docena performed similar evaluations of four of the rehabilitated schools in the Shia south, away from the growing Sunni insurrection, they found essentially unusable facilities inhabited by bitter educators whose anger toward the occupation had grown exponentially in the few months since the fall of the Hussein regime.[42]

The reporters' inspection at one of these schools managed to capture in a single site the full range of inefficiency, corruption, and deconstruc-tion that characterized the U.S. economic effort in Iraq:

> This is Hawa School, run by Batool Mahdi Hussain. . . . She . . . is bitter about the contractors. The school has a fresh coat of paint on the outside with all of the characters from the Disney version of Aladdin, complete with the genie and the prince.
>
> But, she says, things are worse than under Saddam. "UNICEF painted our walls and gave us new Japanese fans. They painted the cartoons outside. When the American contractors came, they took away our Japanese fans and replaced them with Syrian fans that don't work," she says angrily.
>
> The headmistress takes us to the toilets where a new water system has been installed, pipes, taps and a motor to pump the water. The problem is the motor doesn't work so the toilets reek with unflushed sewage. She then uncovers a new drain cover to show us that it is nothing but a cover. She walks quickly, not waiting for the camera to catch up, a whirlwind of show-and-tell. "These doors, the hinges are broken. We were supposed to get steel doors, we got wooden doors. The new paint is peeling off. There isn't enough power to run our school." . . .
>
> As we bid farewell, she walks us out of the gate and points to the con-struction debris in the road. . . . "They didn't even take their rubbish with them. They gave us no papers to tell us what they had done and what they did not do. We had to pay to haul the trash. Honestly, the condition of our school was better before the contractors came."[43]

Other "fully reconstructed" schools exhibited similar problems. Al-Harthia school administrator Huda Sabah Abdurasiq spoke for many other educators when she said: "I could fix everything here for just $1,000. Mr. Jeff [a Bechtel subcontractor] spent $20,000" and left the school with leaking ceilings, shorted power, peeling paint, and a "re-paired" floor that was worse than before reconstruction began.[44]

The many painful deficiencies in the Bechtel project were exemplified by a new water pump that did not work but could no longer be fixed or maintained by local technicians, a power source that did not generate enough electricity to run the school but also could not be locally repaired, and—most of all—the continuing negative conditions that led many teachers and other professionals to flee the school, the city, and the country.

· By 2007 UNICEF reported that one-sixth of all Iraqi children—and the majority of displaced children—were not being educated. Among those who were enrolled, as many as two-thirds were attending irregularly.[45] For girls the onslaught of patriarchal fundamentalism created an added burden, making it dangerous for them to travel to school or, in some locations, to find a school that would accept them. In early 2007 the United Nations Children's Fund estimated that only 30 percent of girls were attending regularly.[46] In provinces with high levels of violence, many teachers were unable to get to work, leaving a large proportion of the remaining students without instructors. Matters became even more desperate when institutional erosion at the Ministry of Education made payment of both government officials and classroom teachers sporadic, spurring an accelerated rate of staff departures.[47] In December 2007 Iraqi teachers called a national strike to protest low and irregular salaries, lack of security, and decaying physical conditions in the schools.[48]

The accelerating decline was crystallized in spring 2007 when only 28 percent of Iraq's seventeen-year-olds sat for their final exams, and less than half of those who attended passed. Ultimately a little over 10 percent of the class of 2007 qualified for academic diplomas.[49] Save the Children Foundation warned that without drastic changes, a substantial proportion of Iraqi children were in danger of remaining uneducated.[50]

The situation at the universities might have been even more desperate. De-Baathification at the beginning of the occupation expelled about one thousand lecturers and researchers. With professors a preferred target of kidnappers seeking ransom and assassins assaulting alleged U.S. collaborators, as well as subjects for U.S. black-ops if they were critical of the occupation, many hundreds were killed in the next few years. The Iraqi minister of education identified 296 professors killed in 2005 alone.[51] Kawther Ahmed Fadel, a nineteen-year-old student at al-Mustansiria University in Baghdad, told independent reporter Zaineb Naji, "The violence targeted the best of the professors. . . . Not a week goes by without an announcement that a professor or other teaching staff member has been killed."[52]

The Iraqi Ministry of Higher Education estimated that more than three thousand professors had left the country by early 2006, with the rate of exodus accelerating.[53] According to Tariq al-Bakaa, who served as minister of higher education until 2004, "the government had shut down 153 academic specializations because there were no longer any experts in those fields." Medical schools were "totally devastated by the lack of expertise." Promises of increased wages and improved security by the Iraqi government failed to induce the return of exiled professors. Beyond the issue of personal danger, academics found that conditions abroad were better than those in Iraq.[54]

Baghdad University, with eighty thousand students, became an unfortunately typical example of the decay that threatened to undermine the viability of Iraqi education. The 2007–8 school year began during a dramatic decline in violence in the city and on the campus, allowing attendance to rebound from less than 50 percent to a still problematic but nevertheless dramatically better 80 percent. This encouraging development, however, brought into focus the debilitated substructure of the university. Many "seasoned professors" did not return and were replaced by "inexperienced lecturers." The laboratories had only "meager equipment." The students were forced to use Xerox copies of obsolete textbooks. Class discussion (as well as lunchroom gossip) was severely constrained by religious orthodoxy. Those who survived these degraded conditions to graduation found that their education offered little promise of professional employment: they entered "a barren job market" in Iraq, and their "degrees were not recognized" in neighboring countries.[55]

Education, in contradiction of its special mission of replenishing human capital, was instead becoming a source of degraded human capital.

Brain Drain

The job backgrounds of an extraordinary proportion of Iraqi refugees in Syria were professional, managerial, or administrative. They had vital skills that would be needed to sustain, repair, and eventually rebuild their country's ravaged infrastructure. In Iraq, approximately 10 percent of adults had attended college, but more than one-third of the refugees in Syria were university educated. Whereas less than one percent of Iraqis had a postgraduate education, nearly 10 percent of refugees in Syria had advanced degrees, including 4.5 percent who had doctorates. At the opposite end of the economic spectrum, fully 20 percent of all Iraqis had no schooling, but only a relative handful of the refugees arriving in Syria (3 percent) had no education.[56] These disparities were probably even more striking in more distant receiving lands where entry was more difficult.

The reasons for this remarkable brain drain are not hard to find. Even the desperate process of fleeing one's home turns out to require resources, and so refugees from most disasters who travel great distances tend to be disproportionately prosperous, as the aftermath of Hurricane Katrina in New Orleans so painfully illustrated.

In early 2006 the United States Committee on Refugees and Immigrants estimated that a full 40 percent of Iraq's professional class had left the country. Universities and medical facilities were particularly hard hit, with some reporting less than one in five of needed staff on hand.[57] The oil industry suffered from what the *Wall Street Journal* called a "petroleum exodus" that included the departure of two-thirds of its top one hundred managers as well as significant numbers of managerial and professional workers.[58]

Even before the huge 2007 exodus from Baghdad, the UN High Commissioner of Refugees warned that "the skills required to provide basic services are becoming more and more scarce," pointing particularly to doctors, teachers, computer technicians, and skilled craftspeople such as bakers.[59]

By mid-2007 the loss of these resources was apparent. Medical facilities commonly required patients' families to act as nurses and technicians and yet were still unable to perform many services. Schools were often closed, or opened only sporadically, because of an absence of qualified teachers. Universities postponed or canceled required courses or qualifying examinations because of inadequate staff. At the height of the cholera epidemic in summer 2007, water purification plants were idled because needed technicians could not be found.[60]

The most devastating impact of the Iraqi refugee crisis, however, was probably its impact on the capacity of the national government, which de-Baathification and privatization had already left in a fragile state. In every area that a government is expected to operate, the missing managerial, technical, and professional expertise had a devastating effect, with postwar "reconstruction" particularly hard hit. Even the ability of the government to disperse its income (mostly from oil revenues) was crippled by what cabinet ministers termed "a shortage of employees trained to write contracts" and "the flight of scientific and engineering expertise from the country."[61]

The depths of the problem could be measured by the fact that the electrical ministry spent only 26 percent of its capital budget in 2006. The remaining three-quarters went unspent or was siphoned off into the personal accounts of corrupt officials. Even with this dismal record, it nevertheless outperformed most other government agencies and ministries, which spent an even smaller proportion of their budgets on appropriate activities.[62] Under pressure from occupation officials to improve performance in 2007, the government made concerted efforts to increase both its budget and its disbursements for reconstruction. Despite initially optimistic reports, the news was grim by year's end. Actual expenditures on electrical infrastructure were below the previous year and might have slipped to 1 percent of the budgeted amount. Other ministries experienced similar downturns.[63]

Even more symptomatic were the few successes in infrastructural rebuilding found by *New York Times* reporter James Glanz in a survey of capital construction throughout the country. Most of the successful programs he reviewed were initiated and managed by officials connected to local and provincial governments, often in areas that had only antagonistic relationships to the Green Zone government. Glanz concluded that successful reconstruction projects often depended on avoiding *any* interaction with the ineffective and corrupt central government. The governor of Babil province, Sallem al-Mesamawe, described the key to his province's success: "We jumped over the routine, the bureaucracy, and we depend on new blood— a new team." They had learned this lesson after using provincial money and local contractors to build a school only to have it remain closed because the national government was unable to provide the necessary furniture.[64]

The government's staggering institutional incapacity was certainly a complex phenomenon, with many contributing factors beyond the drain of human capital. The flood of managers, professionals, and technicians out of the country, however, had acute long-term implications because their departure created a critical obstacle to productive reconstruction. Combined with the decay of the once-formidable education system, the departure of so many crucial individuals was to a considerable extent irreversible, constituting a brain drain on a scale seldom seen in the last century.

Many exiles intended to—even longed to—return to Iraq, when or if the country regained its equilibrium. But time is often the enemy of such intentions. The moment an individual arrives in a new country, he or she begins creating new social ties. This is even truer for those who leave with their families, as so many Iraqis did. As this network-building process continues, the probability of return fades. Meanwhile those with marketable skills, even in the dire circumstances facing most Iraqi refugees, keep seeking work that exploits their training. The most marketable are the most likely to succeed and to begin building new careers in exile.

The Displacement Tsunami

The scale of failure and corruption in 2007 was an unmitigated disaster for Iraqi society as well as an embarrassment for the occupation. From the point of view of long-term U.S. goals in Iraq, however, this situation had a silver lining. The Iraqi government's incapacity to perform at almost any level became further justification for the claims made by L. Paul Bremer at the very beginning of the occupation—that the country's reconstruction would be handled best by private enterprise. Moreover, the mass flight of Iraqi professionals meant that expertise for reconstruction was simply unavailable inside the country. This in turn validated Bremer's claim that foreign-owned multinational companies were the only viable vehicles for reconstructing Iraq.

This neoliberal imperative was brought into focus in late 2007, as the last of the money allocated by the U.S. Congress for Iraqi reconstruction was being spent. The "petroleum exodus" had long before determined that most of the engineers needed for maintaining the decrepit oil industry were already foreigners, mostly "imported from Texas and Oklahoma."[65] The foreign presence had in fact become so pervasive that the main headquarters for maintenance and development of the Rumaila oil field in southern Iraq (the source of more than two-thirds of the country's oil at that time) ran on both Iraqi and Houston time. The U.S. firms in charge of the field's maintenance and development had been utilizing a large number of subcontractors, most of them U.S. or British, very few of them Iraqi.

Within months, when the money ran out, vast new funds would be needed just to sustain Rumaila's production at its already depressed level.[66] According to Harper's senior editor Luke Mitchell, who visited the field in summer 2007, Iraqi engineers and technicians were "smart enough and ambitious enough" to sustain and "upgrade" the system once the U.S. contracts expired, but such a project would require upward of two decades due to of the compromised condition of the central government and the shortage of skilled local engineers and technicians. The likely outcome when U.S. money departed was either an inadequate effort in which work proceeded "only in fits and starts" or, more likely, the establishment of new contracts in which foreign companies would "continue their work," paid for by the Iraqi government.[67]

With regard to the petroleum industry, therefore, what the refugee crisis guaranteed was long-term Iraqi dependence on outsiders. The Iraqi government, when and if it made independent decisions about economic development, would have its choice of proceeding in "fits and starts" or fulfilling the original vision of the occupation—that the Iraqi economy would be fully integrated into and dependent on foreign multinational corporations.

Most horror stories come to an end, but in 2008 there was no relief in sight for the Iraqis. The refugees faced a miserable life in limbo, as Syria and other receiving countries exhausted their meager resources and sought to expel all but the most valuable. Those seeking shelter within Iraq faced the depletion of already minimal support systems in host communities whose residents could themselves be threatened with displacement. The ongoing U.S. presence guaranteed wave after wave of misery.

Part IV

Sovereignty Lost

Chapter Fourteen

Who's Sovereign Now?

As Washington prepares to hand over power, U.S. administrator L. Paul Bremer and other officials are quietly building institutions that will give the U.S. powerful levers for influencing nearly every important decision the interim government will make. In a series of edicts issued earlier this spring, Mr. Bremer's Coalition Provisional Authority created new commissions that effectively take away virtually all of the powers once held by several ministries.

—*Wall Street Journal*

Sovereignty stands on three legs. To achieve it a government must obtain a near monopoly on the means of coercion, it must have the resources needed to keep the country's social and economic infrastructure functioning, and it must sustain an administrative apparatus capable of overseeing and administering policy. If it has these three capabilities, it will almost always acquire a fourth prerequisite for orderly government: its citizens will believe in its legitimacy—that is, its right to demand their compliance to duly constituted government rules. And, finally, under these circumstances the government is likely to acquire yet another essential attribute: the recognition by other countries, particularly neighbors, of its ability to make binding international commitments and to defend its borders.

For all the international hatred of Saddam Hussein's regime, its sovereignty was not questioned for the many years he ruled Iraq. Hussein was fanatical in assuring his monopoly on violence, he made certain that the economy kept functioning (if only sometimes barely, and if only to assure his own disproportionate share of the rewards), and he built an elaborate state apparatus that was not only capable of administering government policy but also of intruding into many other aspects of people's lives. As a consequence of these structural attributes, the Iraqis, no matter how much they detested him and his government, rarely questioned his right to demand their compliance. The international community, particularly his neighbors, was not only confident but also fearful of his ability to fulfill the various threats and promises he made on the international stage.

The beginning of the U.S.-led invasion placed all three facets of Iraqi sovereignty into question. As soon as the bombing attack began, there was no longer a monopoly on the means of coercion and as long as fighting between the two armies continued, coercive privileges were contested. During that period of fighting the country's basic services ceased to function—the shock-and-awe campaign mounted by the U.S. Air Force at the beginning of the war was successful in creating an initial disruption, which was irremediable at least while the Hussein regime was deposed. When U.S. soldiers crossed into Iraq the administrative apparatus also began to collapse, with those responsible for governmental functions abandoning their posts until the fighting stopped or longer. As a consequence most Iraqis were not sure who had the right to impose order, particularly in the many areas where U.S. troops rushed through without establishing an enduring presence. This confusion was highly visible to soldiers in the advancing army, because Iraqi citizens vacillated between treating them as new sovereigns or as dangerous interlopers.[1]

What was less visible, however, was the situation once "major combat operations" were over and the Baathist regime had "passed into history."[2] For a time the occupation might have achieved a kind of sovereignty. In April and May 2003, before the economic depression hit with full force and insurgency made its presence felt, the occupation had an apparent monopoly on the means of violence. This monopoly appeared to make most Iraqis willing to comply with governmentlike decisions made by the CPA.[3]

The other elements of control and legitimacy, however, were never present. Whether or not the occupation might have been able to keep the Iraqi economy going during this transitional period, the Bush administration chose policies that were at best indifferent to this effort. The massive looting—the most visible sign of this indifference—not only disrupted normal life but also ate away at Iraq's economic and social infrastructure, assuring a prolonged period of disorder. The shuttering of government-owned industrial enterprises and massive layoffs of soldiers paralyzed the economy. The dismantlement of Baathist government structure removed the very form that the occupation might have used to assert its administrative presence. As time passed the initial inclination of the Iraqi people to legitimate the rule of the occupation began to dissipate. In areas like Fallujah, where the insurgency grew strong, it disintegrated completely.[4]

Such collapses are not unfamiliar in history, and we can find these moments of "unsovereignty" in many instances of transition from one government to another, particularly when the transition has been animated by an invading army. Often time heals the incapacities of the new government and validates its sovereign claims. L. Paul Bremer, the U.S. proconsul during that 2003 to 2004 period of direct foreign rule, sought to accomplish this transition. His main strategy was to use the full force of the U.S. military to assert the occupation's monopoly on the means of coercion. He also sought to reactivate and reconstruct the economic and social infrastructure, using the many billions of dollars allocated by the U.S. Congress and about an equal amount captured from Saddam Hussein's treasury.[5] In addition he sought to construct a new, privatized administrative apparatus aimed at managing all enterprises from prisons to the electrical grid.

The judgment of history has not been particularly favorable to Bremer's effort, characterized by former Iraqi finance minister Ali K. Allawi as a "slapped-together administration" that "veered uncomfortably between considering itself a caretaker administration" that would play the role of "benign tutor for Iraq's induction into the democratic camp" and a revolutionary regime engineering "a radical overhaul of the country's laws, institutions, and political culture."[6] The increasing alienation of the Iraqi people (already registering vast majorities in favor of U.S. withdrawal) demonstrated that two of the prerequisites for sovereignty—the monopoly on violence and the sense of legitimacy—were in tatters.

After a year, the CPA effectively conceded its failure to create an apparatus capable of establishing sovereignty by shifting to a new plan for governing the country. The hallmark of this shift was the announcement that the United States would transfer responsibility for administering Iraq to an Iraqi government. Bremer and his CPA colleagues, with UN approval and participation, devised an eighteen-month transition to a parliamentary democracy. In the first step the United States would appoint a caretaker government with limited legislative authority in summer 2004. This interim administration would apply existing laws (promulgated by Bremer) until the first national election, held in January 2005, selected a parliament with two key responsibilities—to oversee the drafting of a new constitution and to choose a new cabinet to replace the appointed ministers. Once the constitution was ratified in a second national election, a third election in December 2005 would bring to power a new parliament that would rule the country.

After weeks of contentious negotiation the UN Security Council unanimously passed the fifth version of the U.S.-United Kingdom resolution mandating this procedure and designated June 30, 2004, as the day when "sovereignty" would be transferred to the newly appointed Iraqi Interim Government.

Two key elements of the enabling legislation for the transition reflected the larger U.S. goals in Iraq: that the new Iraqi state should not have the encompassing power of its Baathist predecessor (or even the power of its Middle Eastern neighbors) and that its newly formed administrative apparatus should be constrained and guided by U.S. advisors. Building these principles into the new state apparatus assured Washington's planners that when and if a truly sovereign government emerged from the Iraqi cauldron, it would pursue the sort of political and economic policies that the United States advocated for Iraq, and that it would be well integrated into the global economy. In short, the United States sought to establish a client state in Iraq.

The Transition to a Client State

The client status of the new Iraqi state was visible during the transition process. Keeping in mind that one of the three foundations of sovereignty lay in the monopoly over violence, it is particularly important to scrutinize the way U.S. officials structured the relationship between U.S. military forces stationed in Iraq and the new Iraqi army and police forces.

This issue was a point of contention during the UN debate over the transition plan. Prime Minister Tony Blair argued that the Iraqis should have a veto over the disposition of U.S. military power: "If there's a political decision as to whether you go into a place like Falluja in a particular way, that has got to be done with the consent of the Iraqi government. . . . That's what the transfer of sovereignty means."[7] Secretary of State Colin Powell, on the other hand, argued that Iraqis should not have such veto power: "Obviously we would take into account whatever they might say at a political or military level. . . . And to make sure that that happens, we will be creating coordinating bodies, political coordinating bodies and military-to-military coordinating bodies, so that there is transparency with respect to what we are doing."[8] Although Powell's position was ultimately upheld, it made little difference since this was a purely symbolic argument. Historically, U.S. troops had never been subject to the command of a foreign power except in rare, highly delimited circumstances, and this situation was not one of those exceptions. Since the U.S. military would be far more powerful than any Iraqi army that the United

States itself created, a UN-mandated paper veto over U.S. military activity would have been unenforceable. As long, therefore, as the U.S. military chose to operate inside Iraq, the Iraqis would not only fail to achieve a monopoly on the means of coercion, they would not even be able to contend with the U.S. forces for preeminence.

Does this mean that sovereignty is compromised any time foreign troops are stationed in a country? Yes. But the degree of compromise is larger or smaller depending on the circumstances. In Korea, Japan, and Germany, the examples of long-term U.S. occupations most often invoked by Washington politicians as precedents for the occupation of Iraq, troops remained active within the countries only briefly after the end of hostilities. They were then moved to bases or to unsecured borders. They acted as soldiers only on their own insulated bases and inter acted with local citizens as civilians when off the bases.[9] Though the soldiers were technically not subject to local sovereignty and sometimes escaped prosecution for violation of local laws, these were rare events that did not define their presence within the country.

In the case of Iraq, sovereignty was fatally compromised by the pervasive presence of U.S. soldiers operating as the visible means of social control over the Iraqi population, as providers of social services, and as consumers of Iraqi products and services while at the same time holding themselves exempt from Iraqi law or custom. As long as this dynamic continued no Iraqi government (appointed or elected) could claim dominance over the means of coercion.

This point was forcefully made by conservative columnist Jed Babbin in the *National Review*. He labeled the troops the most important "hole" in the Bush administration's plan "to turn Iraq over to free Iraqis":

> The president insisted that the "turnover" of Iraqi sovereignty would be complete. But how can that be when, as he said, 138,000 American troops will remain there as long as necessary, under American command? If they are not subjected to the law and authority of the new Iraq provisional government, how can they be anything other than an occupation force? Though the "Coalition Provisional Authority" will cease to exist on June 30, changing the sign over the door but leaving American troops there under American command (the only way they could possibly stay) continues the occupation.[10]

The legitimacy of the Iraqi government was further undermined when mercenary security personnel, notably those associated with Blackwater, emerged as an additional source of coercion that was not subject to Iraqi authority or command. The mercenaries' exemption from Iraqi law, which was briefly disputed in late 2007 after Blackwater personnel killed more than a dozen civilians in a busy intersection in downtown Baghdad, meant that Iraqi citizens were confronted on a daily basis with visible evidence of their government's lack of coercive primacy. The pervasive presence of mercenaries became another daily confirmation of the absence of sovereignty within the country.[11]

But what about the Iraqi police and army? It is significant that the UN Security Council debate featured a disagreement over who should command these forces. CPA administrator L. Paul Bremer had originally insisted that Iraqi personnel be trained and commanded by U.S. personnel until the United States declared them ready to operate independently. This policy would have made them a functional part of the U.S. military for as long as the U.S. command believed it necessary, with the Iraqi government powerless to declare otherwise despite the fact that all other members of the Security Council opposed this procedure. The UN eventually adopted an apparent compromise that in practice left the Iraqi army and police under U.S. command.

U.S. domination was assured by three key features of the compromise plan. The most important feature was the modest strength of the new army, numbering no more than forty thousand soldiers and equipped only with light armaments and no tanks, airpower, or armored vehicles.[12] Such a force was incapable of securing the country. At the time of the transition in early 2004, occupation forces consisted of well over one hundred sixty thousand troops from the United States and its "coalition of the willing" allies, utilizing the full range of heavy weapons. These numbers were augmented by tens of thousands of private security contractors. The Iraqi military, even fully trained, would be capable of replacing only a modest proportion of this force. The plan therefore assumed a dominating and ongoing U.S. presence at least until the insurgency was wholly subdued. At a minimum, therefore, the Iraqi government—even if it actually controlled its military forces—could not be expected to achieve a monopoly on the means of coercion for years to come.

Even in the long run, the Iraqi military would not be self-sustaining. Such limited forces would make it the weakest in the Middle East. Iraq's four important neighbors—Syria, Iran, Turkey, and Saudi Arabia (all with historically frictional relationships with Iraq)—maintained armies of between two hundred thousand and six hundred thousand soldiers. Moreover, these armies were fully equipped with armored vehicles and missile systems that the U.S. plan denied to the Iraqi military. Even the tiny United Arab Emirates, with only three million people, maintained a fully equipped force of fifty thousand troops.[13] As long as Iraq's army remained small, and as long as it lacked modern heavy weapons, it would require an ongoing U.S. presence to make it an adequate force for national defense.

These plans, unaltered during the next three years of the occupation, expressed the first element in the Bush administration's goal: to deprive Iraq of a military force comparable to that wielded by Saddam Hussein, which could be used to fuel aggressive foreign adventures. Any serious international confrontation would require active U.S. cooperation, while any serious domestic disturbances would require at least U.S. armaments and logistics and perhaps U.S. personnel. In other words, the Iraqi government would be unable to undertake any serious military activity without the active involvement of the United States, which meant it could not undertake any military activity that the United States did not support.

Beyond this, the military plan also sought to assure seamless coordination between Washington's policy and Iraqi military and police activities. This would be accomplished by placing the U.S. military in charge of financing, recruiting, training, and supplying Iraqi military and police forces. This dense set of administrative ties assured that—even after Iraqi units were fully trained (and presumably delivered to Iraqi command)—they could not function without the continued flow of U.S. funding and logistics. Lieutenant General James Dubik, in charge of training the Iraqi armed forces, told the House Armed Services Committee in January 2008 that Iraq's military would be unable to take full responsibility for defending its borders until 2018 or later.[14]

The significance of these sinews of control was not lost on occupation administrators, who told New York Times reporters John F. Burns and Thom Shanker that if there were ever disagreement over military or police policy, "The American commander would only have to say, 'O.K., we're out of here,' and the Iraqis would back down."[15] Almost four years later nothing had changed. Nor was the significance lost on the Iraqi government, which in early 2008 attempted to buy heavy military equipment from Serbia and other countries outside the U.S. orbit. During the ensuing controversy an Iraqi senior official told New York Times reporter Solomon Moore that their efforts to acquire such equipment from the United States had met with insurmountable obstacles, and that many in the government believed that "the U.S. is trying to keep us unarmed so that we'll always be in need of the Americans."[16]

A sense of how the system would ultimately work was evident as early as May 2004, when the U.S. military organized a raid on the office of Ahmad Chalabi, a member of the Iraqi Government Council (the predecessor group to the interim government), who had previously played a key role in prewar invasion plans.[17] Chalabi was suspected by the Bush administration of cooperating with various Iranian efforts to influence Iraqi politics, though top Iraqi officials vehemently denied that he had engaged in any wrongdoing. The U.S. military organized a coordinated raid on Chalabi's house aimed at collecting incriminating evidence, utilizing occupation military personnel, mercenary security officers from the private U.S. company DynCorp, and Iraqi police.[18]

The description of the raid offered by occupation spokesman Dan Senor provided a vivid picture of how the Iraqi police took their orders from the U.S. command structure even when the Iraqi government was opposed to the action. Senor told *Washington Post* reporter Renae Merle that the raid was conducted by Iraqi police, with U.S. forces providing needed backup in case the lightly equipped Iraqis met violent resistance. The four DynCorp operatives were there "to observe and advise the Iraqi police during this operation, as they do on numerous operations."[19] The Iraqi police knew that the Iraqi Governing Council, the officials who technically commanded the Iraqi personnel involved in the raid, would oppose this attack on one of its members. But they also knew that U.S. commanders wanted the raid completed. The combination of their dependence on the occupation for equipment, logistics, and backup and the presence of DynCorp operatives within the units created a smoothly functioning coordination between U.S. commanders and the Iraqi police. The distant protests of the Iraqi government could not compete with the multifaceted leverage of the United States.

Ali A. Allawi, who served as minister of defense in the subsequent Iraqi governments, concluded from his experience that the "Iraqi army appeared to be entwined with the MNF [occupation forces] and would not normally accede to the orders of the Iraqi government."[20]

Controlling the Budget

The second facet of sovereignty, the maintenance of the fundamentals of social and economic life, depended on restoring Iraq's damaged physical infrastructure, which had been severely compromised during the Hussein regime but was headed toward free fall after the invasion. We have already chronicled the continued infrastructural decay, and that by itself reveals the failure of the new Iraqi government to fulfill this aspect of sovereignty.[21] In 2004 when Washington transferred official power to the new Iraqi Interim Government, this decay, though clearly visible, might still have been reversible. But in order to undertake the reconstruction needed to restore the foundations of Iraqi social life, the new government needed to access sufficient revenues to fund these projects, funds that could only be obtained by claiming a large proportion of oil revenues. CPA leader Bremer was adamantly opposed to allowing the untested Iraqi government unfettered discretion over the flow of oil funds. Washington's proposal to the UN therefore advocated that the United States maintain direct control even after the transfer of power. When this aspect of the Bush administration proposal was defeated by the UN Security Council, CPA authorities sought and received approval for a set of constraints that would ensure that the newly formed government was guided into acceptable decisions concerning oil revenues.

One key constraint placed the management of Iraqi oil revenues in the hands of an independent regulatory commission, the Development Fund for Iraq (DFI). The group consisted of ten foreigners and one Iraqi, all appointed by Bremer. The UN resolution called for this group—with Bremer's appointees remaining in office—to continue its work for five more years, thus guaranteeing that both the U.S.-appointed Interim Government of Iyad Allawi and the subsequently elected governments headed by Ibrahim al-Jaafari and Nouri al-Maliki would have no direct control over the actual spending of oil revenues during the critical period when reconstruction was desperately needed and sovereignty needed to be consolidated.[22]

The insertion of the DFI into the policy process for oil revenues could not by itself eliminate Iraqi government influence over disposition of the funds. In principle, the government could change broad policies relating to oil revenues, including how much to allocate to reconstruction and whether to expand oil production, and then pass the administration of these policies over to the DFI for implementation. To forestall this, government policy-making authority was severely limited by other measures built into the UN resolution. In the short run, the Interim Government was explicitly prohibited from making changes to the oil policy developed by the EPA. The newly appointed premier, Iyad Allawi, and his U.S.-appointed cabinet were required to continue the policies established by Bremer until they were replaced by an elected government— that is, "until such time as an internationally recognized, representative government of Iraq is properly constituted."[23] UN official Lakhadar Brahimi, who was a key figure in the transition, explained that this was not an attempt to limit Iraqi sovereignty but rather to protect the soon-to-be-elected permanent government from ill-conceived policies enacted by an appointed caretaker administration. The interim government, he explained, "should refrain from tying the hands of the elected government that will follow it."[24]

Ironically the Iraqi Interim Government, in one of its very first major acts, entered into the draconian contract with the IMF which severely compromised the autonomy of its successor governments. This agreement, completed just before the elected Parliament took office in January 2005, was part of the negotiated abrogation of loans that Saddam Hussein had executed with the Paris Club group of lenders to finance his various military adventures. The main condition for forgiving $32 billion of Hussein's $120 billion debt was that Iraq accept IMF policies with regard to oil revenues and economic development.

The resulting agreement not only specified general and specific principles that would be followed, but also gave the IMF ongoing oversight of the details of Iraqi economic and social policy, thus (to reprise Brahimi's vivid imagery) severely "tying the hands of the elected government" that took power just after the agreement was executed. An illustration of the quality of this oversight can be found in the IMF's successful demand that the Nouri al-Maliki government implement a 50 percent reduction in the national food basket during the deepening refugee crisis in 2007, a policy change that threatened the health and welfare of a substantial portion of the Iraqi population. In keeping with the IMF's concern for Iraq's standing in the global economy, these reductions were deemed necessary to maintain adequate funds for debt service and other international trade obligations.[25]

Because of these encumbrances on the disposition of oil funds, the bulk of Iraqi oil revenues were committed to paying the remaining debt and continuing the neoliberal reforms that Bremer and the CPA had begun. As a consequence, even though the price of oil tripled during a two-year period and continued to rise thereafter, the amounts of oil revenue available for immediate or long-term infrastructural reconstruction were far below the threshold for meaningful progress.[26] Just one example will illustrate how much constraint this placed on Iraqi government actions. The DFI and the other U.S. supervised institutions were so insistent on following a policy demanding maximum oil exports that in early 2008, 33 percent of Iraq's already inadequate electrical capacity was idled because of inadequate supplies of oil to run them.[27]

Given these constraints on Iraqi government expenditures, the bulk of the funds for Iraqi reconstruction during the first four years after the fall of Saddam Hussein derived from the one-time-only 2003 U.S. Congressional allocation of $18.4 billion. Dispersal of this money was in the hands of U.S. officials, depriving Iraqis of any real control over the allocation of the funds or choice of contractors who would be doing the work. This incapacity was ameliorated by the promise that at some point oil revenues might be sufficiently increased or sufficiently disencumbered to provide the economic basis for an independent Iraqi government. Since neither of these eventualities had materialized, the financial leverage of the

United States and its IMF ally remained fully intact as of 2008. As one of L. Paul Bremer's top aides told the *New York Times* at the time of the sovereignty transfer, "American troops will act as the most important guarantor of American influence. In addition . . . the $18.4 billion voted for Iraqi reconstruction last fall by the United States Congress—including more than $2 billion for the new Iraqi forces—will give the Americans a decisive voice."[28] In these circumstances the Iraqi governments that succeeded the CPA did not have the capacity to sustain the infrastructural prerequisites of sovereignty. Such sustenance required the active cooperation of the U.S.-appointed DFI and the IMF.

Who Administers What?

History is strewn with the wreckage of occupying powers that established military and financial control but did not have the administrative capacity to sustain their rule. Various U.S. military commanders in Iraq made this point over the first years of the war, complaining about "political" failures that undermined the effective "kinetic" work of their soldiers. In the first year of the occupation, these complaints were directed at the CPA, which was unable to deliver sufficient supplies, equipment, expertise, and labor power to the various projects that were designed to validate and therefore consolidate U.S. rule. The combination of this administrative inadequacy and the catastrophic economic situation led to the discontent that nurtured and protected the insurgents who rose to oppose the U.S. presence.

The May 2004 transfer of power from the United States to the Iraqi Interim Government was in part an attempt to correct the administrative failures of the CPA by transferring responsibility for day-to-day implementation of policy to Iraqi administrators who would be hired and supervised by the new government. That is, the Iraqi Interim Government's job would be to construct the administrative apparatus needed to implement the policies developed and promulgated by the U.S. occupation.

The sort of policy-making oversight conferred by the IMF agreement, however, left a great deal of room to maneuver for those in charge of implementing policy. Although the DFI insulated oil policy from administrative control, the remainder of the Iraqi governmental apparatus was scheduled to be staffed and supervised by Iraqi bureaucrats. This administrative structure conferred on these administrators the possibility of altering, subverting, or even reversing policies enunciated by the United States and/or the IMF. In short, if the Iraqis constructed an elaborate bureaucracy that carried most or all of the implementation responsibility, those involved in this structure would eventually develop policy-making power.[29]

The possibility that the Iraqi government administration might develop an independent dynamic was anticipated by L. Paul Bremer's planners. CPA officials set in place an elaborate coordination system that placed U.S. functionaries in the offices of most major Iraqi administrators. Their job was to guide the development and day-to-day operation of the Iraqi government.

Colin Powell's vision of "cooperation" deserves recapitulation in this context, since it was a crystalline expression of the general principles the U.S. intended to apply in creating a client regime: "we will be creating coordinating bodies, political coordinating bodies and military-to-military coordinating bodies."[30] In other words, the Iraqi administrative apparatus was going to be under constant surveillance and supervision by representatives of the U.S. embassy.

A more detailed portrait of how this coordination would work was offered by *Wall Street Journal* reporters Yochi Dreaven and Christopher Cooper:

> As Washington prepares to hand over power, U.S. administrator L. Paul Bremer and other officials are quietly building institutions that will give the U.S. powerful levers for influencing nearly every important decision the interim government will make. In a series of edicts issued earlier this spring, Mr. Bremer's Coalition Provisional Authority created new commissions that effectively take away virtually all of the powers once held by several ministries. The CPA also . . . put in place a pair of watchdog institutions that will serve as checks on individual ministries and allow for continued U.S. oversight. Meanwhile, the CPA reiterated that coalition advisers will remain in virtually all remaining ministries after the handover.[31]

This administrative coordination was even intended to reach into local government. Speaking at the Army War College in May 2004, President Bush assured his audience that the United States would maintain "regional offices in key cities [that] will work closely with Iraqis at all levels of government."[32]

With certain sensitive sectors, notably the media, Bremer's team established independent commissions such as the DFI that effectively supervised the functioning of the agency for which they were responsible. The *Wall Street Journal* offered an unvarnished description of these commissions: "The authority to license Iraq's television stations, sanction newspapers and regulate cell phone companies was recently transferred to a commission whose members were selected by Washington. The commissioners' five-year terms stretch far beyond the planned 18-month tenure of the interim Iraqi government that will assume sovereignty on June 30."[33]

The most dramatic evidence of the administrative intentions of the U.S. occupation came in the form of the elaborate U.S. embassy dubbed "George W.'s Palace" by Iraqis, the "The Mega-Bunker of Baghdad" by *Vanity Fair,* and the "Colossus of Baghdad" by independent journalist Tom Engelhardt.[34] The largest embassy ever built by any country, the cost of the Colossus had exceeded its $600 million budget by nearly $150 million when its opening was "delayed indefinitely" in late 2007.[35] With as many as three thousand employees, the embassy was designed to provide housing for an unprecedented one thousand U.S. administrators. These officials were not part of the military effort but rather state department personnel with civilian responsibilities more consistent with a colonial administration. In fact the projected number of administrators was almost equal to the number of British administrators who oversaw colonial India in 1900, when its population was ten times that of present-day Iraq.[36]

When a report by the International Crisis Group, a Washington, D.C. think tank, asserted that most Iraqis saw the embassy's size and fortress-style architecture "as an indication of who actually exercises power in their country," reporters began for a brief moment questioning U.S. officials about its imposing size. The responses made it clear that the large embassy and U.S. presence in the Iraqi government bureaucracy were part of an effort to institutionalize Washington's influence. Embassy officials told the *Times of London* that the "size and scale of the embassy reflects very much our expectation of a strong long-term relationship with Iraq."[37] State Department spokesman Justin Higgins emphasized that this presence was not temporary, telling the Associated Press that "It's somewhat self-evident that there's going to be a fairly sizable commitment to Iraq by the U.S. government in all forms for several years."[38]

A large administrative presence by itself does not confer control over a huge collection of bureaucracies, even with an imposing presence in both Baghdad and in regional cities. These liaisons were, however, embedded in the larger control system reviewed above, including the ongoing U.S. military presence, the financial control conferred by the DFI administration of oil revenues, the ongoing IMF leverage over the economy, and the U.S. control of reconstruction finance. Taken together these tools were designed to assure that the new Iraqi government would be faithful to the principles and policies that the United States would seek to implement even after the CPA was dismantled.

Ali K. Allawi, who served as both trade and defense minister during this high-constraint period, described Iraqi government decision making under this regime as a process of rubber-stamping policies created by U.S. officials and agencies: "The situation of a sovereign government that by and large was incapable of administrating the state was camouflaged by behind-the-scenes efforts by foreign advisers to hammer out policy and programme positions covering a bewildering array of sectors. These would then be passed off as Iraqi government initiatives, often translated verbatim into a strange 'techno-Arabic', without any serious internal discussions." [39]

Sovereignty Lost

The U.S. invasion of Iraqi sought from the beginning to establish a friendly Iraqi government that would welcome ongoing Washington influence and presence, would be integrated into the global economy, and would nurture a privatized economic and noninterventionist government. The new government would, among other policies, dramatically increase oil production by transferring responsibility for the development and extraction of the country's hydrocarbon resources to the market-driven professionalism of the largest and most successful international petroleum companies, perhaps even taking Iraq out of the OPEC cartel. With their eyes on these prizes, it is not surprising that occupation officials sought to guide the appointed interim government and its elected successors toward these objectives. Nor should it come as a surprise that Iraq's new government, as it was designed and implemented in 2004, had no prospect of developing a monopoly on the means of coercion as long as the U.S. military was present and in command of Iraqi armed forces and police. The new government had only minimal influence over the disposition of its financial resources as long as IMF and U.S. personnel were the final arbiters of economic policy, and the DFI and other outsider-controlled committees oversaw the oil, communication, and other industries. And the new government had little independent administrative capacity as long as the United States maintained an elaborate coordinating structure designed to monitor and guide the government bureaucracy.

Thus the Iraqi government could not gain legitimacy with the Iraqi population. For most Iraqis the client relationship with the United States was obvious. Like the size and structure of the U.S. embassy, the elaborate control relationships were "an indication of who actually exercises power" over the military, the oil revenues, and the bureaucracy.[40] These power arrangements, which all Iraqis confronted regularly, ensured that the government could not obtain the legitimacy that is proof and substance of sovereignty.

For Iraq's neighbors these same arrangements led to their unwillingness to officially acknowledge an Iraqi government that was clearly unable to either defend itself or make binding commitments without U.S.
approval. The Gulf States therefore refused to recognize the succession of
governments in Baghdad and always sought official Washington approval
on any matters affecting their relationship with Iraq. As long as it could
not develop the three facets of sovereignty, then, the Iraqi government
was unable to gain legitimacy with either its citizens or its neighbors.

As the client government that the Bush administration sought to construct kept losing credibility, the U.S. occupation—so intimately intertwined with the failing structure—also lost credibility. Failure to produce a
successful client regime became conclusive evidence that the United States
itself lacked the capacity to rule the country. The U.S.-armed and -trained
Iraqi police, working together with the U.S. military, could not establish
even a modicum of "law and order." Quite the contrary: most cities were
more peaceful when the U.S. military and its Iraqi allies were busy elsewhere. Washington's guidelines for dispensing Iraq's oil revenues did not
produce visible repair of the country's decaying infrastructure. Indeed,
whatever improvements were made derived from local efforts and not from
the occupation or the central government. U.S. coordination with the
Iraqi bureaucracy did not produce a viable administrative presence.
Instead the atrophied Iraqi government withdrew into the insular Green
Zone in Baghdad and was visible only when various corruption scandals
hit the newspapers.

The 2004 "transfer of sovereignty" had devolved by 2008 into sovereignty lost.

Chapter Fifteen

The Creation of Shia City-States

At the point where the U.S. came in, the Shiites kind of tolerated them and even welcomed them in many instances. Over the last three years, that's changed dramatically, and right now what we see and what we've heard is that the Shiites no longer have any use for the Americans. They have built up the security forces [local militias] enough, and they've gotten control of local government, and they feel that at this point, the Americans, as well as the British down in the south . . . are causing more trouble than they're worth, and they would like the Americans to get out.

—*Los Angeles Times* **reporter Borzou Daragahi**

As the U.S. template for a dependent Iraqi government was implemented, the larger, unintended pattern of sovereignty decay was made visible in many of the newsworthy moments that found their way into the establishment media. One of these was the rise of death squads in Baghdad, which by 2006 had become a staple of mainstream news from Iraq as the bodies of hundreds then thousands of Sunnis were found dumped in prominent public places hours or days after being arrested by "men dressed in Iraq police uniforms."[1] A second symptomatic media moment occurred when U.S. military personnel raided Iraqi government detention centers, accusing them of torturing and mistreating prisoners.[2] A third occurred in late summer when Basra, the oil port at the southern tip of the country, far from the insurgency, burst into the news because of a sustained battle between the British Army and the local police.[3]

All these incidents—and many less well-publicized ones—involved the Iraqi Ministry of the Interior, which had administrative jurisdiction over the Special Forces and the police. These events appeared to be symptomatic of both an abuse of power by the ministry and the distinct autonomy of these units from control by the U.S. occupation.

A closer look at these controversies, however, reveals that while the abuse of power may have been all too real, the perception of independence was misleading and that coordination between the occupation and the Interior Ministry remained largely intact. A different kind of independence was developing—a less visible one in which various localities around the country had broken away from both the occupation and the Iraqi government, forming autonomous governing units either at city or provincial levels. These formations had a variety of relationships with the occupation and its Iraqi clients, but all of them sought to exclude both the U.S. military and the Iraqi government from their domains. In other words, as the weakness of central authority (including the occupation) became a fact of Iraqi life, local governments sought an explicit separation from the decaying center, even demanding that funds for national programs and reconstruction be handed unfettered to them for disbursement.

Several examples illustrate the ongoing but uncomfortable unity between the occupation and the Baghdad government. The death squads, though sometimes denounced by the U.S. military, had been established within the Interior Ministry early in 2005 under the supervision of U.S. State Department functionaries who had worked with such units in Central America.[4] They were designed as an extrajudicial method of capturing and killing suspected Sunni insurgents but by the middle of the year had expanded their scope of operations, most visibly as the cutting edge of ethnic cleansing.[5] The official U.S. alarm at this development conveyed the impression that this was a policy developed and enacted by the Iraqi government—or at least the Iraqi Ministry of the Interior—contrary to the policy preferences of the U.S.-led occupation.

The mainstream media portrayed participants in the death squads as members of Shia sectarian militias, notably the Badr Brigade run by the Supreme Council of the Islamic Revolution in Iraq and the Mahdi Army run by the Sadrists. But these characterizations ignored the fact that many, perhaps most, participants utilized uniforms, equipment, and even facilities of the Interior Ministry. They could not have done this without the cooperation of the Iraqi government.[6] And considering that U.S. officials had organized the original death squads and that the occupation maintained a swarm of advisors in the ministry, it is difficult to escape the conclusion that U.S. officials at least tacitly endorsed all the activities of the death squads. This view is strengthened when we realize that their brutal campaign against Sunni residents of Baghdad was consistent with the U.S.

military campaign against the Sunni insurgency, which also targeted all fighting-age men in communities where the insurgency was strong. The fact that the death squads operated without any significant government intervention is best seen not as a sign of Iraqi government independence, but rather as yet another symptom of the fact that the Iraqi government's activities were almost always consistent with U.S. policy.[7]

The official outrage registered by U.S. officials when the mainstream media revealed the existence of rogue detention centers where Iraqi security personnel were abusing prisoners suggested that the Iraqi government might indeed have acted independently of U.S. control in maintaining these torture facilities. The outrage, however, had a hypocritical ring, since the occupation itself had been accused repeatedly of similar abuses toward its more than twenty thousand prisoners.[8] The hypocrisy was deepened when news emerged that U.S. forces had been central to "recruiting, training, supporting, and directing the forces responsible for these atrocities."[9] Occupation officials told the *Los Angeles Times* that they had "known of the police abuses for years but want the Iraqis to solve the problem."[10]

The significance of the furor therefore lay in the decision to force a change in Iraqi government policy, and—more to the point—in the rapidity with which the U.S. military was able to impose its will on Iraqi security forces. In only a few days the detention centers were reformed, and the occupation announced a drastic change in the structure and functioning of Interior Ministry forces. The headlines in U.S. newspapers just after the U.S. press broke the story made U.S. dominance clear: "G.I.s to Increase Supervision of Iraqi Police" (*New York Times*),[11] "U.S. to Restrict Iraqi Police" (*Los Angeles Times*),[12] and "U.S. Troops to Mentor Iraqi Police" (*Washington Post*).[13] The subsequently implemented plan increased the number of U.S. troops assigned to Iraqi police and special service units by a factor of ten, with as many as five hundred U.S. soldiers working together with a brigade of twenty-five hundred or so Iraqis, with as always—ultimate command residing in U.S. officers.[14] This episode exemplified the tight control exercised by the occupation over the policing functions of the Iraqi government.

At about the same time, another incident further highlighted the inability of the Iraqi government to act on its own. Abdul Aziz Hakim, the leading figure in the Supreme Council, the dominant political party of the government, complained bitterly that the United States was preventing the Iraqi government from mounting an aggressive campaign against Sunni insurgents, apparently because such a campaign would interfere with U.S. efforts in the same areas. He told *Washington Post* reporter Ellen Knickmeyer: "The ministries of Interior and Defense want to carry out some operations to clean out some areas [in Anbar province]. There were plans that should have been implemented months ago, but American officials and forces rejected them."[15]

This comment makes clear that the Iraqis could not undertake autonomous action even when they sought to use only Iraqi personnel. Any significant military or police action was routinely vetted by U.S. military leaders, and U.S. decisions were final even if the highest Iraqi officials vehemently disagreed with them.

More significantly, Hakim's complaint pointed to the larger impotence of both Iraqi and U.S. forces. His call for more drastic measures than the United States would sanction was symptomatic of the degree to which the coordinated efforts of the U.S. military and the Iraqis had failed to prevent insurgent strongholds in Anbar province from becoming independent of the government—a blunt declaration that there was no governmental or occupation sovereignty in Anbar province, or in other areas where the insurgency was strong.

Finally, consider the draconian response of the British to their confrontation with the Basra police. The precipitating incident involved two British soldiers disguised as local citizens, who were arrested by local police in a car equipped with explosive devices usually utilized by terrorists. The British military command demanded their release and local authorities refused. British troops mounted an offensive that involved a sustained assault on local government buildings and a firefight before they successfully freed the detainees. They then announced that they would disband the entire 25,000-man Basra police force and "replace it with a new military-style unit capable of maintaining law and order."[16] They expected so much resistance that their plan for enforcing this reform involved massing almost all the British military forces stationed at that time in the south of Iraq. To generate this show of force they abandoned a long-standing plan "that could have seen UK forces withdrawn by [mid-2006]. Instead, it now seems certain Prime Minister Tony Blair will have to keep British troops in the country until 2007 at the earliest."[17] This delay did in fact occur, but even with the troops they had, the British were unable to implement their plan to disband the local police force.

These events were indisputable evidence of the decay of occupation-government sovereignty. In Basra, far away from Baghdad, center of death squads, or Anbar province, center of the Sunni insurgency, an independent local Shia government was at loggerheads with the British Army and the central Baghdad government around a whole host of issues. The Basra provincial council insisted on regulating (and siphoning off part of) the oil that flowed through its port, controlling whether the electricity produced at its power station was shipped to other regions, and asserting its right to arrest British soldiers (thus producing the incident that triggered the crisis). In asserting these sovereign rights the council regularly refused to honor demands from either the Baghdad government or British military commanders, using the police force as part of their resistance. The British plan to dismantle the Basra police force was thus part of a larger effort to rein in what had become a semi-sovereign government in the richest oil province in the country. This local government was reminiscent of the city-states that comprised ancient Greece, in its demand that it have the final say over nearly all the decisions that impacted its citizens.

Unlike the Greek city-states, however, Basra had to contend with an occupying army and a central government that contested its sovereignty. These events and many others during 2005 and 2006, pointed to the nature of this no-win contest. The daily struggle, however, meant that the Baghdad government and the military occupation that was central to its claims had little capacity to control and administer events in Basra or other predominantly Shia provinces. Nor did it have much capacity to assert administrative or military control in the predominantly Sunni areas where the insurgency flourished. Even in Baghdad its authority was at best problematic; the ethnic dislocations that swept through the city during 2006 took place largely in neighborhoods where antigovernment Sunni militias had established a dominant presence. All over Iraq, except during specific times when occupation troops were active in the area, local communities were governed by ethno-religious political groupings whose actions and intentions were antithetical to the occupation and resentful of the neoliberal policies that had created widespread economic distress.[18]

To understand how the Iraqi political system lost its sovereign center, we must consider each region of the country separately.

Shia Fundamentalism Dominates the Iraqi South

With the exception of Karbala and Najaf, the occupation treated the southern cities of Iraq, where the population was overwhelmingly Shia, with a lighter touch.[19] After the CPA disbanded the Hussein regime, these cities, like others all around the country, were left with no institutional or police structures. The CPA assigned its military forces to protect oil facilities and search Sunni areas for remnants of the defeated army, while the British, given control of four mainly Shia southern provinces, took a distinctly hands-off approach, at first making no systematic attempt to reestablish a state or police structure. A crime wave swept the cities and it was left to the individual provinces and communities to reestablish order.

This neglect affected the whole country except in the Kurdish north, where a preexisting governing structure with its own armed forces seamlessly continued an autonomous existence.[20] In the rest of Iraq the vacuum of power was filled by ad hoc governments and militias affiliated with local tribes and/or mosques, the two overlapping institutions that were the center of Iraqi civil society. The arrangements differed between cities and between ethnic enclaves, but they generally attended to three broad sets of issues, offering a minimal set of (poorly funded) social services such as food baskets and infrastructural repair, developing and enforcing a rigorous Shari'a (religious) court system that adjudicated personal issues based on clerical interpretation of Islamic law, and assigning police functions to locally recruited militias loosely controlled by tribal or clerical leaders. In Sunni areas the development of these local governments was delayed, interrupted, or ended by U.S. military incursions aimed at rooting out both the militias and their tribal-clerical leadership, which politically and militarily opposed the U.S. presence and policies.[21]

With the exception of two major battles in the Karbala and Najaf areas, neither U.S. nor British forces mounted major military drives to assert control of the predominantly Shia cities in the south. In these areas, therefore, the newly formed local institutions became the de facto government, and the January 2005 elections allowed the leaders of these institutions to gain official control of the newly established provincial councils and other elected bodies. In early 2005 London *Telegraph* reporters Jack Fairweather and Haider Samad commented on the results of this process: "A silent and largely undocumented social revolution has transformed the Shia-dominated south of Iraq into a virtual Islamic state in the two years since the US army invaded."[22]

This process extended to Sadr City, the vast Shia slum in Baghdad, which was dominated by the Sadrist movement led by young "firebrand" cleric Muqtada Al Sadr and effectively policed by their militia, the Mahdi Army. *New York Times* reporter Edward Wong described the embrace of the Mahdis by Sadr City culture and—by extension—the role of these militias throughout the Shia south: "For many poor Shiites, and even some in middle-class enclaves ... the Mahdi Army is a defender of the faith and a populist force. Its members have permeated every aspect of Iraqi life, from the uniformed police forces to student groups at Baghdad's campuses, where they enforce strict Islamist codes, like head scarves for women."[23]

What Happened in Basra?

The city of Basra, the southern oil hub and second-largest city in Iraq, illustrates the origins and character of locally based power in Shia areas, its problematic relationship to the occupation and its Iraqi allies in Baghdad, and the ways in which this contentious relationship contributed to the decay of sovereignty.[24]

The British, whose troops were placed in control of Basra after the fall of the Hussein regime, initially adopted a laissez-faire approach to local politics and problems throughout the Shia areas of the south. For the first year after the collapse of the Hussein regime, they spent most of their time in bases outside the city. The city was almost devoid of the checkpoints and convoys that disrupted daily life in the Sunni areas assigned to U.S. troops, and the British did not mount the aggressive armored patrols and violent home invasions that played such an important role in generating Sunni rebellion. When they did patrol inside the city, they walked through the neighborhoods without armored vehicles, wearing berets instead of shielded helmets and flak jackets.[25] This strategy avoided the sort of provocation that had set Fallujah and other Sunni cities onto the path toward active rebellion, but it did not resolve the power vacuum created when the CPA dissolved the police force, dismantled the national government, and shuttered all government-owned businesses that were not oil-related. As in other Iraqi cities, local civil society leaders sought to fill this power and economic vacuum.

Various Shia factions sought dominance using a combination of political organizing (including patronage and social welfare programs), the provision of law and order (by organizing mosque- and tribal-based militias), and the liberal application of violent repression against contesting parties. By mid-2004 the Supreme Council for the Islamic Revolution in Iraq (the same group that would soon control the Interior Ministry) established an uncomfortable hegemony over the city, alternately aided and opposed by the Fadhila, a local fundamentalist group. Muqtada Al Sadr's Mahdi Army, though weak at first, aggressively organized in the neighborhoods, gaining influence as the occupation continued. All three major factions and fifteen or so smaller groups claimed specific parts of the city and its environs as their own, and sent their militia members into the police force. By fall 2005 an Iraqi government official estimated that 90 percent of the local police were loyal primarily to local leaders rather than the national government that technically employed them.[26] Neither the national government nor the occupation had an administrative or law enforcement presence in the city.

The dominant groups were ensconced as elected officials by late 2005. The economic and social integration of the country, however, severely limited the local government's ability to impact the major quality-of-life issues that faced the city. For example, an ambitious project to decontaminate the city's rivers had made no progress by late 2007, frustrated by both lack of local resources and upstream sources of pollution.[27] The local regime instead focused attention on rigorously enforcing its religious agenda, which involved the application of fundamentalist Shari'a law to the Basra community. The London *Telegraph* reported that "in Basra's courthouses, Shari'a law is now routinely used in place of civil codes. Politicians work with the tacit approval of the Shia clergy and refer many important decisions to religious leaders."[28] The city, which had been a center of secular and cosmopolitan culture, was transformed into a showcase for traditional Shia cultural values. Alcohol disappeared from stores, the nightlife of the city vanished, and women only appeared in public with escorts and wearing scarves. A deadly incident in which a gender-mixed group of picnicking students was attacked by Fadhila activists gave international publicity to the change in Basra culture.[29] In late 2007 the Basra police chief reported that "at least 40 women had been killed during the previous five months," mainly by Shari'a vigilantes.[30]

The local Basra government could extract few resources from the national government or from the occupation's reconstruction budget and did not have the administrative or monetary wherewithal to manage many of the economic problems itself. Services previously provided by the national government, which in Iraq included provision of medical supplies and infrastructural maintenance of all sorts, were therefore further degraded.[31] These failures ultimately motivated the provincial government to institute measures designed to acquire more power and resources. Various forms of tax collection developed, including extralegal ones. The local government resolved to save all electricity produced in Basra, the largest output in the country, for local use rather then sending it into the national grid.[32] Most dramatically, various local groups and the local government began siphoning off part of the oil that passed through the city, and demanded that these activities be made legal. In February 2006 fifteen thousand workers and engineers in the state-owned Southern Oil Company wrote to Baghdad demanding that the company's entire operation be placed under "an energy council operating directly within the provincial government of Basra."[33]

In late 2005 the British sought to reverse these and other developments with military intervention. It was this new aggressiveness that led to the battle between local police and British troops and to the British decision to disband the police force. In response the Basra provincial council voted to stop cooperating with the British on all matters of local policy, setting the stage for many months of armed confrontation.[34]

During much of 2006 the British tried to pacify Basra militarily, using the strategies and tactics that the U.S. military had been applying in Sunni areas of Iraq.[35] Before this operation there had been a high but not intolerable level of violence in the city, caused by substantial criminal activities that were not fully suppressed by local militias and police, ongoing friction, and occasional battles among contending parties. The new British offensive, given the racist title "Operation Sinbad" by British commanders, triggered a period of far greater violence—"the deadliest period" since the initial invasion.[36]

The British utilized the full force of their armored vehicles, ordered their soldiers to exchange their berets for flak jackets and helmets, and invaded the strongholds of their various adversaries. The Mahdi Army, which had been particularly aggressive during the previous year in sniping at British patrols and setting roadside bombs aimed at armored vehicles, was the main target. In fighting the Mahdis and other groups, the British used artillery and missiles to attack buildings harboring the insurgents, and the resistance responded with rocket-propelled grenades (RPGs). Street and community life in the city became untenable: residents fled the city or waited behind closed doors, hoping that their homes would not be hit.

The British offensive also triggered far greater violence among the contending factions. With some twenty militias active in the city, British efforts to subdue one group provided tempting opportunities for other groups to claim new territory or members. A cycle of attack and retribution began escalating, turning many neighborhoods into war zones with several different parties, including the British, seeking dominance.

Operation Sinbad created a crescendo of violence in which the British become only one of many contending parties. Lieutenant Simon Brown, commander of the British Second Battalion, described the situation as a kind of war of all against all: "We are in a tribal society in Basra and we are, in effect, one of these tribes. As long as we are here the others will attack us because we are the most influential tribe."[37] This image perhaps better than any other describes the devolution of the victorious invaders of 2003 into just another contender for power. In Basra sovereignty had simply disappeared.

Toward the end of 2006, the British gave up their efforts to pacify the city.[38] In September, after two months of regular RPG attacks, they abandoned their headquarters in the Basra Palace and retreated to their bases outside the city. Four months later they stopped all patrols into the city. In August 2007 they officially withdrew from the province. Although the U.S. and British military commands insisted that these withdrawals were signs of success, the Basrans treated them as an "ignominious defeat" of the British by the local militias.[39]

Perhaps more important, during the year of warfare, "the militias lost little or nothing of their authority," and quickly reclaimed local leadership. Because they were the chief target of the British, the Sadrist Mahdi Army could claim to be the key architects of the victory, and therefore emerged as a much stronger force inside the city.[40]

As soon as the British left, Basra experienced a dramatic drop in violence, particularly in those areas where the British had been most active. Reuters reporter Aref Mohammed visited a neighborhood near the Basra Palace just after the British abandoned it, and found that local residents had "begun strolling the waterfront streets again." Housewife Kariya Salman told him, "The situation these days is better. We were living in hell . . . the area is calm since their withdrawal."[41]

After the British departure the city returned to an unsettled condition. Within a few weeks the contending parties negotiated a cease-fire of their own, redividing the city into spheres of influence based on the new balance of forces, with the Sadrists gaining important ground. The various factions continued to struggle with the larger issues of the decaying infrastructure and the dormant economy without the resources to address them. They renewed their confrontation with the national government over distribution of electrical power and oil and sought resources to address the many issues facing the city. And soon enough they renewed their occasionally violent struggle for political control, with the Sadrists continually expanding their areas of domination mainly at the expense of the Supreme Council, which suffered from its association with the hated central government.

Through all of this, the national government in Iraq had been little more than a figurehead presence. During the military confrontations, a contingent of government troops had entered Basra and quickly retreated. After the British withdrawal the national government denounced the local Basra government for hoarding its electricity, but could do nothing to reverse the decision. For many months it was simply accepted that Basra would remain autonomous.

In early 2008 United Press International reporter Ben Lando, one of the most informed Western observers of Iraqi politics, reported on the completion of successful negotiations among the local contenders: "Last year ended on what seemed to be a high note. A week before the British handed over the security file to Iraqi officials; the leading political and religious parties signed an agreement on the division of power and rights in a relatively sovereign Basra."[42] The national government was not a party to either the final British withdrawal from the province or the new agreement among local powerholders.

By the spring of 2008 Basra's autonomy had become an active threat to the occupation and its Baghdad allies.[43] With local elections looming in October, it was virtually certain that the Sadrists would claim control of the provincial government, use it as a platform to energize their campaign to replace the pro-U.S. national leadership, and assert their demand for complete U.S. withdrawal. In the fall of 2007 U.S. military commanders had begun planning a U.S.-Iraqi assault on the city. In March 2008 Iraqi units took the lead, with logistics, artillery, air support, and advisors provided by the U.S. military. The assault focused on Sadrist-controlled areas of the city but was quickly repulsed. As many as 30 percent of the government forces refused to fight, and the remaining units were routed or surrounded by the Mahdi Army fighters. U.S. troops moved into the city to rescue the surrounded units while U.S. airpower pounded Sadrist neighborhoods with 30mm cannons, laser-guided cannons and up to 2,000-pound bombs. With the battle still undecided, Baghdad officials called on Iran to mediate a cease-fire. The settlement allowed the government to maintain a military presence in the city but left the Sadrists in control of large sections of the city. So they continued to threaten to take official control of the provincial council when the elections arrived. Local governance remained in the hands of local leaders. This joint U.S.-Iraqi effort to subdue the Basra city-state, like that of its British predecessors, was unsuccessful.

City-States in the Shia South

Basra's history echoed across the southern cities and provinces of Iraq. In Maysan province, home of the Marsh Arabs, a twenty-five-year-old rebellion led by the Sadrists against the Hussein regime continued unabated when the British took over.[44] Since the British were inactive initially, there was some disruption as local frictions expressed themselves, but the area was generally peaceful. Later British attempts to gain control led to ferocious fighting. At one point there were battles between the British and local fighters in the capital city of Amara for 250 consecutive days. In these and other cases throughout the south, the Iraqi national government made no attempt to influence local events or, when it did, had its meager efforts forcibly rebuffed.[45] In one typical instance a police chief appointed by the Baghdad government sought to use the local police to dislodge the local Sadrist leadership. He was promptly assassinated.[46]

The U.S. response was similarly detached. The long-running guerrilla war waged by Marsh Arabs against Saddam Hussein had led the Baathist regime to drain the marshes that had provided economic sustenance for the province, driving tens of thousands of Maysan residents to Baghdad and other cities. After the invasion the local guerrillas had blown up the dams and dikes and reflooded their historic land only to discover that a host of problems needed attention before the area could become economically viable. Once the area became a stronghold for the Mahdi Army, U.S. funding for restoration was discontinued and money was reallocated to other projects.[47] As the local community struggled on its own to restore the land, occupation officials, like their Iraqi clients, remained far away and uninterested in the Baghdad Green Zone. Like Basra, Maysan province was becoming a city-state.

Across the Shia-dominated south, even in areas where the British made no effort to pacify obstreperous local governments, relations with the Green Zone degenerated over time as economic issues plaguing the localities intensified. Each area had specific issues, like Basra's oil facilities and Maysan's marsh projects, but they all shared general problems, like the inadequate electrical grid, contaminated water system, degenerating medical facilities, and failing schools.[48] These multiple crises led local and provincial governments to make unfulfillable demands on both the Iraqi government and the U.S.-led occupation, which then led to overt friction over the neoliberal policies enacted by the United States and its Iraqi allies. Local governments seeking to revive their local economies demanded that shuttered state-owned enterprises be reopened to create jobs and commerce, thus challenging the privatization campaign. They insisted that food and fuel subsidies be restored, maintained, or increased to ease the economic crisis, thus challenging the IMF-mandated reduction in government subsidies, and they demanded that state protection for local agricultural products be reinstated to vivify local agriculture, thus challenging U.S. plans for free trade. All localities sought to access large chunks of oil revenues for local reconstruction, thus placing them at odds with the system by which oil policy was overseen by the IMF and administered by the Development Fund for Iraq, the Bremer-appointed body that consisted of nine foreigners and one Iraqi.[49]

Tangled together with these economic issues was the question of Iran. Though the Sadrists and some other Shia groups had historically strained relations with Iran, most of the Shia political formations, most notably the Supreme Council that dominated the ruling coalition in the national government, had long-standing friendly relations with Iraq's closest neighbor. All groups had an unwavering commitment to establishing political, cultural, and economic relations to the only Shia regime in the Middle East.

The yearly visits of millions of Iranian pilgrims to various Shia shrines in Iraq, revived after the fall of the Saddam Hussein regime, gave initial substance to these relationships. They were further enhanced as local merchants renewed trade relationships across the Iranian border that had been dormant during the decades of antagonism between the two countries. In Basra the liquor dealers, unable to sell imported North American alcohol due to newly introduced Shari'a law, smuggled their goods across the border to sell on the Iranian black market. Local militias established training and supply relationships with Iran, creating further antagonism between local governing groups and the Green Zone, which kept complaining about Iranian support for its insurgent enemies.[50]

The Iraqi national government, in a rare act of independence from its U.S. sponsors, gave official support to the increasingly dense economic relationships when, starting in 2006, it signed a series of trade and economic agreements with Iran. These took on greater meaning as the increase in oil prices strengthened the Iranian economy and allowed it to offer tangible economic aid—targeted to the southern cities—including an airport and other capital construction in the shrine cities of Karbala and Najaf. The national government, however, was tightly constrained by explicit U.S. directives about the nature of these relationships, creating yet another motivation for local governments and civil groups to forge their own cross-border relationships. These Iranian relationships were one of the main vectors that led to a movement spearheaded by the Supreme Council to establish an autonomous region in the Shia south.[51]

In early 2006 *Los Angeles Times* reporter Borzou Daragahi described the situation in the Shia south as uniformly hostile to the occupation:

> At the point where the U.S. came in, the Shiites kind of tolerated them and even welcomed them in many instances. Over the last three years, that's changed dramatically, and right now what we see and what we've heard is that the Shiites no longer have any use for the Americans. They have built up the security forces [local militia] enough, and they've gotten control of local government, and they feel that at this point, the Americans, as well as the British down in the south . . . are causing more trouble than they're worth, and they would like the Americans to get out.[52]

The decline of sovereignty in the Green Zone was not offset by an equal and opposite rise of local sovereignty claimed by the city-states in the predominantly Shia south. Instead it conferred a kind of quasi-sovereignty upon these local entities, which were able to provide a modicum of law and order (when the occupation was not actively trying to conquer them) but were unable to address long-term needs in a consistent and orderly way. By 2007 the situation in southern Iraq had fallen into an unstable stalemate. Local administrations, though often riven with internal divisions and dependent on militias for police enforcement, offered reasonably stable daily government.[53] People could safely shop for food or clothes if they had money, drive around the city and province if they could afford fuel, and feed their families if they could find a job. Local governments could not, however, make significant progress against the larger crises, including the decaying infrastructure, the 30 percent to 70 percent unemployment, the absence of funds or expertise for reconstruction. The declining conditions therefore set in motion protests and claims against these local governments that undermined their legitimacy, while also undermining the legitimacy of the distant governments located in Baghdad's Green Zone. The escalating crises led to ongoing instability and ongoing displacement as individuals, families, and communities confronted increasingly serious problems without any government that could claim the wherewithal to credibly address them.

Chapter Sixteen

Semisovereign Kurdistan

Kurdish leaders have inserted more than 10,000 of their militia members into Iraqi army divisions in northern Iraq to lay the groundwork to swarm south, seize the oil-rich city of Kirkuk and possibly half of Mosul, Iraq's third-largest city, and secure the borders of an independent Kurdistan.

—Knight Ridder reporter Tom Lasseter

The original plans for the 2003 invasion of Iraq had called for a large force to enter Iraq from Turkey, drive southward through Iraqi Kurdistan, and meet the northward-moving main force in or around Baghdad.[1] These plans had to be altered in early 2003 when the Turkish parliament voted against allowing U.S. military units to gather inside its borders, the most visible evidence of the resistance among Middle Eastern states to the invasion.

The Turkish refusal meant little in terms of the ultimate assault on the Baathist regime, since Baghdad fell quickly and without sustained resistance. But it took on special significance for later political and military developments because it was the first—and perhaps most telling—indication of the autonomy that Kurdistan would enjoy in post-Hussein Iraq.

In place of the large contingent of forces that might have passed through the north, the U.S. military delegated the liberation of that area to the peshmerga, the one-hundred-thousand-strong Kurdish militia that had been formed several decades earlier and had fought against Saddam Hussein for many years. With the help of U.S. Special Forces, the peshmerga performed its assigned task effortlessly, reflecting the fact that the region had been politically insulated from the Baathists since the end of the 1991 Gulf War.

At the end of that earlier war, President George H. W. Bush had decided against directly ousting Saddam Hussein. He had instead invited the Kurds in the north and the Shia in the south to revolt against the regime.[2] Both groups took up his suggestion. In the south, Hussein utilized his elite Republican Guard and the surviving elements in his air force to attack Shia strongholds, killing tens of thousands and ultimately defeating the rebellion. In Kurdistan however the U.S. Air Force imposed a no-fly zone that prevented the Baathist regime from using its airpower or its ground troops to quell the revolt. With this assist the Kurds were able to expel the Baathist military and dismantle its administrative apparatus in the three provinces where they predominated, though the region remained economically integrated with Iraq. The two (often warring) Kurdish nationalist groups, the Kurdish Democratic Party and the Patriotic Union of Kurdistan, jointly ruled the region in an unstable coalition during the last ten years of the Hussein regime.

The peshmerga, which had been a guerrilla force before the Gulf War, became the official militia of the Kurdish regional government and the dominant military presence in the region. As part of their responsibility for fighting in the northern and western areas of the country during the 2003 U.S. invasion, they ranged outward from the Kurdish provinces and expanded their sphere of influence. When the initial fighting ended, the Kurds were an occupying army in a number of key cities outside their previous domain. The most significant was Kirkuk, a key commercial hub with a diverse ethnic history, the northern oil capital of Iraq, and, according to the Kurds, historically and demographically the capital of Iraqi Kurdistan. They also became a dominant force in Mosul, the third-largest city in the country, which became a center of sectarian violence as Kurds, Arabs, and Turkmen struggled for domination.[3]

Autonomous Kurdistan

Once the Hussein regime was deposed, law and order in the Kurdish regions was maintained by members of the peshmerga, which was absorbed whole into the nascent Iraqi national army. While this technically placed the peshmerga under the command of U.S. military commanders and—later on—the Iraqi government, it remained loyal to the Kurdish leadership and was still governed by officers who had led it before the invasion. As *Washington Post* reporters Anthony Shadid and Steve Fainaru put it, these forces were only "nominally under the authority of the U.S.-

backed Iraqi army."[4] Very few U.S. military units ventured into Kurdistan, and in fact peshmerga troops, intact with their Kurdish leadership,
were soon being recruited for counterinsurgency efforts in Sunni and
even Shia hot spots.

In the meantime the two dominant Kurdish political parties continued their political leadership in the three Kurdish provinces, seeking to
protect and extend the autonomy they had achieved under Saddam
Hussein. The regional government—divided though it was between the
two leading parties—continued to function even after the CPA dismantled the Iraqi state, so the region was therefore protected from the economic fallout of neoliberal reforms. As a consequence Kurdistan
experienced little of the looting, administrative chaos, and sudden unemployment that plagued other regions of the country.

The most significant early symptom of the degree of autonomy that
the Kurds retained was the unilateral development of the oil fields within
their domain, described by *Der Spiegel* reporter Bernhard Zand in mid-
2006: "The Kurds are already pursuing a largely independent oil policy
with almost no regard for the central government in Baghdad. Some of
the Turkish, Canadian and Norwegian companies drilling for oil in
Kurdish northern Iraq signed contracts directly with the regional administration in Arbil, bypassing the oil minister in Baghdad."[5]

Despite early alarm and ongoing opposition from the central Iraq government and the occupation, the Kurds continued to negotiate these contracts, including a particularly controversial agreement with Hunt Oil, a
Houston-based firm with strong ties to the Bush administration.[6]

These contracts and the internal stability that facilitated them suggested that the Kurds were achieving a degree of sovereignty unmatched
either by the Iraqi national government or by the city-states in the Shia
south.[7] By early 2008 Kurdistan had signed fifteen contracts with twenty
international companies while the Iraqi government had failed to complete a single agreement, despite energetic effort and the active participation of the U.S. occupation.[8]

These failures were in large part a consequence of deteriorating security in non-Kurdish Iraq. Oil companies refused to risk financial and other
resources in locations where their investment, workers, or machinery
might be in jeopardy. This problem was so enduring that in spring 2008
the occupation assigned commanding general David Petraeus to "get the
ball rolling" with "senior leaders in the corporate world," attempting to
convince them that non-Kurdish Iraq was a secure investment.[9]

Security, however, was only the most visible issue that prevented the
Iraqi government from successful negotiation with international compa-

nies. According to the *Financial Times*, oil company reluctance also derived from "the weakness of the central government and its patchy control over the southern part of the country, home to 80 percent of proven oil reserves."[10] This reluctance highlights the contrast with the Kurdish provinces. The Kurds had a stronger administrative presence throughout their domain, with no question about their physical control of the oil reserves. The "patchy control in the south" referred particularly to the obstreperous local leadership of Basra province, which—inspired by Kurdish success—was seeking to negotiate its own unilateral oil contracts.[11]

The Battle over Kirkuk

The successful negotiation of oil contracts signaled that Kurdistan stood on the cusp of independence—so close in fact that some foreign oil companies, though not the major multinational firms, were willing to trust the region's ability to enter into binding international contracts. In the meantime the issue of Kurdish independence had become one of the central issues of Iraqi politics, with the city of Kirkuk at the center of the friction. While most Iraqis were willing to accept that Kurdistan would retain the political autonomy it had achieved under the last years of the Hussein regime, there was considerable controversy over full independence, particularly because such proposals inevitably included the Kurdish demand that Kirkuk be incorporated into (and made the capital of) their domain.

Historically Kirkuk was a polyglot city including very large contingents of Turkmen and Kurds, significant but smaller concentrations of Assyrians and Christians, and a smattering of Sunni and Shia Arabs.[12] Because of its importance as an oil hub and commercial center, various earlier regimes had driven out Turkmen and Kurds and sent colonizing Arabs to take their place. After the Gulf War led to the establishment of autonomous Kurdistan, Saddam Hussein accelerated these efforts, displacing more than one hundred thousand Kurds in an effort to "Arabize" the city.[13] By 2003, after many decades of ethnic replacement, these efforts had produced not only a substantial number of Arab settlers, but also large numbers of Kurdish and Turkmen refugees living uncomfortably in surrounding areas.

The Kurdish campaign to annex Kirkuk became a violent point of controversy almost immediately among various ethnic groups within the city. The main friction at first was between Kurds and Arabs. The Kurds sought repatriation of all Kurdish exiles and the expulsion of Arab colonists, even those born in the city. Turkmen and Assyrians allied with the Arabs because they saw the Kurdish efforts as ethnic cleansing, expecting that they too would soon be expelled. Turkey—defending its own interests as well as those of the ethnically related Turkmen—repeatedly threatened to intervene.[14]

The Iraqi national government, with the approval of the United States, proposed to settle this friction with a December 2007 referendum in Kirkuk in which local citizens would vote whether or not to merge into Kurdistan. Subsequent events, however, underscored the irrelevance of this and other decisions made in the Green Zone about this dispute. The Kurds, whose military dominance of the city was soon augmented by a political victory in provincial elections, gained control over the local police, giving them the same kind of autonomy that local Shia leadership had achieved in southern cities. Echoing his counterpart in Basra, General Tuhan Yusuf Abdel-Rahman, the Baghdad-appointed chief of the Kirkuk police, told *Washington Post* reporters Steve Fainaru and Anthony Shadid, "The main problem is that the loyalty of the police is to the [Kurdish political] parties and not the police force. . . . They'll obey the parties' orders and disobey us."[15]

Another element of the Kurdish effort to annex Kirkuk was the return of Kurds displaced by the Hussein regime and repatriated by the Kurdish-controlled local government. By late 2004 as many as one hundred thousand Kurds had arrived in a city of one million that had no ability to absorb them. Tales of misery among newly arrived families, relegated to shantytowns "just as wretched as those they left" in refugee camps in Kurdistan, helped to fuel the efforts of the provincial government to expel descendents of the Arab colonists, many of whom had been born and raised in the city.[16]

By the end of 2005 these measures had provoked violent opposition that threatened to make Kirkuk the focal point of a civil war. The resistance centered on the Turkmen who, like the Kurds, had been targeted by the Hussein regime's ethnic cleansing. Unlike the Kurds, however, they had no institutional support to repatriate the Turkmen refugees scattered around the surrounding region. Afraid that Kurdish annexation would lead to their expulsion from the city or from its economic and political life, they formed an alliance with the less numerous Sunni Arabs—who in turn had numerous contacts to the ongoing Sunni resistance in nearby cities. By mid-2005 this opposition constituted a serious threat to the Kurdish program, and they began protesting against what they considered to be state terrorism by the Kurds.

In June 2005 the *Washington Post* reported on a "confidential State Department cable" that detailed a pattern of "extra-judicial detentions," which were "part of a 'concerted and widespread initiative' by Kurdish political parties 'to exercise authority in Kirkuk in an increasingly provocative manner.'" [17] The *Post* reported that "police and security units, forces led by Kurdish political parties . . . have abducted hundreds of minority Arabs and Turkmens in this intensely volatile city and spirited them to prisons in Kurdish-held northern Iraq." [18] This campaign, directed at those protesting the impending annexation of Kirkuk, augmented the ongoing efforts to force Arabs out of Kirkuk and make room for repatriated Kurds.

The Iraqi government had no resources or authority to intervene on either side of the growing violence. It had no functioning military or police in Kirkuk, since both were under Kurdish control. It had no administrative apparatus; the local government, insofar as it functioned, had been constructed and controlled by the Kurds. And it had no national institutions that could intervene in the various disputes. The legal structure that was supposed to adjudicate claims of Arabs and Turkmen and Kurds concerning housing and residence never began to function. Eligibility for election was to be decided by local officials appointed by the Kurds, and the "extra-judicial detentions" were located in Kurdistan, where the government had no presence.

The United States had only a marginally greater ability to impact the conflict, save a major military campaign. Local government policy in Kirkuk was determined by the interaction between the Kurdish-controlled government and the various insurgent groups, with the United States maintaining just a small group of military advisers attached to the Kurdish forces. As in the south, only the occupation's overwhelming military strength could generate leverage against the local Kurdish-controlled government. [19]

By mid-June 2005 the lines were firmly drawn between the two sides. Hamid Afandi, a leader of the Kurdistan Democratic Party, articulated the Kurdish side to Knight Ridder reporter Tom Lasseter: "Kirkuk is Kurdistan; it does not belong to the Arabs. . . . If we can resolve this by talking, fine, but if not, then we will resolve it by fighting." [20] Lasseter, one of most informed reporters in Iraq, summarized the Kurdish posture: "Kurdish leaders have inserted more than 10,000 of their militia members into Iraqi army divisions in northern Iraq to lay the groundwork to swarm south, seize the oil-rich city of Kirkuk and possibly half of Mosul, Iraq's third-largest city, and secure the borders of an independent Kurdistan." [21]

The other side was expressed by Aissa Ramadan, a Kirkuk Arab whose eighty-seven-year-old father had been taken—along with his three brothers and two sons—in an "extra-judicial detention." He told reporters Fainaru and Shadid: "If you could see our house on any day, you'd see that we're having funerals without the corpses. . . . Children are looking for their fathers, wives don't know the fate of their husbands, and mothers are dying 40 times a day." Ramadan then uttered a call to arms: "Tomorrow, I could recruit the entire tribe. . . . I could block the street in Kirkuk and kidnap 40 Kurds. When you lose patience, you can do anything."[22]

By the end of 2005 Kirkuk had become an ongoing battlefront replete with car bombs, attacks on police stations, and the full complement of IEDs. In mid-February 2006 insurgents assassinated the police chief.[23]

The fighting in Kirkuk waxed and waned during the next two years. As the date for the annexation referendum drew near, it became clear that the vote would settle nothing and might make the situation worse, and it was postponed indefinitely. As in so many other areas of Iraqi life, the status quo became one of endemic disequilibrium.

Sovereign Kurdistan?

When the Iraqi constitution was crafted during 2005, Kurdish autonomy was enshrined in Iraq's fundamental law by allowing for a form of federalism that included a guarantee that 17 percent of the government's revenues would be delivered unconditionally to the Kurdish regional government.[24] At the same time Kurdish leaders were integrated into the newly formed national government, assuming the presidency as well as key cabinet positions. This combination of integration and separation embodied perfectly the ambiguous historical and contemporary relationship of Kurdistan to the Iraqi nation.[25]

The issue of just how sovereign the Kurdish provinces were was spotlighted by tensions with Turkey, which spilled over into military warfare in late 2007.[26] The Kurdish provinces within Iraq had long maintained ethnic and political ties with the twenty million Kurds in Iran to the east and Turkey to the north and west. This affinity also implied political and military alliances with Kurdish movements in those countries, notably the Kurdish Workers Party (PKK), which had been fighting the Turkish government since 1980.

The Turkish government kept a close eye on all developments within Kurdish Iraq, fearing they would strengthen the PKK and nationalist demands among its Kurdish minority. Turkey's most consistent public posture was adamant opposition to full Kurdish independence, but they had threatened intervention around any number of issues, including a promise of military support for the Turkmen minority in Kirkuk and Mosul. One of these issues was the PKK's use of the mountainous country just inside the Iraqi border as a safe rear area for its military operations inside Turkey. Turkey's decision to invade northern Kurdistan was justified as an effort to suppress these incursions.

One significant aspect of this incursion lay in the reactions of the Kurds, the Bush administration, and the Iraqi government. The Kurds, including those in leadership in the central government, forcefully denounced the Turkish action, calling it naked aggression and promising a full military resistance to the invading troops. Washington, on the other hand, endorsed the right of Turkey to suppress the PKK—a group that the U.S. State Department had officially designated as a terrorist organization—while calling for a rapid end to the incursion. Non-Kurdish Iraqi leaders spoke on both sides of the issue without taking a definitive position.

By tolerating an invasion of foreign troops into its territory, the Iraqi government failed to respond to a fundamental challenge to the country's sovereignty. Even if we accept the denunciations by the Kurdish officeholders as official policy of the Iraqi government, this means that the Iraqi government's response was strictly rhetorical, akin to the sort of lip-service statements that countries make when they are unwilling to defend an ally. This, perhaps, best expresses the attitude toward the Kurdish region—it was an arm's-length ally for which the central government took little actual responsibility. The behavior of the United States was similarly revealing. In a sense the Kurds had been cast adrift by both the occupation and the Iraq national government, and were left to fend for themselves in international affairs.

All this would appear to suggest that the Kurds had, under the cover of chaos within the country, achieved a kind of sovereignty. With no U.S. troops stationed in the region, the peshmerga gave them a virtual monopoly on the means of coercion except in disputed areas such as Kirkuk. Their full control of regional and city governments provided them with the administrative capability needed to govern. But a number of issues prevented them from achieving real legitmacy.

Though few of Iraq's dismantled bureaucracies and industrial plants were located in the northern Kurdish provinces, the Kurdish economy had nevertheless been intimately tied to the larger Iraqi economy. State-owned factories, which comprised 35 percent of the pre-invasion economy, had utilized Kurdish companies for supplies and as customers, and the shuttering process, though it did not produce the immediate shock experienced elsewhere, eventually had a profound impact on Kurdish firms, many of which could not survive the demise of their dominant trading partners. The deep depression that swept through the rest of the country also impacted Kurdistan. The dependence of Kurdistan's fate on broader Iraqi conditions was further underscored by the cholera crisis of 2007.[27]

The cholera epidemic started in Kurdistan because the Kurdish government could not prevent the dysfunctional sewage and water purification system from contaminating the region's water. And the disease spread through the Kurdish provinces because the regional government could not muster the medical staff and water purification engineers to halt it.[28]

Electrical service in Kurdistan, as in other regions, declined in the course of the occupation. As part of the national electrical grid, the Kurds had insufficient independent electrical production to supply themselves. They sought to remedy this problem by importing electricity from Turkey in exchange for oil exports, but this effort was insufficient for Kurdish needs and ultimately foundered when the Kurds could not sustain the exports, which depended on refineries and pipelines that were located in other parts of the country.

As the national infrastructure decayed, so did the infrastructure in Kurdistan, undermining and weakening the legitimacy of the government. And as the decay continued, legitimacy eroded further, undermining the potential for the Kurdish region to achieve viability. In Kurdistan, as in the Shia south, sovereignty was being lost.

Unlike the Shia south, Kurdistan could conceivably execute a divorce from the larger polity and climb out of the cycle of decay. Such a divorce, which by late 2007 was supported by public opinion among the Kurds,[29] would probably require the annexation of Kirkuk, the hub of the northern oil fields and a commercial crossroads that would lend viability to an independent Kurdish economy. That annexation, already problematic, also raised a larger issue. Although the occupation had not intervened in the ongoing fighting there, or in the confrontation with Turkey, the possibility of major military intervention (by the occupation) loomed, a constant reminder of the force that had been applied in key Sunni cities such as Fallujah and Ramadi or Shia cities such as Najaf. As long as the U.S. military remained in the country, the Kurds could not establish the conditions needed to construct a sovereign, independent state without the tacit or explicit approval of the United States. The Kurds could only seek a sovereign existence if Washington stopped opposing it.

In the first five years of the occupation, the United States failed to establish its own sovereignty or that of the Iraqi government. Yet it continued to prevent any other entity, regional or national, from establishing an alternate sovereignty, leaving Iraqis with no viable government institutions.

Chapter Seventeen

Rebellious Sunni Cities

The Iraqi resistance is something and the terrorism is something else. We don't kidnap journalists and we don't sabotage the oil pipelines and the electric power stations. We don't kill innocent Iraqis. We resist the occupation.

—Abdullah Janabi, insurgent leader in Fallujah

The Sunni Resistance

What the world came to call the "insurgency" in Iraq was concentrated in Baghdad and its southern suburbs and in the Sunni-dominated cities north and west of the capital. Other regions resisted U.S. policy ambitions and Iraqi government control, but—as we have seen—neither the Kurds nor the Shia mounted a sustained war against the occupation.

While the major media focused public attention on the Sunni insurgency, the actual nature of the war was largely unreported. Instead, news coverage dwelled on certain spectacular moments: a few major battles—in Fallujah, Tal Afar, and a handful of other cities—and the most destructive car bombs and other suicide attacks aimed at civilian targets, mostly Shia. The U.S. media rarely mentioned the grinding war of attrition—the multitude of small-scale confrontations between resistance fighters and patrolling occupation troops that accounted for the vast majority of violent incidents. (See chapters 6 to 9.)

Except during the height of the battle of Baghdad (see chapter 18), the bulk of the fighting, dying, and destruction was taking place in the four

Sunni provinces that formed a wedge-shaped area between Baghdad and the Syrian border, dubbed by the occupation the "Sunni Triangle." This war was fought between the U.S. military and the resistance, with Iraqi troops under U.S. command playing a smaller but not inconsequential role. The Iraqi government had no operational control over the Iraqi forces, nor did Iraqi leadership play any significant part in the military and political planning for the various campaigns. They were rarely mentioned in the accounts of the anti-insurgency effort.

The occupation in the meantime was unable to establish orderly administrative control over any of the cities in the Sunni Triangle. In Fallujah after the U.S. offensive in November 2004, a long-term occupation sustained by thousands of troops never managed to extinguish an obstreperous resistance. (See chapter 8.) By 2008 Fallujah was a virtual prison in a city of ruins, accessible only to authorized individuals passing through heavily fortified military checkpoints. U.S. efforts to develop compliant local administrations capable of managing viable economic and social life in other cities were no more successful.

On the other side, except in Fallujah during the brief period between the two battles, the insurgency could not establish even the semi-stable government that the local Shia leadership achieved in Basra and elsewhere in the south. (See chapter 7.) The persistent efforts of the occupation to pacify Sunni cities prevented even this level of government. Each side thwarted the other from consolidating its rule.

To the outside observer, the surprising element of this situation was the ability of the resistance to reach such a stalemate with the United States, given the overwhelming kinetic advantage that the U.S. military—equipped with awesome firepower—had over the insurgents, who were armed with Kálashnikov rifles, rocket-propelled grenades, and improvised roadside bombs. The occupation "won" every armed confrontation (that is, ended with possession of the arena of battle), but the insurgents could claim truthfully that they were the dominant day-to-day presence in these disputed cities.

The Political Organization of the Local Sunni Insurgency

To understand the power and leverage that the resistance exercised, we need to look at the organization of the Sunni resistance in the many cities of Iraq where the war became an ongoing part of life.

Consider first Fallujah, before the U.S. military conquered the city after protracted house-to-house fighting in November 2004.[1] U.S. troops had withdrawn from Fallujah after an abortive battle the previ-

ous April, leaving the city in the hands of the Fallujah Brigade, a group
made up mostly of Baathist Army veterans who were assigned the job of
pacifying the city. Instead of acting as a proxy for the occupation, however, the Fallujah Brigade gave support to a group of local religious leaders who were allied with the insurgency. During the succeeding months
this group evolved into a local government that borrowed its organizational skeleton from the local tribes and Sunni mosques (including the
Shari'a courts), using the resistance fighters and the Fallujah Brigade as
a police force.

Until the November 2004 battle, Fallujah was ruled by this government in a way that strongly resembled the Basra government—with only
tenuous ties to the national administration and no ties at all to the occupation.[2] Like Basra, there was conflict within the city. One significant element was the tension between the jihadists, who wanted to establish
Fallujah as a safe rear area for their larger goals including violent subju-
gation of the Shia, and the local resistance, which was determined to
keep the occupation out but opposed attacks on Shia civilians.[3] There
was also friction between the government and a large minority of citizens who felt constrained by newly enforced religious orthodoxy: head
scarves for women, facial hair for men, and the abolition of liquor and
Western music.

Despite this friction, however, the amount of street crime was negligible
and armed confrontations were rare. April to November 2004 was the most
peaceful period in Fallujah during the first five years of the occupation.

This Fallujah interlude points to a key fact about the occupation. In
almost every locality—Sunni as well as Shia—tribal leaders and local
clerics constituted a protogovernment, capable of leading an orderly (if
fundamentalist) lifestyle. Because they could utilize mosques and tribal
oganizations to assure local coordination, they were generally able to
provide locally controlled city services (such as garbage collection and
traffic control) but unable to provide services that depended on infrastructural support from the larger political economy (such as electricity,
potable water, sewage disposal, or social programs). By organizing local
militias and instituting Shari'a courts, they could effectively sustain
law and order, adjudicate domestic disputes, and suppress crime. But
the militias—in Fallujah and elsewhere—could only maintain a monopoly on coercion if they were not challenged by the U.S. military.
Their credibility varied with the frequency of occupation patrols and
larger incursions.

Violence occurred precisely when occupation troops invaded the city
to capture insurgents or, more ambitiously, to wrest control from these

local forces. These U.S. operations were disruptive even when they did not trigger sustained battles. Relatively uneventful U.S. incursions, punctuated by an IED, sniper fire, or no resistance at all, still drove the local militia underground—often for considerable periods—and therefore deprived the community of normal policing functions. This not only meant increases in street crime, it also gave leave for organized criminal gangs, an increasingly intrusive part of daily Iraqi life, to kidnap prominent citizens, attack strategic targets, and otherwise disrupt routine life. This secondary danger led the local militias to fight more insistently, attempting to make their area a "no-go" zone for foreign troops.

Fighting in Sunni cities therefore correlated directly to the presence of the U.S. military.[4] Ordinarily, when occupation forces entered a city, fighting began in the form of remotely exploded roadside bombs, supplemented with sniper and hit-and-run attacks, designed to deter or delay U.S. patrols. When the U.S. forces discontinued their assault, usually because they moved on to another town, control of the city reverted back to local tribal leaders and clerics with their rule enforced by the resistance fighters, who now acted as informal police forces.

At no time in this process did the Iraqi government figure as a partisan or mediating force. Occasionally, a governor or police chief was appointed by the central government, but these functionaries quickly discovered (just as the police chiefs in Basra and Kirkuk discovered) that the de facto law enforcement apparatus was allied with (or controlled by) the local resistance. Such functionaries, therefore, either accepted this reality and worked with the local power structure, resigned in protest over their lack of authority, or became the target of assassination attempts.[5]

In a sense, then, the difference between Sunni cities—most of which were at least partially destroyed by intense fighting—and cities in the Shia and Kurdish regions of the country was the determination of the Bush administration to pacify the Sunnis, even while it tolerated quasi-rebellious local governments in the Shia south and officially embraced the autonomy of the Kurdish north.

The Guerrilla War in Baiji

Events in the city of Baiji offer an illustration of how the insurgency effectively resisted occupation efforts at pacification.[6] Though its population was only seventy thousand, the city was the site of the largest oil refining plant in Iraq and therefore crucial to the Iraqi economy.

When U.S. proconsul L. Paul Bremer shuttered all non-oil–government enterprises, the refinery remained open but the surrounding industrial plants did not. Unemployment swept through Baiji, generating deep bitterness among local residents and inspiring a variety of protests.[7]

In late 2003, in response to the growing discontent, the United States initiated what *Washington Post* reporter Ann Tyson characterized as "heavy-handed sweeps through Baiji by U.S. forces . . . [that] left many people angry, frightened and humiliated." Tyson quoted Adil Faez Jeel, the director of the oil refinery in the town, saying that these sweeps, along with the economic depression, solidified local support for armed resistance: "Most of the people fighting the Americans tell me they do nothing for us but destroy the houses and capture people. . . . There are no jobs, no water, no electricity."[8]

By late 2004 Baiji guerrillas, supported by local clerics and tribal leaders, were strong enough to seek control of the town. In addition to skirmishes with U.S. troops and Iraqi police, the guerrillas sabotaged pipelines bringing oil to the local refinery and hijacked trucks transporting refined petroleum produced at the plant. The biggest battle occurred in the center of town, when guerrillas launched a mortar attack against a joint U.S.-Iraqi patrol, triggering two days of battles. A doctor at the local hospital told the Agence-France Presse that at least ten civilians were killed and twenty-six wounded.[9]

For the next year Baiji was out of the news, largely because the U.S. military was busy with military sweeps in the west of Anbar province. This quiescence ended in late 2005 when the the U.S. military returned to Baiji, characterized by *Washington Post* reporter Tyson as "long neglected by American forces and still firmly in the grip of insurgents."

The new attempt at pacification was provoked, according to occupation sources, by suspicions that local guerrillas were using Baiji as a staging area for attacks in Mosul and Baghdad, and—more immediately—by growing evidence that the guerrillas had shifted their oil operations from sabotage to appropriation. According to U.S. sources, Iraqis were siphoning off a measurable proportion of the oil refinery output for sale on the black market and/or to finance the resistance. A resistance supporter in Baiji, speaking to Inter Press Service reporters Brian Conley and Isam Rashid, justified these siphoning activities as an attempt to stop U.S. theft of Iraqi oil: "This petrol will go to Turkey and is stolen by occupation force; or, when Turkey buys this petrol, the money is taken by the occupation forces."[10]

The occupation sent in the Army's 101st Airborne Division to close the refinery. Their attempt to retake the town, however, was unsuccessful. Sergeant First Class Danny Kidd, a veteran of both the Afghan and Iraqi war, attributed the hard going to the fact that Baiji residents supported the guerrilla fighters: "They have the place locked down. We have almost no support from the local people. We talk to 1,000 people and one will come forward." [11]

This observation summarizes U.S. experiences throughout the Sunni triangle: hidden insurgents could be found only if local residents pointed them out to patrolling soldiers, but the occupation found few who would help in this identification. The incursions were therefore fruitless and commanders were driven to utilizing terrorist tactics—intimidating, arresting, or even torturing residents in an attempt to either break the wall of silence or sweep up the insurgents in a dragnet that detained the bulk of the local male population. [12]

The degree of support for the resistance by local residents was illustrated in a gruesome incident that took place during the early weeks of 2006. Captain Matt Bartlett, accompanied by a convoy of tanks and personnel carriers, sought information from a tribal chief about a group of bomb-makers that were suspected of operating in the chief's domain. The convoy was cordially greeted by the sheik's children, who accepted the officers' gifts and "traded high-fives with them." Captain Bartlett was told, however, that the sheik was hosting a large gathering and could not meet that day. When the Americans turned to leave, they found the street blocked by people and cars that were apparently part of the gathering. The people "waved the soldiers down an alternative, dirt route along the Tigris nicknamed 'Smugglers' Road.'"

This turned out to be an elaborate ruse designed to lure the occupation troops into an ambush:

> A few hundred yards down the road, bordered by fields, the convoy was hit by a massive explosion.
>
> Behind the blast, [First Sergeant Robert] Goudy jumped out of his Humvee and ran forward toward the huge cloud of smoke and debris. As it cleared, he was confused by what he found.
>
> "I saw this big piece of flesh and thought it was a goat or cow. I thought, 'Wow, these guys put an IED in a dead animal,'" he recalled. He went on, hoping to find his men sitting in the truck. But as he got closer, he recalled, "I didn't see the truck. I started seeing limbs and body parts." Goudy tripped over what was left of one soldier. Then he found the only survivor of the five soldiers in the Humvee, blinded and screaming.
>
> "It was horrible," Bartlett said. "We had to pick up body parts 200 meters away." The Humvee was "ripped in half and shredded," he said, by a monster bomb later found to contain 1,000 pounds of explosives and two antitank mines, with a 155mm artillery round on top. [13]

Sergeant Goudy and the other survivors were "convinced Iraqis living nearby knew about the bomb but did nothing to warn them." In fact, it appears that they participated in luring the convoy into a trap. The sol-

diers' thoughts naturally turned to revenge: "I felt so angry and violated. . . . We all wanted to go out and tear up the city, kick down the
doors, shoot the civilians, blow up the mosque." [14]

The reports from Baiji contain no accounts of such revenge, but the
incident and the failure of other strategies to pacify the city led to an official escalation of the U.S. assault. According to the *Army Times*, the strategy subsequently adopted was modeled after "walls built around Fallujah
and Samarra in recent months [that] have quelled restive insurgent cells."
U.S. forces constructed an earthen barrier around Siniyah, the most rebellious neighborhood in the city. Checkpoints were set up to stop "all vehicles leaving or entering . . . as soldiers look for known insurgents,
bomb-making materials and illegal weapons." [15] These draconian measures interrupted all normal life in the area. Anyone with business outside
the community could not reliably pass through the checkpoint: college
students were forced to drop out of school, employees lost their jobs.

One resident told the Inter Press Service that "we live in a very big jail
for three thousand," while a local cleric told the *Army Times* that Siniyah
had become "a concentration camp." [16] This strategy became the standard
in Sunni insurgent areas and was subsequently adapted to Baghdad
neighborhoods during Operations Together Forward I and II and their
more famous successor known as the "surge." [17] Only in Fallujah, however, did the occupation make the severe lockdown a permanent feature
of life in the captive areas. In Baiji and other insurgent strongholds, the
U.S. presence was relaxed after a time, with a small contingent of occupation troops attempting without much success to keep the insurgency
in check. The occupation presence however did prevent the local resistance from establishing the sort of overt control that came to be a fact of
life in Shia cities in the south. This prevented local tribal leaders and clerics from organizing consistent services and law enforcement and left
them less able to attend to even a reduced list of local needs.

In Baiji, for example, the insurgent protogovernment operated almost
clandestinely. A reputed leader of the resistance was the brother of the official mayor and they apparently carried on various cooperative relationships despite the presence of U.S. troops. [18] The insurgency discontinued
attacks on the oil production facilities, preferring instead to finance their
military and social welfare operations by hijacking trucks carrying as
much as one-third of the production. Other economic operations also
developed under the radar, with elected and appointed officials including
the police chief and the provincial governor taking part of the operation.

According to the U.S. Army commander in Baiji, Captain Joe
DaSilva, the refinery where his men were stationed was "the money pit

of the insurgency." Nevertheless, the network of connections was so elaborate and involved so many local officials that he was unable to make a dent in the operation.[19]

Through the many different phases of the battle for control of Baiji, the enduring constant was support of the insurgency by local citizens. The ambush of Captain Bartlett's unit required the cooperation of the entire surrounding community, and the unwillingness of residents to identify insurgents was an ongoing symptom that there were almost no citizens willing to help the occupation. This absence of collaborators was also a necessary precondition for successfully siphoning off a substantial proportion of refinery oil, and it demonstrated the loyalty of one very important constituency—the employees in the refinery—to the black-market operation. In the Sunni cities in central Iraq, the insurgency rested on the committed support of the vast majority of the population.

Popular support gave the insurgency in Baiji and elsewhere the means to survive and even expand, despite the full opposing force of the occupation. It did not however provide local leaders with sufficient resources to reconstruct destroyed communities like Siniyah, to restore the lost jobs and disrupted economy that were the dual legacy of Bremer's economic shock treatment and each U.S. attempt at pacification, or to deal with the ongoing physical, emotional, and structural debilitation of the people and infrastructure. The jerry-rigged local governments had few resources with which to address these problems, especially since most required national resources.

Despite periods of relative stability, the physical, economic, and infrastructural decline was more or less continuous; the absence of resources and control meant that each confrontation left the cities further degraded. For the residents of Baiji, conditions continued to decline, fueling their anger at the occupation and at the Iraqi government. As the years wore on and the logic of national decay created a parallel logic of local decay, desperation intensified, producing amplified displacement as people left looking for a better life, greater insurgency as people sought to lift the ongoing burden of the occupation, and new demands on local leadership—insurgent and civilian—as the crisis deepened.

Jihadists versus Guerrillas:
The Origins of the Anbar Awakening

For consumers of U.S. media the so-called Anbar Awakening sprang suddenly into full-blown existence, seemingly from the head of U.S. General David Petraeus, in summer 2007. It was during that surge summer, when fighting in Baghdad was at its most ferocious as thousands of U.S. soldiers invaded neighborhood after neighborhood, that the occupation military officially announced that it was paying "Concerned Local Citizens" to attack and subdue various jihadist groups, which Washington designated under a single title, al-Qaeda in Iraq. By early 2008 this apparently successful ploy was being credited with turning Anbar province from the center of the Sunni insurgency into one of the quietest and most pacified areas of the country.

In fact, however, the Awakening—in Anbar and beyond—was rooted in the history of the insurgency and in the divisions and frustrations that matured during the five years that local resistance fighters sought to expel the occupation from their communities.

From the beginning of the insurgency, there were strong and visible differences between the bulk of the guerrilla fighters, whose main purpose was to expel the United States, and the relatively small minority of jihadists (estimated at less than 15 percent of all fighters),[20] who sought to establish a "caliphate" throughout the Arab Middle East embodying the principles of Salafi Islam.[21] The key military difference between the nationalist insurgents and the jihadists was expressed in their respective attitudes toward attacking civilians, especially Shia.[22]

For the jihadists, the Shia were not only apostate believers in a false religious doctrine, but also—mainly due to their support of the Iraqi government that had abandoned its electoral promise to end the occupation—the key internal support of the ongoing presence of the U.S. military. For jihadists, therefore, the Shia were unredeemable enemies. Moreover, in their view the occupation could not survive without the validation provided by the Iraqi government, particularly the Iraqi troops—almost all Shia—who were mobilized to fight the insurgency under U.S. leadership. As al-Qaeda's Ayman al-Zawahiri put it, these Shia troops were "the Crusader occupier's paws, used to strike at Muslims in Iraq."[23] If, under the pressure of attack, Shia civilians would abandon their support for the government and stop joining the military, the occupation would unravel. The jihadists' logic was similar to that applied by the occupation in Fallujah—that civilians who supported the enemy would withdraw that support once they experienced the agony of punishment.[24]

This logic—and the very different logic embraced by the non-jihadist, nationalist insurgency—is vividly illustrated by a terrorist attack during the run-up to the first Iraqi election in January 2005. As the *New York Times* reported at the time:

Gunmen assassinated a representative of Iraq's most powerful Shiite cleric, grand ayatollah Ali al-Sistani, and five other people in an attack south of

> Baghdad on Wednesday. . . . sheik Mahmoud al-Madaini was killed along
> with his son and four guards after leaving sunset prayers at a mosque in
> Maidan, a Sunni-dominated city about 12 miles south of the capital, said
> an official in the ayatollah's office.[25]

In a statement posted on several Web sites, the jihadist group Ansar al-Islam claimed responsibility for killing the cleric, describing it as part of a campaign to prevent Shia citizens from participating in the election. According to *Washington Post* reporter Anthony Shadid, the group called al-Madaini "one of the main supporters of the election and reiterated their threats to target voters and candidates and to attack polling stations."[26]

The *New York Times* also reported the decidedly negative reaction to the assassination of the most visible Sunni representatives of the nationalist insurgents:

> The powerful Association of Muslim Scholars denounced Madaini's killing
> as the work of "criminal agents." The association has called for a boycott of
> the elections and includes members who advocate violent resistance to the
> American occupation. Its statement Friday, however, buttressed the theory
> that domestic militants and those with foreign links have diverging goals.[27]

The Association of Muslim Scholars (AMS) was a group made up of Sunni clerics with very close ties to the guerrilla movement. This statement then was as close to a general policy as the Sunni guerrilla movement could make, considering its decentralized and localized nature. It captured the more general attitude of the nationalist resistance, which believed in attacking only occupation military forces and sought to avoid all Iraqi civilian casualties.

The underlying logic of the AMS was quite opposite to that of the jihadists. They saw the Shia as potential allies against the occupation. Instead of attacking them for their involvement in the government, the AMS hoped to gain their support for the electoral boycott, as well as fighting together with them against occupation troops. Toward that end, the AMS had played a key role in organizing Sunni-Shia alliances around the fighting in Fallujah in April 2004. (See Chapter 8.) With this orientation—that there would be a long-term alliance between Sunni and Shia to expel the United States—the AMS and the insurgents who fought under the nationalist banner were vigorously opposed to the terrorist campaign mounted by the jihadists.

Moreover many nationalists, though themselves believers in fundamentalist versions of Islam, were uncomfortable with the larger jihadist goal of reorganizing the internal life of insurgent communities according to their very specific Salafist views of appropriate behavior. These disagreements had led, for example, to considerable friction in Fallujah during the period when the insurgency ruled the city, and they became visible to the outside world as the second battle of Fallujah approached. Just before that battle, *Washington Post* reporter Rajiv Chandresekaran talked with various Fallujah guerrilla leaders and reported their unhappiness with the presence of the jihadists, who at that time were commanded by Abu Musab al-Zarqawi:

> Many Fallujah residents appear to be growing weary of Zarqawi's followers, according to residents interviewed by telephone. Zarqawi's agenda appears to extend well beyond the goal of residents, who want to keep U.S. forces out of the city. He and his supporters have turned the city into a base for wider attacks, particularly against Iraqi officials and security forces. His loyalists, many of whom adhere to the strict Salafi school of Islam, also have attempted to instill hard-line social restrictions, demanding that women cover their hair and hectoring men for not growing beards. Although Fallujah is a deeply religious city, many residents follow mystical Sufi beliefs, such as praying by the graves of relatives, which Salafis regard as blasphemous.
>
> In what may be the strongest sign of tension between residents and foreigners, the head of the Shura Council, Abdullah Janabi, who had invited foreigners to the city in April, issued a statement on Friday calling Zarqawi a "criminal."
>
> "We don't need Zarqawi to defend our city," said Janabi, who sought to draw a distinction between what he called "Iraqi resistance fighters" and foreign fighters engaged in a campaign against Iraq's infrastructure, foreign civilians and Iraqi security forces. "The Iraqi resistance is something and the terrorism is something else. We don't kidnap journalists and we don't sabotage the oil pipelines and the electric power stations. We don't kill innocent Iraqis. We resist the occupation." [28]

During abortive negotiations with the occupation aimed at avoiding the impending battle, the insurgent leadership of Fallujah offered to expel the jihadists in exchange for U.S. forbearance—an offer that underscored the degree of alienation between the two groups. The U.S. military refused the offer, apparently viewing the nationalist guerrillas as at least as great an obstacle to occupation goals as the jihadists. They were not willing to tolerate the insurgents' continued domination of the city. [29]

Even after the second battle of Fallujah, which enhanced jihadist sentiment throughout Sunni areas, the nationalists continued to view attacks on Shia civilians as both criminal and detrimental to the goal of expelling the United States. On February 4, 2005, a summit meeting of the Anti-Occupation Patriotic Forces led by the AMS and the Shia insurgents loyal to Muqtada al-Sadr called for a broad alliance that would "lead to the withdrawal of the Americans from our country." A central component of the manifesto issued by the meeting called for a clear "separation between resistance and terrorism, because some are trying to relate the Iraqi resistance to the Zarqawi group and loyalists of the former regime." The demands that subsequently emanated from this meeting embodied both these principles and were signed by twenty-one groups, including secular and religious Shia and Sunni organizations.[30]

The opposition of the nationalists to the jihadists was not only rhetorical. The friction in Fallujah during the period between the two battles was replicated elsewhere whenever there was enough stability in local communities for religious, philosophical, and strategic differences to emerge in everyday practice. In areas where the jihadists were particularly strong, they sought to impose dress and behavioral codes and to harness local resources to their broader campaign against the Shia, using the more-than-occasional application of violence against local opposition to their plans.

One dramatic instance of this conflict was described by embedded *Washington Post* reporter Ellen Knickmeyer during an offensive in western Anbar province. Local guerrillas reached out to the occupation forces, requesting help in expelling the jihadists from the town of Husaybah, but the U.S. military refused the alliance. Instead they halted their advance on the city and waited for the subsequent battle between the two groups to be completed:

> For four days this month, U.S. Marines were onlookers at just the kind of fight they had hoped to see: a battle between suspected followers of Abu Musab Zarqawi, a foreign-born insurgent, and Iraqi Sunni tribal fighters at the western frontier town of Husaybah. In clashes sparked by the assassination of a tribal sheik, which was commissioned by Zarqawi, the foreign insurgents and the Iraqi tribal fighters pounded one another with small weapons and mortars in the town's streets as the U.S. military watched from a distance.[31]

By mid-2005, as U.S. offensives utilized more and more Shia troops to fight against Sunni guerrillas, the jihadists gained greater numbers of adherents who agreed that the Shia were a legitimate target. They were able to recruit larger numbers of suicide bombers inside and outside of Iraq, and therefore able to mount increasing numbers of car bombings and other spectacular attacks against Shia civilians. At the same time they asserted their views more forcefully within local Sunni communities. While the jihadists were far from being the majority of the resistance, they were sometimes able to contend for power within these communities, particularly given their violent tactics against local adversaries.

The Husaybah battle was atypical in one important respect, however: the occupation forces did not usually restrain themselves in order to allow friction between jihadist and nationalist forces to mature. When U.S. troops entered an area, they moved quickly to pacify it without any attention to the internal divisions within the community. The occupation presence therefore tended to suppress the conflict, as the two sides joined to fight the common enemy. As long as the occupation persisted in trying to pacify the centers of Sunni insurgency, the conflict between jihadists and nationalists remained substantially suppressed.

The Awakening

The prevalent image in the U.S. media that the occupation was the initiator of the so-called Anbar Awakening ignored not only the history of division between the nationalists and the jihadists, but also the process by which the tension between the guerrillas and the jihadists developed. Even before relaxation of the U.S. presence, tension amplified as the insurgency grew, and amplified further as sectarian friction became a central feature of the national scene. As the attacks on Shia increased, many Sunni insurgents became convinced of the pernicious impact of the jihadists, feeling that they "undermined the image of the Sunni resistance and imposed Islamic laws that were too restrictive."[32]

The organizational aspects of what became known as the Anbar Awakening began to coalesce after the February 2006 bombing of the Golden Dome, a major Shia shrine located in the predominantly Sunni city of Samarra.[33] The crescendo of Shia death-squad activity that swept through Baghdad after the bombing of the shrine resulted in daily harvests of dead Sunnis and a flood of Sunni refugees seeking safe haven in Anbar province. Initially these events lent further credibility to jihadist claims that the Shia were unredeemable enemies. Among the many results of this enhanced sectarian friction was retaliatory ethnic displacement in the Sunni-dominated cites of Anbar. The relativly small Shia populations in these cities, though never a threat to Sunni political dominance, became targets of local jihadists who, with the support of many local residents, forced large numbers of Shia to leave.

As the jihadists increased their presence and power in Sunni cities, they sought more forcefully to enforce their version of Shari'a law, creating significant friction with local residents who did not share their religious vision. As this dynamic sparked conflict, the jihadists applied increasing doses of violence to the mix, assassinating local insurgents or political leaders who opposed them and even engaging in suicide attacks against these adversaries.

In mid-2006, as this tension was escalating, the occupation began shifting combat troops from Anbar to Baghdad as part of Operation Together Forward I, aimed at recapturing the city from the various sectarian militias operating there.[34] Occupation offensives in Anbar and Diyala provinces became smaller and less frequent, and the large contingents of U.S. troops in or near various cities were reduced or withdrawn.

This relaxation of the occupation military presence provided local nationalist leaders with the opportunity to root out the jihadists. They could use their vast numerical advantage to overwhelm the jihadists without exposing themselves to a U.S. attack. Moreover, unlike the U.S. military, these local leaders never had a problem identifying the jihadists. Their base in the local community, as well as growing resentment by locals over the imposing behavior of the jihadists, guaranteed that the nationalists knew exactly who their adversaries were.

By summer 2006 various local leaders, calling themselves the Sahwa, were beginning to organize coordinated attacks on the jihadists. This coordination was imperative, since the jihadists' mobility allowed them to survive by moving to another location and using their new headquarters to retaliate against old adversaries. Coordination allowed the local leaders to counter this tactic and successfully expel or liquidate jihadists, who were forced to disband or find new bases far away.

Although the Sahwa, rendered in English as "the Awakening," had become a visible force in the country as a whole by late 2006, the U.S. military did not officially acknowledge their existence. The occupation continued its policy of invading insurgent strongholds, seeking to capture or kill all insurgents without discriminating between nationalists and jihadists.

While certain local U.S. commanders in Anbar province responded to the Sahwa organization by relaxing attacks on their communities, the top officers remained mystified observers of these developments. In April 2007, when Sahwa leaders met to form a political party to press their demands against the Iraqi government, the occupation had no foreknowledge of the meeting. Major Jeff Pool, a spokesman for the U.S. military command in Anbar, told the Associated Press that he had no information about the meeting. He called it "an all-Iraqi event. . . . We are hoping to find out the details later this week."[35]

As the pressure to transfer additional troops from Anbar to manage the battle of Baghdad increased, the U.S. military leadership began to consider formalizing the live-and-let-live approach to the Anbar insurgency that a few local U.S. commanders had implicitly adopted. Officially the new system was described by top military commanders as a new local law enforcement operation financed by the occupation. They dubbed the local groups Concerned Local Citizens (CLCs) and announced that they would be given responsibility for enforcing law and order in their own neighborhoods, with a special mandate to suppress, arrest, or kill local jihadist cadre.

The label "Concerned Local Citizens" implied a group of previously passive or even intimidated local residents, energized by the prospect of U.S. military support to take back their neighborhoods from violent jihadist interlopers. But this imagery was completely misleading: the vast majority of CLC members had hardly been passive citizens; they were instead active insurgents who had only a few days or weeks earlier been fighting against the United States, often for many years. Moreover, a large proportion had already been fighting the jihadists and had even subdued or expelled them before the occupation even acknowledged their activity, while a smaller proportion had themselves been jihadists not too long before. Partly, then, Washington was acknowledging a fait accompli by supporting the Sahwa groups, since the process of suppressing the jihadists was well along before the U.S. military formally endorsed the movement.[36]

Nevertheless, the official embrace of the Sahwa movement by the United States was a momentous development in the war: a negotiated cease-fire between the U.S. military and the Sunni insurgency in large parts of the Sunni triangle.

A typical agreement was constructed around the occupation's agreeing to concede local law enforcement authority to the Awakening group in a city or the neighborhood. In practice this meant that the U.S. military agreed to discontinue violent incursions into the insurgents' domain. This constituted a huge concession to the guerrillas and to the residents of these areas, since their main purpose through years of warfare had been to prevent such raids.

In exchange the insurgents agreed to suppress what the Bush administration labeled "terrorist attacks" emanating from their neighborhood, which in practice involved two very different activities. First the Sahwas agreed to eliminate jihadist activity in their areas; that is, they agreed to stop the jihadists from building and exporting car bombs and staging terrorist attacks targeting civilians (mostly Shia) outside the neighborhood. Second, they agreed to end their own offensive operations against the occupation, notably mortar attacks on U.S. forward bases, IED attacks on convoys, and ambushes in the community or at checkpoints.

In addition to this military cease-fire the occupation promised to pay the insurgents a wage of about $300 per month, with promises that they would eventually be offered permanent employment by the Iraqi government in law enforcement or some other state agency. Beyond this a larger goal loomed: that the cease-fire with the occupation would allow long-suffering Sunni cities to acquire the resources for an economic revival, with jobs, infrastructure, services, and commerce reemerging in areas that had been decaying for years.[37]

The U.S. media emphasized the decline in violence in the key areas of the Sunni insurgency. There is no doubt that this decline was real. U.S. military officers stationed in Anbar told the *New York Times* that violent confrontations in Anbar had declined from more than five hundred a week in December 2006 to fewer than thirty per week in early 2008. These figures express the effect of the cease-fire rather than suppression of the jihadists. (Violence due to terrorism was located in Shia areas in and around Baghdad and was not reflected in Anbar province figures.) With the occupation discontinuing incursions and home invasions, the primary source of violence was eliminated. This in turn rendered unnecessary the vast majority of all insurgent-initiated violence—IEDs, sniper fire, and other actions aimed at delaying and deterring U.S. patrols. Local guerrillas by and large honored their commitment to discontinue offensive operations and discontinued their attacks on convoys and forward bases, thus eliminating almost all the remaining attacks by insurgents.

As for the jihadists, they disappeared from most of the cities where the Sahwa had organized but continued to operate in Baghdad and other areas where the occupation undertook offensive operations. The number of jihadist bombings continued to increase during the first half of 2007 and did not decline until the United States began recognizing CLCs in Baghdad.[38]

The decline in violence in Anbar represented a major improvement in the lives of the residents there. It greatly reduced the threat of house break-ins, artillery barrages, and attacks. It virtually eliminated the daily violence that the occupation's presence had generated. And it held out the promise that the cities might begin to revive.

As soon as violence began to decline, the newly ascendant guerrillas and their local political allies focused their attention on consolidating control of official power. In most locations the insurgent leadership became the formal political leadership, a process that had been limited during the period when U.S. opposition prevented them from establishing local administrative control.[39] In its report to Congress in December 2007, the Pentagon acknowledged this new reality, concluding that the Sahwa movement "is demonstrating its ability to affect multiple levels of government in Anbar, including influencing the appointment of key officials such as the governor and the provincial chief of police."[40]

This newly won power, however, served to underscore the intractability of the underlying economic and social issues facing Sunni cities. The new leaders could not begin to address the manifold issues without a huge infusion of resources and services from the national government.[41] Such an infusion was an impossibility. Partly this failure reflected the sectarian divisions that separated the Shia national government from Sunni localities. But at a deeper level it reflected the overarching inca-pacity of the government itself, fostered by the original U.S. design and then consolidated in the years of destruction that followed the accession of Iraqi leadership.

The nature of the problem was forcefully expressed by Kamal Nouri, a leader of the Anbar Sahwa Council: "We thought that when security was established in Anbar, then the situation would turn to development and reconstruction, but we're surprised to see neglect from the govern-ment." His constituent, Salam Faraj, was more personal, blaming the problem on Prime Minister Nouri al-Maliki: "Where is the prime minis-ter? Does he know what we have to do to earn a living to feed our fami-lies? Call this a job? The government has failed." [42]

Another Sahwa leader, Ali Hatem Sulaiman, accused the Anbar Provincial Council, which was beholden to the national government, of embezzling reconstruction funds: "Do you know that the projects in Anbar are only ink on paper?" he asked *Los Angeles Times* reporter Ned Parker. "The reality," he said, was that the funds for the projects were "stolen by the provincial council." [43]

Almost immediately the revival of local politics sparked antagonism to the Iraqi national government and its local affiliates, contributing to an atmosphere of sectarian polarization. [44] Many Iraqis therefore turned their attention to strengthening the local governments, in effect follow-ing the Basra model in which cities would seek to serve the needs of their citizens without relying on the national government. They demanded discretion over government funds allocated to their areas, appropriated (as Baiji did) whatever resources could be siphoned off from local com-merce, and established local initiatives, as Basra did, that would work without the aid or interference of the national government. That is, they sought to become city-states with local sovereignty.

In the meantime the growing antagonism to the Iraqi government created tense relationships with the occupation as well. When the Baghdad government agreed to incorporate only twenty thousand of the eighty thousand Sahwa members into local police forces, discontent ex-ploded into a threatened strike. By spring 2008 many local Sahwa groups, having endured several months without pay, were threatening to break the cease-fire and reengage in armed resistance. [45] Abu Addul-Aziz, the leader of the Sahwa in Abu Ghraib, told the *Guardian*: "The Americans got what they wanted. We purged al-Qaida for them and now people are saying 'why should we have any more deaths for the Americans.' They have given us nothing." [46]

The cease-fire that the occupation had negotiated with the Anbar resistance had strengthened the Sunni insurgency in several ways. It had conceded local control to the guerrillas and their political allies, allowed them to claim formal leadership of neighborhoods and cities, and armed them to make claims for resources from the national government. As these institutional arrangements matured, they had strengthened the base of support for the insurgency while amplifying their alienation from the occupation and its client government. In many areas local insurgent leadership had been able to acquire a preponderance of authority, becoming power brokers and incipient warlords.[47]

The dynamics unleashed by the Sahwa were succinctly summarized by Joost Hiltermann of the International Crisis Group: "Iraq is moving in the direction of a failed state, a highly decentralized situation—totally unplanned, of course—with competing centers of power run by warlords and militias. The central government has no political control whatsoever beyond Baghdad, maybe not even beyond the Green Zone."[48]

Chapter Eighteen

The Battle of Baghdad

Baghdad looks like a city out of the Middle Ages, divided into hostile townships. Districts have been turned into fortresses, encircled by walls made out of concrete slabs. Police and soldiers check all identities at the entrances and exits.

—**Patrick Cockburn,** *Independent* **reporter**

During the first five years of the war, Baghdad, the capital city of Iraq, was transformed from a metropolis into an urban desert of half-destroyed buildings, dotted by partially deserted, mutually hostile minighettos that used to be neighborhoods, surrounded by cement barriers reminiscent of medieval fortifications. The most prominent of these ghettos, the only one with an intact infrastructure, was the heavily fortified city inside a city dubbed the Green Zone, where Iraq's most fearsome militia, the U.S. military, was headquartered.

The remaining ghettos, large and small, were governed by local militias, most of them sworn enemies of the United States and the Maliki regime. In the expanding Shia areas of the capital, the local guardians were usually members of the Mahdi Army, the militia of cleric Muqtada al-Sadr that had opposed the occupation since it began. In the shrinking Sunni-controlled parts of the city, the local guardians were usually members of the Sahwa forces (the Awakening or, in U.S. military jargon, Concerned Local Citizens). The Bush administration had ceded to them control of their cement-enclosed domains as long as they discontinued attacks elsewhere. As London *Guardian* reporter Ghaith Abdul-Ahad described it, most Baghdad residents "now live in walled, effectively ethnically cleansed, communities. Traveling across the city means hopping from one frontline to another and negotiating countless militia-controlled fiefdoms."[1]

The residents of these fiefdoms lived in homes with "rats and clogged toilets but no electricity or hot water, and no air conditioning or heating."[2] They were "drowning in sewage, thirsty for water and largely powerless," unable to reach jobs or schools across impassable cement barriers, and increasingly hungry because local stores could not obtain sufficient shipments of food.[3] Men could not visit friends and family who "live five minutes away" beyond the cement barriers, and women stayed home "unless it's absolutely necessary" to avoid vigilante enforcement of strict Shari'a law.[4] According to Baghdad professor Abdul Majeed Hassan, "You have to bid farewell to your family each time you go out to buy bread because you don't know if you are going to see them again. . . . If we're lucky, we get a few hours of electricity a day, barely enough drinking water, no health care, no jobs to feed our kids."[5]

In mid-2008—as tens of thousands of residents per month were following hundreds of thousands of their neighbors who had already fled the city—Baghdad waited for either a definitive military confrontation or some less violent change that would bring its long ordeal to an end.

How did this all come to be?

The Do-Nothing Government

For eighteen months, from June 2004 until the end 2005, Iraqi sovereignty was unclear. The appointed Iraqi Interim Government of Iyad Allawi and the elected transitional government of Ibrahim al-Jaafari were explicitly caretaker operations, so their records of inaction were—at least in principle—understandable.[6] With the new constitution in place, however, national elections in December 2005 were hailed as the moment when Iraqis would take control of their own destiny. President Bush evoked the larger Bush administration ambition of transforming the region when he designated the elections "a turning point in the history of Iraq, the history of the Middle East and the history of freedom."[7] The newly elected permanent government would begin asserting its sovereignty over the country, building an administrative infrastructure, and rising to the challenge of governing an unruly, rebellious, and often violent constituency. It would also, if Bush's vision was accurate, begin constructing the modernized and privatized neoliberal oil economy that would become a model for Iraq's neighbors and a lever for the transforming the rest of the Middle East.

Only three months later this hopeful vision was in ruins. While multiple crises exploded around their Green Zone sanctuary, various parliamentary factions had occupied themselves with tortuous negotiations over who would be the next prime minister, abetted by the interventions of Washington's activist ambassador Zalmay Khalilzad.[8]

While the U.S. media focused on this parliamentary maneuvering, some of the underlying crises flashed in and out of the headlines, including a controversy over illegal detention and torture sites run by Shia in the Ministry of the Interior, a rising wave of insurgent attacks in Baghdad, and most dramatically the bombing of the "Golden Dome" mosque in Samarra, which triggered retaliatory attacks against Sunni mosques, nationwide demonstrations calling for the withdrawal of U.S. forces, and a wave of death-squad murders that lasted for the better part of two years.

As described earlier, other crises continued to build without benefit of the media spotlight: a multiethnic conflict over control of Kirkuk, the northern oil hub and projected capital of a future Kurdistan; the steady escalation of battles between guerrilla fighters and occupation troops; a huge spike in U.S. air strikes against Sunni cities; a further degeneration in the delivery of electricity, potable water, fuel, and most of the other basics of modern life; an exponential growth rate in the number of homeless refugees; the ongoing exodus of professionals; and unremitting unemployment levels, variously estimated at between 30 percent and 70 percent of the workforce.[9]

In dealing with all these crises, the Iraqi government was notable mainly for its absence. This irrelevance was of course not new. The predecessor governments of Allawi and Jaafari had been just as irrelevant. Locked inside the Green Zone with no capacity to reach beyond its cement borders, Iraq's government had none of the resources needed to exercise sovereignty.

In no area was this incapacity more visible than in the failure of the government to play even a minor role in the escalating violence within Baghdad. Just outside the Green Zone's fifteen-foot cement barrier, a spectacular car-bomb campaign organized by Sunni jihadists against Shia citizens engulfed Baghdad with full force in 2006. Back in 2004 most car bombs had targeted government officials or employees, with particular attention to the applicants for police and military positions who gathered in vulnerable places outside recruiting centers. By late 2005 however, the jihadists had shifted their attention to Shia civilians as punishment for their support for the succession of Iraqi governments allied with the occupation. In the eyes of the jihadists, this systematic assault on civilians was justified by the illegality of the occupation and the fact that the government had betrayed its electoral promise to set a date certain for U.S. withdrawal.[10] In their view the campaign was necessary to force the Shia to withdraw that support from the puppet government, clearing the way for the insurgents to drive the United States out of Iraq.[11]

The January 2006 bombing of the Golden Dome became the trigger for a massive increase in the Shia retaliation against the Sunnis. Death squads were the main agency for this counterattack.[12] Originally organized by U.S. operatives inside the Iraqi Ministry of the Interior, by 2006 they had proliferated inside and outside the special police forces commanded by the ministry. (See chapter 7.) Imposters as well as authentic police used checkpoints to search for suspected jihadists, and employed police vehicles and uniforms to apprehend accused insurgents and possible sympathizers.

The death squads typically applied torture to extract confessions of terrorist activity and summarily executed the "convicted" terrorists. The bodies were often deposited in highly visible locations around the city as a warning to prospective jihadists. In the eyes of the death-squad commanders, this campaign was necessary because the Iraqi government and its U.S. sponsors had failed to quell the constantly escalating car-bomb campaign against Shia civilians. In their view, systematic application of this form of state terrorism would eventually deter Sunni jihadists from organizing any further attacks against them.

Ethnic Cleansing in Baghdad

When the occupation of Baghdad began in April 2003, about half the city's neighborhoods had no predominant ethnic or religious character.[13] In late 2004, however, tens of thousands of Sunnis, driven out of Fallujah and other insurgent strongholds by U.S. offensives, began arriving in Baghdad. In these increasingly crowded neighborhoods ethnic friction rose, fueled by Sunni anger at a Shia-dominated government that sent its troops into battle beside occupation forces.[14]

Sunni militias, originally organized to deal with local crime (after the occupation dismantled the Iraqi police force) began to turn on Shia residents in the capital's two hundred mixed neighborhoods. Eventually, scattered acts of harassment were transformed into systematic campaigns of expulsion, justified by the housing needs of the rapidly growing multitudes of Sunni refugees, and as retaliation for government-supported assaults on Sunni cities. During 2005 the first stream of expelled Shia began arriving in Baghdad's vast, already overcrowded Shia slum of Sadr City and in the Shia cities of southern Iraq.

In January 2006 the bombing of the Golden Dome mosque in Samarra triggered sweeping Shia reprisals against Sunni communities.

In the capital the struggle for the dominance of mixed neighborhoods escalated dramatically. Deadly battles between Shia and Sunni militias involved every available weapon and method, including car bombs and death squads. Minority groups, including Christians, Kurds, and Palestinians, became targets in these drives for ethnic purity and were forced to flee or be killed. Ethnic cleansing had become central to the spiraling violence in Baghdad.

The number of violent encounters and fatalities resulting from car bombs and death squads kept increasing, but these numbing totals did not approach the destructiveness of the violence involving the U.S. military—which was still pursuing its goal of conquering and pacifying insurgent strongholds in Sunni cities and neighborhoods. Car bombs and death squads nevertheless came to dominate the news coverage, at least in the United States, partly because they were designed as public displays of brutality, and partly because they fit the tendency of the U.S. media to view violence in Iraq principally as a consequence of ethnic and religious antagonism.[15]

From the time it began in early 2005 until mid-2006, the escalating violence in Baghdad generated little visible reaction from either the succession of Iraqi governments or the occupation authorities. Transitional Prime Minister Ibrahim al-Jaafari and his permanent successor Nouri al-Maliki both spoke about cracking down on bombers and other jihadists, but no actual programs were organized.

As for the death squads, neither Jaafari nor Maliki took a strong stand against them. When they were mentioned it was usually to explain their activities as reasonable responses to the unrestrained jihadists. Maliki, for example, told the *New York Times* that the death squads were a "reaction . . . [to] Saddamists and terrorist groups."[16] This was not surprising since many death squads remained under the stewardship of the Ministry of the Interior and thus followed the global pattern of government-sponsored paramilitary terror.[17]

The ascension of the Maliki regime, which President Bush trumpeted as "a turning point in the history of Iraq, the history of the Middle East and the history of freedom" became instead just more evidence that sovereignty did not reside in the new government.[18]

This was hardly news to many Iraqis, who had witnessed the impotence of the new regime from its inception. What might have been more surprising was the discovery that sovereignty had also slipped away from the United States, even when it sought to assert it with the full force of its military firepower.

The U.S. Military Intervention

By mid-2006 the dire situation in Bagdad forced the United States to accept the challenge of halting ethnic dislocation and restoring law and order. In order to do so, the U.S. military and civilian officials had to reverse a two-year-old policy, initiated when the Iraqi Interim Government was formed, that enabled the occupation to camouflage its influence through the Iraqi government with the exception of designated hot spots, mostly in the Anbar province, where the Sunni insurgency was strongest. Initiating an offensive in Baghdad constituted an admission that the transition to Iraqi administration was not effective and that many Baghdad neighborhoods could not be controlled by the Iraqi government. Decisive U.S. intervention to halt this disintegration constituted an admission that sovereignty—even the limited version imagined when the plan was formulated—had not been transferred to the Iraqis but remained instead in the hands of the occupation.

The year-long effort aimed at restoring law and order and reversing ethnic dislocation in Baghdad was therefore a systematic, almost explicit, attempt to assert U.S. sovereignty. Instead it accomplished the opposite. It amplified rather than suppressed violence. It increased rather than reduced the rate of displacement. It escalated rather than reversed ethnic expulsion. It further degraded Baghdad's infrastructure. And it ultimately strengthened both the Sunni and Shia militias that opposed both the occupation and the Iraqi government it had sponsored.

Eventually during summer 2007 the campaign was abandoned (without any formal announcement) in favor of accommodation with both the Sunni and Shia insurgents, a new strategy that involved arming both sides of the sectarian conflict and facilitating the creation of ethnically homogeneous neighborhoods surrounded by cement barriers that prevented any semblance of normal economic or social life in the city. No central government exercised integrative economic, administrative, or military leadership over the city of Baghdad. The capital became a disintegrated collection of mutually hostile, feudallike townships, each woefully lacking in the key prerequisites for viable government.

The U.S. campaigns—Operation Together Forward I and II initiated in summer 2006 and the "surge" begun in January 2007—only exacerbated the crisis. Perhaps the only accomplishment of these campaigns was to convince Iraqis—and Iraq's neighbors—that, as independent journalist Nir Rosen put it, "the Americans are just one more militia lost in the anarchy."[19]

The United States Enters the Battle

Systematic U.S. intervention in Baghdad began in May 2006 with the transfer of several brigades of combat troops from Anbar province to the capital city. Although Anbar was still the active base of the Sunni insurgency, the thinly stretched U.S. military resources were more urgently needed in the capital.

The strategy in Baghdad reflected both the larger goals of the occupation and the military principles that the occupation forces had applied elsewhere during the previous two years. The occupation did not, for example, seek to introduce a policelike presence in disputed neighborhoods to protect them from car bombs, death squads, or ethnic expulsions. Nor did they adopt a "hearts and minds" approach that replaced or augmented military action with ameliorative programs to provide housing and other services for homeless or vulnerable families. These strategies might have worked to address the immediate problem of sectarian violence, but they would not have addressed the longer-term U.S. goals of rooting out Sunni insurgents and dismantling the Mahdi Army. Indeed, because ameliorative strategies would not have targeted the strongholds of Sunni insurgents and the Mahdi, they might have encouraged America's chief adversaries to further consolidate their power in these neighborhoods, making them more difficult to dislodge later. In this scenario, ameliorative strategies were particularly risky, since whoever controlled local areas would attempt to take credit for having forced the occupation to implement such reforms.

To bring order to Baghdad while pursuing the larger goals of eliminating the insurgency, U.S. military leadership sought to apply the strategy they had used in Fallujah and subsequently applied in other hinterland cities. This involved invading the strongholds of the Sunni insurgency and the Sadrist militias in an attempt to dislodge them once and for all. In principle these offensives would eliminate the organizations and leaders who were planning and executing the car bombs, death squads, and ethnic expulsion, while simultaneously rooting out key sources of resistance to both the occupation and the newly formed Iraqi government.

Operation Together Forward I, the first of these campaigns, was devised as a joint operation in which Iraqi units were paired with U.S. units under the command of U.S. officers. Applying the template developed in Anbar, designated communities were surrounded by troops and barriers and then systematically canvassed by armed patrols searching for signs of insurgency, including weapons caches, bomb factories, and insurgent literature. Suspected insurgents were apprehended, snipers or IED explosions were met with overwhelming firepower from foot patrols and armored vehicles, and the occasional sustained resistance was answered with airpower, including missiles and bombs ranging up to two thousand pounds.

In May 2006 occupation forces first joined "the battle for Baghdad" in a significant way. With the initiation of Operation Together Forward I, the U.S. military began transferring combat brigades to the capital in an attempt to take control of Sunni and Shia militia strongholds.

This strategy quickly proved itself ineffective. In August 2006 the *New York Times* reported that sectarian violence was "spiraling out of control." By the fall, the number of insurgents attacks in Baghdad had increased by 26 percent and violent deaths reported by the city morgue had quadrupled.[20]

The seeming paradox of a pacification campaign generating more violence can be explained by looking at the mechanics of the offensive.

Despite their involvement in ethnic violence, the Sunni and Shia militias that the U.S. military sought to root out were also the forces of law and order in Baghdad's otherwise lawless neighborhoods. They directed traffic, arrested and/or punished common criminals, and mediated disputes. They also protected neighborhoods from outsiders, including occupation or Iraqi soldiers, suicide bombers, death squads, and criminal gangs.

Before the U.S. military entered the fray, ethnic violence was largely restricted to contested mixed neighborhoods where no militia was dominant. Militia strongholds, in contrast, had been relatively invulnerable to sectarian attack because the streets were saturated with armed men on the lookout for enemies. Car bombers and death squads were spotted quickly and easily neutralized so they rarely attempted attacks. U.S. military targeted these previously quiescent communities and quickly overwhelmed the local militias, chasing surviving militia members off the streets or even out of neighborhoods. Without their local police and defense forces these communities became vulnerable to sectarian attack.

This vulnerability was vividly illustrated in Sadr City, the stronghold of the Sadrist movement. As the home base of the Mahdi Army, this city within a city had not experienced a car bomb attack in two years until U.S. troops sealed it off in October 2006, set up checkpoints at key entrance and exit points, and began patrols aimed at hunting down Mahdi Army members they suspected of participating in death squads and of kidnapping a U.S. soldier.[21] Local residents told *New York Times* reporter Sabrina Tavernise that the operation had "forced Mahdi Army members who were patrolling the streets to vanish." Soon after, the first car bombs were detonated.[22]

The violence reached a crescendo in November 2006 when a coordinated set of five car bombs killed at least 215 and wounded 257 Iraqis.[23]

Qusai Abdul-Wahab, a Sadrist member of parliament, spoke for many residents of the community when he told the Associated Press that "occupation forces are fully responsible for these acts."[24]

Such events generated immense bitterness among Shia, who took them as proof that the occupation and the Iraqi government were concerned only with attacking the Mahdi, not suppressing jihadist attacks. This encouraged their support of the death squads, which sought to exact retribution on the Sunni communities they believed were harboring the bombers. U.S. intervention again contributed to further escalation of sectarian violence.

The occupation offensives also facilitated retaliatory attacks of the Shia. Sunni insurgents in the Baghdad suburbs of Balad and Duluiyah, for example, were suspected of slaughtering seventeen Shia workers in a particularly well-publicized instance of sectarian brutality. U.S. troops and their Iraqi allies cordoned off the two districts and invaded the neighborhoods. The invading forces quickly silenced the insurgent militias, leaving the streets unpatrolled. Soon after, Shia death squads made their appearance. Some of them had apparently been organized inside (predominantly Shia) Iraqi military units that accompanied the U.S. military into Sunni communities. According to the *Washington Post*, "a police officer in Duluiyah, Capt. Qaid al-Azawi, accused U.S. forces of standing by in Balad while [Shia] militiamen in police cars and police uniforms slaughtered Sunnis."[25] In the face of these attacks large numbers of residents fled, adding to the river of refugees flooding the country. The U.S. pacification campaign had become its opposite, escalating the cycle of slaughter, while neighborhoods were emptied of the members of whichever sect was losing local ground.

As with many other developments in the war, this unmitigated disaster for Baghdad residents was a lesser one for the occupation. For the Bush administration, the storm of violence in the Iraqi capital had at least one benefit: the occupation's two main enemies were now at each other's throats. As a U.S. intelligence official told investigative reporter Seymour Hersh, "The White House believes that if American troops stay in Iraq long enough—with enough troops—the bad guys will end up killing each other."[26]

The Surge

As Operation Together Forward I continued, intense violence spread across the city. U.S. combat fatalities reached a two-year high of 113 in November 2006, not in itself surprising since occupation troops were entering militia strongholds. Other statistics, however, defied Washington's expectations.

The number of insurgent attacks, which should have declined, increased dramatically. A little under one hundred per day through the first half 2006, they jolted up to 140 soon after the offensive started and then hovered between 160 and 180 per day for the rest of the year. The number of lethal bombings, a main target of the offensive, also rose. According to U.S. military statistics published by the Brookings Institution, in late 2005 they rose from under twenty to more than forty per month and then started upward again as the U.S. offensive began in the late spring 2006, reaching sixty-nine in December. Deaths associated with these bombings soared from under five hundred per month in early 2006 to almost one thousand per month in the second half of the year.[27] Population displacement also reached new heights—especially in communities where occupation forces were most active.[28]

In response the U.S. military sought a new plan for pacifying Baghdad, which would become known as "the surge." Rather than altering the fundamental premises of Operation Together Forward I and II,[29] the architects of the surge argued that the previous campaign had failed because insufficient force had been applied. Now, tens of thousands of new U.S. troops would be sent to Baghdad, using tactics borrowed from the 2004 assault on the Sunni city of Fallujah. Each target area would first be surrounded to prevent insurgents from escaping. Then, once the battle was joined, overwhelming firepower would be brought to bear. As Captain Paul Fowler had explained to *Boston Globe* reporter Anne Barnard during the Fallujah fighting, "The only way to root out [the insurgents] is to destroy everything in your path."[30]

As in Fallujah the new surge plan also called for invading forces to remain in the community to prevent the insurgents from returning and to supervise the Iraqi army units they had led into battle.

The Battle of Haifa Street

The template for the surge was first applied in January 2008, even before Bush's official speech to the nation, in the battle of Haifa Street.

Haifa Street, a moderately prosperous two-mile-long avenue just outside the U.S.-controlled Green Zone in Baghdad, had been a center of Sunni resistance since early in the war. Like most insurgent strongholds, it had largely been quiet since the fall of Hussein except when occupation troops attempted to pacify it.

Soon after the fall of Baghdad, local leaders in the area constructed militias to combat the wave of criminal violence that swept through the capital after the CPA dismantled the Iraqi military and police. By early

2004 the militia leaders, together with clerics from neighborhood mosques, were the de facto local government. Although they institutionalized their form of Sunni fundamentalism, until mid-2005 they tolerated the presence and practices of a substantial Shia minority, which continued to live peacefully among the Sunni majority.

During the first year after the fall of the Hussein regime, serious violence occurred only when occupation troops entered the area. When the U.S. military arrived, they were met by snipers and roadside bombs that sought to divert the intruders from their goal of arresting or killing suspected insurgents.[31] The battles that often followed these incidents were so ferocious that U.S. soldiers dubbed the neighborhood "Death Street," and the patrols dwindled as Haifa Street became one of many no-go areas in the capital, "off-limits for American and even Iraqi soldiers."[32]

In November 2004 an IED exploded near one of the occasional occupation patrols, demolishing a Humvee and triggering a cascading set of events that culminated with a U.S. helicopter shooting into a crowd and killing Mazen Tomeizi, a Palestinian reporter for the Al Arabiya satellite news network of Dubai. Because when Tomeizi was shot he was filming his follow-up to the earlier incident, his death became one of the most horrific and widely viewed images of the war—at least in the Middle East—with his blood splattering on the camera as he cried, "I'm going to die, I'm going to die."[33] This incident convinced the U.S. military command to make another attempt to pacify Haifa Street.[34]

Under the headline "A Violent Street Finds Calm," *Christian Science Monitor* reporter Scott Peterson described how the U.S. military took control of the neighborhood in a six-month military offensive that included "rooftop snipers" and other "tough measures that reportedly included abuse of detainees."[35] This running battle, which began in January 2005, qualified as the most violent period in Haifa Street history—until the surge arrived. But in the U.S. media the emphasis was on the pacification and quiescence achieved, once—by late spring 2005—the occupation had suppressed the active resistance.

Sprinkled among positive stories of grateful residents welcoming the end of the fighting were telltale signs of an unpopular military occupation: some residents would "glower" when U.S. troops passed by; "tensions [were] a little higher" whenever occupation troops entered a street; and graffiti slogans proclaiming "Long Live the Mujahideen" were quickly restored after the soldiers tried to obliterate them. Nevertheless in June 2005 ABC News reporter Nick Watt declared that "Death Street is indeed a thing of the past."[36]

Occupation control, however, ultimately collapsed because the Haifa

Street guerrillas had melted into the population while waiting to reclaim the community. Just before the declarations of success were issued, they had initiated their own "surge of violence" before melting back into the neighborhood. Even at the moment when ABC reporter Watts was offering an obituary to "Death Street," U.S. troops and their Iraqi counterparts were conducting dozens of weekly patrols, breaking into homes in the Haifa Street neighborhood to arrest or kill residents suspected of membership in or support for the revived insurgency.[37] These patrols, together with a massive increase in unemployment, the precipitous deterioration of public services, and economic shocks generated by the removal of government food and fuel subsidies, insured increased support for and membership in the resistance.

In February 2006, with violence exploding all over Baghdad in response to the Golden Dome bombing, the occupation withdrew its troops from Haifa Street, leaving a contingent of government troops in charge. Very quickly afterward, the guerrillas resurfaced and expelled the Iraqi army, putting an end to the military patrols, home invasions, arrests, and detentions, as well as the battles they had generated. Haifa Street once again became an enemy enclave suspected of "harboring terrorists." As *New York Times* reporter Marc Santora put it in early 2007: "For the past two years, [Haifa Street] has been relatively quiet, but in recent months, as the sectarian fighting has intensified, Iraqi and American military officials suspected it was being used as a base of operations for insurgents concentrating on the Shiite civilian population and American forces."[38]

Occupation Forces Reenter Haifa Street, Bringing Sectarian Violence with Them

Haifa Street's relative calm was sustained even while ferocious sectarian violence erupted elsewhere in the capital. Ethnic cleansing, so prevalent in other parts of the city, had not yet transformed the neighborhood and most of the Shia members of the community remained in their homes.

When adjoining neighborhoods also calmed down, an uneasy but genuine peace settled over the area. The foundation of this truce was no mystery: Haifa Street militia members, freed from defensive fights against the U.S. military and strengthened by their victory over the Iraqi military, were mobilized to protect and defend the larger community against Shia death squads. In fact, all around Baghdad Sunni militias had responded to the escalating Shia death squad activity by focusing on preventing any police personnel from entering their neighborhoods, since death squads most often came in official uniforms and vehicles. As *Asia Times* commentator Mahan Abedin put it, "The residents widely welcome the presence of the guerrillas as vital protection against Shi'ite paramilitaries (often operating as Iraqi security forces)."[39]

The success of these measures—as well as comparable measures by the Mahdi Army in similarly well-organized Shia communities—was one component of the focus that both car bombers and death squads gave to poorly defended mixed neighborhoods. In 2006 and 2007 this competition for mixed neighborhoods had yielded victory after victory for the Shia. Their greater numbers, their integration into the official security forces, and the focus of Operation Together Forward I and II on Sunni insurgents combined to produce a tide of Sunni expulsions from mixed neighborhoods. The newly consolidated Shia areas then became fresh strongholds and amplified the Shia advantages, generating a more and more embattled posture among the remaining Sunni communities, which also faced the problem of trying to integrate a flood of new refugees expelled from previously mixed neighborhoods.

In the meantime Muqtada al-Sadr's Mahdi Army was a key force in expanding the Shia areas of Baghdad. As violence spread into contested neighborhoods, the Mahdi had also spread, participating in the ethnic expulsions and consolidating local leadership independent of the official government, which they continued to oppose as an instrument of the occupation. Eventually, mixed areas in and around Haifa Street had become consolidated Shia strongholds, with the Mahdi moving displaced Shia families from other areas into the vacated Sunni dwellings. The Mahdi, like their Sunni counterparts, patrolled the streets to guard against sectarian intruders, thus preventing any reversal of the ethnic displacements. These patrols also created a form of mutual deterrence on both sides of the sectarian divide that now characterized the Haifa Street section of town. Though not all Shia had yet left the Sunni sections of the community, borders between neighborhoods were well established and neither side had the strength to attack the other.

The Occupation Surge into Haifa Street

During Operation Together Forward I occupation forces had focused their attacks on Sunni strongholds despite the growing strength of Sadrists and their militia, the Mahdi Army. During Operation Together Forward II this focus shifted, and U.S. incursions and attacks on Shia areas become more common. One such incursion took place in early January 2007, when troops entered a border area near Haifa Street and arrested a senior Mahdi leader, apparently the local commander in that part of the city.[40]

The removal of this key officer compromised the effectiveness of the Mahdi protective patrols. Quoting an unnamed U.S. military official, *New York Times* reporter Marc Santora noted that: "The arrest . . . created an opening for Sunni insurgents, and they began aggressively singling out Shiites who had relocated south from the neighborhood of Kadhimiya."[41]

These attacks may or may not have originated in Haifa Street, but when twenty-seven Shia bodies were dumped there on January 6 it became the occasion for the first U.S. offensive in Bush's soon-to-be-announced "surge." As U.S. military spokesman Lieutenant Colonel Scott Bleichwehl explained, "It's an area that needed to be brought back under Iraqi security control."[42] Ali al-Dabaggh, a spokesman for Iraqi Prime Minister Nouri al-Maliki, was blunter: "This area must be cleansed," he said, suggesting that the solution lay in removing all Sunni from the neighborhood.[43]

Haifa Street Sunni residents believed al-Dabaggh, particularly after U.S. commanders mentioned the 2005 battle of Tal Afar as the model of their new strategy.[44] In Tal Afar, a city of about three hundred thousand near the Syrian border, the entire population of pro-insurgent neighborhoods was moved out as part of the pacification process.

Iraqi military forces were sent in first but within a couple of days they had been repulsed. These battles and the growing sectarian violence in border areas shattered the fragile foundation of sectarian peace within Haifa Street, and the small remaining Shia minority began receiving threats that they would be killed "if they did not leave immediately."[45]

The Denouement

Before dawn on January 9, after sealing off the area, the occupation forces attacked, backed by helicopters and jets and followed by Iraqi soldiers. *Washington Post* reporters Sudarsan Raghavan and Joshua Partlow offered this description of the battle, quoting Major Jesse Pearson and Sergeant Israel Schaeffer:

> In the pre-dawn darkness, the joint forces took control of the buildings surrounding Tallil Square, a key target of the operation.
> "We showed up in their living room for breakfast," Pearson said.
> About 7 am, the trouble began. "As soon as the sun came up, the insurgents began shooting," he said.
> "We started taking it from all sides," Schaeffer recalled.
> From rooftops and doorways, the gunmen fired AK-47 assault rifles and machine guns. Snipers also were targeting the U.S. and Iraqi soldiers. U.S. soldiers started firing back with 50-caliber machine guns mounted on their Stryker armored vehicles. They used TOW missiles and Mark-19

grenade launchers. The F-15 fighter jets strafed rooftops with cannons, while the Apaches fired Hellfire missiles.[46]

After eleven hours of death and devastation, the occupation forces prevailed and one thousand U.S. and Iraqi troops began house-to-house searches, arresting and killing suspected insurgents.

The next day, CBS News reporter Lara Logan provided horrifying visual evidence of conditions on Haifa Street in a report that only appeared online. It showed demolished buildings, deserted neighborhoods, and the results of sectarian torture on both sides. It concluded with a resident who blamed the United States for the plight of his community: "They told us they would bring democracy. They promised life would be better than it was under Hussein. But they brought us nothing but death and killing. They brought mass destruction to Baghdad."[47] According to McClatchy reporters Youssef and Obeid, "a U.S. military spokesman said he had no reason to believe Haifa Street residents' accounts." Meanwhile, U.S. ambassador Zalmay Khalilzad told a press conference, "I am encouraged by what I have seen"[48]

One week later the battle for Haifa Street continued.[49] More and more residents were fleeing the area, trying to escape U.S. airstrikes, to avoid the cross-fire between the occupation and insurgents, or to elude the death threats made by both sides of the sectarian divide.

Reflecting on the battle for a neighborhood that "the United States has now fought to regain from a mysterious enemy at least three times in the past two years," Sergeant First Class Marc Biletski told New York Times reporters Damien Cave and James Glanz, "This place is a failure. . . . Every time we come here, we have to come back."[50]

The Results of the Surge

Haifa Street would become typical of many Baghdad communities that soon felt the full impact of the surge offensive. A year later the neighborhood still bore all the marks of battle. There had been no effort to restore public services including the electrical grid or the water-treatment system; there were no medical services, nor was there any public transportation.

The New York Post's Ralph Peters summarized the posture of the Maliki government inside the Green Zone: "Iraq's government isn't much help—none, as far as Haifa Street's revival is concerned." The U.S. military commander on Haifa Street told him that the U.S. was relying on "spontaneous economic development"—local citizens were expected to develop the area through their own efforts with the help of a limited number of microloans (a few hundred dollars each) from the military's meager noncombat funds. It was no surprise then that aside from a few food markets, there was no economy to speak of.[51] In the meantime tens of thousands of mainly Sunni residents had left, with large parts of the area transformed from Sunni to Shia and smaller sections moving in the other direction.[52] A large contingent of U.S. soldiers remained in the area while a vast cement barrier with a handful of heavily armored gates was put in place, effectively separating the community from the rest of the city. The dislodged insurgents retreated into intermittent guerrilla war, organizing some twenty attacks on U.S. forces each month—a sharp reduction from the seventy-four much larger battles they had fought in January. U.S. forces mounted an average of thirty-four combat patrols each day aimed at capturing or suppressing them.[53]

In January 2008 Lieutenant Colonel Tony Aguto, the U.S. commander in Haifa Street, estimated that some fifty thousand of the area's one hundred fifty thousand residents had been displaced in the previous year.[54] In Baghdad as a whole, the United Nations High Commissioner on Refugees estimated that the heavy surge fighting in the first half of 2007 was producing ninety thousand refugees a month, the bulk from Baghdad; the 2007 total reached eight hundred thousand.[55]

As ethnic cleansing in Haifa Street and elsewhere was completed, the rate of refugee production began to drop, declining to thirty thousand by December 2007. Displaced Baghdad residents, searching desperately for places to settle, faced the overwhelming challenge of supporting families in a largely dormant economy with dwindling government support. This was not, commented Lieutenant Colonel Aguto, a problem the occupation needed to address. "It is," he said, "the job of the Iraqi government to sort this out."[56]

The Ebb of the Surge

As the battle of Haifa Street illustrated, the surge amplified violence in the capital significantly. For six months U.S. forces invaded one community after another, using all the firepower at their command. When heavy fighting ended the occupation sought to consolidate their military victory by erecting the ubiquitous concrete barriers, ensuring the ethnic segregation of each neighborhood or partial neighborhood. These became demarcation lines and no-go boundaries in the city's civil war. The walls ensured that there would be little or no physical, social, or economic contact among ghettoized, ethnically cleansed areas, even ones that had previously depended on such intercourse for daily sustenance. The city's already compromised economy thus suffered another blow. Residents of these new ghettos, unable to travel to jobs, became increasingly desperate. Many, searching for solutions, joined or supported the local militias that spoke and acted on their behalf and also provided employment and a hope for change. Shia militiaman Abu Mustafa al-Thahabi told *Washington Post* reporter Sudarsan Raghavan, "People have reached a point that they will sell their refrigerator to buy a rocket launcher to shoot and kill the Americans."[57]

As sectarian displacement continued, the Shia militias essentially moved east to west across Baghdad, creating more Shia-dominated areas out of previously mixed and Sunni neighborhoods. Mainly in the western and southern parts of Baghdad, the Sunni militias persevered, consolidating their control in areas that the occupation did not invade.

The ghettoization of Baghdad, which had begun relatively modestly in early 2005, reached a crescendo in early 2007 with the surge and was largely completed by the fall 2007. By that time what had once been a city split between Sunnis and Shia had been transformed into a 75-percent-Shia capital. The U.S. military made its presence felt at checkpoints, at many small bases established around the city, and by patrols into neighborhoods now demarcated by cement barriers. The localities however were still governed by the local militias in what was no longer an integrated city, but a ghettoized collection of ethnically cleansed enclaves.

The End of the Surge

After a spring and summer of heavy fighting, the occupation was still far from pacifying Baghdad. In a way the surge had worsened the situation. Before it began, in many neighborhoods neither Sunni nor Shia militias were dominant. By mid-2007 nearly every community had its own mini-government, usually dominated by a militia that was hostile both to the occupation and the central government. To assert centralized authority over the city, each neighborhood would have to be invaded again.

Without announcing a change in policy, the U.S. military abandoned the surge in late summer 2007 in favor of a live-and-let-live program. On the Sunni side of the street, the occupation pursued a version of the Awakening movement that had arisen without occupation encouragement in Anbar province the previous year, and then had been embraced by U.S. military commanders attempting to coopt the Sunni insurgency in those cities.[58] In Baghdad, as in Anbar, these so-called Concerned Local Citizens groups (CLCs) were created by negotiating armed truces with insurgent adversaries on a community-by-community basis.

On the Shia side the occupation essentially negotiated a temporary cease-fire with the Mahdi Army, described publicly as a unilateral stand-down by its leader Muqtada Al Sadr. The Sadrists curtailed the planting of lethal roadside bombs against the U.S. military and no longer sought to ambush occupation and Iraqi army troops moving through their neighborhoods. The U.S. military curtailed its raids and offensives in Sadrist neighborhoods and spent far less effort hunting down and arresting Sadrist leaders.

The result of this twofold détente was a dramatic reduction in violence in Baghdad. With the U.S. military keeping its side of the bargain, the huge running battles associated with occupation attacks on Sunni strongholds like Haifa Street declined, and even the smaller battles resulting from attempts to capture specific insurgents subsided. In return both Sunni and Shia insurgents reduced their attacks against U.S. forward bases and convoys in Baghdad, and the jihadists, largely expelled from Sunni insurgent communities, either demobilized or moved to northern Iraq where negotiations with insurgents had not taken place.

This was, however, little more than a fragile, armed truce among enemies, a truce that actually strengthened the militias within their own communities. The Sunni insurgents, now validated as legitimate police and even paid and armed by the U.S. military, began making political demands for restoration of services as well as for infrastructure reconstruction and job-creation programs for their desperate constituents, all the while denouncing the Iraqi government as a client of U.S. and Iranian policy.

The Mahdi Army militias, having extended their influence into previously mixed neighborhoods, used the truce to spread their own meager but meaningful social service programs and demand increased access to resources that might revive the economy of the city. Their national spokespeople continued to insist that the country could not begin genuine reconstruction until the United States left. Although many Baghdad communities experienced their lowest levels of violence in two years, the cement barriers made social and economic life nearly impossible. Most people were locked into ghettos, terrified of strangers, afraid to send their children to schools, and unable to reach (and consequently to hold) jobs. Employers, deprived of workers and customers, shuttered their establishments. The economy barely existed.[59]

For most of Baghdad, like the rest of the country, the Iraqi government had become irrelevant. It had no administrative apparatus in any communities and made no attempt to restore needed services. Its only presence, the Iraqi army, was only occasionally visible and was usually commanded or controlled by U.S. officers. When Iraqi soldiers appeared as independent forces they were populated predominantly with Shias and led by Shia militia commanders, not by the central government. In neighborhoods just a few hundred feet from the Green Zone, the Iraqi government did not exist.

The occupation had long since lost any semblance of sovereignty. It maintained the most fearsome of the militias in Baghdad, capable of militarily overwhelming any adversary, but incapable of creating stable rule, even in cement-encircled ghettos like Haifa Street. Occupation forces could not deliver electricity, water, or jobs—or even safe passage to the next neighborhood.

As early as May 2006, Nir Rosen presciently described the U.S. military's position in this way: "[T]he American Army is lost in Iraq, as it has been since it arrived. Striking at Sunnis, striking at Shias, striking at mostly innocent people. Unable to distinguish between anybody, certainly unable to wield any power, except on the immediate street corner where it's located . . . [T]he Americans are just one more militia lost in the anarchy."[60]

In spring 2008 the residents of Baghdad were waiting. They were waiting for the walls around their neighborhoods to come down, public transportation to be restored, and roads to be reopened so they could begin to move around the city. They waited for public services to be rebuilt so they could count on being able to turn on the lights, have clean water come out of taps, and perhaps even contribute to "spontaneous economic development." They waited for employers to begin rehiring so they could begin to support their suffering families.[61]

They were waiting for the United States to leave.

Conclusion

The River of Resistance: How Washington's Dream Foundered in Iraq

Always remember that the spirit of the people is greater than the man's technology.
—Huey P. Newton

On February 15, 2003, ordinary citizens around the world poured into the streets to protest George W. Bush's onrushing invasion of Iraq. Demonstrations took place in large cities and small towns globally, including a tiny but spirited protest at the McMurdo Station in Antarctica. Up to thirty million people, who sensed impending catastrophe, participated in what the author Rebecca Solnit called "the biggest and most widespread collective protest the world has ever seen."[1]

The first glancing assessment of history branded this remarkable planetary protest a record-breaking failure, since the Bush administration, less than one month later, ordered U.S. troops across the Kuwaiti border and on to Baghdad.

And it has since largely been forgotten or (perhaps better put) obliterated from official and media memory. Yet popular protest is more like a river than a storm; it keeps flowing into new areas, carrying pieces of its earlier life into other realms. We rarely know its consequences until many years afterward, when, if we're lucky, we finally sort out its meandering path.[2] Speaking for the protesters back in May 2003, only a month after U.S. troops entered the Iraqi capital, Solnit offered the following:

> We will likely never know, but it seems that the Bush administration decided against the 'Shock and Awe' saturation bombing of Baghdad because

we made it clear that the cost in world opinion and civil unrest would be too high. We millions may have saved a few thousand or a few tens of thousand of lives. The global debate about the war delayed it for months, months that perhaps gave many Iraqis time to lay in stores, evacuate, brace for the onslaught.[3]

Whatever history ultimately concludes about that unexpected moment of protest, once the war began, other forms of resistance arose—mainly in Iraq itself—that were equally unexpected. Their effects on the larger goals of Bush administration planners can be more easily traced. In a land the size of California, with twenty-six million people, an amalgam of Baathists, fundamentalists, former military men, union organizers, democratic secularists, local tribal leaders, politically active clerics, and outraged ordinary citizens—often at each others' throats—managed to thwart the plans of the self-proclaimed New Rome, the "hyperpower" and "global sheriff" of planet Earth. This fact, even in the first glancing assessment of history, may indeed prove historic.

The New American Century Goes Missing in Action

It's hard now even to recall the original vision George W. Bush and his top officials had of how the conquest of Iraq would unfold as an episode in the Global War on Terror. In the minds of the war's planners, the invasion was sure to yield a quick victory, to be followed by the creation of a client state in Iraq that would house crucial "enduring" U.S. military bases from which Washington would project power throughout what it called "the Greater Middle East."[4]

In addition, Iraq would quickly become a free-market paradise, replete with privatized oil flowing at record rates onto the world market. Like falling dominos, Syria and Iran, cowed by such a demonstration of U.S. might, would follow suit, either from additional military thrusts or because their regimes—and those of up to sixty countries worldwide—would appreciate the futility of resisting Washington's demands.[5] Eventually, the "unipolar moment" of U.S. global hegemony that the collapse of the Soviet Union had initiated would be extended into a "New American Century" (accompanied by a generational Pax Republicana at home).[6]

This vision is now, of course, long gone, largely thanks to unexpected and tenacious resistance within Iraq. This resistance consisted of far more than the initial Sunni insurgency, which had tied down what Donald Rumsfeld boast labeled "the greatest military force on the face of the earth."[7] It is already not a rash statement to suggest that, at all levels of society, usually at great sacrifice, the Iraqi people frustrated the imperial designs of the world's greatest superpower.

Consider, for example, the myriad ways in which the Iraqi Sunnis resisted the occupation of their country from almost the moment it became clear that the Bush administration intended to dismantle the governing apparatus of Saddam Hussein's Baathist regime. The predominantly Sunni city of Fallujah, like most other communities around the country, spontaneously formed a new government based on local clerical and tribal structures. Like many of these cities, it avoided the worst of the postinvasion looting by encouraging the formation of local militias to police the community. Ironically, the orgy of looting that took place in Baghdad was, at least in part, a consequence of the U.S. military presence, which delayed the creation of such militias there. Eventually, however, sectarian militias brought a modicum of order even to Baghdad.

In Fallujah and elsewhere, these same militias soon became effective instruments for reducing, and—for a time—eliminating, the presence of the U.S. military. The militias' effectiveness depended, however, on the support given them by their members' relatives, friends, and neighbors—that is, the ordinary citizens of each community—who risked their own safety by hiding the fighters, by supplying them with food and armament, and by refusing to divulge their identities to the occupation.

For the better part of a year, faced with IEDs and ambushes from insurgents and the protective secrecy of the community, the U.S. military declared Fallujah a no-go zone, withdrew to bases outside the city, and discontinued violent incursions into hostile neighborhoods. This retreat was matched in many other cities and towns. The absence of patrols by occupation forces saved tens of thousands of suspected insurgents from the often deadly violence of home invasions and spared their relatives and neighbors from wrecked homes and detention.

Even the most successful U.S. military campaign in that period, the second battle of Fallujah in November 2004, could be seen—if viewed from quite a different perspective than the one presented by the establishment media—as a successful act of resistance. Because the United States was required to mass a significant proportion of its combat brigades for the offensive (even transferring British troops from the south to perform logistical duties), most other cities were left alone and therefore, for some months, not subject to the violent incursions of the occupation. Many of these cities, moreover, used this respite to establish or consolidate quasi-governments and defensive militias, making it all the more difficult for the occupation to attack and control them.

Fallujah itself was, of course, destroyed, with 70 percent of its buildings turned to rubble, thousands killed, and tens of thousands of its residents permanently displaced—an extreme sacrifice that nevertheless had the unexpected effect of taking pressure off other Iraqi cities, if only for a while.[8] Perhaps the most fortunate beneficiaries of the Fallujans' sacrifice were the Shia cities of the south. The ferocity of the resistance in Fallujah and other Sunni cities forced the U.S. military to wait almost four years before renewing its initial 2004 efforts to pacify the well-organized Sadrist-led resistance in the predominantly Shia areas of the country.

The Rebellion of the Oil Workers

In another arena entirely, consider the Bush administration's dreams of harnessing Iraqi oil production to its foreign policy ambitions.[9] The immediate goals, as Bush administration planners saw it, were to double prewar output and begin the process of transferring control of production from state ownership to foreign companies. Three major energy initiatives designed to accomplish these goals had, by late 2007, been frustrated by resistance from virtually every segment of Iraqi society. Iraq's well-organized oil workers played a key role in this long campaign by using their ability to bring production to a virtual standstill. Only a few months after the United States toppled Saddam Hussein's regime, the oil union stopped all oil shipments to abort the transfer of the southern oil port of Basra to the management of KBR (still at that point a Halliburton subsidiary). Faced with an indefinite interruption in oil shipments, the occupation returned control to the government owned oil company.

This and other early acts of labor defiance turned back the initial assault on the Iraqi government-controlled system of oil production. Such acts also laid a foundation for successful efforts to prevent the passage of oil policies shaped in Washington that were designed to transfer energy exploration and production to foreign companies. In these efforts, the oil workers were joined by both Sunni and Shia resistance groups, local governments, and finally the new national parliament.

This same sort of resistance extended to the whole roster of neoliberal reforms sponsored by the U.S.-controlled CPA. From the beginning of the occupation there were protests against mass unemployment caused by the dismantling of the Baathist state, the shuttering of state-owned factories, and other CPA initiatives. Much of the armed resistance was a response to the occupation's violent suppression of nonviolent protests.

Perhaps more significant were local efforts to replace the government services discontinued by the CPA. The same local quasi-governments that had nurtured the militias sought to sustain or replace Baathist social programs, often financing them by siphoning off oil destined for export and selling it on the black market. The result was the creation of virtual city-states wherever U.S. troops were not present, leading to the inability of the occupation to pacify any substantial portion of the country.

The Sadrist movement and the Mahdi Army militia of the cleric Muqtada al-Sadr were probably the most successful—and most anti-occupation—of the Shia political parties-cum-militias that systematically sought to develop quasi-government organizations. They tried to meet, however minimally, the basic needs of their communities, supplying food baskets and housing services, and performing a host of other functions previously promised by the Baathist government but forsworn by the U.S. occupation and the Iraqi government that the United States installed when "handing over" sovereignty in June 2004.[10]

U.S. occupation authorities expected that their plans for the rapid privatization and transformation of the state-driven economy would indeed generate resistance, but they were convinced that this would subside quickly once the determination of the occupation military was demonstrated and the new economy kicked into gear. Instead, as the economic depression deepened and military repression grew more destructive, demands for relief grew more strident and insistent, while the country itself, in chaos and near collapse, became visible evidence of the failure of the Bush administration's free-market policies.

An Iraqi Agenda for Withdrawal

Occupation officials faced the same dilemma in the political realm. The original goal of the Bush administration was a stable, pro-Washington government, stripped of its economic and political dominance over Iraqi society, but a bastion of resistance to Iranian regional power and the host to an extensive network of "enduring" U.S. military bases. Under the weight of Iraqi resistance, this vision, like its military and economic cousins, had been wholly frustrated four years later.

Take, for example, the two high-profile Iraqi elections, celebrated in the mainstream media as a unique Bush administration accomplishment in the otherwise relentlessly autocratic Middle East. Inside Iraq these elections had quite a different look. It is important to remember that the United States initially planned to sustain its direct rule—through CPA—until Iraq was fully pacified and its economic reforms completed.[11] When the CPA became a hated symbol of an unwanted occupation, planning shifted to the idea of installing an appointed Iraqi government, based on community meetings that only supporters of the occupation could attend. Full-scale elections would be postponed until winners fully supportive of the Bush agenda were assured. But an outpouring of protest from the predominantly Shia areas of the country, led by Grand Ayatollah Ali al-Sistani, forced CPA administrators to shift to an election-based strategy.

The first election in January 2005 delivered a sizeable parliamentary majority with platforms specifying strict timetables for a full U.S. military withdrawal from the country. Bush administration representatives then forcefully pressured the newly installed cabinet to abandon this position.

The second parliamentary election in December 2005 followed a similar pattern. This time, the backroom bargaining was only partially effective. The newly installed prime minister, Nouri al-Maliki, reneged on his campaign promises by publicly supporting an ongoing U.S. military presence, which caused deep fissures in the ruling coalition. After a year of unproductive negotiations, the thirty Sadrists in parliament, originally a key part of Maliki's ruling coalition, withdrew from both the coalition and the cabinet in protest over the prime minister's refusal to set a date for an end to the occupation. Subsequent parliamentary demands for a certain date for withdrawal were ignored by both the government and U.S. officials. While Maliki continued in office without a parliamentary majority, the controversy contributed to the soaring popularity of the Sadrists and waning support for the other Shiite governing parties. .

By early 2008, with provincial elections looming in November, there was little doubt that the Sadrists would sweep to power in many predominantly Shia provinces, most critically Basra, Iraq's second largest city and southern oil hub. To prevent this debacle, Iraqi government troops, supported and advised by the U.S. military, sought to expel the Sadrists from key areas of Basra, launching a major assault in March.[12]

This use of military force to prevent electoral defeat was only one of many indications that the Iraqi government was feeling the pressure of public opinion. Another was the reluctance of Prime Minister Maliki to maintain an antagonistic stance toward Iran. Despite fervent Bush administration efforts, his government promoted social, religious, and economic relationships between Iraqis and Iranians. These included facilitating visits to the holy cities of Karbala and Najaf by hundreds of thousands of Iranian Shia pilgrims, as well as supporting extensive oil transactions between Basra and Iranian firms, including distribution and refining services that promised to integrate the two energy economies. A formal military relationship between the two countries was vetoed by U.S. authorities, but this did not reverse the tide of cooperation. (In fact, Iran brokered the cease-fire that concluded the joint U.S. and Iraqi assault on Basra.[13])

The River of Resistance

As the occupation wore on, the Bush administration found itself swimming against a tide of resistance of a previously unimaginable sort, and was ever further from its goals. By mid-2008, cities and towns around the country were largely under the sway of Shia or Sunni militias that, even when trained or paid by the occupation, remain militantly opposed to the U.S. presence. Moreover, though the prostrate Iraqi economy had been formally privatized, these local militias—and the political leaders they worked with—continued to raise demands for vast government-funded reconstruction and economic development programs, often threatening to appropriate the resources unilaterally if the government did not comply.

The formal political leadership of Iraq, locked inside the heavily fortified, U.S.-controlled Green Zone in Baghdad, remained publicly compliant with Bush administration plans to transform Iraq into a Middle Eastern outpost—including the continued presence of U.S. troops on a series of megabases in the heart of the country.[14] The rest of the government bureaucracy and the bulk of Iraq's grass roots were increasingly insistent on an early departure date and a reversal of the economic policies first introduced by the occupation.

In Washington, for Democratic as well as Republican politicians, the outpost idea remained at the heart of the policy agenda for Iraq in the 2008 election campaign, along with the idea of forging a neoliberal economy in Iraq, featuring a modernized oil sector in which multinational firms applied state-of-the-art technology to maximize the country's lagging oil production.

Iraqi resistance of every kind and on every level had already frustrated this vision for four years. Because of the Iraqis, the metaphoric Global War on Terror had been transformed into an endless, hopeless actual war.

But the Iraqis have paid a terrible price for resisting. The invasion and the social and economic policies that accompanied it have destroyed Iraq, leaving its people essentially destitute. In the first five years of this endless war, Iraqis suffered more for resisting than if they had accepted and endured U.S. military and economic dominance. Whether consciously or not, they sacrificed themselves to halt Washington's projected military and economic march through the oil-rich Middle East on the path to a New American Century that now will never be.

It is now past time for the rest of the world to shoulder at least a small share of the burden of resistance. Just as the worldwide protests before the war were among the sources of the Iraqi resistance-to-come, so now others, especially residents of the United States, should resist the very idea that Iraq could ever become the headquarters for a permanent U.S presence that would, in the words of Bush speechwriter David Frum, "put America more wholly in charge of the region than any power since the Ottomans, or maybe even the Romans." [15] Unlike the Iraqis, after all, the people of the United States are uniquely positioned to bury this imperial dream for all time.

Notes

Introduction

This chapter epigraph is drawn from Neil Smith, *The Endgame of Globalization* (New York: Routledge, 2005), 53.

1. Tom Engelhardt, "The $100 Barrel of Oil vs. the Global War on Terror," Tom-Dispatch, January 8, 2008, http://www.tomdispatch.com/post/174878/if_the_gwot_were_gone. Internal quotes are to Jane Perlez, "After the Attacks: U.S. Demands Arab Countries 'Choose Sides,'" *New York Times*, September 15, 2001, "US 'Threatened to Bomb' Pakistan," British Broadcasting Corporation, September 22, 2006, http://news.bbc.co.uk/2/hi/south_asia/5369198.stm.
2. R. W. Apple, Jr., "After the Attacks: No Middle Ground," *New York Times*, September 14, 2001, quoted in Engelhardt, "The $100 Barrel of Oil."
3. "Top Bush Officials Push Case Against Saddam," CNN, September 9, 2002, http://archives.cnn.com/2002/ALLPOLITICS/09/08/iraq.debate/.
4. George W. Bush, "State of the Union Address," January 20, 2003, http://www.whitehouse.gov/news/releases/2003/01/20030128-19.html.
5. Ibid.
6. Ibid.
7. Paul Wolfowitz, "Wolfowitz Interview with *Vanity Fair*'s Tannenhaus," United States Department of Defense (Press Release, May 30, 2003), http://www.defenselink.mil/transcripts/2003/tr20030509-depsecdef0223.html.
8. Alan Greenspan, *The Age of Turbulence: Adventures in a New World* (New York: Penguin, 2007), 463.
9. Jeremy Earp and Sut Jhally, *Highjacking Catastrophe: 9/11, Fear and the Selling of the American Empire* (Immediate Pictures, Media Education Foundation, 2005), documentary film.
10. Naomi Klein, *The Shock Doctrine: The Rise of Disaster Capitalism* (New York: Metropolitan Books, 2007), especially 7–9.

11. Colin Powell, who studied under Ullman, called him a "rarity, a scholar in uniform, a line officer qualified for command at sea, also possessed of one of the best, most provocative minds I have ever encountered." Quoted in John T. Correll, "What Happened to Shock and Awe?" *Air Force Magazine* 86 (November 2003), http://www.afa.org/magazine/nov2003/1103shock.asp.

12. Quoted in Eduardo Mendieta, "The Axle of Evil: SUVing Through the Slums of Globalizing Neoliberalism," *City* 9 (July 2005): 223. See also James Wade and Harlan Ullman's influential book, *Shock and Awe: Achieving Rapid Dominance* (Washington, D.C.: Center for Advanced Concepts and Technology, 1996), and Jeremy Earp and Sut Jhally, *Hijacking Catastrophe: 9/11, Fear, and the Selling of American Empire* (Northampton, MA: 2004).

13. Quoted in Correll, "What Happened to Shock and Awe?"

14. This point is brilliantly made by philosopher Eduardo Mendieta in "The Axle of Evil," 224. Mendieta cites Paul Virilio as the source of this argument (Paul Virilio, *Strategy of Deception* [London: Verso, 2000], 15.)

15. Kenneth Rizer, "Bombing Dual-Use Targets: Legal, Ethical, and Doctrinal Perspective," *Air and Space Power Chronicles* 5 (January 2001): 176–77, http://www.airpower.maxwell.af.mil/airchronicles/cc/Rizer.html.

16. Ruth Blakeley, "Bomb Now, Die Later," *Commentary*, 2003, http://www.geocities .com/ruth_blakeley/bombnowdielater.ht (quoted in Graham, "Switching Cities Off," 174).

17. Mike Davis, "Planet of Slums: Urban Involution and the Informal Proletariat," *New Left Review* 26 (March/April, 2004): 5–34; Mike Davis, *Planet of Slums*, (New York: Verso, 2006).

18. Stephen Graham, "Switching Cities Off: Urban Infrastructure and U.S. airpower," *City* 9 (July 2005), 169. See also Stephen Graham, "Cities and the 'War on Terror,'" *International Journal of Urban and Regional Research* 30 (June 2006): 255–76.

19. Milton Friedman, *Capitalism and Freedom* (Chicago: University of Chicago Press. 1962, 1982), 2, quoted in Klein, *Shock Doctrine*, 6.

20. Klein, *Shock Doctrine*, 7–8. Internal quote is to Ullman and Wade, *Shock and Awe*, xxviii.

21. This account of initial U.S. strategy is taken from Graham, "Switching Cities Off," 180–88; and Correll, "What Happened to Shock and Awe?"

22. United States General Accountability Office (USGAO), *Rebuilding Iraq: Enhancing Security, Measuring Program Results, and Maintaining Infrastructure Are Necessary to Make Significant and Sustainable Progress*, (GAO-06-179T) (Washington, D.C.: U.S. Government Accountability Office, October 18, 2005), 5.5, http://www.gao.gov/htext/d06179t.html.

23. Quoted in Correll, "What Happened to Shock and Awe?"

24. Ibid.

25. Mendieta, "The Axle of Evil," 223.

26. For a well-reasoned example of this argument, see Paul D. Eaton, "For His Failures, Rumsfeld Must Go," *New York Times* (March 20, 2006) On Shinseki, see Thomas Ricks, *Fiasco: The American Military Adventure in Iraq* (New York: Penguin, 2006), 68–74.

27. Davis, "Planet of Slums," 16–17.

28. President George W. Bush, "Remarks by the President from the USS Abraham Lincoln At Sea Off the Coast of San Diego, California," White House press release, May 1, 2003, http://www.whitehouse.gov/news/releases/2003/05/20030501-15.html.

Chapter One

Greenspan, *Age of Turbulence*, 463.

George Packer, "Dreaming of Democracy," *New York Times Magazine*, March 2, 2003, 49; quoted in Anthony Arnove, *Iraq: The Logic of Withdrawal* (New York: The New Press, 2006), 7.

1.   This account is largely based on Michael Klare's *Blood and Oil: The Dangers and Consequences of America's Growing Dependency on Imported Petroleum* (New York: Metropolitan Books, 2004). See also his *Resource Wars: The New Landscape of Global Conflict* (New York: Metropolitan Books, 2001).

2.   Tariq Ali, *Bush in Babylon* (New York: Verso, 2003), chapters 2–3.

3.   Greg Muttit, "Crude Designs—The Rip Off of Iraq's Oil Wealth," Platform November 2005, 7, http://www.carbonweb.org/documents/crude_designs_large.pdf.

4.   Klare, *Blood and Oil*, xv.

5.   For a lucid account of the activities of OPEC, see Dilip Hiro, *Blood of the Earth: The Battle for the World's Vanishing Oil Reserves* (New York: Nation Books, 2006), 111–37. See also Greenspan, *Age of Turbulence*, 444–49.

6.   On the coup, see Hiro, *Blood of the Earth*, 92–98; on the revolution, see Misagh Parsa, *Social Origins of the Iranian Revolution* (Brunswick, NJ: Rutgers University Press, 1989).

7.   In addition to Klare, *Blood and Oil*, an excellent treatment of the pre-2000 foundations of the Bush policy toward Iraq can be found in a series of articles by James A. Paul: "Iraq: the Struggle for Oil," Global Policy Forum, August 2002 (revised December, 2002), http://www.globalpolicy.org/security/oil/2002/08jim.htm; "Oil in Iraq: the Heart of the Crisis," Global Policy Forum, December 2002, at http://www.globalpolicy.org/security/oil/2002/12heart.htm; and "The Iraq Oil Bonanza: Estimating Future Profits," Global Policy Forum, January 28, 2004, http://www.globalpolicy.org/security/oil/2004/0128oilprofit.htm.

8.   Klare, *Blood and Oil*, 46.

9.   Michael Klare, "The Pentagon as an Energy-Protection Racket," TomDispatch, January 14, 2007, http://www.tomdispatch.com/index.mhtml?emx=x&pid=157241.

10.   For the oily foundations of the Gulf War, see Klare, *Blood and Oil*, 49–50.

11.   "President Clinton Explains Iraq Strike," Cable News Network, December 16, 1998, found at http://www.cnn.com/ALLPOLITICS/stories/1998/12/16/transcripts/clinton.html; "Clinton Manufactured Iraq Crisis, Violated Constitution," The Wisdom Fund, January 4, 1999, http://www.twf.org/News/Y1998/19981222-IraqAttack.html.

12.   Baker Institute, "Running on Empty? Prospects for Future World Oil Supplies," Baker Institute for Public Policy (Rice University), November 2000, http://www.bakerinstitute.org/publications/study_14.pdf.

13.   Charles Krauthammer, "The Unipolar Moment," *Foreign Affairs: America and the World* 70 (No. 1, 1990/91).

14.   Klare, *Blood and Oil*, 67f.

15.   Project for a New American Century (PNAC), "Letter to the President," January 26, 1998, http://www.newamericancentury.org/iraqclintonletter.htm; Project for a New American Century, *Rebuilding America's Defenses: Strategy Forces and Resources for a New Century* (Washington D.C.: PNAC, September 2000), http://www.newamericancentury.org/RebuildingAmericasDefenses.pdf, 4, 75, passim.

16.   Project for a New American Century, "Letter to the President."

17.   Ibid.; PNAC, *Rebuilding America's Defenses*, 2, 11.

18. PNAC, *Rebuilding America's Defenses*, 2, 11.
19. This account based on Hiro, *Blood of the Earth*, 127–31.
20. U.S. imports came mainly from non–Middle East producers. Nora Macaluso, "Imported Oil Dependency Reaches Record 51% of U.S. Consumption," *Oklahoma City Journal Record* (Bloomberg Business News), January 16, 1997.
21. David Strahan, "Slippery Slope," *Guardian* (UK), October 3, 2007, http://www.truthout.org:80/issues_06/100307EA.shtml.
22. Greenspan, *Age of Turbulence*, 440.
23. Barbara Starr, "U.S. to Move Operations from Saudi Base," Cable News Network, April 29, 2003, http://www.cnn.com/2003/WORLD/meast/04/29/sprj.irq.saudi.us.
24. Hiro, *Blood of the Earth*, 134.
25. Matthew Simmons, *Twilight in the Desert* (Hoboken, NJ: Wiley, 2006).
26. Baker Institute, "Running on Empty," 10; see also pages 2, 6, passim.
27. Ron Suskind, *The Price of Loyalty* (New York, 2004), 85; quoted in Hiro, "It's the Oil, Stupid."
28. For a very useful account of the group's secret deliberations by a participant (Treasury Secretary Paul O'Neill), see Suskind, *The Price of Loyalty*, especially 143–56. For an excellent analysis of the task force's role in developing U.S. Middle East policy, see Mark LeVine, "Waist Deep in Big Oil," *Nation*, December 12, 2005 (posted November 22, 2005). See also Paul, "Oil Companies in Iraq."
29. Muttit, "Crude Designs," 7–8.
30. Antonia Juhasz, "Whose Oil Is It Anyway?" *New York Times*, March 13, 2007; Klare, *Blood and Oil*, 75–84.
31. Klare, *Blood and Oil*, 82.
32. Jane Mayer, "Contract Sport: What did the Vice-President Do for Halliburton?" *New Yorker*, February 16, 2004.
33. Suskind, *Price of Loyalty*, 129.
34. Ibid, 184–91, 204, 306–07.
35. Greenspan, *Age of Turbulence*, 463.
36. "Bush vs. Greenspan: White House Fires Back," ABC News, September 16, 2007. Later in 2007, Greenspan was joined in his claim by General John Abizaid, CentCom commander from 2003 to 2006, who told a Stanford University audience, "Of course it's about oil, we can't really deny that." This comment, however, attracted no media attention. Gerry Shih and Susana Montes, "Roundtable Debates Energy Issues," *Stanford Daily*, October 15, 2007.
37. Greenspan, *Age of Turbulence*.
38. Bob Woodward, "Greenspan: Ouster of Hussein Crucial for Oil Security," *Washington Post*, September 17, 2007.
39. Alan Greenspan and Naomi Klein, "Alan Greenspan vs. Naomi Klein on the Iraq War, Bush's Tax Cuts, Economic Populism, Crony Capitalism and More," *Democracy Now!*, September 24, 2007.
40. Paul Krugman, "Things to Come," *New York Times*, March 18, 2003.
41. For a clear statement of this intention, see PNAC, *Rebuilding America's Defenses*, passim, and 4, 11–12, 30, 61, 75.
42. "Interview with Vice-President Dick Cheney," *Meet the Press*, transcript for March 16, 2003," http://www.mtholyoke.edu/acad/intrel/bush/cheneymeetthepress.htm.
43. Suskind, *Price of Loyalty*, 85.
44. George Packer, "Dreaming of Democracy," *New York Times Magazine*, March 2, 2003, 49, quoted in Anthony Arnove, *Iraq: The Logic of Withdrawal* (New York:

New Press, 2006), 7.
45. "Wolfowitz Interview," I.S. DOD press release.
46. PNAC, *Rebuilding America's Defenses*, 11, 10–12.
47. Ibid., 12.
48. Ibid., 14, 74, and passim.
49. Jay Bookman, "The President's Real Goal in Iraq," *Atlanta Journal-Constitution*, September 29, 2002.
50. David E. Sanger and Eric Schmitt, "Threats and Responses: A Plan for Iraq; U.S. Has a Plan to Occupy Iraq, Officials Report," *New York Times*, October 11, 2002.
51. Ibid.
52. Tom Engelhardt, "A Basis for Enduring Relationships in Iraq," TomDispatch, December 2, 2007, http://www.tomdispatch.com/post/174869/a_basis_for_enduring_relationships_in_iraq. For a discussion of Saudi Arabia as an unreliable hub of U.S. influence, see Klare, *Blood and Oil*, 86f.
53. Ron Suskind, *The One-Percent Solution* (New York: Simon and Schuster, 2007), quoted in Mark Danner, "Taking Stock of the War on Terror," TomDispatch, March 25, 2008, http://www.tomdispatch.com/post/174910/mark_danner_generals_bin_laden_and_bush.
54. Klein, *Shock Doctrine*, Part 6, especially 361–65.
55. William Booth and Rajiv Chandrasekaran, "Occupation Forces Halt Elections Throughout Iraq," *Washington Post*, June 28, 2003, quoted in Klein, *Shock Doctrine*, 363.
56. Thomas E. Ricks and Karen DeYoung, "Ex-Defense Official Assails Colleagues Over Run-Up to War," *Washington Post*, March 9, 2008.
57. Booth and Chandrasekaran, "Occupation Forces Halt Elections Throughout Iraq"; Klein, *Shock Doctrine*, 363–65.
58. Quoted in Dexter Filkins, "Tough New Tactics by U.S. Tighten Grip on Iraq Towns," *New York Times*, December 7, 2003.

Chapter Two

Mike Davis, "Planet of Slums: Urban Involution and the Informal Proletariat," *New Left Review* 26 (March/April 2004), pp.16-17.
Quoted in Smith, Neil Smith, *The Endgame of Globalization* (New York: Routledge, 2005), 178.
1. Ricks, *Fiasco*, 128, 212, see also 87, 118.
2. Rajiv Chandrasekaran, "Mistakes Loom Large as Handover Nears," *Washington Post*, June 20, 2004.
3. Graham, "Switching Cities Off," 175. The internal quote is to Thomas Barnett, *The Pentagon's New Map* (New York: Putnam, 2004).
4. Ricks, *Fiasco*, 128.
5. For a lucid discussion of the trajectory of neoliberal reform as a global expression of U.S. policy, see David Harvey, *The New Imperialism* (New York: Oxford, 2003); Harvey, *A Brief History of Neoliberalism* (New York: Oxford, 2005); and Smith, *Endgame of Globalization*.
6. Alan Greenspan, head of the very powerful U.S. Federal Reserve, held firmly to this belief. See his *Age of Turbulence*, chapter 24. For an analysis of this position, see Klare, *Blood and Oil*, chapter 4.
7. Smith, *Endgame of Globalization*.
8. Harry Magdoff, *The Age of Imperialism* (New York: Monthly Review Press,

1969). A vivid example of how this liberalization process functioned can be found in the impact of neoliberal reforms on milk production in Jamaica during the 1990s. In 1987, the Jamaican government had instituted high tariffs against imported milk, using the proceeds to subsidize local producers who relied on a unique hybrid cow, the Jamaica Hope, which could produce three times as much milk as other dairy cows on the island. Local production, which had increased a healthy 15 percent to 20 million liters during the first part of the decade, enjoyed spectacular growth under the new program, recording a 95 percent increase to 39 million liters in the next five years.

Unfortunately for the local milk industry, Jamaica negotiated what is called a *structural adjustment loan* with the World Bank in 1990. In exchange for funds needed to cover pressing economic problems, it agreed to a sweeping set of reforms designed to liberalize the economy—that is, to replace government control with unregulated market forces. Among the changes dictated by the loan agreement was the removal, by the end of 1992, of both the milk tariffs and the subsidies to local dairy farms.

Sure enough, 1992 marked the high point of local production. The market was flooded with inexpensive milk products from the European Union, which, ironically, were heavily subsidized by their home governments, and local dairy farming collapsed. After several years in which local farmers gave away and even destroyed large amounts of milk, production declined sharply, falling more than 60 percent from 39 million to 14 million liters between 1992 and 2005. Farmers slaughtered their devalued cows for food, the land under their farms depreciated catastrophically, and the number of dairy farms declined from just over four thousand to just over one hundred in thirteen years. The displaced farmers and their workers joined the already large army of the unemployed in Jamaica, unable for the most part to afford the milk that they used to produce. With so many unemployed dairy workers, the handful of much larger remaining farms lowered wages of their dwindling workforce, but still made little progress in matching the prices of the imports.

Perhaps the saddest indication of the destruction of the Jamaican dairy industry occurred in 2005, when the price of imported milk products rose sharply, a pattern that is all too common once local competition to imports dwindles. Fifteen years earlier, these price increases would have infused life into the local industry, increasing production, market share, and profits. In its weakened state, however, the moribund local industry registered another loss in production and market share.

In the vision of the advocates of liberalization, severe contraction of the dairy industry should have been offset by the expansion of another, more competitive sector, for example, tourism. With government barriers to investment eliminated, a cost-effective sector like tourism should be able to attract large infusions of foreign capital that were previously unavailable, creating new, better, and more plentiful jobs and entrepreneurial opportunities. Unfortunately in Jamaica (as in other countries), the expansion of tourism did not come close to offsetting the losses in the dairy industry and other declining areas—at least not in the first fifteen years of neoliberal policies. Then, in 2005, price increases in milk products began to bite into the modest price declines that had been the only benefit reaped by Jamaicans from structural adjustment. The one enduring result of neoliberal reform was the increased market share and profits of the European Union milk product firms. This account is based on Jamaica Dairy Development Board, *Dairy Facts and Figures*, 2005–2006 (Jamaica, 2006), http://www.moa.gov.jm/statbod/data/dairy_

facts_figures_05_06.pdf; Jamaica Dairy Development Board, *Dairy Facts and Figures*, 2002–2003 (Jamaica, 2003), http://www.moa.gov.jm/statbod/data/dairy_facts_figures_02_03.pdf; European Solidarity Towards Equal Participation of People, "Dumping in Jamaica," Eurostep, November 1999, http://eurostep.antenna.nl/detail_pub.phtml?page=pubs_position_coherence_jamaicad; Zadie Neufville, "GLOBALISATION: Dairy Farmers Pit 'Jamaica Hope' Against Subsidies," Inter Press Service, March 17, 2004, http://ipsnews.net/interna.asp?idnews=22910.

9. Smith, *Endgame of Globalization*, 193. For a list of interventions, see Zoltan Grossman, "A Century of US Military Interventions," ZNet (September 20 2001), http://www.zmag.org/crisescurevts/interventions.htm.

10. The best treatment of Garner's ideas about reconstructing Iraq can be found in Charles Ferguson's film, *No End in Sight* (Magnolia Pictures and Red Envelope Entertainment, 2007).

11. Suskind, *Price of Loyalty*, 85.

12. Chandrasekaran, "Mistakes Loom Large."

13. For more detailed discussions of these policies, see Naomi Klein, "Baghdad: Year Zero," *Harper's* (September 24, 2004); Klein, *Shock Doctrine*, part 6; Susan Roberts, Anna Secor, and Matthew Sparke, "Neoliberal Geopolitics," *Antipode* 35 (2003): 887–97; Barnett, *Pentagon's New Map*.

14. Chandrasekaran, "Mistakes Loom Large."

15. Smith, *Endgame of Globalization*, 178.

16. Harvey, *Brief History*, 118, 159. See also Harvey, *New Imperialism*.

17. Harvey, *Brief History*, 159.

18. Harvey, *New Imperialism*, chapter 4 (137–82).

19. Jackie Smith, "Economic Globalization and Strategic Peacebuilding," in Daniel Philpot and Gerard Powers, eds., *Strategies for Peace* (New York: Oxford, forthcoming).

Chapter 3

Quoted in Thomas E. Ricks, *Fiasco: The American Military Adventure in Iraq* (NY: Penguin, 2006), 165.

1. Ibid. For a full discussion of demobilization and de-Baathification, see chapter 8, especially 158–166. For a discussion of the deliberate erosion of state administrative capacity, see Paul Brinkley, "A Cause for Hope: Economic Revitalization in Iraq."

2. Brinkley, "A Cause for Hope: Economic Revitalization in Iraq," *Military Review* 87, 4 (July/August 2007); 2–12. See Ricks, *Fiasco*, part II, for a comprehensive discussion of de-Baathification and dismantling the military. The best account of the early economic policies of the CPA can be found in Klein, "Baghdad: Year Zero"; See also Naomi Klein, *Shock Doctrine*, Part 6; Pratap Chatterjee, *Iraq, Inc.* (New York: Seven Stories Press, 2004), especially 175–82; Herbert Docena, "How the U.S. Got Its Neoliberal Way in Iraq," *Asia Times* (September 1, 2005); and "The Economic Restructuring of Iraq: What Dreams May Come," *Al-Ahram Weekly*, March 23–29, 2006; Antonia Juhasz, "The Economic Colonization of Iraq," World Tribunal on Iraq, May 8, 2004, http://www.ifg.org/analysis/globalization/IraqTestimony.html; and Antonia Juhasz, *The Bush Agenda: Invading the World, One Economy at a Time*, (New York: Regan Books, 2006).

3. On Russia, see Joseph Stiglitz, "The Insider: What I Learned at the World

Economic Crisis," *New Republic* (April 17, 2000); and Boris Kagarlitsky, *Russia under Yeltsin and Putin: Neo-liberal Autocracy.* (Sterling, VA: Pluto, 2002). On Argentina, see Guillermo Perry and Luis Serven, "La anatomía de una crisis múltiple: qué tenía Argentina de especial y qué podemos aprender de ella," *Desarrollo Economico—Revista de Ciencias Sociales Ides, Buenos Aires* 42 (October–December, 2002): 323–75 and Hector Schamis, "Argentina: Crisis and Democratic Consolidation," *Journal of Democracy* 13, 2 (2002): 81–94.

4. Juhasz, "Economic Colonization of Iraq."

5. Ibid.

6. Peter McPherson, "Financial Reconstruction in Iraq: The CPA View," *Middle Eastern Economic Survey* Volume 46, 45 (November 10, 2003), (Report delivered to U.S. Senate Subcommittee on International Trade and Finance, November 4, 2003, http://www.menafn.com/qn_news_story_s.asp?StoryId-33852.

7. Brian Mockenhaupt, "Kurdistan, the Iraq Worth Fighting For," *Esquire* (online), September 25, 2007, http://www.esquire.com/features/esquire-100/kurdistan 1007.

8. Chatterjee, *Iraq, Inc.*, 180; Juhasz, "Economic Colonization of Iraq"; David S. Cloud, "Top General in Iraq Aims to Shoot Less, Rebuild More," *New York Times*, April 1, 2006.

9. Cloud, "Top General In Iraq."

10. This account is based on Brinkley, "A Cause for Hope"; Cloud, "Top General in Iraq"; Rajiv Chandrasekaran, "On Iraq, U.S. Turns to Onetime Dissenters"; *Washington Post*, January 14, 2007; and Mockenhaupt, "Kurdistan."

11. Chandrasekaran, "On Iraq."

12. Brinkley, "A Cause for Hope."

13. United States Department of Defense, *Measuring Stability and Security in Iraq, December 14, 2007* (Report to Congress, Department of Defense Appropriations Act, 2007), http://www.defenselink.mil/pubs/pdfs/FINAL-SecDef%20Signed-20071214.pdf.

14. Brinkley, "A Cause for Hope." See also Stephen Farrell, "U.S. Market Seen for Iraqi-Made Clothes," *New York Times*, August 13, 2007.

15. McPherson, "Financial Reconstruction in Iraq"; Klein, "Baghdad: Year Zero"; Juhasz, "Economic Colonization of Iraq"; Klein, *Shock Doctrine*, 339, Edmund L. Andrews, "After Years of Stagnation, Iraqi Industries Are Falling to a Wave of Imports," *New York Times*, June 1, 2003.

16. Thomas B. Edsall and Juliet Eilperin, "Lobbyists Set Sights on Money-Making Opportunities in Iraq," *Washington Post*, October 2, 2003, quoted in Klein, *Shock Doctrine*, 340.

17. James Glanz, "Devising Survival at Factory in Iraq," *New York Times*, April 15, 2008.

18. See below. For a vivid portrait of both the failure to reconstruct infrastructure and the angry reaction to it, see Zaid Al-Ali, "Iraq–The Lost Generation," *Open Democracy*, July 10, 2004, http://www.opendemocracy.net/debates/article-2-114-2143.jsp.

19. Faiza Al-Araji and Eman Ahmad Khamas, "Iraqi Women Make Rare Trip to U.S. to Tell Their Stories of Life Under Occupation," *Democracy Now!*, March 6, 2006. On education, see below as well as Al-Ali, "Iraq–The Lost Generation," and Ahmed Janabi, "Iraq's Education Setback," Aljazeera.net (English-language), May 28, 2004.

20. Klein, *Shock Doctrine*, 346, 355.

21. On unemployment, see Brinkley, "A Cause for Hope"; Klein, *Shock Doctrine*, 349–53; Joseph Stiglitz and Linda Bilmes, "The Three Trillion Dollar War," *Democracy Now!*, February 29, 2008.

22. Quoted in Ricks, *Fiasco*, 165.
23. This account based on Klein, *Shock Doctrine*, 351–65. See also David Teather, "US Begins Iraq Crackdown as Soldiers Found Dead," *Guardian*, June 30, 2003.
24. L. Paul Bremer III, "New Risks in International Business," *Viewpoint: The Marsh and McLennan Companies Journal* (No. 2, 2001).
25. Bremer, "New Risks."
26. Al-Ali, "Iraq—The Lost Generation."
27. Baiji, the oil refinery center discussed in chapters 6 and 8, was a typical example. See below and Ann Scott Tyson, "In Iraqi Oil City, a Formidable Foe: Airborne Soldiers Struggle to Break Grip of Insurgents," *Washington Post*, January 19, 2006.
28. Edmund Blair, "Anger Mounts after US Troops Kill 13 Iraqi Protesters," Reuters, April 29, 2003.
29. Ibid.
30. Ali A. Allawi, *The Occupation of Iraq: Winning the War, Losing the Peace* (New Haven: Yale University Press, 2007), 186. The quote is Allawi's paraphrasing of the report's findings.
31. John Murtha, "Representative Murtha Holds a News Conference on the War in Iraq," *Washington Post* Online, November 17, 2005; Brookings Institute, *Iraq Index*, August 30, 2007: 8.
32. Michael Schwartz, "A Government with No Military and No Territory: Iraq's Sovereignty Vacuum (Part 1)," TomDispatch, March 9, 2006, http://www.tom dispatch.com/index.mhtml?pid=66969.

Chapter 4

Iraqi Labor Union Leadership, "Iraqi Trade Union Statement on the Oil Law," Platform, December, 14, 2006, found at http://www.carbonweb.org/showitem .asp?article=222&parent=4.

1. Sean Loughlin, "Rumsfeld on Looting in Iraq: 'Stuff Happens,'" CNN, April 12, 2003.
2. Joshua Holland, "Bush's Petro-Cartel Almost Has Iraq's Oil," AlterNet, October 25, 2006. http://www.alternet.org/story/43045/ (Part I), http://www.alternet.org/ waroniraq/43077 (Part II).
3. Paul Wolfowitz, "Testimony," U.S. House of Representatives, Committee on Appropriations, March 27, 2003, http://www.structuredmethods.com/drop/ wolfowitz.html.
4. On Iraqi resistance to privatization, see Hiro, *Blood of the Earth: The Battle for the World's Vanishing Oil Resources* (New York: Nation Books, 2007), 144–48; for Iraqi public opinion, 145.
5. Ben Lando, "Baghdad vs. Irbil Begins . . . Lukoil Getting Itchy for W. Qurna . . . The Fate of Basra and Kirkuk . . . ," *Iraq Oil Report*, December 12, 2007, http:// iraqoilreport.com/2007/12/12/baghdad-vs-irbil-begins-lukoil-getting-itchy-for-w- qurna-the-fate-of-basra-and-kirkuk/.
6. United States Energy Information Administration, "Country Analysis Briefs: Iraq," (last updated June 2006) http://www.eia.doe.gov/emeu/cabs/Iraq/Full.html.
7. See Matthew Simmons, *Twilight in the Desert* (Hoboken, NJ: Wiley, 2006); Jingyao Gong and Larry Gerken, "GIS in an Overview of Iraq Petroleum Geology," *Search and Discovery* 10041 (2003), http://www.searchanddiscovery .net/documents/gong03/images/gong03.pdf.
8. James A. Paul, "Oil in Iraq – The Heart of the Crisis," Global Policy Forum, December 2002, http://www.globalpolicy.org/security/oil/2002/12heart.htm. See

also, James A. Paul, "The Iraq Oil Bonanza: Estimating Future Profits," Global Policy Forum, January 28, 2004, http://www.globalpolicy.org/security/oil/2004/0128oilprofit.htm.

9. Even if the most pessimistic estimates were validated and Iraq had only one third the reserves that were officially listed, this news, combined as it would be with news of reduced reserves all over the Middle East, would guarantee huge price increases beyond those already reached in 2007. In those circumstances, the price of oil would soar well past the $100 mark, perhaps reaching the $200 per barrel that many oil economists were predicting. In that case, even a reserve of one third the announced size would be worth about several trillion dollars.

10. Michael Klare, *Blood and Oil,* (New York: Holt, 2004), 94–7; Hiro, *Blood of the Earth,* 117–45.

11. Wolfowitz, "Testimony."

12. Greg Muttit, "When It Comes to Oil, the U.S. Administration Is Bypassing Democracy in Iraq," *Foreign Policy in Focus,* August 28, 2006, http://www.carbonweb.org/showitem.asp?article=208&parent=39.

13. For an excellent discussion of PSAs, see Greg Muttit, "Crude Designs: The Rip-Off of Iraq's Oil Wealth," Platform (with Global Policy Forum), November 2005, http://www.globalpolicy.org/security/oil/2005/crudedesigns.htm; see also Muriel Mirak-Weissbach, "Cheney's Oil Law for Iraq Is Neocolonial Theft," Global Research.ca, October 8, 2007, http://www.globalresearch.ca/index.php?context=va&aid=7008.

14. Christian Parenti, "Who Will Get the Oil?," *Nation,* March 19, 2007.

15. Muttit, "Crude Designs."

16. Greenspan and Klein, "Alan Greenspan vs. Naomi Klein," On the Iraq War, Bush's Tax Cuts, Economic Populism, Crony Capitalism and More," *Democracy Now!,* September 24, 2007, http://www.democracynow.org/article.pl?sid=07/09/24/1412226.

17. Holland, "Bush's Petro-Cartel Almost Has Iraq's Oil."

18. Klare, *Blood and Oil,* 99–105; Mirak-Weissbach, "Cheney's Oil Law for Iraq Is Neocolonial Theft."

19. David Bacon, "Oil for Freedom," *Progressive,* October 2005.

20. Michael Schwartz, "How the Bush Administration Deconstructed Iraq," TomDispatch, May 18, 2006, found at http://www.tomdispatch.com/post/84463/michael_schwartz_on_dismantling_iraqi_life.

21. Klein, *Shock Doctrine,* 347–49.

22. Steve Quinn, "Safe Iraq Said Needed for U.S. Investment," Associated Press, June 27, 2006. United States Energy Information Administration, "Country Analysis Briefs: Iraq," (updated June 2006), http://www.eia.doe.gov/emeu/cabs/Iraq/Full.html.

23. Brookings Institution, *Iraq Index: Tracking Variables of Reconstruction & Security in Post-Saddam Iraq,* (Washington D.C.: Brookings Institution, August 30, 2007), http://www3.brookings.edu/fp/saban/iraq/index20070830.pdf, 29.

24. Ibid., 39, see also Brookings, Iraq Index, October 29, 2007, 39.

25. Juan Cole, "A Mixed Story," Informed Comment, January 30, 2005, http://www.juancole.com/2005/01/mixed-story-im-just-appalled-by.html.

26. This account based on Zaid Al-Ali, "The IMF and the Future of Iraq," Middle East Report Online, December 7, 2004, http://www.merip.org/mero/mero120704.html, and Basav Sen and Hope Chu, "Operation Corporate Freedom: The IMF and World Bank in Iraq," 50 Years Is Enough Network, May 17, 2006, http://www.50years.org/cms/updates/story/320.

27. Sen and Chu, "Operation Corporate Freedom."

28. Al-Ali, "The IMF and the Future of Iraq."

29. Holland, "Bush's Petro-Cartel Almost Has Iraq's Oil."

30. Al-Ali, "The IMF and the Future of Iraq."

31. Holland, "Bush's Petro-Cartel Almost Has Iraq's Oil."

32. Iraq Study Group (James A. Baker III and Lee H. Hamilton, Co-chairs), *The Iraq Study Group Report* (New York: Vintage Books, 2006); for an account of the report and its impact, see Linda McQuaig, "U.S. Troops Should Leave Country, but How Will America Then Keep Control of Oil Fields?" *Toronto Star*, December 18, 2006.

33. For more information on resistance to the proposed law see Mirak-Weissbach, "Cheney's Oil Law for Iraq Is Neocolonial Theft"; Parenti, "Who Will Get the Oil?"; and Tina Susman, "Iraqis Resist US Pressure to Enact Oil Law," *Los Angeles Times*, May 13, 2007.

34. For an English translation of the law, see Iraq Government, "Draft Hydrocarbon Law," (translated by Raed Jarrar), posted February 18, 2007, http://www.box.net/public/2y7kkf4tzn. For analysis, see Raed Jarrar, "The New Oil Law Will Increase Violence in Iraq," posted on Raed in the Middle (blog), April 23, 2007, http://raedinthemiddle.blogspot.com/2007/04/new-oil-law-will-increase-violence-in.html.

35. Platform, "Cabinet Readies Iraqi Oil for Privatisation," ZNet, February 27, 2007, http://www.zmag.org/content/showarticle.cfm?ItemID=12248; Holland, "Bush's Petro-Cartel Almost Has Iraq's Oil."

36. On resistance to the oil law, see Parenti, "Who Will Get the Oil?"; Mirak-Weissbach, "Cheney's Oil Law For Iraq Is Neocolonial Theft;" and Susman, "Iraqis Resist US Pressure to Enact Oil Law."

37. "Satterfield: Iraq Oil Law Will Pass," United Press International, March 28, 2007, http://www.earthtimes.org/articles/show/45126.html.

38. Parenti, "Who Will Get the Oil?"

39. Ewa Jasiewicz, "Iraqi Workers Kick Out KBR! Begin Autonomous Reconstruction," Infoshop News, December 12, 2003, http://www.infoshop.org/inews/article.php?story=03/12/12/1992450; Lotte Folke Kaarsholm, Charlotte Aagaard, and Osama Al-Habahbeh, "Iraqi Port Weathers Danish Storm," CorpWatch, January 31, 2006, http://www.corpwatch.org/article.php?id=13196; Greg Muttit, "Iraq's Other Resistance: Oil Workers in Basra Are Ready to Fight Privatisation," *Guardian*, June 3, 2005.

40. Iraqi Labor Union Leadership, "Iraqi Trade Union Statement on the Oil Law," Platform, December 14, 2006 http://www.carbonweb.org/showitem.asp?article=222&parent=4.

41. Chip Cummins and Hassan Hafidh, "Iraqi Oil Wealth Stays Locked Up," *Wall Street Journal*, February 21, 2007.

42. Emad Mekay, "Iraq: New Oil Law Seen as Cover for Privatization," Inter Press Service, February 27, 2007, http://ipsnews.net/print.asp?idnews=36754.

43. Pepe Escobar, "US's Iraq Oil Grab Is a Done Deal," *Asia Times*, February 28, 2007; Parenti, "Who Will Get the Oil?"

44. James Glanz, "Compromise on Oil Law in Iraq Seems to Be Collapsing," *New York Times*, September 13, 2007.

Chapter 5

David Swanson, "A Peace Movement Demanding the Rule of Law," Truthout, January 7, 2006, http://www.truthout.org/docs_2006/010706G.shtml.

1. See chapters 2–4 for a detailed discussion of the economic impact of the occupation.

2. On looting, see Thomas E. Ricks, *Fiasco: The American Military Adventure in Iraq* (New York: Penguin, 2006). On kidnapping, see Naomi Klein, *The Shock Doctrine: The Rise of Disaster Capitalism* (New York: Metropolitan Books, 2007), 373.

3. Paul Bremer, interview by Peter Sissons, *Breakfast with Frost*, BBC, June 29, 2003.

4. For the first report on these bases, see Thom Shanker and Eric Schmitt, "Pentagon Expects Long-Term Access to Four Key Bases in Iraq," *New York Times*, April 19, 2003. For more complete analyses of their purpose, development, and evolution, see Tom Engelhardt's reporting, including "A Permanent Basis for Withdrawal?," TomDispatch, February 14, 2006, http://www.tomdispatch.com/index.mhtml?pid=59774, and "A Basis for Enduring Relationships in Iraq," TomDispatch, December 2, 2007, http://www.tomdispatch.com/post/174869/a_basis_for_enduring_relationships_in_iraq.

5. Naomi Klein, "Let's Make Enemies," *Nation*, April 9, 2004.

6. Graham, Bradley, "Commander's Plan Eventual Consolidation of U.S. Bases in Iraq," *Washington Post*, May 22, 2005.

7. Nir Rosen, "The Occupation of Iraqi Hearts and Minds," Truthdig, June 28, 2006, http://www.commondreams.org/views06/062820.htm. For a more complete description of this patrol and others by American soldiers during the early part of the war, see Rosen's book, *In the Belly of the Green Bird*, (New York: Free Press, 2006), chapter 3.

8. Rosen, "The Occupation of Iraqi Hearts and Minds."

9. Ibid.

10. Chris Hedges and Laila Al-Arian, "The Other War: Iraq Vets Bear Witness," *Nation*, July 30, 2007.

11. Ewen MacAskill, "Sunni Insurgents Form Alliance Against U.S.," *Guardian*, October 12, 2007.

12. See below. Dahr Jamail, in *Beyond the Green Zone: Dispatches from an Unembedded Journalist in Occupied Iraq* (Chicago: Haymarket Books, 2007), 7–100, has an excellent discussion of collective punishment as the American strategy in the war.

13. See below, chapter 8.

14. Rosen, "The Occupation of Iraqi Hearts and Minds"; Ellen Knickmeyer, "In Haditha, Memories of a Massacre," *Washington Post*, May 27, 2006. See also Dahr Jamail, "How to Control the Story, Pentagon-Style," TomDispatch, November 26, 2007, http://www.tomdispatch.com/post/174866/tomdispatch_dahr_jamail_how_to_control_the_story_pentagon_style.

15. Paul von Zielbauer, "Officer Says Civilian Toll in Haditha Was a Shock," *New York Times*, May 9, 2007.

16. Ibid.

17. Ibid.

18. Paul von Zielbauer, "Two Marines Deny Suspecting Haditha War Crime," *New York Times*, May 3, 2007.

19. Paul von Zielbauer, "US General Says His Staff Misled Him on Haditha Killings," *New York Times*, May 11, 2007.

20. "U.S.: At least 5 killed at Iraq roadblocks," Associated Press, November 27, 2007.

21. Giuliana Sgrena, *Friendly Fire: The Remarkable Story of a Journalist Kidnapped in Iraq, Rescued by an Italian Secret Service Agent, and Shot by U.S. Soldiers* (Chicago: Haymarket Books, 2006).

22. Michael Massing, "Iraq: The Hidden Human Costs," *New York Review of Books* 54 no. 20 (December 20, 2007). Internal quotes are to Evan Wright, *Generation Kill: Devil Dogs, Iceman, Captain America, and the New Face of American War* (New York: Penguin, 2005).

23. Jeremy Scahill, "A Very Private War," *Guardian*, August 1, 2007. For a comprehensive discussion of Blackwater and other private contractors, see Scahill, *Blackwater: The Rise of the World's Most Powerful Mercenary Army* (New York: Nation Books, 2007).

24. Anonymous, "Last Night," Operation Truth, downloaded January 23, 2005, http://www.optruth.org/main.cfm?actionId=globalShowStaticContent&screen Key=hear&htmlId=1234. The author withheld his name from the blog.

25. Ibid.

26. Paul von Zielbauer, "US General Says His Staff Misled Him on Haditha Killings."

27. Richard A. Oppel Jr. and Omar Al-Neami, "U.S. Strike on Home Kills 9 in Family, Iraqi Officials Say," *New York Times*, January 4, 2006; Ellen Knickmeyer and Salih Saif Aldin, "U.S. Raid Kills Family North of Baghdad," *Washington Post*, January 4, 2006.

28. See chapter 8 for an account of the insurgency in Baiji.

29. Oppel and Al-Neami, "U.S. Strike . . ."

30. Ibid.

31. Knickmeyer and Aldin, "U.S. Raid . . ."

32. Ibid.

33. Paul von Zielbauer, "Investigator Said to Find Case Against Marine Weak," *New York Times*, October 5, 2007.

34. Charles W. Hoge et al., "Combat Duty in Iraq and Afghanistan, Mental Health Problems and Barriers to Care," *New England Journal of Medicine* 351 (July 1, 2004): 13–22.

35. Brookings Institution, *Iraq Index: Tracking Variables of Reconstruction & Security in Post-Saddam Iraq* (Washington D.C.: Brookings, August 30, 2007), 7–12; Nicolas J. S. Davies, "Setting the Record Straight on the U.S. Invasion and Destruction of Iraq," *Z Magazine* (September 2007), 22.

36. Opinion Research Business, "More than 1,000,000 Iraqis Murdered," *Opinion Research Business*, September 2007, http://www.opinion.co.uk/Newsroom_details. aspx?NewsId=78. Tables 1, 3.

37. Michael Schwartz, "Is the United States Killing 10,000 Iraqis Every Month?" After Downing Street, July 5, 2007, found at http://www.afterdowningstreet.org/ ?q=node/24310.

38. ABC News/BBC/NHK, "Iraq: Where Things Stand," ABC News, September 10, 2007, http://abcnews.go.com/images/US/1043a1IraqWhereThingsStand.pdf.

39. Alex Horton, "One Angry Dude in Iraq: Stupid Shit of the Deployment Awards!" Army of Dude (blog), August 27, 2007, http://armyofdude.blogspot.com/2007/08/ stupid-shit-of-deployment-awards.html.

40. Juan Cole, "Iraq and Vietnam," Informed Comment, March 21, 2005, http://www.juancole.com/2005/03/iraq-and-vietnam-although-martin-van.html.

41. David Swanson, "A Peace Movement Demanding the Rule of Law," Truthout, January 7, 2006, http://www.truthout.org/docs_2006/010706G.shtml.

42. Zielbauer, "Two Marines . . ."

43. Dexter Wilkins, "Tough New Tactics by U.S. Tighten Grip on Iraq Towns," *New York Times*, December 7, 2003.

44. Michael Hirsh and John Barry, "The Salvador Option: The Pentagon May Put Special-Forces-Led Assassination or Kidnapping Teams in Iraq," *Newsweek*, January 8, 2005.

45. Rick Atkinson, "If You Don't Go after the Network, You're Never Going to Stop These Guys. Never." *Washington Post*, October 3, 2007.

46. James Paul and Celine Nahory, *War and Occupation in Iraq* (London: Global Policy Forum, June 2007), http://www.globalpolicy.org/security/issues/iraq/occupation/report/full.pdf; Eulàlia Iglesias, "U.N. Food Expert Condemns U.S. Tactics in Iraq," (Inter Press Service,) November 12, 2005, http://www.commondreams.org/headlines05/1112-02.htm; Gareth Porter, "US Military Still Runs with Dreaded Wolf Brigade," Inter Press Service, January 2, 2006, http://www.ipsnews.net/news .asp?idnews=31639. See also Massing, "Iraq: The Hidden Human Costs," and Hedges and Al-Arian, "The Other War."

47. Marjorie Cohn, "The Quaint Mr. Gonzales," Truthout, November 13, 2004, http://www.truthout.org/docs_04/111304A.shtml, and John Barry, Michael Hirsh, and Michael Isikoff, "The Roots of Torture," *Newsweek*, May 24, 2007.

48. Geneva Conventions, Protocol Additional to the Geneva Conventions of 12 August 1949, and relating to the Protection of Victims of International Armed Conflicts (Protocol I), June 8, 1977 (Geneva: International Committee of the Red Cross), http://www.icrc.org/ihl.nsf/WebList?ReadForm&id=470&t=art; Articles 43, 50.

49. Merriam-Webster Online Dictionary, http://m-w.com/dictionary/terror.

50. Jeff Goodwin, "A Theory of Categorical Terrorism," *Social Forces* 84 (No. 4, 2006): 2027–46.

51. Quoted in Dahr Jamail, "Missing Voices in the Iraq Debate," TomDispatch, January 27, 2008, http://www.tomdispatch.com/post/174886/dahr_jamail_missing_voices_in_the_iraq_debate.

52. Nir Rosen, *In the Belly of the Green Bird* (New York: Free Press, 2006), 92.

53. L. Paul Bremer (interviewed by Peter Sissons), "BBC Breakfast with Frost Interview with Paul Bremer," *Breakfast with Frost*, December 7, 2003.

54. Brookings Institute, *Iraq Index*.

Chapter 6

Scahill, *Blackwater*, 82.

1. This history of Fallujah until summer of 2004 is based on Dahr Jamail, *Beyond the Green Zone: Dispatches from an Unembedded Journalist in Occupied Iraq* (Chicago: Haymarket Books, 2007), 127–41; Michael Schwartz, "Why the U.S. is Losing the War in Iraq," *Contexts* 3 (January, 2005): 1–12; and Jeremy Scahill, *Blackwater: The Rise of the World's Most Powerful Mercenary Army* (New York: Nation Books, 2007), 50–60, 90–115.

2. Jamail, *Beyond the Green Zone*, 131–33; Rosen, *In the Belly of the Green Bird*, chapter 5, esp. 139f.

3. Scahill, *Blackwater*, 50–60; Rosen, *In the Belly of the Green Bird*, chapter 5, esp. 139f; see also Rosen's other accounts of Fallujah, "Letter from Falluja: Home Rule, A Dangerous Excursion into the Heart of the Sunni Opposition," *New Yorker*, June 28, 2004; "Falluja: Inside the Iraqi Resistance," *Asia Times* (seven-part series beginning July 15, 2004), www.atimes.com/atimes/Front_Page/FG16Aa02.html.

4. Quoted in Tom Engelhardt, "Dreaming of George: Optimism Then, Optimism Now," TomDispatch, April 16, 2004, http://www.tomdispatch.com/post/print/1384/Dreaming%2520of%2520George (Originally posted on AlterNet.org, April 13, 2004).

5. Bremer, "BBC *Breakfast with Frost* interview with Paul Bremer"; Naomi Klein, "Let's Make Enemies," *Nation*, April 9, 2004.

6. Rosen, *In the Belly of the Green Bird*, 152–53.

7. Seymour Hersh, "The Gray Zone: How a Secret Pentagon Program Came to Abu Ghraib," *New Yorker*, May 24, 2004; see also Seymour Hersh, *Chain of Command: The Road from 9/11 to Abu Ghraib* (New York: HarperCollins, 2004), 59.

8. Rosen, *In the Belly of the Green Bird*, 153.

9. Rahul Mahajan, "Report from Fallujah—Destroying a Town in Order to Save it," Common Dreams, April 12, 2004, http://www.commondreams.org/views04/0412-01.htm. See also Rosen, *In the Belly of the Green Bird*, 152f; Scahill, *Blackwater*, 80–90.

10. Scahill, *Blackwater*, 81–2.

11. Rajiv Chandrasekaran and Anthony Shadid, "U.S. Targeted Fiery Cleric in Risky Move—As Support for Sadr Surged, Shiites Rallied for Fallujah," *Washington Post*, April 11, 2004.

12. Scahill, *Blackwater*, 92.

13. Ibid.

14. Peter McPherson, "Financial Reconstruction in Iraq: The CPA View," *Middle Eastern Economic Survey*, 46 (No. 45 November 10, 2003), Report delivered to U.S. Senate Subcommittee on International Trade and Finance, November 4, 2003, http://www.menafn.com/qn_news_story_s.asp?StoryId=33852. See chapter 3.

15. Scahill, *Blackwater*, 82.

16. Rosen, *In the Belly of the Green Bird*, chapter 5.

17. Quoted in Scahill, *Blackwater*, 82.

18. Chandrasekaran and Shadid, "U.S. Targeted Fiery Cleric."

19. This account is largely based on Scahill, *Blackwater*, 82–104.

20. Quoted in Ibid., 82.

21. This account of U.S. military strategy is based on Seymour M. Hersh, "Moving Targets: Will the Counter-Insurgency Plan in Iraq Repeat the Mistakes of Vietnam?" *New Yorker*, December 15, 2003; Dexter Filkins, "Tough New Tactics by U.S. Tighten Grip on Iraq Towns," *New York Times*, December 7, 2003; Karl Vick, "Iraqi Holy City Left Broken by Urban Warfare," *Washington Post*, August 27, 2004.

22. Vick, "Iraqi Holy City Left Broken."

23. Ibid.

24. Quoted in Scahill, *Blackwater*, 142.

25. Filkins, "Tough New Tactics."

26. Excellent accounts of the first siege can be found in Jamail, *Beyond the Green Zone*, 127–42; Rosen, *In the Belly of the Green Bird*, chapter 5; Scahill, *Blackwater*, 134–44.

27. Jeffrey Gettleman, "The Struggle for Iraq: Combat Marines in Falluja Still Face and Return Relentless Fire," *New York Times*, April 14, 2004; Gettleman, "Marines Use Low-Tech Skill to Kill 100 in Urban Battle," *New York Times*, April 15, 2004"; John F. Burns and Ian Fisher, "U.S. Troops Shut Long Sections of 2 Main Routes to Baghdad," *New York Times*, April 18, 2004. See also Scahill, *Blackwater*, 141–44. *New York Times*, April 17, 2004.

28. Gettleman, "The Struggle for Iraq."

29. Ibid.

30. Burns and Fisher, "U.S. Troops Shut."

31. Gettleman, "Marines Use Low-Tech Skill."

32. Jamail, *Beyond the Green Zone*, 127–14; Mahajan, "Report from Fallujah"; Rahul Mahajan, "Fallujah and the Reality of War," CommonDreams.org, November 6, 2004, http://www.commondreams.org/views04/1106-22.htm. See also the excellent description in Scahill, *Blackwater*, 133–42.

33. Quoted in Sheila Samples, "I Know Who I Am, and Who I May Be, If I Choose,"

Allen L. Roland's Radio Weblog, Salon.com, http://blogs.salon.com/0002255/2004/12/10.html.

34. Editorial, "The Falluja Stakes," *Wall Street Journal*, April 26, 2004.
35. Thomas E. Ricks, *Fiasco: The American Military Adventure in Iraq* (New York: Penguin, 2006), 335–6,343–6; Ashley Smith, "The Invasion and Occupation of Iraq: Anatomy of an Imperial War Crime," *International Socialist Review* 55, (November–December 2007); Michael Schwartz, "Guerrilla Warfare in Sadr City," *Against the Current* 20 (January/February 2005), 26–40; Michael Schwartz, "What Triggered the Shia Insurrection," TomDispatch, April 12, 2004 http://www.tomdispatch.com/index.mhtml?pid=1371.
36. Ricks, *Fiasco*, 345.
37. "The Falluja Stakes," *Wall Street Journal*.
38. Jamail, *Beyond the Green Zone*, chapter 0–11; Rosen, *In the Belly of the Green Bird*, chapter 5. Ricks, *Fiasco*, 335–36, 343–46; Smith, "The Invasion and Occupation of Iraq."
39. Michael Schwartz, "What Triggered the Shia Insurrection?" TomDispatch, April 12, 2004; Burns and Fisher, "U.S. Troops Shut."
40. Burns and Fisher, "U.S. Troops Shut."
41. Ibid.

Chapter 7

Erik Eckholm, "Residents Trickle Back, but Fallujah Still Seems Dead," *New York Times*, January 6, 2005.

1. Dahr Jamail, *Beyond the Green Zone: Dispatches from an Unembedded Journalist in Occupied Iraq* (Chicago: Haymarket Books, 2007), 169–70.
2. Ali A. Allawi, *The Occupation of Iraq: Winning the War, Losing the Peace* (New Haven: Yale University Press, 2007), 279; Nir Rosen, *In the Belly of the Green Bird: The Triumph of the Martyrs in Iraq* (New York: Free Press, 2006), 152–73.
3. Allawi, *The Occupation of Iraq*, 277.
4. "Use of Iraqi POWs by GIs Probed: *60 Minutes* II Has Exclusive Report on Alleged Mistreatment," *60 Minutes II*, CBS, April 28, 2004.
5. The key evidence documenting torture as a policy can be found in two articles and a subsequent book by Seymour Hersh: "Moving Targets: Will the Counter-Insurgency Plan in Iraq Repeat the Mistakes of Vietnam?" *New Yorker*, December 15, 2003; Seymour Hersh, "The Gray Zone: How a Secret Pentagon Program Came to Abu Ghraib," *New Yorker*, May 24, 2004; and Seymour Hersh, *Chain of Command: The Road from 9/11 to Abu Ghraib* (New York: HarperCollins, 2004).
6. An earlier version of this argument about the dynamics of torture appeared in Michael Schwartz, "Why the Abu Ghraib Torture Should Be No Surprise," ZNet, May 11, 2004, http://www.zmag.org/content/showarticle.cfm?ItemID=5505.
7. See chapter 7, and Jeremy Scahill, *Blackwater: The Rise of the World's Most Powerful Mercenary Army* (New York: Nation Books, 2007), 92.
8. Unless otherwise indicated, this discussion of the development of the torture system is based on Hersh's "Moving Targets" and "The Gray Zone," and on Naomi Klein, *The Shock Doctrine: The Rise of Disaster Capitalism* (New York: Holt, 2007), 365–74. For a more general history of the development of U.S. torture techniques, see Greg Grandin, *Empire's Workshop: Latin America, the United States, and the Rise of the New Imperialism*, (New York: Metropolitan Books, 2007).
9. Dexter Filkins, "Tough New Tactics by U.S. Tighten Grip on Iraq Towns," *New York Times*, December 7, 2003.
10. Greg Grandin, "The Unholy Trinity," TomDispatch, December 11, 2007,

http://www.tomdispatch.com/post/174873/greg_grandin_on_the_torturable_
and_the_untorturable.

11. Hersh, "The Gray Zone."

12. On the controversy over clandestine torture, see Mark Mazzetti, "CIA Destroyed Two Tapes Showing Interrogations," *New York Times*, December 7, 2007; Dan Froomkin, "Did Torture Work?" *Washington Post*, December 11, 2007. On various names for the methods used, see Tom Engelhardt, "Greg Grandin, On the Torturable and the Untorturable," TomDispatch, December 11, 2007, http://www.tomdispatch.com/post/174873/greg_grandin_on_the_torturable_ and_the_untorturable.

13. Hersh, "Moving Targets," "The Gray Zone."

14. Hersh, "The Gray Zone"; Klein, *Shock Doctrine*, 365–74.

15. Hersh, "The Gray Zone."

16. Ibid.

17. Ibid.

18. Hersh, "Moving Targets."

19. Rajiv Chandrasekaran, "U.S. to Form Iraqi Paramilitary Force: Unit Will Draw from Party Militias," *Washington Post*, December 3, 2003.

20. Nir Rosen, "On the Ground in Iraq: The Roots of Sectarian Violence," *Boston Review*, March/April 2006.

21. Michael Hirsh and John Barry, "The Salvador Option," *Newsweek*, January 8, 2005. For background on the Latin American origins of U.S. death squad development, see Grandin, *Empire's Workshop*, and "The Unholy Trinity." For death squads in Iraq, see Jamail, *Beyond the Green Zone*, 244–47; Mussab al-Khairalla, "UN Raises Alarm on Death Squads and Torture in Iraq," Reuters, September 8, 2005.

22. Grandin, "The Unholy Trinity."

23. Hersh, "Moving Targets."

24. Allawi, *Occupation of Iraq*, 340.

25. "Interview with Vice-President Dick Cheney," *Meet the Press* (Tim Russert, interviewer), March 16, 2003."

26. Reuel Marc Gerecht, a key scholar at the American Enterprise Institute, frequently argued for the importance of Shia support for the occupation. See, for example, "Getting It Right, Despite Ourselves," *Weekly Standard*, June 7, 2004.

27. Rosen, *In the Belly of the Green Bird*, 130–45. Jamail, *Beyond the Green Zone*, 152–60.

28. Anthony Shadid, *Night Draws Near: Iraq's People in the Shadow of America's War* (New York: Picador, 2007), 449, quoted in Ashley Smith, "The Invasion and Occupation of Iraq—Anatomy of an Imperial War Crime," *International Socialist Review* 55 (November–December 2007).

29. Rosen, *In the Belly of the Green Bird*, 149, and Patrick Cockburn, *The Occupation* (London: Verso, 2006), 144, quoted in Smith, "The Invasion and Occupation of Iraq."

30. Allawi, *The Occupation of Iraq*, 275, quoted in Smith, "The Invasion and Occupation of Iraq."

31. Rosen, *In the Belly of the Green Bird*, 118–36; Smith, "The Invasion and Occupation of Iraq."

32. Video by Zawahiri, summarized and posted (in Arabic) by the United States Government Open Source Center, translation by Juan Cole, posted at Juan Cole, "Zawahiri: Iraq Main Field of Jihad Attacks Iran, Muqtada, Nasrallah," Informed Comment, December 18, 2007, http://www.juancole.com/2007/12/usg-open-source-center-summarizes-main.html.

33. Michael Schwartz, "Contradictions of the Iraqi Resistance: Guerilla War vs.

Terrorism," *Against the Current* 120 (January/February 2006): 19–26.

34. Summarized by U.S. Government Open Source Center, quoted in Cole, "Zawahiri. . . ."

35. Jeff Goodwin, "A Theory of Categorical Terrorism," *Social Forces* 84 (2006), 2027–46.

36. Ricks, *Fiasco*, 338–341; Allawi, *Occupation of Iraq*, 276.

37. Reported by Major General Paul Eaton, who was in charge of training Iraqi military forces during 2003, 2004; quoted in Ricks, *Fiasco*, 339.

38. Rosen, *In the Belly of the Green Bird*, 143–85.

39. Michael Schwartz, "Guerrilla Warfare in Sadr City," *Against the Current* 20 (January–February 2005), 26–40.

40. Earlier versions of this analysis of the destruction of Fallujah were published in Michael Schwartz, "Fallujah–City Without a Future?" TomDispatch, January 14, 2005, and Michael Schwartz, "Neo-Liberalism on Crack: Cities Under Siege in Iraq," *City: Analysis of Urban Trend* 11 (April 2007): 21–69. For a portrait of the battle from the point of view of the resistance, see Abhay Mehta, "Fallujah: the End of Warfare," *Outlook India*, December 20, 2004, http://www.outlookindia.com/full.asp?fodname=20041220&fname=Fallujah&sid=1.

41. Erik Eckholm, "Residents Trickle Back, but Fallujah Still Seems Dead," *New York Times*, January 6, 2005.

42. Doug Sample, "Fallujah Secure, But Not Yet Safe, Marine Commander Says," *American Forces Press Service*, November 19 2004, http://209.157.64.200/focus/f-news/1283788/posts.

43. Allawi, *Occupation of Iraq*, 339–40.

44. Ann Barnard, "Inside Fallujah's War: Empathy, Destruction Mark a Week with US Troops," *Boston Globe*, November 28, 2004.

45. IRIN (Integrated Regional Information Networks), "Death Toll in Fallujah Rising, Doctors Say," United Nations Office for the Coordination of Humanitarian Affairs, January 7, 2005.

46. Al Jazeera, "Falluja's Destruction Continues," Al–Jazeera (English language), January 2, 2005, http://english.aljazeera.net/NR/cxeres/23FBDBB2-C104-4E69-BA80-F476CC64C4A1.htm.

47. Ali Fadhil, "City of Ghosts," *Guardian*, January 11, 2005.

48. Dahr Jamail, "Iraq Is Burning with Wrath, Anger, and Sadness," Electronic Iraq, November 12, 2004, http://electroniciraq.net/news/1705.shtml.

49. Mike Davis, "Planet of Slums: Urban Involution and the Informal Proletariat," *New Left Review* 26 (March/April 2004): 16–17.

50. Jamail, *Beyond the Green Zone*, chapter 15.

51. Omer al-Mansouri, "U.S. Offensives on Falluja Have Disabled 500 Children," *Azzaman*, April 12, 2008, http://www.azzaman.com/english/index.asp?fname=news%5C2008-04-12%5Ckurd.htm.

52. Barnard, "Inside Fallujah's War."

53. Ken Gewertz, "Looking at Germany, Japan, Iraq: A Tale of Three Occupations," *Harvard Gazette*, March 18, 2004.

54. Rajiv Chandrasekaran, "Mistakes Loom Large as Handover Nears," *Washington Post*, June 20, 2004.

55. Tony Perry, "After Leveling City, U.S. Tries to Build Trust," *Los Angeles Times*, January 7, 2005.

56. Robert F. Worth, "In Falluja's Ruins, Big Plans and a Risk of Chaos," *New York Times*, December 1, 2004.

57. Doug Sample, "Iraq Reconstruction Progresses," *American Forces Press Service*, December 16, 2004, http://editorials.arrivenet.com/government/article.php/3095

.html. For a full description of the security system installed in Fallujah, see Michael Schwartz, "The Sinister U.S. Plans in Falluja," TomDispatch, December 17, 2004; and Schwartz, "Fallujah—City Without a Future?"

58. Charlie Hess, "Special Defense Department Briefing on Iraq Reconstruction Update" U.S. Department of Defense (Office of the Assistant Secretary of Defense [Public Affairs]), December 15, 2004, http://www.dod.mil/transcripts/2004/tr20041215-1802.html.

59. These estimates are based on material from Schwartz, "Fallujah–City Without a Future?"; Worth, "In Falluja's Ruins"; and Stephan Said, "Iraq—A Silenced Majority," Truthout, December 19, 2004, http://www.truthout.org/docs_04/122004Y.shtml.

60. Worth, "In Falluja's Ruins."

61. Joel Brinkley "Closer Look at Fallujah Finds Rebuilding Is Slow," New York Times, April 14, 2005. See also Mike Whitney "The New York Times in Fallujah— You Call This Normal?" Peace, Earth and Justice News, April 18, 2005. http://www.pej.org/html/modules.php?op=modload&name=News&file=article&sid=2380&mode=thread&order=0&thold=0; Ann Scott Tyson "Increased Security in Fallujah Slows Efforts to Rebuild," Washington Post, April 19, 2005; and Andrew North "Falluja's Struggle for Recovery," BBC, April 14, 2005.

62. Dahr Jamail "Life Goes On in Fallujah's Rubble," Inter Press Service, November 24, 2005.

63. Katarina Kratovac, "Security Checks to Greet Fallujah's Returning Residents," Associated Press, December 10, 2004.

64. This discussion is based on Jamail "Life Goes on in Fallujah's Rubble"; Dahr Jamail and Ali Fadhil, "Rebuilding Not Yet Reality for Fallujah," Inter Press Service, June 25, 2006, http://www.dahrjamailiraq.com/hard_news/archives/hard_news/000408.php. See also Jamail, Beyond the Green Zone.

65. Jamail and Fadhil, "Rebuilding Not Yet Reality for Fallujah."

66. Ibid.

67. Ibid.

68. Jeffrey D. Barnett, "Musings on Falluja," New York Times (online) [Frontlines – Dispatches from U.S. Soldiers in Iraq], March 17, 2006, http://frontlines.blogs.nytimes.com/2006/03/17/musings-on-falluja/.

69. "Can a Lull Be Turned into a Real Peace?," Economist, December 13, 2007. On the strength of the U.S. garrison, see "Falluja Lacks Necessary Requirements to Rise," Asumaria, December 21, 2007, http://www.alsumaria.tv:80/en/Iraq-News/1-11760-.html.

70. Mike Lanchin and Mona Mahmoud, "Iraq Government 'Failing Falluja,'" BBC, December 12, 2007, news.bbc.co.uk/go/pr/fr/-/2/hi/middle_east/7152991.stm.

71. Lanchin and Mahmoud, "Iraq Government 'Failing Falluja.'"

72. "Muslim Hands Feedback 2006/2007," Muslim Hands International, December 7, 2007, http://www.reliefweb.int/rw/RWB.NSF/db900SID/SSHN-79YHBT?OpenDocument.

73. Patrick Cockburn, "A Week in Iraq: 'People Say Things Are Better, but It's Still Terrible Here,'" Independent, February 3, 2008.

Chapter 8

Nir Rosen, In the Belly of the Green Bird (New York: Free Press, 2006), 98.

1. Les Roberts, Riyadh Lafta, Richard Garfield, Jamal Khudairi, and Gilbert Burnham, "Mortality Before and After the 2003 Invasion of Iraq: Cluster Sample

Survey" *Lancet* 364 (October 30, 2004 [posted October 28]).

2. They visited a random set of homes and asked the residents if anyone in their household had died in the last few years, recording the details and inspecting death certificates in the vast majority of cases. By comparing the rates for violent deaths before and after the invasion, they could calculate how many more violent deaths ("excess violent deaths") had occurred since the war began than would have occurred if the Hussein regime had remained in power.

3. Nicolas J. S. Davies, "Burying the *Lancet* Report . . . and the Children," *Online Journal*, December 14, 2005, http://onlinejournal.com/artman/publish/article_333.shtml; Les Roberts, "Co-Author of Medical Study Estimating 650,000 Iraqi Deaths Defends Research in the Face of White House Dismissal," *Democracy Now!*, October 12, 2006.

4. Les Roberts, "Study Shows Civilian Death Toll in Iraq More Than 100,000," *Democracy Now!*, December, 2005.

5. Gilbert Burnham, Riyadh Lafta, Shannon Doocy, and Les Roberts, "Mortality After the 2003 Invasion of Iraq: A Cross-Sectional Cluster Sample Survey," *Lancet*, early online publication October 12, 2006.

6. Joshua Holland, "Iraq Death Toll Rivals Rwanda Genocide, Cambodian Killing Fields," AlterNet, September 18, 2007; for later studies, see Opinion Research Business, "More than 1,000,000 Iraqis Murdered," *Opinion Research Business*, September 2007, http://www.opinion.co.uk/Newsroom_details.aspx?NewsId=78; and Opinion Research Business, "New Analysis Confirms 1 Million + Iraq Casualties," *Opinion Research Business*, January 28, 2008, http://www.opinion.co.uk/Documents/Revised%20Casulaty%20Data%20-%20Press%20release.doc. For an ongoing estimate of Iraqi deaths, as well as methodology for computing the estimates based on the *Lancet* study, see the Just Foreign Policy Web site. Estimates and explanations can be found at http://www.justforeignpolicy.org/iraq/iraqdeaths.html. In early 2008 another study using similar methods offered a much lower estimate of Iraqi violent deaths: Iraq Family Health Survey Study Group, "Violence Related Mortality in Iraq from 2002 to 2006," *New England Journal of Medicine* 358 (January 9, 2008): 484–93. The inconsistencies between the studies appear to be explained by the nexus of factors that led the *NEJM* study to severely underestimate mortality due to the use of government-employed interviewers. See Matthew Chavez, "Q & A: Les Roberts," Daily Lobo, January 30, 2008, found at http://www.dailylobo.com:80/news/2008/01/30/Opinion/Qa.Les.Roberts-3176859.shtml.

7. Juan Cole, "Hopkins Study," Informed Comment, October 11, 2006.

8. BBC, "Huge Rise in Iraqi Death Tolls," BBC News, October 11, 2006; for Bush's estimates of Iraqi deaths, see CBS, "30,000 Iraqis Killed in War," *CBS News*, December 12, 2005.

9. Chalmers Johnson, "Tom Graham: Chalmers Johnson, Ending the Empire," "TomDispatch, May 15, 2007.

10. "Americans Lowball Iraqi Death Toll," Associated Press, February 24, 2007, quoted in Holland, "Iraqi Death Toll. . . ."

11. These statistics gotten directly from the authors of the *Lancet* study.

12. Tom Engelhardt, "Escalation by the Numbers," TomDispatch, August 13, 2007.

13. Rick Atkinson, "'The Single Most Effective Weapon Against our Deployed Forces" *Washington Post*, September 30, 2007.

14. Brookings Institution, *Iraq Index: Tracking Variables of Reconstruction & Security in Post-Saddam Iraq* (Washington, D.C.: Brookings Institution, March 29, 2007), 8.

15. Atkinson, "The Single Most Effective Weapon."

16. Joshua Partlow, "Body Count in Baghdad Up in June," *Washington Post*, July 5, 2007.

17. Partlow, "Body Count in Baghdad Up in June."

18. Brookings Institution, *Iraq Index*, August 30, 2007, 9–11. These figures received a confirmation of sorts when the U.S. military, in early 2008, revealed its own estimates on Al-Qaeda in Iraq (AQI) bombings to the *Washington Post*. According to occupation authorities, AQI, the perpetrator of the vast majority of car bombings, accounted for 3,870 Iraqi civilian deaths in its most prolific year, 2007. While this is a prodigious figure, it is dwarfed by even the monthly totals for the U.S. military. See Karen DeYoung, "Papers Paint New Portrait of Iraq's Foreign Insurgents," *Washington Post*, January 21, 2008.

19. In 2007, multiple-fatality bombings reached new heights, killing more than 500 people in five different months that year. Even so, this was only a fraction of the U.S. totals, which were still marching along at considerably more than ten thousand per month. Brookings, *Iraq Index*, 10.

20. Brookings Institution, *Iraq Index*, 2007, 5.

21. Rosen, *In the Belly of the Green Bird*, 98.

22. Juan Cole, "Iraq and Vietnam," Informed Comment (web site), March 21, 2005.

23. Pepe Escobar, "Roving in The Red Zone."

Chapter 9

Brian Conley, "Ramadi becomes another Fallujah," Inter Press Service, June 5, 2006, found at http://www.ipsnews.net/news.asp?idnews=33489.

Andy Mosher and Bassam Sebti, "Another Year of Living Misery in Baghdad," *Washington Post*, June 23, 2005, found in http://www.washingtonpost.com/wp-dyn/content/article/2005/06/23/AR2005062301963.html.

1. Eduardo Mendieta, "The Axle of Evil: SUVing Through the Slums of Globalizing Neoliberalism," *City* 9 (July 2005): 194–204.

2. Patrick Cockburn, "A Week in Iraq: 'People Say Things Are Better, but It's Still Terrible Here,'" *Independent*, February 3, 2008.

3. "Can a Lull Be Turned into a Real Peace?," *Economist*, December 13, 2007.

4. The process was also hampered by the exclusion of necessary products, particularly tools and other metal products, which were deemed "dual use" for the U.S. occupation—that is, they might be useful to the ongoing resistance. Such items were confiscated at checkpoints, interfering with various reconstruction tasks and daily life.

5. Thom Shanker and Eric Schmitt, "Terror Command in Falluja Is Half Destroyed, US Says," *New York Times*, October 12, 2005.

6. See chapter 8.

7. Brookings Institution, *Iraq Index: Tracking Variables of Reconstruction & Security in Post-Saddam Iraq* (Washington, D.C.: Brookings Institution, May 2006).

8. For accounts of various U.S. offensives, see Dahr Jamail, "Violence Leads Only to More Violence," Iraq Dispatches, October 8, 2005, http://dahrjamailiraq.com/weblog/archives/dispatches/000293.php; Dahr Jamail, "Operation 'Steel Curtain,'" Iraq Dispatches, November 7, 2005, http://dahrjamailiraq.com/weblog/archives/dispatches/000315.php#more; IRIN (Integrated Regional Information Networks), "Thousand of Civilians Flee Military Offensive Near Syrian Border," United Nations Office for the Coordination of Humanitarian Affairs, October 4), http://www.irinnews.org/report.asp?ReportID=49327&SelectRegion=Middle_East&SelectCountry=IRAQ; Jonathan Finer, "5,000 US and Iraqi Troops Sweep into

City of Tall Afar," *Washington Post*, September 3, 2005.

9. Ellen Knickmeyer, Jonathan Finer, and Omar Fekeiki, "US Debate on Pullout Resonates as Troops Engage Sunnis in Talks," *Washington Post*, November 30, 2005.

10. This account of the war in Ramadi is based on Conley, "Ramadi Becomes Another Fallujah;" Dahr Jamail and Ali Fadhil, "Residents Struggle to Survive, in and out of Ramadi," Inter Press Service, June 22, 2006; and Louise Roug and Peter Spiegel, "Hopes for Iraq Pullback Fading," *Los Angeles Times*, May 31, 2006.

11. Conley, "Ramadi Becomes Another Fallujah."

12. Roug and Spiegel, "Hopes for Iraq Pullback Fading." Zarqawi was not a leader of the Ramadi resistance; at best he was an uncomfortable ally. In early 2006, reports from Iraqi sources indicated that local resistance fighters had become active enemies of Zarqawi's terrorist organization; and *Al-Hayat* newspaper on January 26, 2006, reported that "Six armed groups belonging to 'the Iraqi resistance' recently declared war on Zarqawi's 'terrorist' organization . . . in order to expel them to Syria." Quoted in Gilbert Achcar (trans.), "Sunni Clans Take the Initiative of Launching a Campaign to Expel Zarqawi's Followers and 'Foreigners and Intruders,'" *Al-Hayat* (London), January 26, 2006, http://www.juancole.com/2006/01/split-in-sunni-guerrilla-movement.html.

13. Conley, "Ramadi Becomes Another Fallujah."

14. Ibid.

15. Kenneth R. Rizer, "Bombing Dual-Use Targets: Legal, Ethical, and Doctrinal Perspectives," *Air & Space Power Journal*, May 2001, http://www.airpower.maxwell.af.mil/airchronicles/cc/Rizer.html.

16. Conley, "Ramadi Becomes Another Fallujah."

17. Ibid.

18. Juan Cole, "Senate Rejects Withdrawal; Bombings in Basra, Baghdad, Diyala; 25 Executed at Mosul," June 23, 2006, Informed Comment, http://www.juancole.com/2006/06/senate-rejects-withdrawal-bombings-in.html.

19. Jamail and Fadhil, "Residents Struggle."

20. Conley, "Ramadi Becomes Another Fallujah."

21. Ibid.

22. Knickmeyer, Finer, and Fekeiki, "US Debate on Pullout."

23. This account of the war in Baiji is based on information found in Brian Conley and Isam Rashid, "Siniyah Isolated and Simmering," Inter Press Service, February 9, 2006, http://ipsnews.net/news.asp?idnews=32100; Ellen Knickmeyer and Salih Saif Aldin, "US Raid Kills Family North of Baghdad," *Washington Post*, January 4, 2006; Ryan Lenz, "Troops Build Wall of Sand to Keep Insurgents in Their Homes," *Army Times*, January 9, 2006; Ann Scott Tyson, "In Iraqi Oil City, a Formidable Foe: Airborne Soldiers Struggle to Break Grip of Insurgents," *Washington Post*, January 19, 2006; Oliver Poole, "Corrupt Iraq Officials 'Fund Rebels,'" *Telegraph*, February 7, 2006; "Developments in Iraq on April 9," Reuters, April 9, 2006. An earlier version was published in Michael Schwartz, "The Campaign to Pacify Sunni Iraq: Iraq's Sovereignty Vacuum (Part 2)," TomDispatch, March 12, 2006.

24. Tyson, "In Iraqi Oil City. . . ." For analysis of U.S. plans to privatize all new oil development, see chapters 2 and 3.

25. Tyson, "In Iraqi Oil City. . . ."

26. Indy Bay, "Clashes Erupt in Iraqi Oil City of Baiji," San Francisco Independent Media Center, November 11, 2004, http://www.indybay.org/news/2004/11/1704793.php.

27. Tyson, "In Iraqi Oil City. . . ."

28. Conley and Rashid, "Siniyah Isolated and Simmering."

29. Poole, "Corrupt Iraq Officials 'Fund Rebels.'" Some Iraqi government officials claimed that the national black market in oil added up to "more than ?10 billion a year in direct losses and missed opportunities" with the proceeds split among criminal gangs, local and national political leaders, and the resistance. See Jim Muir, "Iraqi Oil Gangs Siphon off Billions," *Telegraph*, April 28, 2006.
30. Tyson, "In Iraqi Oil City."
31. Lenz, "Troops Build Wall."
32. Conley and Rashid, "Siniyah Isolated and Simmering."
33. Lenz, "Troops Build Wall."
34. Michael Storper and Richard Walker, *The Capitalist Imperative* (New York: Basil Blackwell, 1989).
35. James Glanz and Robert F. Worth, "Attacks on Iraq Oil Industry Aid Vast Smuggling Scheme," *New York Times*, June 4, 2006.
36. During the Great Depression in the United States, for example, unemployed coal miners extracted coal from coal mines for their own use and for sale on the black market. (See Alfred Winslow Jones, *Life, Liberty, and Property* (Akron, OH: University of Akron Press, 1993).
37. During the occupation, the same siphoning process was also a fixture in the southern oil hub, Basra (Sabrina Tavernise and Qais Mizher, "Iraq's Premier Seeks to Control a City in Chaos," *New York Times*, June 1, 2006).
38. Mosher and Sebti, "Another Year of Living Misery in Baghdad."

Chapter 10

James Glanz, "Rebuilding of Iraqi Pipeline as Disaster Waiting to Happen," *New York Times*, April 25, 2006.
1. For an account of the geography of the fighting, see Michael Schwartz, "A Government with No Military and No Territory: Iraq's Sovereignty Vacuum (Part 1)," TomDispatch, March 9, 2006, Michael Schwartz, "The Campaign to Pacify Sunni Iraq: Iraq's Sovereignty Vacuum (Part 2)," TomDispatch, March 12, 2006.
2. For accounts of battles in Najaf and Sadr City, see Michael Schwartz, "Guerrilla Warfare in Sadr City," *Against the Current* 20 (January/February 2005) 26–40. For accounts of Maysan province and Basra, see Schwartz, "A Government with No Military and No Territory," Michael Schwartz, "Forgotten Iraq: The War in Maysan Province on What We Don't See in Iraq," TomDispatch, November 2, 2005, and Sabrina Tavernise and Qais Mizher, "Iraq's Premier Seeks to Control a City in Chaos," *New York Times*, June 1, 2006.
3. Schwartz, "A Government with No Military and No Territory."
4. Frederick Barton and Bathsheba Crocker, "Estimated Breakdown of Funding Flows for Iraq's Reconstruction: How Are the Funds Being Spent?" Center for Strategic and International Studies: Post Conflict Reconstruction Project (December 2004), http://www.csis.org/isp/pcr/iraq_funds.pdf. CSIS is a well-connected Washington, D.C., think tank with a mandate to "advance global security and prosperity," populated by former high-ranking government officials, and not given to criticism of government policy (http://www.csis.org/about/).
5. See, for example, Pratap Chatterjee and Herbert Docena, "Occupation, Inc.: *Southern Exposure* Investigates the New War Profiteers," *Southern Exposure* 31 (Winter 2003/2004) http://www.southernstudies.org/reports/OccupationInc—WEB-2.htm, and Andrea Buffa and Pratap Chatterjee, "Houston, We Still Have a Problem: An Alternative Annual Report on Halliburton," Corporation Watch,

May 2005, http://www.corpwatch.org/downloads/houston.2005.pdf.

6.   Glanz, "Rebuilding of Iraqi Pipeline as Disaster Waiting to Happen." See also Llewellyn H. Rockwell, Jr., "Don't Let the Planners Take Charge of Energy," Lew Rockwell.Com, April 29, 2006, http://www.lewrockwell.com/rockwell/energy-planners.html.

7.   Glanz, "Rebuilding of Iraqi Pipeline as Disaster Waiting to Happen."

8.   Ibid.

9.   Michael Schwartz, "Fallujah—City Without a Future?" TomDispatch, January 14, 2005; Schwartz, "The Campaign to Pacify Sunni Iraq."

10. United Nations Environment Program, Report on Iraq, May 2005, (New York: United Nations, 2005), quoted in Joel Kovel, "Ecological Implications of the War," World Tribunal on Iraq, June 24, 2005, http://www.worldtribunal.org/main/popup/kovel_eco.doc; Brookings Institution. Iraq Index: Tracking Variables of Reconstruction & Security in Post-Saddam Iraq (Washington, D.C.: Brookings, May 18, 2006), www.brookings.edu/iraqindex:21.

11. Tom Engelhardt, "Icarus (Armed with Vipers) Over Iraq," TomDispatch, December 12, 2004.

12. For a detailed analysis of U.S. intentions to integrate the Iraqi economy into the nexus of globalized capital, see chapters 1-3. See also Antonia Juhasz, The Bush Agenda: Invading the World, One Economy at a Time (New York: Regan Books: 2006), and Joshua Holland "The Great Iraq Oil Grab," AlterNet, May 24, 2006.

13. Naomi Klein, "Baghdad: Year Zero," Harper's, September 24, 2004; Herbert Docena, "The Economic Restructuring Of Iraq: What Dreams May Come," Al-Ahram Weekly, March 23–29, 2006, http://www.zmag.org/content/showarticle.cfm?SectionID=15&ItemID=9998.

14. Houston Chronicle, April 29, 2003, quoted in Chatterjee, Iraq Inc., 48.

15. Glanz, "Rebuilding of Iraqi Pipeline as Disaster Waiting to Happen."

16. For a detailed discussion of the prevalence of these sorts of inefficient and counterproductive overspending deriving from cost-plus contracting, see Pratap Chatterjee, Iraq, Inc. (New York: Seven Stories Press: 2004), 25–60. See also Buffa and Chatterjee, "Houston, We Still Have a Problem," and Ed Harriman, "Where Has All the Money Gone?" London Review of Books 27 (July 7, 2005).

17. Harriman, "Where Has All the Money Gone?"

18. Glanz, "Rebuilding of Iraqi Pipeline as Disaster Waiting to Happen."

19. United States General Accountability Office (USGAO), Rebuilding Iraq: Stabilization, Reconstruction, and Financing Challenges (Washington, D.C.: U.S. Government Accountability Office, February 8, 2006), http://www.gao.gov/htext/d06428t.html.

20. Buffa and Chatterjee, "Houston, We Still Have a Problem."

21. Glanz, "Rebuilding of Iraqi Pipeline as Disaster Waiting to Happen."

22. Farah Stockman, "Success Is Elusive in Iraq's Oil Fields," Boston Globe, January 22, 2006.

23. Stockman, "Success Is Elusive in Iraq's Oil Fields."

24. "Iraq Oil Pipeline Sabotaged," Agence France Press, December 17, 2007; "At Least 34 Killed in Iraq Suicide Attacks," Telegraph (UK), December 26, 2007.

25. For a general treatment of political-economic "lock-in" effects, see Vivek Chibber, Locked in Place: State-Building and Late Industrialization in India (Princeton, NJ: Princeton University Press, 2004).

Chapter 11

Stephen Farrell, "U.S. Market Seen for Iraqi-Made Clothes," *New York Times*, August 13, 2007.

1. The amount of leftover oil revenues may have been as high as $20 billion, though much of it was allocated to other purposes besides reconstruction. A large portion of the funds was never accounted for by the CPA, which was given custodianship over them. For a detailed discussion of the oil revenues inherited from the Hussein regime, see Ed Harriman, "Where Has All the Money Gone?" *London Review of Books* 27 (July 7, 2005). For statistics on U.S. allocations as well as pledges and actual payments from other countries, see Brookings Institution, *Iraq Index: Tracking Variables of Reconstruction & Security in Post-Saddam Iraq*. (Washington D.C.: Brookings Institution, May 18, 2006), http://www.brookings.edu/fp/saban/iraq/index20060530.pdf, 30–5.

2. United States General Accountability Office (USGAO), *Rebuilding Iraq: Stabilization, Reconstruction, and Financing Challenges* (Washington D.C., U.S. Government Accountability Office, February 8, 2006), http://www.gao.gov/htext/d06428t.html.

3. Paul Wolfowitz, Testimony to House Appropriations Committee, March 27, 2003, quoted in Ali A. Allawi, *The Occupation of Iraq: Winning the War, Losing the Peace* (New Haven, CT: Yale University Press, 2007), 114.

4. Anthony Shadid, *Night Draws Near: Iraq's People in the Shadow of America's War* (New York: Holt, 2005), 134.

5. This summary is based on USDOD, Measuring Stability and Security in Iraq, December 2007, and Brookings Institution, *Iraq Index* (December 21, 2007), 37.

6. United States Department of State, Bureau of Near Eastern Affairs, Iraq Weekly Status Report, January 16, 2008 (Washington D.C., USDOS, 2008), http://www.state.gov/documents/organization/99563.pdf, 19; quoted in Ben Lando, "Analysis: Iraqis Without Fuel, Power," United Press International, January 22, 2008.

7. Ahmed Ali and Dahr Jamail, "Iraq: The Lights Have Gone Out, Who Cares," Inter Press Service, February 15, 2008, www.ipsnews.net/news.asp?idnews=41217.

8. Ibid.

9. Farrell, "U.S. Market Seen for Iraqi-Made Clothes."

10. This discussion based on Steven Hurst, "Power Cuts Worsen as Iraqi Grid Nears Collapse," *Guardian*, August 6, 2007; and James Glanz and Stephen Farrell, "Militias Seizing Control of Iraqi Electricity Grid," *New York Times*, August 23, 2007. See also USDOD, Measuring Stability and Security in Iraq, December 14, 2007, 13, and Allawi, *The Occupation of Iraq*, 257–59.

11. Hurst, "Power Cuts Worsen as Iraqi Grid Nears Collapse." See also Alexandra Zavis, "A Different Kind of Power Struggle in Iraq," *Los Angeles Times*, March 24, 2008.

12. Glanz and Farrell, "Militias Seizing Control of Iraqi Electricity Grid."

13. "Iran Commits to Iraq's Power Sector," United Press International, January 3, 2008.

14. Quoted in Ben Lando, "Japan-Iraq Relations: Investment and Presence," Iraq Oil Report (blog), March 31, 2008, http://www.iraqoilreport.com/2008/03/31/basra-break-in-violence-allows-oil-workers-to-leave-head-to-work%e2%80%a6/.

15. UN & IMPDC, "Iraq Living Conditions Survey 2004."

16. The original allocation was $5.1 billion from the U.S. reconstruction fund and $3.8 billion from the oil revenues recovered from the Hussein regime. Not all diversion from the original amount have been recorded. "U.S. Cites Failures in Paying Iraq Tribes to Secure Power Grids," Associated Press, June 23, 2007;

Brookings Institution, *Iraq Index: Tracking Variables of Reconstruction & Security in Post-Saddam Iraq*, (Washington D.C.: Brookings Institution, May 30, 2006), http://www.brookings.edu/fp/saban/iraq/index20060530.pdf, 35; Harriman, "Where Has All the Money Gone?"

17. Sabah Ali "Behind the Steel Curtain: The Real Face of the Occupation," Iraq Dispatches, December 19, 2005, http://www.truthout.org/docs_2005/ 121905Q .shtml.

18. Nelson Hernandez, "New Iraqi Power Plant Feeds a Feeble Grid Rising Demand, Attacks on Infrastructure Limit Impact of U.S.-Funded Project." *Washington Post*, May 1, 2006; James Glanz, "Rebuilding of Iraqi Pipeline as Disaster Waiting to Happen," *New York Times*, April 25, 2006.

19. This account is taken from Pratap Chatterjee, *Iraq, Inc.* (New York: Seven Stories Press: 2004), 61–62; and Herbert Docena "Iraq Reconstruction's Bottom-Line," *Asia Times*, December 23, 2003.

20. Docena, "Iraq Reconstruction's Bottom-Line."

21. Ibid.

22. Ibid.; Chatterjee, *Iraq, Inc.*, chapter 2, esp. 61–69.

23. Ali, "Behind the Steel Curtain"; Harriman, "Where Has All the Money Gone"; USGAO, *Rebuilding Iraq* (February 8, 2006).

24. Deborah Haynes, "Iraq Needs $20 Bln to End Chronic Electricity Crisis," Middle East Online, January 18, 2006.

25. Jonathan Finer, "Report Measures Shortfall in Iraq Goals: Shifting of Funds Blamed for Abandoned Projects," *Washington Post*, January 27, 2006.

26. Chatterjee, *Iraq, Inc.*, 68–69.

27. This account is based on T. Christian Miller, "U.S. Missteps Leave Iraqis in the Dark," *Los Angeles Times*, December 25, 2005. See also David Bacon, "NPR's *Science Friday* Used to Justify the Plunder of Iraq's Power Grid," U.S. Labor Against the War, February 10, 2006, http://dbacon.igc.org/Art/ 2006sciencefriday.html.

28. Miller, "U.S. Missteps Leave Iraqis in the Dark."

29. This account based on: Ross Colvin, "Power Cuts Plague Iraq, Hurt Oil Production," Reuters, January 18, 2008; Abdulatif al-Mawsawi, "Production Halted at Two Major Iraqi Refineries," Azzaman, January 18, 2008, http://www .azzaman.com/english/index.asp?fname=news\2008-01-17\kurd.htm; Ben Lando, "Analysis: Iraqis Without Fuel, Power," United Press International, January 22, 2008; Reuters, "Iraq Halts Oil Exports to Turkey Temporarily," Guardian, January 28, 2008; Ben Lando, "Iraq Refineries Face Perfect Storm," United Press International, January 28, 2008.

30. Colvin, "Power Cuts Plague Iraq;" Glenn Zorpette, "Oil and Electricity Ministries Won't Mix," *International Herald Tribune*, March 10, 2008.

31. Colvin, "Power Cuts Plague Iraq."

32. Lando, "Analysis: Iraqis without Fuel, Power."

33. "Update 1: Shell Seeks Iraq Gas Deal, Decision Soon—Minister," Reuters, January 31, 2008.

34. "Iraq: No Let-Up in the Humanitarian Crisis," International Committee of the Red Cross, March 17, 2008, http://www.reliefweb.int/rw/RWFiles2008.nsf/ FilesByRWDocUnidFilename/YSAR-7CQN6P-full_report.pdf/$File/full_report .pdf.

35. Basil Adas, "Ex-Dictator's Rule 'Was Better than Al-Maliki's'," *Gulf News*, December 30, 2007, http://archive.gulfnews.com/articles/07/12/30/10178316.html

Chapter 12

Dahr Jamail, *Beyond the Green Zone: Dispatches From an Unembedded Journalist in Occupied Iraq* (Chicago: Haymarket Books, 2007), 197.

1. A good account of the prewar background and initial reconstruction efforts in water and sewage can be found in United States General Accountability Office (USGAO), "Rebuilding Iraq: Water and Sanitation Efforts Need Improved Measures for Assessing Impact and Sustained Resourced for Maintaining Facilities" (GAO-05-872),U.S. Government Accountability Office (September 7, 2005), http://www.gao.gov/new.items/d05872.pdf.

2. According to the U.S. Government Accountability Office, "Operation Iraqi Freedom largely spared water and wastewater treatment plants; however, water networks were seriously damaged." (USGAO, "Rebuilding Iraq," (September 7, 2005), 7n4.)

3. Dahr Jamail, "Iraq: The Devastation," TomDispatch, January 7, 2005, http://www.tomdispatch.com/index.mhtml?pid=2109.

4. Quoted in Dahr Jamail, *Bechtel's Dry Run: Iraqis Suffer Water Crisis,* a special report of Public Citizen's Water for All Campaign (Washington, D.C.: Public Citizen, April, 2004), http://www.citizen.org/documents/bechteliniraq.pdf.

5. USGAO, "Rebuilding Iraq" (September 7, 2005).

6. Pratap Chatterjee, *Iraq, Inc* (New York: Seven Stories, 2004), 80–84; Stephen Farrell "Fear of Fanatics Overshadows Problems of Everyday Life," *Times* (London), December 22, 2005; Michael Schwartz, "Forgotten Iraq: The War in Maysan Province on What We Don't See in Iraq," TomDispatch, November 2, 2005, http://www.tomdispatch.com/index.mhtml?pid=32961.

7. Brookings Institution, *Iraq Index: Tracking Variables of Reconstruction & Security in Post-Saddam Iraq,* May 18, 2006 (Washington D.C.: Brookings Institution, 2006), http://www.brookings.edu/fp/saban/iraq/index20060530.pdf, 41.

8. Ibid.

9. For discussions of the health consequences of the collapse of the Iraqi sewage and water treatment systems, see Jamail, "Iraq: The Devastation"; Dahr Jamail, "Iraqi Hospitals Ailing Under Occupation," World Tribunal on Iraq, June 23, 2005, http://www.uruknet.info/?p=m12845&l=i&size=1&hd=0; Joel Kovel, "Ecological Implications of the War," World Tribunal on Iraq (June 24, 2005), http://www.worldtribunal.org/main/popup/kovel_eco.doc; Antonia Juhasz, "The Economic Colonization of Iraq," World Tribunal on Iraq, May 8, 2004, http://www.ifg.org/analysis/globalization/IraqTestimony.html.

10. USGAO, "Rebuilding Iraq," 7.

11. Stuart W. Bowen, Jr., Report *to Congress of the Special Inspector General for Iraq Reconstruction* (Washington D.C.: U.S. Congress, 2005), http://www.sigir.mil/reports/QuarterlyReports/pdf/Jan05/SIGIR%20Jan05%20-%20Report%20to%20Congress.pdf, quoted in Harriman "Where Has All the Money Gone?"

12. T. Christian Miller, "Millions Said Going to Waste in Iraq Utilities," *Los Angeles Times,* April 11, 2005.

13. Ali A. Allawi, *The Occupation of Iraq: Winning the War, Losing the Peace* (New Haven, CT: Yale University Press, 2007), 260.

14. James Rainey, "Aiming for a More Subtle Fighting Force," *Los Angeles Times,* May 9, 2006. See also Brookings, *Iraq Index,* May 18, 2006, 50; and Kovel, "Ecological Implications of the War."

15. Chatterjee, *Iraq, Inc.,* 81. This account is based on Chatterjee, *Bechtel's Dry Run,* and on Jamail, *Beyond the Green Zone,* 91–94.

16. Chatterjee, *Iraq, Inc.,* 81–82.

17. Jamail, *Beyond the Green Zone*, 93.
18. Miller, "Millions Said Going to Waste in Iraq Utilities."
19. United States General Accountability Office (USGAO), *Rebuilding Iraq: Stabilization, Reconstruction, and Financing Challenges* (Washington, DC: U.S. Government Accountability Office, February 8, 2006), http://www.gao.gov/htext/d06428t.html. The internal footnote is to another GAO report: United States General Accountability Office (USGAO), *Rebuilding Iraq: Enhancing Security, Measuring Program Results, and Maintaining Infrastructure Are Necessary to Make Significant and Sustainable Progress* (GAO-06-179T) (Washington, DC: U.S. Government Accountability Office, October 18, 2005), http://www.gao.gov/htext/d06179t.html. See also John Ward Anderson and Bassam Sebti, "Billion-Dollar Start Falls Short in Iraq," *Washington Post*, April 16, 2006.
20. See also Anderson and Sebti, "Billion-Dollar Start Falls Short in Iraq."
21. Rajiv Chandrasekaran, "Mistakes Loom Large as Handover Nears," *Washington Post*, June 20, 2004.
22. Amit R. Paley and Karen DeYoung, "Iraqis' Quality of Life Marked By Slow Gains, Many Setbacks," *Washington Post*, November 30, 2007.
23. United States Department of Defense (USDOD), "Measuring Stability and Security in Iraq," (Report to Congress in accordance with the Department of Defense Appropriations Act 2007 [Section 9010, Public Law 109-289]), December 14, 2007, 13, http://www.defenselink.mil/pubs/pdfs/FINAL-SecDef%20Signed-20071214.pdf .
24. U.S. claims cited in Bobby Caina Calvan, "Most Iraqis Still Don't Have Access to Clean Water," *McClatchy Newspapers*, November 19, 2007, http://www.contracostatimes.com/nationandworld/ci_7504787?nclick_check=1. UN report cited in Oxfam International and NGO Coordination Committee in Iraq, *Rising to the Humanitarian Challenge in Iraq* (Briefing Paper 105), July 30, 2007, 11, http://www.oxfam.org/en/policy/briefingpapers/bp105_humanitarian_challenge_in_iraq_0707.
25. USDOD, "Measuring Stability and Security in Iraq," December 14, 2007, 13.
26. Miller, "Millions Said Going to Waste in Iraq Utilities."
27. Calvan, "Most Iraqis Still Don't Have access to Clean Water."
28. Associated Press, "Cholera Outbreak Highlights Iraq's Plight," October 5, 2007; World Health Organization, "Daily Situation Report on Cholera Outbreak in Northern Iraq," WHO, September 19, 2007, http://www.reliefweb.int/rw/RWFiles2007.nsf/FilesByRWDocUnidFilename/LSGZ-778GJS-Full Report.pdf/$File/ Full_Report.pdf; Ben Lando, "Oil-Rich Iraqis Face Cholera Still," United Press International, December 21, 2007; James Glanz and Denise Grady, "Cholera Epidemic Infects 7,000 People in Iraq," *New York Times*, September 12, 2007.
29. For a similar conclusion about Kurdish health care, see MedAct, *Rehabilitation Under Fire: Health Care in Iraq 2003–7* (London: MedAct and Physicians for the Prevention of Nuclear War), January 21, 2008, http://www.medact.org/content/violence/MedactIraq08final.pdf, 1.
30. Lando, "Oil-Rich Iraqis Face Cholera Still."
31. "Iraq: No Let-up in the Humanitarian Crisis," International Committee of the Red Cross, March 17, 2008, http://www.reliefweb.int/rw/RWFiles2008.nsf/FilesByRWDocUnidFilename/YSAR-7CQN6P-full_report.pdf/$File/full_report.pdf.
32. Glanz and Grady, "Cholera Epidemic Infects 7,000 People in Iraq."
33. This discussion of Iraqi health care is taken mainly from Jamail, "Iraqi Hospitals Ailing Under Occupation."

34. Jamail, "Iraqi Hospitals Ailing Under Occupation." See also Jamail, *Beyond the Green Zone*.

35. Dahr Jamail, "Hospitals Come Under Siege," Inter Press Service, November 29, 2005, http://www.dahrjamailiraq.com/hard_news/archives/hard_news/000327 .php. For discussions of U.S. attacks on health care facilities, see also Jamail, "Iraqi Hospitals Ailing Under Occupation"; Ali, "Behind the Steel Curtain"; Zaid Al-Ali, "Iraq—The Lost Generation," Open Democracy, July 10, 2004, http://www.open democracy.net/debates/article-2-114-2143.jsp; Michael Schwartz, "Guerrilla Warfare in Sadr City," *Against the Current* 20 (January/February 2005), 26–40, http://www.atimes.com/atimes/Middle_East/ GA12Ak02.html.

36. Jamail, *Beyond the Green Zone*, 151.

37. As in other sectors, a surprising amount of medical equipment and drugs were defined as "dual use"—that is, as having a military application—and were therefore prohibited by the UN sanctions.

38. Karen DeYoung, "Petraeus, Crocker Testify Before Impatient Lawmakers," *Washington Post*, April 8, 2008.

39. MedAct, *Rehabilitation Under Fire*, 8. On Iraqi officials' resistance to Bush administration and IMF dictates, see page 4 of this report.

40. James Glanz "US pays for 150 Iraqi Clinics and Manages to Build 20," *New York Times*, April 30, 2006.

41. World Bank, "Iraqi Needs up to $8 Billion to Revive Health Sector," January 13, 2006, http://www.noticias.info/asp/aspComunicados.asp?nid=135350&src=0.

42. Calculated from Brookings, *Iraq Index*, May 18, 2006, 33, 36, and Glanz, "US Pays for 150 Iraqi Clinics and Manages to Build 20."

43. Ali A. Allawi, *The Occupation of Iraq: Winning the War, Losing the Peace* (New Haven: Yale University Press, 2007), 426–67.

44. Dahr Jamail, "Iraqi Healthcare Given a New Look," Antiwar.com, December 8, 2004, http://www.antiwar.com/jamail/?articleid=4128.

45. Jamail, *Beyond the Green Zone*, 197.

46. Jamail, "Hospitals Come Under Siege."

47. Joshua Partlow, "For Broken Iraqis, a Haven for Healing," *Washington Post*, February 9, 2008. See also ICRC, "Iraq: No Let-up in the Humanitarian Crisis."

48. Partlow, "For Broken Iraqis, a Haven for Healing."

49. MedAct, *Rehabilitation Under Fire*, 5.

50. See, for example, USDOD, *Measuring Stability and Security in Iraq*, December 14, 2007, 14.

51. World Bank, "Iraq Needs up to $8 Billion to Revive Health Sector."

52. Ellen Knickmeyer, "U.S. Plan to Build Iraq Clinics Falters; Contractor Will Try to Finish 20 of 142 Sites," *Washington Post*, May 3, 2006.

53. Ibid. [Emphasis added.]

54. USDOD, Measuring Stability and Security in Iraq, December 14, 2007, 14.

55. Oxfam, *Rising to the Humanitarian Challenge in Iraq*, 11; MedAct, *Rehabilitation Under Fire*, Introduction.

56. Oxfam, *Rising to the Humanitarian Challenge in Iraq*, 11; MedAct, *Rehabilitation Under Fire*, 2, 5.

57. "Little Respite for Iraq's Children in 2007," UNICEF, December 21, 2007, http://www.unicef.org/media/media_42256.html.

58. Brookings, *Iraq Index* (May 16, 2006), 40; Naomi Klein, *Shock Doctrine: The Rise of Disaster Capitalism* (New York: Holt, 2007), 373; Dahr Jamail, *Beyond the Green Zone*, 285–86.

59. Ali al-Fadhily, "'Arrowhead' Becomes Fountainhead of Anger," Inter Press Service, July 10, 2007, http://www.dahrjamailiraq.com/hard_news/archives/iraq/000608.php.

60. Associated Press, "Violence Creates Doctor Shortage in Iraq," September 11, 2007.

61. Daniel McGrory, "Exodus of the Iraqi Middle Class," *Times Online* (London), May 11, 2006.

62 "U.S. Embassy in Baghdad Unsafe?" United Press International, January 12, 2008.

63. Stephen Farrell, "Iraq Must Rebuild Itself After £11bn Fund Is Exhausted," *Times* (London), January 3, 2006.

64. Anderson and Sebti, "Billion-Dollar Start Falls Short in Iraq."

65. Neil MacDonald, "Billions Pour into Iraqi Reconstruction Efforts," *Financial Times*, December 7, 2005.

66. Doug Smith and Borzou Daragahi, "'Marshall Plan' for Iraq Fades," *Los Angeles Times*, January 15, 2006.

67. USDOD, *Measuring Stability and Security in Iraq*, December 14, 2007, 8.

68. Matthew Rothschild, "IMF Occupies Iraq, Riots Follow," *Progressive*, January 3, 2006.

69. Farrell, "Iraq Must Rebuild Itself After £11bn Fund Is Exhausted."

70. Dana Hedgpeth, "Report Says Iraq Lags on Rebuilding: Special Inspector Derides Iraqi Government's Lack of Responsibility," *Washington Post*, July 29, 2007.

71. This discussion of conditions in 2007 is taken from United Nations Assistance Mission for Iraq, Human Rights Report, (January 1–3; March 31, 2007), 19–20, http://www.uniraq.org/FileLib/misc/HR%20Report%20Jan%20Mar%202007%20EN.pdf; Brookings, Iraq Index (May 16, 2006): 32; Paley and DeYoung, "Iraqis' Quality of Life Marked by Slow Gains, Many Setbacks"; Oxfam, Rising to the Humanitarian Challenge in Iraq, 10–11.

72. United States Department of State, Bureau of Near Eastern Affairs, *Iraq Weekly Status Report*, January 16, 2008 (Washington D.C., USDOS, 2008), 19, http://www.state.gov/documents/organization/99563.pdf; quoted in Ben Lando, "Analysis: Iraqis Without Fuel, Power," United Press International, January 22.

73. United Nations, *Human Rights Report*, 19–20.

74. Ahmed Ali and Dahr Jamail; "Iraq Slashes Food Rations, Putting Lives at Risk," Inter Press Service, December 28, 2007, http://www.commondreams.org/archive/2007/12/28/6033; Dahr Jamail, "Iraq Progresses to Some of Its Worst," Inter Press Service, December 31, 2007, http://www.commondreams.org/archive/2007/12/31/6076.

75. Ali and Jamail, "Iraq Slashes Food Rations, Putting Lives at Risk."

76. Ibid.

77. See, for example, the reaction to the unusually cold winter of 2007–8. Hamza Hendawi, "Discontent Surges in Iraq," Associated Press, January 19, 2008, http://www.truthout.org/docs_2006/printer_012008C.shtml.

Chapter 13

Quoted in Khalid Jarrar, "As if There Were No Tomorrow, Sunnis Leaving Iraq," Islam On Line, March 5, 2006, http://www.uruknet.de/?s1=1&p=21257&s2=06.

1. Quoted in Khalid Jarrar, "As if There Were No Tomorrow, Sunnis Leaving Iraq." See also Sami Alkhojaand Charles Racknagel, "Professionals Increasingly Eye Emigration as Security Problems Continue," [Radio Free Europe Online,]

August 3, 2004, http://www.rferl.org/featuresarticle/2004/08/599df9b5-9ee0-4d0e-947d-ba92bf7156cb.html. and Daniel McGrory, "Exodus of the Iraqi Middle Class," *Times* Online (London), May 11, 2006.

2. James Paul and Celine Nahory, *War and Occupation in Iraq* (London: Global Policy Forum, June 2007), http://www.globalpolicy.org/security/issues/iraq/occupation/report/full.pdf. Internal footnotes are to United Nations, Emergency Working Group – Falluja Crisis (December 19, 2004); "Iraq: Displaced in the West Need More," United Nations Integrated Regional Information Networks (November 16, 2005); Yasin al-Dulaimi and Daud Salman, "Ramadi: Mass Exodus Amid Rising Tensions," Institute for War and Peace Reporting (June 15, 2006).

3. Ali A. Allawi, *The Occupation of Iraq: Winning the War, Losing the Peace* (New Haven, CT: Yale University Press, 2007), 447.

4. James Glanz and Stephen Farrell, "More Iraqis Said to Flee Since Troop Increase," *New York Times*, August 24, 2007. The *Washington Post* used maps to chart the process of neighborhood changing: Gene Thorp and Dita Smith, "Changing Baghdad," *Washington Post*, December 15, 2007.

5. Allawi, *Occupation of Iraq*, 387.

6. Riverbend's work can be found at her blog, Baghdad Burning: . . . I'll meet you 'round the bend my friend, where hearts can heal and souls can mend . . . , http://riverbendblog.blogspot.com, two books of her collected essays, *Baghdad Burning: Girl Blog from Iraq* (New York: Feminist Press, 2005) and *Baghdad Burning II: More Girl Blog from Iraq* (New York: Feminist Press, 2006), and a play based on her work: "Iraqi Woman's Blog Adapted for Stage," *BBC News*, August 14, 2006, http://news.bbc.co.uk/2/hi/entertainment/4790577.stm.

7. Riverbend, Baghdad Burning (blog), September 6, 2007.

8. Sabrina Tavernise, "For Iraqis, Exodus to Syria and Jordan Continues," *New York Times*, June 14, 2006; UNHCR "Statistics on Displaced Iraqis Around the World," United Nations High Commissioner for Refugees, September 2007, http://www.unhcr.org/cgibin/texis/vtx/home/opendoc.pdf?tbl=SUBSITES&id=470387fc2.

9. Oxfam International and NGO Coordination Committee in Iraq, *Rising to the Humanitarian Challenge in Iraq* (Briefing Paper 105), July 30, 2007, http://www.oxfam.org/en/policy/briefingpapers/bp105_humanitarian_challenge_in_iraq_0707, 14; Glanz and Farrell, "More Iraqis Said to Flee Since Troop Increase."

10. Patrick Cockburn, "UN Warns of Five Million Iraqi Refugees," *Independent*, June 10, 2007.

11. UNHCR "Statistics on Displaced Iraqis around the World."

12. A change in policy, announced in early 2007, created a new quota of seven thousand Iraqi refugees per year. Matt Weaver, "U.S. to Welcome 7,000 Iraqi Refugees," *Guardian*, February 14, 2007.

13. Hannah Godfrey, "From Baghdad to Britain," *Guardian*, March 20, 2008.

14. Glanz and Farrell, "More Iraqis Said to Flee Since Troop Increase."

15. UNHCR, "Statistics on Displaced Iraqis around the World"; Jennifer Pagonis, "Iraqi Refugees: Fresh Research Studies," United Nations High Commissioner on Refugees, December 14, 2007, http://www.unhcr.org/cgi-bin/texis/vtx/iraq?page=briefing&id=47626dbe14; Riverbend, Baghdad Burning (blog), October 22, 2007. For a vivid description of refugee life in Syria, see Deborah Campbell, "Exodus: Where Will Iraq Go Next?" *Harpers*, April 2008, 50–6.

16. Campbell, "Exodus"; Cara Buckley, "Iraq Premier Sees Families Returning to Safer Capital," *New York Times*, November 12, 2007; Karen DeYoung, "Balkanized Homecoming: As Iraqi Refugees Start to Trickle Back, Authorities

Worry About How They Will Fit into the New Baghdad," *Washington Post*, December 16, 2007.

17. UNHCR, "Statistics on Displaced Iraqis around the World."

18. Olivier Beucher, "Vital Role of Legal Assistance for Displaced Iraqis," *Forced Migration Review*, June 2007, 49.

19. Alissa J. Rubin, "Shiite Refugees Feel Forsaken in Their Holy City," *New York Times*, October 19, 2007.

20. Haroon Siddiqui, "Humanitarian Tsunami Sweeping Across Iraq," *Toronto Star*, November 4, 2007.

21. IPSOS, "Second IPSOS Survey on Iraqi Refugees," November 2007, quoted in Hannah Allam, "Survey: Many Iraqis in Syria Fled During U.S. Troop Buildup," McClatchy, December 14, 2007 http://www.mcclatchydc.com/iraq/story/23159.html.

22. Maki al-Nazzal and Dahr Jamail, "Iraq: Poverty Gets the Survivors," Inter Press Service, April 26, 2008 http://www.commondreams.org/archive/2008/04/26/8544.

23. Oxfam, *Rising to the Humanitarian Challenge in Iraq*, 15.

24. Campbell, "Exodus."

25. Allam, "Survey. Many Iraqis in Syria Fled During U.S. Troop Buildup."

26. Carolyn Bancroft, "Becoming a Refugee," Iraq Voices In Cairo, American University in Cairo (website), http://www.aucegypt.edu/ResearchatAUC/rc/fmrs/iraqivoicesincairo/Pages/becomingarefugee.aspx.

27. IPSOS, "Second IPSOS Survey on Iraqi Refugees."

28. "Deborah Campbell on the Iraq Refugee Crisis," *Democracy Now!*, March 31, 2008, http://www.democracynow.org/2008/3/31/exodus_where_will_iraq_go_next.

29. Ibid.

30. Beucher, "Vital Role of Legal Assistance for Displaced Iraqis"; Rubin, "Shiite Refugees Feel Forsaken in Their Holy City."

31. Haroon Siddiqui, "Iraq's Little-Known Humanitarian Crisis," *Toronto Star*, November 1, 2007.

32. "Iraq: No Let-up in the Humanitarian Crisis," International Committee of the Red Cross, March 17, 2008 http://www.reliefweb.int/rw/RWFiles2008.nsf/FilesByRWDocUnidFilename/YSAR-7CQN6P-full_report.pdf/$File/full_report.pdf, 3.

33. Ibid.

34. Zaineb Naji, "Iraq's Scholars Reluctant to Return," Institute for War and Peace Crisis Report No. 243, January 18, 2008, http://www.reliefweb.int/rw/RWB.NSF/db900SID/KHII-7B32SJ?OpenDocument.

35. For an analysis of the decline of Iraqi education under Hussein that emphasizes the role of the Gulf War in 1991 and (therefore) U.S. culpability, and which describes recent events from the perspective of the Iraqi resistance, see Ghali Hassan, "The Destruction of Iraq's Education System under US Occupation," Global Research, May 11, 2005, http://globalresearch.ca/articles/HAS505B.html.

36. For a convincing portrait of this renaissance during the first months after the fall of the Baathist regime, see the film *The Dreams of Sparrows* (Hayder Jaffar, director, produced by the Iraq Eye Group, 2005).

37. This discussion is based on Chatterjee and Docena, "Occupation, Inc."; Catherine Taylor, "Contrary to Policy, US Forces Occupy Schools and Church," *Christian Science Monitor*, March 4, 2003; and Center for Economic and Social Rights (CESR), "11. Violation VIII: Failure to Protect the Rights to Food and Education," *Beyond Torture: US Violations of Occupation Law in Iraq* (Brooklyn, NY: Center for Economic and Social Rights, 2004), http://cesr.org/node/238?PHPSESSID=

75fd950a443bd804bcb5ab624794e907.

38. Evan Wright, *Generation Kill*, passim.

39. See chapters 6 and 7, and Edmund Blair, "Anger Mounts After US Troops Kill 13 Iraqi Protesters," *Reuters*, April 29, 2003; Rone Tempest, "Sight of Carnage in Iraq Town Still Haunts Young Marine," *Los Angeles Times*, May 30, 2006.

40. Larry Kaplow, "Bechtel Criticized over School Project in Iraq," Cox News Service, December 14, 2003 http://www.corpwatch.org/article.php?id=11120.

41. "Iraq—An Expensive & Corrupt Vietnam?" *Newsweek*, October 27, 2003.

42. Chatterjee and Docena, "Occupation, Inc."

43. Ibid.

44. Ibid. See also Kaplow, "Bechtel Criticized over School Project in Iraq."

45. "Little Respite for Iraq's Children in 2007," UNICEF, December 21, 2007, http://www.unicef.org/media/media_42256.html; Klein, "The Erasing of Iraq."

46. Dahr Jamail, "Women's Day–Iraq: Surviving Somehow Behind a Concrete Purdah," Inter Press Service, March 6, 2008, http://dahrjamailiraq.com/hard_news/archives/iraq/000757.php.

47. Ahmed Ali, "Living Becomes Hard in a Death City," Inter Press Service, July 23, 2007, http://www.dahrjamailiraq.com/hard_news/archives/iraq/000614.php.

48. Ben Lando, "Iraqi Oil, Health, Teacher Demands Unmet," United Press International, December 21, 2007 http://www.upi.com/International_Security/Energy/Briefing/2007/12/21/iraqi_oil_health_teacher_demands_unmet/6675.

49. UNICEF, "Little Respite for Iraq's Children in 2007."

50. Cited in J. R. A. Williams, "Education Crisis for Iraqi Children," *Forced Migration Review*, June 2007, 45.

51. Nicolas J. S. Davies, "Evidence of an American Dirty War in Iraq," *Peace Review* 19 (September 2007): 435–6; Naji, "Iraq's Scholars Reluctant to Return."

52. Naji, "Iraq's Scholars Reluctant to Return."

53. "Threatened Teachers Fleeing the Country," Integrated Regional Information Networks (IRIN), (United Nations Office for the Coordination of Humanitarian Affairs), August 24, 2006 http://www.alertnet.org/thenews/newsdesk/IRIN/9c65cf0098d9fd852b6cc81cfa749748.htm

54. Naji, "Iraq's Scholars Reluctant to Return."

55. Joshua Partlow, "A Cautious Comeback on Campus at Baghdad University, Students Welcome the Decline in Violence, but Still Look Toward the Future Warily," *Washington Post*, January 15, 2008.

56. International Republican Institute, Survey of Iraqi Public Opinion, November 24–December 5, 2004, http://www.iraqfoundation.org/studies/2004/December IraqiPublicOpinionSurvey.ppt; IPSOS, "Second IPSOS Survey on Iraqi Refugees." See also "Deborah Campbell on the Iraq Refugee Crisis."

57. Jim Lobe, "Iraq Exodus Ends Four-Year Decline in Refugees." Inter Press Service, June 14, 2006, http://www.ipsnews.net/news.asp?idnews=33613. United Nations High Commissioner on Refugees, Update on the Current Iraq Situation, November 2006, (New York: UNHCR, 2006), http://www.internal-displacement.org/8025708F004CE90B/(httpDocuments)/8911DEDCD9E41687C12572 210042D466/$file/Iraq+Situation+Update+Oct+06+Final.pdf; Oxfam, *Rising to the Humanitarian Challenge in Iraq*, 15.

58. Chip Cummins, "Energy Security Is Hostage to Supply of Oil. Professionals," *Wall Street Journal*, August 22, 2006, quoted in Luke Mitchell, "The Black Box," *Harper's*, December 2007, 40. See also Ahmed Rasheed and Simon Webb, "Iraq Oil Flows Faster, But Not Fast Enough," Reuters, March 19, 2008.

59. UNHCR, Update on the Current Iraq Situation.

60. See chapter 12; "Cholera Outbreak Highlights Iraq's Plight," Associated Press, October 5, 2007; Tom Engelhardt, "Having a Carnage Party: We Count, They Don't," TomDispatch, October 12, 2007, http://www.tomdispatch.com/post/174844/having_a_carnage_party; Joshua Partlow, "For Broken Iraqis, a Haven for Healing," *Washington Post*, February 9, 2008.

61. Ben Lando, "Analysis: Iraqis Without Fuel, Power," United Press International, January 22, 2008; James Glanz, "Provinces Use Rebuilding Money in Iraq," *New York Times*, October 1, 2007.

62. Glanz, "Provinces Use Rebuilding Money in Iraq"; Allawi, *Occupation of Iraq*, 426–67.

63. Lando, "Analysis."

64. Glanz, "Provinces Use Rebuilding Money in Iraq."

65. Cummins, "Energy Security is Hostage to Supply of Oil Professionals"; see also Walid Khadduri, "Oil In a Week (The Battle of Basra and its Oil Dimension)," *Al-Hayat*, March 31, 2008, found at http://english.daralhayat.com/business/03-2008/Article-20080331-04eb2134-c0a8-10ed-017c-432453bc65dc/story.html.

66. Ibid., 45, 49. See also Khadduri, "Oil in a Week."

Chapter 14

Yochi J. Dreazen and Christopher Cooper, "Behind the Scenes, US Tightens Grip on Iraq's Future," *Wall Street Journal*, May 13, 2004.

1. Evan Wright, *Generation Kill* (New York: Berkley Caliber, 2004); see, for example, 232–33.

2. George W. Bush, "Major Combat Operations Have Ended," remarks from the USS *Abraham Lincoln*, May 1, 2003, http://www.whitehouse.gov/news/releases/2003/05/20030501-15.html.

3. A. Allawi, *The Occupation of Iraq: Winning the War, Losing the Peace* (New Haven, CT: Yale University Press, 2007). The documentary video by Hayder Mousa Daffar, *The Dreams of Sparrows* (Harbinger Productions, 2003), captures the early postwar mood very effectively.

4. An excellent treatment of the impact of looting on legitimacy can be found in Charles Ferguson's film *No End in Sight* (2007); see also the accompanying book, Charles Ferguson, *No End in Sight* (New York: Public Affairs, 2008).

5. See chapter 3.

6. Allawi, *The Occupation of Iraq*. This discussion of the shift from United States to Iraqi rule is based on Allawi's account.

7. Steven R. Weisman, Patrick E. Tyler, and Warren Hoge, "The Struggle for Iraq: Iraqi Government; Scientist Jailed by Hussein Is Favored for Premier's Post," *New York Times*, May 26, 2004.

8. Ibid.

9. See, for example, Arizona Senator John McCain on *Meet the Press*, January 27, 2008, http://www.msnbc.msn.com/id/21134540/vp/22867420#22867420.

10. Jed Babbin, "Mission Report: Two Steps Forward, One Step Back," *National Review* Online, May 25, 2004, http://www.nationalreview.com/babbin/babbin200405250938.asp.

11. See Jeremy Scahill, *Blackwater: The Rise of the World's Most Powerful Mercenary Army* (New York: Nation Books, 2007); Jeremy Scahill, "Blackwater: Hired Guns, Above the Law," testimony before the Senate Democratic Policy Committee, September 21, 2007, http://www.thenation.com/doc/20071008/scahill0921.

12. This discussion based on John F. Burns, Thom Shanker, and Steven R. Weisman,

"US Officials Fashion Legal Basis to Keep Force in Iraq," *New York Times*, March 26, 2004; Ann Scott Tyson, "Iraq May Need Military Help for Years, Officials Say," *Washington Post*, January 18, 2008; Tom Engelhardt, "The Natives of Planet Earth," TomDispatch, April 3, 2008, http://www.tomdispatch.com/post/174914/the_natives_of_planet_earth.

13. Wikipedia, "List of Countries by Size of Armed Forces," download, February 3, 2008, http://en.wikipedia.org/wiki/List_of_countries_by_size_of_armed_forces.

14. Tyson, "Iraq May Need Military Help for Years."

15. Burns, et al., "US Officials Fashion Legal Basis to Keep Force in Iraq."

16. Solomon Moore, "Secret Iraqi Deal Shows Problems in Arms Orders," *New York Times*, April 13, 2008.

17. This account based on "US under Fire over Chalabi Raid," BBC, May 21, 2004, http://news.bbc.co.uk/1/hi/world/middle_east/3734443.stm; Renae Merle, "Dyn-Corp Took Part in Chalabi Raid," *Washington Post*, June 4, 2004.

18. Merle, "DynCorp Took Part in Chalabi Raid."

19. Ibid.

20. Allawi, *The Occupation of Iraq*, 450.

21. See chapters 5–7.

22. Andrew Cockburn, "Raiding Iraq's Piggy Bank," Salon.com, May 17, 2004, http://fairuse.1accesshost.com/news1/salon12.htm.

23. Ibid.

24. Maggie Farley and Mary Curtius, "U.S., Britain Present Proposal on Iraq to United Nations," *Los Angeles Times*, May 25, 2004.

25. See chapter 13.

26. "History of Illinois Basin Post Crude Oil Prices," http://www.ioga.com/Special/crudeoil_Hist.htm. See chapters 10–13.

27. Glenn Zorpette, "Oil and Electricity Ministries Won't Mix," *International Herald Tribune*, March 10, 2008.

28. Burns et al., "US Officials Fashion Legal Basis to Keep Force in Iraq."

29. Beth Mintz and Michael Schwartz, *The Power Structure of American Business* (Chicago: University of Chicago Press, 1986), chapters 1–3; Robert Jackal, *Moral Mazes: The World of Corporate Managers* (New York: Oxford University Press, 1989).

30. Weisman et al., "Struggle for Iraq."

31. Yochi J. Dreazen and Christopher Cooper, "Behind the Scenes, US Tightens Grip on Iraq's Future," *Wall Street Journal*, May 13, 2004.

32. Ibid.

33. Ibid.

34. Daniel McGrory, "Exodus of the Iraqi Middle Class," *Times* Online (London), May 11, 2006. http://www.timesonline.co.uk/article/0,,3-2174643,00.html; William Langewiesche, "The Mega-Bunker of Baghdad," *Vanity Fair*, November 2007. This account is also based on Tom Engelhardt," A Permanent Basis for Withdrawal?" TomDispatch, February 14, 2006, found at http://www.tomdispatch.com/index.mhtml?pid=59774; Tom Engelhardt, "The Colossus of Baghdad," TomDispatch, May 29, 2007, http://www.tomdispatch.com/index.mhtml?pid=199798; Anne Gearan, "U.S. Embassy in Iraq to be Biggest Ever," Associated Press, May 19, 2007; Martin Fletcher, "Welcome to the New U.S. Embassy," *Times* Online (London), September 1, 2007, http://www.timesonline.co.uk/tol/news/world/iraq/article2364255.ece.

35. Sue Pleming, "US Embassy Opening in Baghdad Delayed Indefinitely," Reuters, October 9, 2007; Warren P. Strobel, "New Baghdad Embassy's Fire-Fighting

System Is Defective," *McClatchy*, January 11, 2008, http://www.mcclatchydc.com/227/story/24626.html.

36. In the early 1900s, Great Britain ruled colonial India, with a population of three hundred million (about ten times the size of present-day Iraq), with an administrative staff of about 1,200. See United States Bureau of Insular Affairs, *Report of the Philippine Commission, 1905, Part I* (Washington, D.C.: U.S. Government Printing Office, 1906), 712.

37. Fletcher, "Welcome to the New U.S. Embassy."

38. Hanley, "Massive New Embassy in Iraq.

39. Allawi, *The Occupation of Iraq*, 349. See also 288, 350f, 450f, passim.

Chapter 15

Borzou Dargahi, "More People Are Dying Violently Now," *Democracy Now!*, May 9, 2006, http://www.democracynow.org/article.pl?sid=06/05/09/1415215.

1. Michael Hirsh and John Barry, "Pentagon May put Special Forces Led Assassination or Kidnapping Teams in Iraq," *Newsweek*, January 8, 2005; Max Fuller, "For Iraq, Salvador Option Becomes Reality," Global Research, http://globalresearch.ca/articles/FUL506A.html.

2. John F. Burns, "Torture Alleged at Ministry Site Outside Baghdad," *New York Times*, November 16, 2005.

3. Tom Regan, "Britain Will Scrap and Replace Police Force in Basra," *Christian Science Monitor*, September 26, 2005. See also Jill Carroll, "Old Brutality Among New Iraqi Forces," *Christian Science Monitor*, May 4, 2005.

4. See chapter 8. For discussions of U.S. primacy in creating the death squads, see Hirsch and Barry, "Pentagon May Put Special Forces–Led Assassination or Kidnapping Teams into Iraq"; Fuller, "For Iraq, Salvador Option Becomes Reality."

5. See chapters 8 and 13.

6. Nir Rosen, "On the Ground in Iraq: The Roots of Sectarian Violence," *Boston Review*, March/April 2006.

7. For a more detailed discussion of death squads, see chapters 6, 7, and 18. See also Dahr Jamail, "The Myth of Sectarianism," *International Socialist Review*, January 4, 2008.

8. See chapter 6.

9. Nicolas J. S. Davies, "Evidence of an American Dirty War in Iraq," *Peace Review* 19 (September 2007), 440.

10. *Los Angeles Times*, July 9, 2006, quoted in "Iraqi Police Rife with Abuse, Corruption: Ministry of Interior Document," Agence-France Presse, July 9, 2006, http://www.lebanonwire.com/0607MLN/06070917MAF.asp.

11. Dexter Filkins, "GIs to Increase US Supervision of Iraqi Police," *New York Times*, December 30, 2005.

12. Louise Roug, "US to Restrict Iraqi Police," *Los Angeles Times*, November 22, 2005.

13. Ellen Knickmeyer, "US Troops to Mentor Iraqi Police," *Washington Post*, December 30, 2005.

14. Filkins, "GIs to Increase US Supervision of Iraqi Police." ·

15. Ellen Knickmeyer, "Shiite Urges US to Give Iraqis Leeway in Rebel Fight," *Washington Post*, November 27, 2005.

16. Tom Regan, "Britain Will Scrap and Replace Police Force in Basra," *Christian Science Monitor*, September 25, 2005.

17. Brian Brady, "Scrap Basra Police and Start Again Orders MoD," *Scotsman*,

September 25, 2005.

18. See below for a more detailed discussion of these issues. A good short summary can be found in Anthony Shadid and Steve Fainaru, "Militias Wresting Control Across Iraq's North and South," *Washington Post*, August 20, 2005.

19. For discussion of the battles in Najaf and Karbala, see Michael Schwartz, "Guerrilla Warfare in Sadr City," *Against the Current* 20 (January/Febuary 2005) 26–40; Jeremy Scahill, *Blackwater: The Rise of the World's Most Powerful Mercenary Army* (New York: Nation Books, 2007), 117–32; Ali A. Allawi, *The Occupation of Iraq: Winning the War, Losing the Peace* (New Haven: Yale University Press, 2007), 316–33.

20. See chapter 16.

21. See chapters 6–8.

22. Jack Fairweather and Haider Samad, "Clerics Become Powerbrokers in the South," *Telegraph*, February 14, 2005.

23. Edward Wong, "Shiite Militiamen Reclaim Mosque from the Sunnis," *New York Times*, March 3, 2003. See also Christian Parenti, "The Rough Guide to Baghdad," *Nation*, July 1, 2004.

24. An excellent analysis of Basra under British occupation can be found in International Crisis Group, "Where Is Iraq Heading? Lessons from Basra," *Middle East Report* 67, June 25, 2007, http://www.crisisgroup.org/library/documents/middle _east___north_africa/iraq_iran_gulf/67_iraq___lessons_from_basra_web.doc.

25. Ghaith Abdul-Ahad, "The British Officer Said: 'We Are Now Just Another Tribe,'" *Guardian*, October 14, 2006.

26. Anthony Shadid and Steve Fainaru, "Militias Wresting Control Across Iraq's North and South," *Washington Post*, August 20, 2005; Bernhard Zand, "British Leaving Basra to the Mahdi Militia," *Spiegel* Online, February 23, 2007, http:// www.spiegel.de:80/international/0,1518,468118,00.html.

27. "Rivers of Basra . . . Pollution and Unfulfilled Promises," Voices of Iraq, December 17, 2007, http://www.iraqupdates.com/scr/preview.php?article=25140.

28. Fairweather and Samad, "Clerics Become Powerbrokers in the South."

29. Catherine Philip, "Death at 'Immoral' Picnic in the Park," *Times* Online (London), February 25, 2005 http://www.timesonline.co.uk/article/0,,7374-1537512,00.html.

30. Dahr Jamail, "Women's Day–Iraq: Surviving Somehow Behind a Concrete Purdah," *Inter Press Service*, March 6, 2008, found at http://dahrjamailiraq.com/ hard_news/archives/iraq/000757.php .

31. International Crisis Group, *Where Is Iraq Heading?*

32. Dana Hedgpeth, "Iraq Far from U.S. Goals for Energy: $50 Billion Needed to Meet Demand," *Washington Post*, September 2, 2007.

33. Bernhard Zand, "Iraq on the Verge of Collapse," *Spiegel* Online, May 1, 2006, http:// service.spiegel.de/cache/international/spiegel/0,1518,druck-413981,00.html.

34. "Basra Council Breaks Ties with Coalition," CNN, February 14, 2006.

35. This account based on International Crisis Group, "Where Is Iraq Heading?"; Abdul-Ahad, "The British Officer Said . . ."; Anthony Shadid, "In a Land Without Order, Punishment Is Power: Conflicts Among Shiites Challenge a Village Sheik in Southern Iraq," *Washington Post*, October 22, 2006; Paul von Zielbauer, "Iraqi and British Troops Clash with Shiite Militias," *New York Times*, August 17, 2008; Thomas Harding, "British to Evacuate Consulate in Basra After Mortar Attacks," *Telegraph*, October 30, 2006.

36. "Iraq Police Block Militia as UK Troops Quit Centre," Reuters, August 26, 2007.

37. Abdul-Ahad, "The British Officer Said . . ."

38. This account of end of the British occupation of Basra is based on International

Crisis Group, Where is Iraq Heading?; Aref Mohammed, "Iraqis Say Basra Quieter After British Troop Pullout," Reuters, October 1, 2006; Harding, "British to Evacuate Consulate in Basra After Mortar Attacks"; Reuters, "Iraq Police Block Militia as UK Troops Quit Centre"; Ghaith Abdul-Ahad, "Welcome to Tehran–How Iran Took Control of Basra," *Guardian*, May 19, 2007; Zand, "British Leaving Basra to the Mahdi Militia"; Sam Dagher, "In the 'Venice of the East,' a History of Diversity" (three parts), *Christian Science Monitor*, September 18–19, 2007; Ben Lando, "Analysis: Iraq's '08 Fate—Basra, Kirkuk," United Press International, January 4, 2008.

39. International Crisis Group, *Where Is Iraq Heading?*
40. Ibid.
41. Mohammed, "Iraqis Say Basra Quieter After British Troop Pullout."
42. Lando, "Analysis: Iraq's '08 Fate."
43. This account of the 2008 battle of Basra is taken from Michael R. Gordon, Eric Schmitt, and Stephen Farrell, "U.S. Cites Gaps in Planning of Iraqi Assault on Basra," *New York Times*, April 3, 2008; Sudarsan Raghavan and Ernesto Londoño, "Basra Assault Exposed U.S., Iraqi Limits Anti-Sadr Gambit Seen Aiding Cleric," *Washington Post*, April 4, 2008; Robert Dreyfuss, "Lessons of Basra," *Nation*, March 31, 2008; Patrick Cockburn, "Violence Erupts in Basra as Iraqi Forces Battle Mehdi Army," *Independent*, March 26, 2008; Patrick Cockburn, "Police Refuse to Support Iraqi PM's Attacks on Mehdi Army," *Independent*, March 29, 2008; Ned Parker, "In Iraq, U.S. Caught in Middle of Shiite Rivalry," *Los Angeles Times*, March 30, 2008.
44. Michael Schwartz, "Forgotten Iraq: The War in Maysan Province," TomDispatch, November 3, 2005.
45. Shadid and Fainaru, "Militias Wresting Control Across Iraq's North and South."
46. "Deadly Clashes Erupt in Second Iraq Town," CNN, October 24, 2006.
47. Ibid.
48. See chapters 9–12.
49. See chapter 14.
50. Michael Schwartz, "The Irony of Conquest," TomDispatch, August 9, 2005; Robert Dreyfuss, "Is Iran Winning the Iraq War?" *Nation*, March 10, 2008.
51. Schwartz, "The Irony of Conquest"; Jonathan Finer and Omar Fekeiki, "Iraq to Build Airport with Help from Iran Loan Would Pay for Project in Shiite Area," *Washington Post*, August 3, 2005.
52. Borzou Dargahi, "More People Are Dying Violently Now," *Democracy Now!*, May 9, 2006.
53. Sudarsan Raghavan, "Shiite Contest Sharpens in Iraq,"

Chapter 16

Tom Lasseter, "Kurds in Iraqi Army Proclaim Loyalty to Militia," Knight Ridder, December 27, 2005.

1. A succinct account of the Kurdish role in the U.S. invasion can be found in Ali A. Allawi, *The Occupation: Winning the War, Losing the Peace* (New Haven, CT: Yale University Press, 2007), 87–93.
2. A succinct account of the post–Gulf War developments can be found in Thomas E. Ricks, *Fiasco: The American Military Adventure in Iraq* (New York: Penguin, 2006), 3–11.
3. Ned Parker, "A Battle for Land in Northern Iraq," *Los Angeles Times*, April 5, 2008.

4. Anthony Shadid and Steve Fainaru, "Militias Wresting Control Across Iraq's North and South," *Washington Post*, August 20, 2005.
5. Bernhard Zand, "Iraq on the Verge of Collapse," *Spiegel* Online, May 1, 2006, http://service.spiegel.de/cache/international/spiegel/0,1518,druck-413981,00.html. For the history of Kurdish oil development, see Borzou Daragahi, "Kurdish Oil Deal Shocks Iraq's Political Leaders: A Norwegian Company Begins Drilling in the North without Approval from Baghdad," *Los Angeles Times*, December 1, 2005; "Dispute over Kurdistan Oil Deals Might Be Solved at Federal Court, Minister Says," Associated Press, March 10, 2008.
6. Jay Price, "U.S. Officials Criticize Hunt Oil's Iraq Deal," McClatchy, September 27, 2007, http://www.mcclatchydc.com/iraq/story/20038.html.
7. This account is based on Roula Khalaf and Steve Negus, "Forbidden Fields: Oil Groups Circle the Prize of Iraq's Vast Reserves," *Financial Times*, March 19, 2008; Ben Lando, "Analysis: Petraeus Makes Iraq Energy Calls," United Press International, March 18, 2008. See also chapter 4.
8. See chapter 4 for a full account of U.S. efforts to develop Iraqi oil. See chapter 1 for the ambitious plans that animated these efforts.
9. Lando, "Analysis: Petraeus Makes Iraq Energy Calls."
10. Khalaf and Negus, "Forbidden fields."
11. Zand, "Iraq on the Verge of Collapse." See chapter 15.
12. Useful background to the friction over Kirkuk can be found in K. Gajendra Singh, "The Kirkuk Tinderbox," Asia Times, January 22, 2005.
13. Ibid.
14. Ibid.
15. Steve Fainaru and Anthony Shadid, "Kurdish Officials Sanction Abductions in Kirkuk," *Washington Post*, June 15, 2005.
16. "Claims in Conflict: Reversing Ethnic Cleansing in Northern Iraq," Human Rights Watch Reports, August 2004, http://hrw.org/reports/2004/iraq0804/7.htm#_Toc78803822; Singh, "The Kirkuk Tinderbox."
17. Fainaru and Shadid, "Kurdish officials sanction abductions in Kirkuk."
18. Ibid.
19. Unlike the south, however, this threat was never visibly activated. The occupation approach in Kirkuk, which was less kinetic than in Shia cities like Najaf and Basra, was illustrated by the official reaction to the *Washington Post* report on the "extra-judicial detentions." When Fainaru and Shadid reported that most Kirkuk residents believed that U.S. military advisers had supported the policy, a U.S. official said they had discovered the practice in May 2005, months after it began; then, according to Major Darren Blagbum, the intelligence officer for the 116th Brigade Combat Team stationed there, "We put a stop to it." Whether or not this was true, it was symptomatic of the way the occupation chose to exercise its limited leverage in Kirkuk.
20. Lasseter, "Kurds in Iraqi Army Proclaim Loyalty to Militia."
21. Ibid. On the struggle for control of Mosul, see Parker, "A Battle for Land in Northern Iraq." Ned Parker, "A Battle for Land in Northern Iraq," *Los Angeles Times*, April 5, 2008.
22. Fainaru and Shadid, "Kurdish Officials Sanction Abductions in Kirkuk."
23. "Police chief in Northern Iraq killed," United Press International, February 19, 2006.
24. In practice the actual proportion was a source of considerable dispute. See "Iraq Crisis Report: Kurdish Frustration with Maliki Grows," Institute for War and Peace Research, January 25, 2008, http://www.iwpr.net/?p=icr&s=f&o=342253&

apc_state=henpicr.

25. Ibid.
26. "Turkey Launches Major Iraq Incursion," CNN, February 23, 2008; Joshua Partlow and Ellen Knickmeyer, "Kurdish Soldiers in Iraq Caught Between Competing Allegiances," *Washington Post*, February 24, 2008; Singh, "The Kirkuk Tinderbox."
27. See chapters 11 and 12.
28. Ben Lando, "Oil-rich Iraqis Face Cholera still," United Press International, December 21, 2007.
29. Anthony H. Cordesman, *Pandora's Box: Iraq Federalism, Separatism, 'Hard' Partitioning, and US Policy* (Washington D.C.: Center for Strategic and International Studies), http://www.csis.org/media/csis/pubs/071009_pandorasbox.pdf.

Chapter 17

Rajiv Chandrasekaran, "Marines Bide Their Time in Insurgent-Held Fullujah," *Washington Post*, September 21, 2004.
1. See chapters 7–8.
2. On Basra, see chapter 16.
3. Michael Schwartz, "Contradictions of the Iraqi Resistance: Guerilla War Vs. Terrorism," *Against the Current*, January–February 2006 (120), 19–26.
4. See chapters 5–7.
5. See chapters 15, 16.
6. This account of Baiji is based, unless otherwise noted, on Ann Scott Tyson, "In Iraqi Oil City a Formidable Foe," *Washington Post*, January 19, 2006; "Clashes Erupt in Iraqi Oil City of Baiji," San Francisco Bay Area Independent Media, November 11, 2004, http://www.indybay.org/news/2004/11/1704793.php; Ryan Lenz, "Troops Build Wall of Sand to Keep Insurgents in Their Homes," *Army Times*, January 9, 2006; Brian Conley and Isam Rashid, "Siniyah Isolated and Simmering," Inter Press Service, February 9, 2006, http://ipsnews.net/news.asp?idnews=32100.
7. See chapter 3. See also Naomi Klein, "Pillaging Iraq in Pursuit of a Neocon Utopia," *Harper's*, September 2004.
9. Cited in IndyBay, "Clashes Erupt in Iraqi Oil City of Baiji."
10. Conley and Rashid, "Siniyah Isolated and Simmering."
11. Ibid.
12. See chapter 6.
13. Tyson, "In Iraqi Oil City a Formidable Foe."
14. Ibid. For a very similar story, see Sam Slavin, "The Devil in Me: Act One, and So We Meet Again," Episode 340 of *This American Life*, (National Public Radio), September 7, 2007, http://www.thislife.org/ Radio_Episode.aspx?sched=1205.
15. Lenz, "Troops Build Wall of Sand to Keep Insurgents in Their Homes."
16. Conley and Rashid, "Siniyah Isolated and Simmering"; Lenz, "Troops Build Wall of Sand to Keep Insurgents in Their Homes."
17. See chapter 17.
18. This account based on Richard A. Oppel, Jr., "Iraq's Insurgency Runs on Stolen Oil Profits," *New York Times*, March 16, 2008.
19. Ibid.
20. Radha Iyengar and Jonathan Monten, "Is There an 'Emboldenment' Effect? Evidence from the Insurgency in Iraq," Princeton Industrial Relations Section, February 2008, http://www.irs.princeton.edu/seminars/pdfs/Iyengar.pdf.
21. Global Security, "Salafi Islam," http://www.globalsecurity.org/military/intro/islam-

salafi.htm.

22. This account of early friction between guerrillas and jihadists is based largely on Michael Schwartz, "Contradictions of the Iraqi Resistance. See also chapter 8.

23. Video by Zawahiri, summarized and posted (in Arabic) by the United States Government Open Source Center, translation by Juan Cole, posted at Juan Cole, "Zawahiri: Iraq Main Field of Jihad; Attacks Iran, Muqtada, Nasrallah," Informed Comment, December 18, 2007.

24. See chapter 8.

25. Christine Hauser, "Shiite Cleric's Representative Killed in Iraq After Prayers," *New York Times*, January 13, 2005.

26. Anthony Shadid, "Sunni Group Says it Killed Shiite Cleric," *Washington Post*, January 15, 2005.

27. Erik Eckholm, "Iraq Militants Claim Murder of Shiite Cleric's Aid," *New York Times*, January 15, 2005.

28. Chandrasekaran, "Marines Bide Their Time in Insurgent-Held Fallujah."

29. Schwartz, "Contradictions of the Iraqi Resistance."

30. "Statement of the Anti-Occupation Patriotic Forces," Informed Comment, March 5, 2005 http://www.juancole.com/2005/03/achcar-allawis-offensive-gilbert.html.

31. Ellen Knickmeyer, "Zarqawi Followers Clash with Local Sunnis," *Washington Post*, May 29, 2005.

32. Sudarsan Raghavan, "New Leaders of Sunnis Make Gains in Influence," *Washington Post*, January 8, 2008.

33. This history of the Sahwa movement is based on Alissa J. Rubin and Damien Cave, "In a Force for Iraqi Calm, Seeds of Conflict," *New York Times*, December 23, 2007; Damien Cave, Michael Kamber, and Diana Oliva Cave, "The Anbar Awakening," (video), *New York Times*, March 30, 2008; United States Department of Defense, *Measuring Stability and Security in Iraq, December 14, 2007* (Report to Congress, Department of Defense Appropriations Act, 2007), http://www.defenselink.mil/pubs/pdfs/FINAL-SecDef%20Signed-20071214.pdf; Raghavan, "New Leaders of Sunnis Make Gains in Influence," "Anbar: US Trophy for Iraq Security Losing Its Shine," Reuters, March 24, 2008; Ned Parker, "Iraq Calmer, but More Divided," *Los Angeles Times*, December 10, 2007; Ahmed Ali and Dahr Jamail, "Sahwa Forces Challenge Govt, and Win," Inter Press Service, March 5, 2008, http://dahrjamailiraq.com/hard_news/ archives/iraq/000751.php; Ahmed Ali and Dahr Jamail, "Tensions Rise Between Sahwa and Govt Forces," Inter Press Service, March 1, 2008, http://dahrjamailiraq.com/hard_news/archives/iraq/000747.php.

34. See chapter 18.

35. "Sunni Sheiks in Anbar to Form New National Party to Oppose al-Qaida," Associated Press, April 20, 2007.

36. Wayne White, "Iraq: Dark Shadows of Things to Come," MEI Commentary, April 3, 2008 http://www.mideasti.org/commentary/iraq-dark-shadows-things-come.

37. Rubin and Cave, "In a Force for Iraqi Calm, Seeds of Conflict."

38. Brookings Institution, *Iraq Index: Tracking Variables of Reconstruction & Security in Post-Saddam Iraq,* (Washington D.C.: Brookings, April 4, 2008), http://www3 .brookings.edu/fp/saban/iraq/index20080404.pdf, 10.

39. Jim Lobe, "Toward National Reconciliation of a Warlord State?" Inter Press Service, November 20, 2007, http://www.ipsnews.net/news.asp?idnews=40140.

40. USDOD, "Measuring Stability and Security in Iraq," 23.

41. Rubin and Cave, "In a Force for Iraqi Calm, Seeds of Conflict."

42. Abbas, "U.S. Trophy for Iraq Security Losing Its Shine."

43. Parker, "Iraq Calmer, but More Divided."

44. See Ali and Jamail, "Sahwa Forces Challenge Govt, and Win," and "Tensions Rise Between Sahwa and Govt Forces."
45. Peter Spiegel, "US Shifts Sunni Strategy in Iraq," *Los Angeles Times*, January 14, 2008.
46. Maggie O'Kane and Ian Black, "Sunni Militia Strike Could Derail US Strategy Against Al-Qaida," *Guardian*, March 21, 2008.
47. Lobe, "Iraq: Toward National Reconciliation or a Warlord State?"
48. Rosa Brooks, "The Walls Around Bush's Iraq Strategy," *Los Angeles Times*, December 20, 2007.

Chapter 18

Patrick Cockburn, "A Week in Iraq: 'People Say Things Are Better, But It's Still Terrible Here,'" *Independent*, February 3, 2008.
1. Ghaith Abdul-Ahad, "Death, Destruction and Fear on the Streets of Cafes, Poets and Booksellers," *Guardian*, March 17, 2008.
2. Leila Fadel, "GIs in Sadr City Under Fire from Friends and Foes," McClatchy, April 18, 2008, http://www.truthout.org/docs_2006/041908A.shtml.
3. "Baghdad Drowning in Sewage: Iraqi Official," Agence-France Presse, February 3, 2008, "They Don't Think About Us," *McClatchy*, March 29, 2008, http://washingtonbureau.typepad.com/iraq/2008/03/they-dont-think.html.
4. Spiegel Staff, "Life in Baghdad Since the Fall of Saddam," *Spiegel Online*, March 17, 2008, http://www.spiegel.de:80/international/world/0,1518,541977,00.html; Mark KacKinnon, "Women: Iraq's Persecuted Majority," *Toronto Globe and Mail*, March 18, 2008.
5. Dahr Jamail, "Missing Voices in the Iraq Debate," TomDispatch, January 27, 2008, http://www.tomdispatch.com/post/174886/dahr_jamail_missing_voices_in_the_iraq_debate.
6. For a detailed discussion of these administrations, see Ali A. Allawi, *The Occupation of Iraq: Winning the War, Losing the Peace* (New Haven, CT: Yale University Press, 2007), especially chapters 16–24.
7. "Bush: 30,000 Iraqis Killed in War: President Hails Iraqi Elections in Speech in Philadelphia," *CBS News*, December 12, 2005.
8. Allawi, *Occupation of Iraq*, 404f.
9. See chapters 3, and 12.
10. On electoral promises of U.S. withdrawal, see Allawi, *Occupation of Iraq*, 340.
11. On the logic of the jihadists, see chapters 8 and 17. See also Michael Schwartz, "Contradictions of the Iraqi Resistance: Guerilla War vs. Terrorism," *Against the Current*, January–February 2006, 19–26.
12. On death squads, see Ali Al-Fadhily and Dahr Jamail, "IRAQ: Govt. Death Squads Ravaging Baghdad," Inter Press Service, October 19, 2006, http://www.ipsnews.net/news.asp?idnews=35159; Kim Sengupta, "Operation Enduring Chaos: The Retreat of the Coalition & Rise of the Militias," *Independent*, October 29, 2006; A. K. Gupta, "New Exit Strategy for Iraq: Civil War," Z Magazine (online), 18 (September 2005), http://zmagsite.zmag.org/Sep2005/ gupta0905.html; Inge Van de Merlen, "The Assault on Adhamiya," Global Research, June 25, 2006, http://www.globalresearch.ca/index.php?context=viewArticle& code=VAN20060625&articleId=2690; Sabrina Tavernise, "Iraq's Leader Jabs at U.S. on Timetables and Militias," *New York Times*, October 26, 2006. On the origins of the death squads, see chapter 8 and Michael Hirsh and John Barry, "The Salvador Option: The Pentagon May Put Special-Forces-Led Assassination or Kidnapping Teams in Iraq," *Newsweek*,

January 8, 2005.

13. Gene Thorp and Dita Smith, "Changing Baghdad," *Washington Post*, December 15, 2007.

14. For an excellent account of the origins and development of ethnic expulsions in Baghdad, see Nir Rosen, "Anatomy of a Civil War: Iraq's Descent into Chaos," *Boston Review*, November/December 2006. See also Allawi, *Occupation of Iraq*, 447–52.

15. See chapter 8.

16. Tavernise, "Iraq's Leader Jabs at U.S."

17. For the origins of this pattern in Latin America, see Greg Grandin, *Empire's Workshop: Latin America, the United States, and the Rise of the New Imperialism* (New York: Metropolitan Books, 2007). For similar developments relating to Hindu-Muslim-Sikh violence in India, see Paul R. Brass, *Forms of Collective Violence: Riots, Pogroms, and Genocide in Modern India* (Palam Vihar, India: Three Essays Collective, 2006).

18. "Bush: 30,000 Iraqis Killed In War: President Hails Iraqi Elections in Speech in Philadelphia," *CBS News*, December 12, 2005.

19. Nir Rosen, "Iraq Is the Republic of Fear," *Washington Post*, May 28, 2006.

20. Edward Wong and Damien Cave, "Iraqi Death Toll Rose Above 3,400 in July," *New York Times*, August 15, 2006; Mark Danner, "How a War of Unbound Fantasies Happened," TomDispatch, November 21, 2006, http://www.tomdispatch.com/index.mhtml?pid=142383.

21. John Ward Anderson and Ellen Knickmeyer, "Twofold Operation Seals Sadr City: Troops Seek U.S. Soldier, Militiaman," *Washington Post*, October 30, 2006.

22. Sabrina Tavernise, "Spate of Bombs Sweep Baghdad—Cleric Faults U.S.," *New York Times*, October 30, 2006.

23. Edward Wong and Kirk Semple, "Iraq Death Toll Rises; Shiites Threaten to Leave Government,"*New York Times*, November 24, 2006.

24. "Two Bombs Explode, Killing 22 in Iraq, Following Bombings in Baghdad Slum That Killed 215," Associated Press, November 24, 2006.

25. Anderson and Knickmeyer, "Twofold Operation Seals Sadr City."

26. Seymour Hersh, "The Next Act: Is a Damaged Administration Less Likely to Attack Iran, or More?" *New Yorker*, November 11, 2006.

27. Brookings Institution, *Iraq Index: Tracking Variables of Reconstruction & Security in Post-Saddam Iraq*, (Washington D.C.: Brookings, August 30, 2007), 5–10.

28. See chapter 13.

29. Michael Schwartz, "Baghdad Surges into Hell: First Results from the President's Offensive," TomDispatch, February 11, 2007, http://www.tomdispatch.com/index.mhtml?pid=165183.

30. Ann Barnard, "Inside Fallujah's War: Empathy, Destruction Mark a Week with US Troops," *Boston Globe*, November 28, 2004; quoted in Gregory, "The Rush to the Intimate."

31. Tom Engelhardt, "Incident on Haifa Street," TomDispatch, September 19, 2004, http://www.tomdispatch.com/index.mhtml?pid=1830.

32. Nick Watt, "Once Notorious Baghdad Street New Peaceful," *ABC News*, June 29, 2005.

33. Engelhardt, "Incident on Haifa Street."

34. Scott Peterson, "A Violent Street Finds Calm," *Christian Science Monitor*, May 26, 2005.

35. Peterson, "A Violent Street Finds Calm."

36. Watt, "Once Notorious Baghdad Street Now Peaceful."

37. Peterson, "A Violent Street Finds Calm."
38. Marc Santora, "US and Iraqis Hit Insurgents in All-Day Fight," *New York Times*, January 10, 2007.
39. Mahan Abedin, "The Surge: Don't Hold Your Breath," *Asia Times*, January 30, 2007.
40. Michael Schwartz, "The Myth of More," TomDispatch, December 6, 2006, http://www.tomdispatch.com/index.mhtml?pid=145524.
41. Santora, "US and Iraqis Hit Insurgents in All-Day Fight."
42. "Ethnic Cleansing in Baghdad: Baghdad Street Becomes New Fallujah," *Australian*, January 10, 2007.
43. Ibid.
44. Peter Grier, "Counterinsurgency Takes Center Stage in Iraq," *Christian Science Monitor*, January 22, 2007.
45. Damien Cave, "'Man Down'—When One Bullet Alters Everything," *New York Times*, January 29, 2007.
46. Sudarsan Raghavan and Joshua Partlow, "Airstrikes Back Troops in Baghdad Clash," *Washington Post*, January 10, 2007.
47. Lara Logan, *CBS News* Online, January 17, 2007, http://www.cbsnews.com/sections/i_video/main500251.shtml?id=2371456n.
48. Youssef and Obeid, "Residents Say Snipers Are Firing at Random."
49. Damien Cave and James Glanz, "In a New Joint U.S.-Iraqi Patrol, the Americans Go First," *New York Times*, January 25, 2007.
50. Ibid.
51. Peters, "Back from Hell."
52. Ibid.
53. Linda Robinson, "For Haifa Street, a Welcome Calm: U.S. Troops Begin a Quiet Drawdown, Hoping that Locals Don't Notice," *U.S. News and World Report*, January 10, 2008.
54. Peters, "Back from Hell."
55. Brookings, *Iraq Index*, March 4, 2008, 12.
56. Robinson, "For Haifa Street, a Welcome Calm."
57. Sudarsan Raghavan, "19 Tense Hours in Sadr City Alongside the Mahdi Army," *Washington Post*, March 29, 2008.
58. See chapter 17.
59. Dahr Jamail, "Iraq: Five Years, and Counting," Inter Press Service, March 18, 2008, http://dahrjamailiraq.com/hard_news/archives/newscommentary/000766.php#more.
60. Rosen, "Iraq Is the Republic of Fear."
61. Cockburn, "A Week in Iraq."

Conclusion

Bobby Seale, *Seize the Time: The Story of the Black Panther Party and Huey P. Newton* (New York: Random House, 1970), 140.
1. This account of the February 15, 2003, demonstrations is taken from Rebecca Solnit, *Hope in the Dark: Untold Histories, Wild Possibilities* (New York: Nation Books, 2004), 54.
2. For a general discussion of the subtle ways that protest movements impact social and political life, viewed through the lens created by the long-term effects of the civil rights movement in Mississippi, see Kenneth T. Andrews, *Freedom Is a Constant Struggle: The Mississippi Civil Rights Movement and Its Legacy*

(Chicago: University of Chicago Press, 2004).

3. Solnit, *Hope in the Dark*, 23. On the reduction of the "shock and awe" campaign, see chapter 5.

4. Tom Engelhardt, "A Permanent Basis for Withdrawal?," TomDispatch, February 14, 2006, http://www.tomdispatch.com/index.mhtml?pid=59774.

5. "American Widens 'Crusade,'" BBC, September 16, 2001 http://news.bbc.co.uk/1/hi/world/americas/1547561.stm; Jane Perlez, "After the Attacks: U.S. Demands Arab Countries 'Choose Sides,'" *New York Times*, September 15, 2001; see also Tom Engelhardt, "The $100 Barrel of Oil vs. the Global War on Terror," TomDispatch, January 8, 2008, http://www.tomdispatch.com/post/174878/if_the_gwot_were_gone_.

6. Donald Kagan, Gary Schmitt, and Thomas Donnelly, *Rebuilding America's Defenses: Strategy, Forces and Resources for a New Century* (Washington D.C.: Project for a New American Century, 2000), http://72.14.205.104/search?q= cache: ruMnHnl98cAJ:www.newamericancentury.org/RebuildingAmericasDefenses.pdf+Rebuilding+America%27s+Defenses&hl=en&ct=clnk&cd=1&gl=us.

7. Donald Rumsfeld, Meet the Press with Tim Russert, *NBC News*, January 20, 2002.

8. See chapter 7.

9. See chapters 1 and 4.

10. See chapters 2 and 3. See also Adam Hochschild and Tom Engelhard, "On Hubris and the Pseudostate," TomDispatch, June 27, 2004, http://www.tomdispatch.com/post/1516/adam_hochschild_on_hubris_and_the_pseudostate.

11. See chapter 3.

12. Juan Cole, "Why al-Maliki Attacked Basra," Salon.com, April 1, 2008, http://www.salon.com/opinion/feature/2008/04/01/basra/index.html.

13. Michael R. Gordon, Eric Schmitt, and Stephen Farrell, "U.S. Cites Gaps in Planning of Iraqi Assault on Basra," *New York Times*, April 3, 2008.

14. Tom Engelhardt, "Baseless Considerations," TomDispatch, November 4, 2007, http://www.tomdispatch.com:80/post/174858/baseless_considerations.

15. Quoted in William Bowles, "So What Gives?" Investigating Imperialism (website), March 12, 2007, http://www.williambowles.info/ini/2007/0307/ini-0475.html.

Acknowledgments

My work on the war in Iraq is intended to reach beyond the scholarly world that I usually inhabit. The essays I have written over the past few years have been mostly topical, designed to address specific issues that were current in the public controversy. This book has a different genesis; I am hoping it will provide people with a broad understanding of the dynamics that produced and sustain the war, its systemic impact on Iraqi society, and the pressure points that might lead to U.S. withdrawal. This different purpose has forced me into a different style of work. While the short essays have been animated by bursts of anger, inspiration, or sadness which carried me through the writing process, the book has required a much more sustained effort. The desire to continue needed to be constantly nurtured and replenished with active encouragement, fresh ideas, sharp criticism, or soothing support. All of this I got from a long list of friends and colleagues.

At the top of this list are Tom Engelhardt and Gilda Zwerman: I know that the book would never have been written without their time-consuming involvement and emotion-draining commitment. Gilda has been my omnipresent friend: my conscience, my sounding board, my critic, my mentor, and the safe place I could go when things were bad. Tom has been my (often unacknowledged) collaborator. In every chapter, the ideas are partly or wholly his, the argument is partly or wholly his, the language is partly or wholly his.

There are many others I relied on for virtues, visible or subtle. A few who come repeatedly to mind are Robert Zussman for his unrelenting intolerance of romanticism; Tyson Smith for patient listening; Cathy Silverstein for commitment to lucidity; Joseph Schwartz for always being there; Naomi Rosenthal for productively channeling hyperventilation; Gabriela Polit-Dueñas for contagious good spirits; Eileen Otis for daily encouragement; Susie Orbach for an aura of inevitability; Jeff Goodwin for timely encouragement; Naomi Gerstel for strategic enthusiasm; Louis Esparza for questioning everything; Jonathan Cutler for trying to figure it all out; Vivek Chibber for supportive criticism; Javier Auyero for encouraging obsession; Anthony Arnove for the last word; Gilbert Achcar for understanding the incomprehensible.

For various other contributions I should also thank Rina Agarwala, Zaid Alrawy, Joel Andreas, Rob Angert, Diane Barthel-Bouchier, Cynthia Bogard, Nitsan Chorev, Lee Clarke, Dan Clawson, Maryann Clawson, Steven Cole, Anthony Di Donato, Francis Di Donato, Greg Durkin, Carolyn Eisenberg, Katie Even, Samuel Farber, Sujatha Fernandes, Francis Fox-Piven, William Futtersak, John Gagnon, Irene Gendzier, Stanley Goff, Kristofer Goldsmith, Jerry Jacobs, A.J. Julius, Michael Kimmel, Michael Kogan, Richard Lachmann, Gene Lebovics, Jake Levich, Daniel Levy, Steven Lukes, Bashir Abu-Manneh, Martin Markowitz, Eduardo Mendieta, Mike Miller, Timothy Moran, Majid Muhammadi, Rene Poitevin, Betty Robinson, Michael Rossman, Ken Sanderson, Magali Sarfatti-Larsen, Stephen Shalom, Anna Sher, Hwa Ji Shin, Marina Sitrin, Jackie Smith, Judy Tanur, Alerie Tirsch, Marilyn Young, Michael Zweig.

In the spring of 2003, the students in my economic sociology seminar insisted that each session begin with a discussion of the political economy of the pending (and then active) Iraq war. The analytic ideas that we collectively developed in that class have structured the conception and execution of this book. Since then, the war has found a place in all my graduate seminars, in hallway discussions, and in the regular departmental colloquium series. I have shamelessly drawn ideas, arguments, and evidence from all these sources. I want to offer special thanks to the students in my freshman seminar, "Understanding the War in Iraq," given four times between 2006 and 2008. The students in these classes have struggled gamely with the complexities of the war and with the confusion created by the U.S. media, and in doing so they have relentlessly drawn my attention to fundamental issues. In myriad ways—too many for me to be conscious of—they pointed me toward both the questions and the answers that are contained in this text. I thank them most for demanding information about the impact of the war on ordinary people in Iraq and the U.S., an issue that is central to the book.

I am not a Middle East scholar and I do not speak or read Arabic or any other Middle Eastern language. Therefore I rely for evidence of the skills of those who are specialists, who live in or travel to Iraq, and who speak Arabic. Like so many others who follow or study the war, my starting place most days is Juan Cole, whose indispensable daily blog, "Informed Comment," contains the news, the blues, and the analysis that so often forms the foundation for understanding what is going on in Iraq. From there I go to TomDispatch, where I look for coverge of the issues that are neglected or suppressed in other outlets. I then turn to a large number of journalists who report the news under often lethal conditions, some of whom have risked their lives to gather evidence that the U.S. government was anxious for them not to find. I am most aware of my debt to the many independent reporters who have refused the protection and the constraints of the U.S. military, and whose work has therefore been indispensable to learning what is going on the ground in Iraq. Dahr Jamail and Nir Rosen are the two who come quickest to my mind, and I make sure to read everything they write. I thank them and many others for their physical bravery in bringing back the story from Iraq, for their moral bravery for speaking truth to power, and for the quality of their reporting, which would be brilliant even under less taxing conditions. To them I would add Patrick Cockburn, who acts like an independent journalist even while his regular columns in the London *Independent* reach audiences across England and the rest of the English speaking world. The work of these westerners is invigorated and elevated by Iraqi reporters and bloggers who write in English and whose contributions are less visible—but no less indispensable. The two I have most admired are Riverbend, the legendary "girl blogger," who is now in silent exile in Syria; and Raed Jarrar, who is now in vocal exile in the United States.

I should also mention reporters on Washington, D.C., beat who so often know what is going on in the darkest depths of official Washington. Jim Lobe and Seymour Hersh are the two I admire most. And then there are the columnists from whom I have borrowed so much of my analysis; Pepe Escobar and Brian Conley are two on whom I have often relied.

Though the coverage of the U.S. corporate media has been often misleading and always incomplete, a surprisingly large proportion of mainstream reporters have regularly overcome the physical dangers of reporting from Iraq and editorial limitations placed on them by their employers. Those I most frequently found myself admiring and using are Anthony Shadid, Nancy Youssef, Ben Lando, and Ellen Knickmeyer, but there are many others whose reporting forms a foundation for my work and that of others who write about the war.

Julie Fain and the other folks at Haymarket Books have worked around the constant delays that I created for them, and still produced a beautiful book in a timely fashion.

Pieces, hunks, and whole sections of various chapters first appeared over the years in other venues, usually TomDispatch. Large parts of chapter 1 were published as part of "The Struggle over Iraqi Oil: Eyes Eternally on the Prize" TomDispatch, May 6, 2007. Parts of chapters 2–4, and 9–12 were first published in "Neoliberalism on Crack: Cities Under Siege in Iraq" in *City* 11 (April 2007). The Haditha story in chapter 5 was first published by ZNet as "What is the Significance of the Haditha Massacre?" (June 11, 2006). Chapter 7 was based largely on "U.S. Hopes for the Fallujah Battle have Already Begun to Unravel," published by ZNet (November 18, 2004), "The Sinister U.S. Plans in Fallujah," published by TomDispatch (December 12, 2004), and "Falluja—City without a future," also published on TomDispatch (January 14, 2005). Much of chapter 8 was published in "Is the United States Killing 10,000 Iraqis Every Month? Or is it More?" published by After Downing Street (July 5, 2007).

Chapter 13 is mostly taken directly from "Iraq's Tidal Wave of Misery: The First History of the Planet's Worst Refugee Crisis," which was first published by TomDispatch (February 10, 2008). Chapter 14 is an augmented blend of "Who's Sovereign Now?" and "Iraq's Sovereignty Vacuum, Part I: A Government with No Military and No Territory," both published by TomDispatch (June 17, 2004, March 9, 2006). "Iraq's Sovereignty Vacuum, Part I: A Government with No Military and No Territory," also formed the foundation for chapters 15 and 16. Chapter 17 is an expansion of "Iraq's Sovereignty Vacuum, Part II: The Campaign to Pacify Sunni Iraq," published by TomDispatch (June 13, 2006), and "Contradictions of the Iraqi Resistance: Guerilla War vs. Terrorism," published in *Against the Current* (January–February 2006).

Chapter 18 is based on three TomDispatch commentaries, "Baghdad Surges into Hell" (February 11, 2007), "Surge and Destroy" (March 11, 2007), and "The Battle of Baghdad" (March 23, 2008). The conclusion was published by TomDispatch under the title, "River of Resistance" (May 22, 2008).

Index

Contributors

About Michael Schwartz

Michael Schwartz received a PhD in Sociology at Harvard in 1971. He has taught at Harvard, UCLA, Edinburgh University, Chuo University in Tokyo, and—for the last thirty-five years—at the State University of New York at Stony Brook, where he was the founding director of the Undergraduate College of Global Studies.

Schwartz has published five books and over fifty articles, including the widely acclaimed *Radical Protest and Social Structure*, a pioneering work in historical sociology and social movement analysis; *The Power Structure of American Business* (with Beth Mintz), an award-winning analysis of American business structure; and *Social Policy and the Conservative Agenda* (edited with Clarence Lo), a collection that analyzed the resiliency of the conservative move in American politics during the Clinton years.

Schwartz has written extensively on the war in Iraq since its inception, analyzing topics as diverse as American military strategy, the nature of the insurgency, and the impact of the war on Iran's position in Middle East politics. His work on Iraq has appeared on numerous internet sites, including TomDispatch, Asia Times, Mother Jones, and ZNET; and in print in *Contexts*, *Cities*, and *Z* magazine.

About TomDispatch.com

Tom Engelhardt launched TomDispatch in November 2001 as an email publication offering commentary and collected articles from the world press. In December 2002, it gained its name, became a project of the Nation Institute, and went online as "a regular antidote to the mainstream media." The site now features Engelhardt's regular commentaries, as well as the original work of authors ranging from Rebecca Solnit, Dahr Jamail, Bill McKibben, and Mike Davis to Chalmers Johnson, Noam Chomsky, Michael Klare, Michael Schwartz, Adam Hochschild, and Karen J. Greenberg among many others. Nick Turse, who also writes for the site, is its associate editor and research director.

TomDispatch is intended to introduce readers to voices and perspectives from elsewhere (even when the elsewhere is here). Its mission is to connect some of the global dots regularly left unconnected by the mainstream media and to offer a clearer sense of how this imperial globe of ours actually works.

Many of the interviews done by Tom Engelhardt for the site have been collected in *Mission Unaccomplished: TomDispatch Interviews with American Iconoclasts and Dissenters*. The first "best of" book from TomDispatch, *The World According to TomDispatch: America in the New Age of Empire*, was published in June 2008 by Verso.

Also From Haymarket Books

Winter Soldier: Iraq and Afghanistan:
Eyewitness Accounts of the Occupations

Iraq Veterans Against the War with Aaron Glantz, foreword by Anthony Swofford • In March 2008, veterans deployed in Iraq and Afghanistan gathered to share firsthand accounts of the brutality of these occupations. This book preserves the testimonies of hundreds of veterans addressing such issues as the U.S. military's changing "rules of engagement," torture of detainees, gender and sexuality within the military's ranks, and the crisis in veterans' health care. ISBN: 978-1-931859-65-3.

Beyond the Green Zone:
Dispatches from an Unembedded Journalist in Occupied Iraq

Dahr Jamail with a foreword by Amy Goodman • As one of the only U.S. journalists to spend time unembedded in Iraq, Jamail has filed indispensable reports chronicling the unfolding disaster there—from the siege of Fallujah to prison torture and the raids of Iraqi homes. Now available in an updated paperback edition. ISBN 978-1-931859-47-9.

The Road from ar-Ramadi:
The Private Rebellion of Staff Sergeant Camilo Mejia

Camilo Mejia with a foreword by Chris Hedges • A courageous, personal account of rebellion within the ranks of the U.S. military in wartime—written by the first soldier to publicly refuse to return to fight in Iraq. ISBN: 978-1-931859-553-0.

Winter Soldiers: An Oral History of the Vietnam Veterans Against the War

Richard Stacewicz • At its height, the 30,000-strong VVAW organized influential campaigns to contest military neglect of veterans, expose the dangers of chemicals defoliants, and testify to the genocidal nature of the war in Vietnam. This study brings readers inside veterans' antiwar efforts—and brings to life the suppressed history of revolt that brought America's longest war to date to an end. ISBN: 978-1-931859-60-8.

Vietnam: The (Last) War the United States Lost

Joe Allen • This history from below analyzes the impact of the war in Vietnam on the region and its people, as well as on American workers, students, and politicians, and discusses the relationship between the era's antiwar, labor, and civil rights movements. Allen identifies the decisive developments that led to defeat and examines the implications evident in U.S. politics today. ISBN: 978-1-931859-49-3.

The Democrats: A Critical History

Lance Selfa • Contesting the dominant two-party binary that shapes U.S. politics, Selfa presents a wide-ranging and well-researched examination of the Democratic Party. He demonstrates the party's historic alignment with business interests, their frequent support for wars, and reluctance to grant reforms, tracing the material circumstances that place the party at odds with rhetorical commitments to minorities, workers, and the poor. ISBN: 978-1-931859-55-4.

Between the Lines:
Readings on Israel, the Palestinians, and the U.S. "War on Terror"

Tikva Honig-Parnass and Toufic Haddad • This compilation of essays—edited by a Palestinian and an Israeli—constitutes a challenge to critically rethink the Israeli-Palestinian conflict. ISBN: 978-1-931859-44-8.

Soldiers in Revolt: GI Resistance During the Vietnam War

David Cortright with a new introduction by Howard Zinn • "An exhaustive account of rebellion in all the armed forces, not only in Vietnam but throughout the world."—New York Review of Books. ISBN: 978-1-931859-27-1.

No One Is Illegal:
Fighting Racism and State Violence on the U.S.–Mexico Border

Justin Akers Chacón and Mike Davis • Countering the chorus of anti-immigrant voices, Davis and Akers Chacón expose the racism of anti-immigration vigilantes and put a human face on the immigrants who risk their lives to cross the border to work in the United States. ISBN: 978-1-931859-35-3.

In Praise of Barbarians: Essays Against Empire

Mike Davis • No writer in the United States today brings together analysis and history as comprehensively and elegantly as Mike Davis. In these contemporary, interventionist essays, Davis goes beyond critique to offer real solutions and concrete possibilities for change. ISBN: 978-1-931859-42-4.

Friendlly Fire: The Remarkable Story of a Journalist Kidnapped in Iraq, Rescued by an Italian Secret Service Agent, and Shot by U.S. Forces

Giuliana Sgrena • The Italian journalist, whose personal story was featured on *60 Minutes*, describes the real story of her capture and shooting in 2004. Sgrena also gives invaluable insight into the reality of life in occupied Iraq, exposing U.S. war crimes there. ISBN: 978-1-931859-39-4.

Welcome to the Terrordome: The Pain, Politics, and Promise of Sports

Dave Zirin • This much-anticipated sequel to *What's My Name, Fool?* by acclaimed sportswriter Dave Zirin breaks new ground in sportswriting, looking at the controversies and trends now shaping sports in the United States—and abroad. Always insightful, never predictable. ISBN: 978-1-931859-41-7.

Sin Patrón: Stories from Argentia's Occupied Factories

The lavaca collective, with a foreword by Naomi Klein and Avi Lewis • The inside story of Argentina's remarkable movement to create factories run democratically by workers themselves. ISBN: 978-1-931859-43-1.

Order these titles and more online at www.haymarketbooks.org or call 773-583-7884.

About Haymarket Books

Haymarket Books is a nonprofit, progressive book distributor and publisher, a project of the Center for Economic Research and Social Change. We believe that activists need to take ideas, history, and politics into the many struggles for social justice today. Learning the lessons of past victories, as well as defeats, can arm a new generation of fighters for a better world. As Karl Marx said, "The philosophers have merely interpreted the world; the point however is to change it."

We take inspiration and courage from our namesakes, the Haymarket Martyrs, who gave their lives fighting for a better world. Their 1886 struggle for the eight-hour day, which gave us May Day, the international workers' holiday, reminds workers around the world that ordinary people can organize and struggle for their own liberation. These struggles continue today across the globe—struggles against oppression, exploitation, hunger, and poverty.

It was August Spies, one of the Martyrs who was targeted for being an immigrant and an anarchist, who predicted the battles being fought to this day. "If you think that by hanging us you can stamp out the labor movement," Spies told the judge, "then hang us. Here you will tread upon a spark, but here, and there, and behind you, and in front of you, and everywhere, the flames will blaze up. It is a subterranean fire. You cannot put it out. The ground is on fire upon which you stand."

We could not succeed in our publishing efforts without the generous financial support of our readers. Many people contribute to our project through the Haymarket Sustainers program, where donors receive free books in return for their monetary support. If you would like to be a part of this program, please contact us at info@haymarketbooks.org.